Modern Saudi Arabia

Recent Titles in Understanding Modern Nations

Modern China
Xiaobing Li

Modern Spain
Enrique Ávila López

Modern Mexico
James D. Huck Jr.

Modern India
John McLeod

MODERN SAUDI ARABIA

Valerie Anishchenkova

Understanding Modern Nations

BLOOMSBURY ACADEMIC
NEW YORK · LONDON · OXFORD · NEW DELHI · SYDNEY

BLOOMSBURY ACADEMIC
Bloomsbury Publishing Inc
1385 Broadway, New York, NY 10018, USA
50 Bedford Square, London, WC1B 3DP, UK
29 Earlsfort Terrace, Dublin 2, Ireland

BLOOMSBURY, BLOOMSBURY ACADEMIC and the Diana logo
are trademarks of Bloomsbury Publishing Plc

First published in the United States of America by ABC-CLIO 2020
Paperback edition published by Bloomsbury Academic 2024

Copyright © Bloomsbury Publishing Inc, 2024

Cover photos: Kaaba in Mecca, Saudi Arabia. Muslim pilgrims. (Sufi70/Dreamstime.com);
Prophet's Mosque, Medina, Saudi Arabia. (numbeos/iStockphoto.com); Saudi Arabia Capital Riyadh skyline.
(Hansmusa/Dreamstime.com); Arabic man with falcon. (Fabio Formaggio/ Dreamstime.com);

All rights reserved. No part of this publication may be reproduced or
transmitted in any form or by any means, electronic or mechanical,
including photocopying, recording, or any information storage or retrieval
system, without prior permission in writing from the publishers.

Bloomsbury Publishing Inc does not have any control over, or responsibility for,
any third-party websites referred to or in this book. All internet addresses given
in this book were correct at the time of going to press. The author and publisher
regret any inconvenience caused if addresses have changed or sites have
ceased to exist, but can accept no responsibility for any such changes.

Library of Congress Cataloging-in-Publication Data
Names: Anishchenkova, Valerie, author.
Title: Modern Saudi Arabia / Valerie Anishchenkova.
Description: Santa Barbara, California : ABC-CLIO, [2020] |
Series: Understanding modern nations | Includes bibliographical references and index.
Identifiers: LCCN 2019056369 (print) | LCCN 2019056370 (ebook) |
ISBN 9781440857041 (cloth) | ISBN 9781440857058 (ebook)
Subjects: LCSH: Saudi Arabia— Encyclopedias.
Classification: LCC DS204 .A673 2020 (print) | LCC DS204 (ebook) | DDC 953.80503— dc23
LC record available at https://lccn.loc.gov/2019056369
LC ebook record available at https://lccn.loc.gov/2019056370

ISBN: HB: 978-1-4408-5704-1
PB: 979-8-7651-2507-6
ePDF: 978-1-4408-5705-8
eBook: 979-8-2161-1873-2

Series: Understanding Modern Nations

To find out more about our authors and books visit www.bloomsbury.com
and sign up for our newsletters.

Contents

Series Foreword	xi
Introduction	xiii

Chapter 1: Geography   1
Overview   1
    Asir   2
    Border Demarcations and Disputes   4
    Climate   6
    Eastern Arabia: Al-Hasa   7
    Environmental Issues after the Gulf War   8
    Fresh Water Reserves and Water Conservancy   9
    Great Deserts   11
    Hijaz and Tihamah   13
    Jeddah   14
    Mecca   16
    Medina   17
    Najd: Central Arabia   18
    Northern Arabia   20
    The Persian Gulf   21
    Population   23
    The Red Sea   24
    Riyadh   26

Chapter 2: History   29
Overview   29
Timeline   30
    The Abbasids   36
    Arab Revolt (1916–1918)   37
    Discovery of Oil   39
    Emirate of Diriyah: The First Saudi State (1744–1818)   40
    Emirate of Najd: The Second Saudi State (1824–1891)   42
    The Golden Age of Islam in Arabia   43

    Ibn Saud   44
    Ikhwan   45
    King Abdullah   47
    The Mamluks and the Ottomans in Arabia   49
    Muhammad, Prophet of Islam   51
    Muhammad ibn Abd al-Wahhab   53
    Nabateans   54
    Najran   55
    Pre-Islamic Arabia   56
    Rashidun: The Righteous Caliphs   58
    The Rise of Islam   60
    Sharifs of Mecca   63
    Third Saudi State: Saudi Arabia in the 20th Century   64
    The Umayyads   65

Chapter 3: Government and Politics   69
Overview   69
    The Arab Spring   71
    Capital and Corporal Punishment   73
    Constitution and Legal Reform   75
    Corruption   77
    Gulf Cooperation Council   78
    Human Rights and Censorship   79
    Law Enforcement and Security   81
    Local Government and Municipal Elections   82
    Military   84
    Political Dissent and Opposition   85
    Political Reform and Modernization   87
    Saudi Monarchy and Branches of the Government   88
    Saudi–U.S. Relations   90
    Sharia Law and Judicial System   93
    Ulama   94
    Wahhabi Ideology   95

Chapter 4: Economy   99
Overview   99
    Agriculture   100
    Diversification and Development Plans   102
    Energy   103
    Financial Institutions and Saudi Riyal   105
    Land and Household Policy   107
    Migrant Workers and Unemployment   108
    Oil Industry and Aramco   110
    OPEC and OAPEC   112
    Petrochemical Industry   113

Public vs. Private Sectors 115
Saudization 117
Science and Technology 119
Taxation 120
Tourism 121
Trade and Exports 123
Transportation 125
Vision 2030 127

Chapter 5: Religion and Thought 129
Overview 129
Five Pillars or the Tenets of Islam 130
Hajj 133
Islamic Calendar 136
Jihad 137
Non-Muslims 138
Quran 139
Shia Community 141
Shia Islam 142
Sunni Islam and Jurisprudence 143

Chapter 6: Social Classes and Ethnicity 147
Overview 147
Bedouins and Nomadism 149
Ethnic Composition 152
Health and Welfare 153
House of Saud 155
Major Tribes 157
Settled Population: *Hadar* 160
Sharif and *Sayyid* 161
Sulubbah 162
Urbanization 163

Chapter 7: Gender, Marriage, and Sexuality 165
Overview 165
Divorce 168
Domestic Violence 170
Gender Segregation 171
Guardianship 172
Hijab and Dress Code 173
Identity Cards 175
Marriage Law and Tradition 176
The *Mutawwa*: Saudi Religious Police 178
Parents and Children 179
Social Life, Kinship, and Friendships 180

    Traditional Wedding — 182
    Women in Public Office — 183
    Women's Mobility and Driving Ban — 186

Chapter 8: Education — 189
Overview — 189
    Education of Women — 191
    Higher Education — 192
    International Schools — 194
    Islamic Education — 195
    Key Universities — 196
    Princess Nourah Bint Abdulrahman University — 199
    Secondary Education — 200

Chapter 9: Language — 203
Overview — 203
    Arabic Alphabet and Script — 205
    Arabic Calligraphy — 206
    Arabic Dialects — 209
    Dialect of Hijaz — 211
    Dialect of Najdi — 212
    Gulf Arabic and Minority Languages — 213

Chapter 10: Etiquette — 215
Overview — 215
    Death Rites — 216
    Dress Etiquette — 218
    Honor — 219
    Majlis — 221
    Social Life — 222
    Workweek and Holidays — 223

Chapter 11: Literature — 227
Overview — 227
    Abdelrahman Munif — 229
    Ghazi al-Gosaibi — 230
    Poetry — 231
    Prose — 233
    Raja Alem — 235
    Turki al-Hamad — 236
    Women Writers — 237

Chapter 12: Art and Architecture — 241
Overview — 241
    Abraj al-Bait — 243
    Bedouin Jewelry — 245

Calligraphic Art	246
Contemporary Art	250
Great Mosque of Mecca	252
Modernization of Saudi Architecture	254
Sadu Weaving	256
Traditional Architecture	257
Traditional Garments	259

Chapter 13: Music and Dance — 263
Overview — 263

Ardha Dance	264
Bedouin Music	266
Contemporary Saudi and *Khaliji* Music	267
Janadiriyah Heritage and Cultural Festival	268
Music of Hijaz and Asir	269
Religious Music	271
Sawt Music	272
Traditional Instruments	273
Wedding Music and Dance	275

Chapter 14: Food — 277
Overview — 277

Arabic Coffee, Tea, and Other Traditional Beverages	280
Islamic Dietary Laws	282
Kabsah	284
Traditional Foods and Regional Variations	285

Chapter 15: Leisure and Sports — 291
Overview — 291

Camel Racing	293
Falconry	294
Golf	296
Horse Racing	297
Maqha: Traditional Coffeehouse	298
Popular Consumerism	300
Soccer	302
Women in Sports	303

Chapter 16: Media and Popular Culture — 307
Overview — 307

Cinema	309
Freedom of Speech	310
Government Censorship	312
Internet and Social Media	314
Printed Press	317

    Television   318
    Tradition vs. Globalization   321

Appendix A: A Day in the Life   323
    A Day in the Life of a Young Professional Woman   323
    A Day in the Life of a Bedouin   325
    A Day in the Life of a Rural Widow   326
    A Day in the Life of a Young Urban Man   328

Appendix B: Glossary of Key Terms   331

Appendix C: Facts and Figures   337

Appendix D: Holidays   343

Selected Bibliography   345

Index   357

Series Foreword

We live in an evolving world, a world that is becoming increasingly globalized by the minute. Cultures collide and blend, leading to new customs and practices that exist alongside long-standing traditions. Advancing technologies connect lives across the globe, affecting those from densely populated urban areas to those who dwell in the most remote locations in the world. Governments are changing, leading to war and violence but also to new opportunities for those who have been oppressed. The *Understanding Modern Nations* series seeks to answer questions about cultures, societies, and customs in various countries around the world.

Understanding Modern Nations is geared toward readers wanting to expand their knowledge of the world, ideal for high school students researching specific countries, undergraduates preparing for studies abroad, and general readers interested in learning more about the world around them. Each volume in the series focuses on a single country, with coverage on Africa, the Americas, Asia and the Pacific, and Europe.

Each country volume contains 16 chapters focusing on various aspects of culture and society in each country. The chapters begin with an Overview, which is followed by short entries on key topics, concepts, ideas, and biographies pertaining to the chapter's theme. In a way, these volumes serve as "thematic encyclopedias," with entries organized for the reader's benefit. Following an Introduction, each volume contains chapters on the following themes:

- Geography
- History
- Government and Politics
- Economy
- Religion and Thought
- Social Classes and Ethnicity
- Gender, Marriage, and Sexuality
- Education
- Language
- Etiquette
- Literature and Drama
- Art and Architecture

- Music and Dance
- Food
- Leisure and Sports
- Media and Popular Culture

Each entry concludes with a list of cross references and Further Reading, pointing readers to additional print and electronic resources that might prove useful.

Following the chapters are appendices, including "A Day in the Life" feature, which depicts "typical" days in the lives of people living in that country, from students to farmers to factory workers to stay-at-home and working mothers. A Glossary, Facts and Figures section, and Holidays chart round out the appendices. Volumes include a Selected Bibliography, as well as sidebars that are scattered throughout the text.

The volumes in the *Understanding Modern Nations* series are not intended to be comprehensive compendiums about every nation of the world, but instead are meant to serve as introductory texts for readers, examining key topics from major countries studied in the high school curriculum as well as important transitioning countries that make headlines daily. It is our hope that readers will gain an understanding and appreciation for cultures and histories outside of their own.

Introduction

Contemporary Saudi Arabia is truly a country of stark contrasts. It is one of the youngest modern states, but its territory had some of the oldest human settlements. It has some of the fastest-growing economies yet some of the most traditional societies. It has some of the vast deserts in the world and some of its tallest buildings. It invests the greatest share of its budget in education, yet it prosecutes any display of free thinking. Understanding this country's contrasts is necessary to understand its unique character and its special place in the history of humankind.

In Western imagination, Saudi Arabia is usually associated with a set of static images—its oil wealth, its controversial royals, and the abuses of women's and human rights. Even the Arabic-speaking media rarely goes beyond the familiar depictions of Saudi Arabia's opulence as the biggest economy of the Middle East, the infamous *fatwas*, the country's aggressive foreign policy, and the video coverage of the annual Hajj. In reality, Saudi Arabia is a country of great nuances, contradictions, and cultural complexities. It is changing now at a rate similar to the time when oil was discovered on the Arabian Peninsula 80 years ago. In contrast to popular beliefs, Saudi Arabia's population and culture show a great deal of regional diversity. The Saudi interpretation of Islam is far from representing its "pure" form but is a complex hybrid of Muslim and tribal customs and cultural codes. Finally, there is a powerful and rapidly growing internal sociocultural movement that challenges its conservative establishment and demands for greater women's rights and the freedom of speech. This book aims to illustrate some of the cultural, historical, and political nuances of Saudi Arabia, inviting the reader to explore the unknown aspects of this country.

During the past century, the Kingdom of Saudi Arabia has experienced an extraordinary transformation, accompanied by a clash between tradition and modernization to a much greater degree than most other countries. Until the turn of the 20th century, the political and geographical center of contemporary Saudi Arabia, Najd, had one of the most isolated societies on earth, situated in one of the harshest environments known to humanity. Unified in 1932 under the banner of Ibn Saud, Saudi Arabia is the only country in the world that carries the name of its royal family. The discovery of oil and the subsequent rapid development of the oil industry have forever changed the fate of the Arabian Peninsula and its people. In this process of transformation, the constant confrontation between the traditional and the modern remained a central feature of the country's identity—perhaps even more so with the turn of the 21st century. This book outlines different aspects—political, social, and cultural—of this transformation and illustrates its effect on different spheres of Saudi life. The volume also aims to show the unique (and often largely unknown to an outsider) features of local culture, including its culinary traditions, architecture, music, and literature. The representation of Saudi Arabia offered in this book focuses on four central aspects that are meant to illustrate the complexity of the country's identity.

First, the cultural identity of Saudi Arabia is a complex amalgam of its tribal and Muslim cultures. It is important to understand that Islamic dogmas practiced in the country represent one particular ultraconservative ideology, the so-called Wahhabism. This term originates from the name of Muhammad Abd al-Wahhab—the 18th-century preacher who is considered the forefather of the doctrine and the reformist religious movement inspired by it. Wahhabism is, in turn, based on the Hanbali school, which is the most conservative of the four schools of Islamic jurisprudence while being the smallest, as it is practiced only in Saudi Arabia, Qatar, and Kuwait. In other words, the religious culture of Saudi Arabia is certainly not representative of Islam as a whole, but rather embodies one of its many manifestations in current times. Moreover, many of the country's most restrictive norms and laws are closely associated with the millennia-long tribal society of the Arabian Peninsula, rather than Islamic culture. Indeed, Islam did not appear in a vacuum, and many of the ancient customs, societal norms, and traditions of the Arabian Bedouins have been incorporated into Islamic dogmas and codified into Sharia law. However, many of the cultural and social norms practiced in Saudi Arabia lie outside of the Islamic culture, and some even contradict it.

Second, understanding the Arabian physical environment and history is essential for understanding the country's contemporary political life, including its internal dynamics and foreign policies. The historic pact between Al Saud and Abd al-Wahhab families, the harsh physical environment, and the centuries-long isolation of the heartland from the rest of the world are the key factors that defined Saudi Arabia's character. There are also many clashing cultural differences that exist between different parts of the peninsula—perhaps a surprising fact for most outsiders, as it is usually perceived as a place of a markedly uniform culture and society.

Third, it is certain that Saudi Arabia is going through a major metamorphosis, but the question of who is behind it largely remains unanswered. Although it may seem that the new generation of royals are driving the change, the massive cultural shift is happening from the bottom up. Young people—who make up over 70 percent of the country's population—are quickly and forcefully taking over. They reject the culture imposed by the conservative *ulama* and demand a more liberal interpretation of Islam. The dramatic changes that would be unthinkable even a few years ago—from the lifting of the driving ban for women to stripping the religious police of its powers to opening cinemas after a prohibition that lasted for 30 years—take place because the educated youth are craving these changes. They may appear in the press as initiatives by a 30-something royal prince, but these are mere formal steps to legalize the demands of the Saudi youth.

Fourth, Saudi women are not hapless victims as they are often portrayed by the Western press, but are powerful agents of change. Saudi Arabia has some of the most repressive systems toward women, including the mandatory full covers, the gender segregation law, the driving ban that lasted until 2018, and most importantly, the male guardianship system that treats women as legal minors throughout their whole life. But at the same time, the country has some of the most vocal and fearless feminists who fight for their rights, even when it costs them their freedom. They went to the election centers demanding their right to vote as citizens, they organized the #IAmMyOwnGuardian campaign and signed their names on the petition to end male guardianship, they drove cars around city streets in protest of the driving ban decades before it was ended—all while knowing that they can be arrested, jailed, and tortured. Some are still in prison today—while the government is flaunting its newly minted "hip and modern" image to the world.

Saudi Arabia is changing. As a society, as a political system, as a culture—it is at a crossroads. It is becoming more and more difficult to resist global cultural influences, accelerated by the growth of new technologies—although it held up its traditional character for a remarkably long time. But whatever the Saudi Arabia of the future will look like on the surface, it will undoubtedly remain a unique place, defined by its aspiring youth, its Islamic character, and its Bedouin roots.

Saudi Arabia

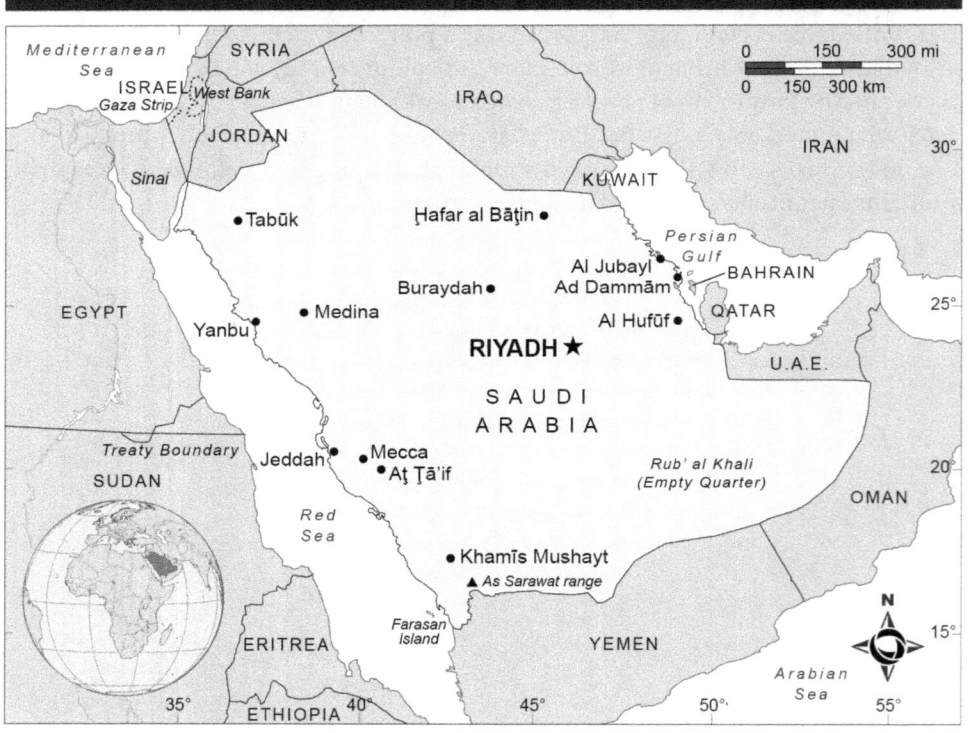

CHAPTER 1

GEOGRAPHY

OVERVIEW

The Kingdom of Saudi Arabia occupies about 75 percent of the Arabian Peninsula. The country's territory is comparable to one-quarter the size of the continental United States. The Saudi government reports that the country occupies 865,000 square miles. Geographically, Saudi Arabia is located in southwestern Asia. Geopolitically, it occupies a central place in the world area currently known as the "Middle East." Saudi Arabia borders eight countries and two seas. Its western coastal border is the Gulf of Aqaba and the Red Sea—one of the most important world trade sea passes. To the east, the country borders the shallow Persian Gulf. Both seas are very important trade arteries. Despite its extensive coastlines, Saudi Arabia does not have strategic control over either of these bodies of water. The Red Sea access is controlled by Egypt in the north via the Suez Canal, and by Yemen and Eritrea on its southern side; whereas Iran's command of the Strait of Hormuz gives it authority over the entry point to the Persian Gulf from the Gulf of Oman. To the north of Saudi Arabia are the Syrian Desert, Iraq, Jordan, and Kuwait. The country's eastern borders are with Bahrain (offshore), Qatar, the United Arab Emirates, and Oman. Its southern neighbors are Oman and Yemen.

The Arabian Peninsula is the world's largest. Saudi Arabia's unique geology is behind the country's enormous oil reserves. The peninsula consists of a single tectonic plate, the Arabian plate, which is slowly moving eastward. Millions of years ago, it was a part of the African continent. The same geological forces that separated the peninsula from Africa continue to rotate it, and scientists believe that in another 10 million years the Persian Gulf will close off as a result of this rotation. When the Arabian plate shifted to the east, it moved above what was a large ancient sea, pushing the seabed deep under the earth's surface. The large sedimentary deposits of marine plant and animal life, which accumulated at this buried sea's floor and came under enormous geological pressure, created the vast oil reserves in the whole Gulf region. Thanks to its favorable geographical location, Saudi Arabia has about 26 percent of the world's oil reserves. Its Ghawar field, which is about 186 miles long, is the world's largest oil field.

Early European geographers divided the Arabian Peninsula into two parts. Arabia Felix, or Fertile Arabia, consists of the relatively moist highlands of Yemen in the south and the mountains of Asir and the Hijaz. The rest of the peninsula was called Arabia Deserta, or Desert Arabia, covering the barren lands that dominate the peninsula's geography. However, despite a persistent stereotype of Saudi Arabia being nothing but a uniform "land of sand," in reality, the desert in its traditionally understood form occupies only about one-third of the country. The rest is made of various oases, wadis, steppe, mountain systems, and the Hijaz countryside that resembles the Mediterranean. Saudi Arabia has two distinct mountain ranges: the Mountains of Hijaz on the Red Sea coast and the Asir range in the south. Geographically, the kingdom can be divided into five areas: (1) Central Arabia, or Najd, where the capital of Riyadh is located; (2) the Hijaz, which includes the provinces of Mecca and Medina; (3) the Asir Mountains neighboring Yemen; (4) Eastern Arabia, or al-Hasa, which contains most of Saudi oil reserves; and (5) Northern Arabia, which geographically constitutes a part of the Great Syrian Desert. Today, the majority of Saudis live in four populated areas: Najd, Hijaz, al-Hasa, and Asir.

An important aspect of Saudi Arabia's geography, which has made a profound impact on its society and culture, is its inaccessibility from the rest of the world, created by various factors, such as long impassable stretches of desert, seacoasts, and high mountain ranges. For instance, Najd was one of the most physically isolated permanently inhabited places on earth prior to the discovery of oil. Over the centuries, this geographical isolation greatly influenced how Saudi Arabia views itself and the world.

Further Reading

Suhail, Mohammad. *Introduction to General Geography and Water Resources of Saudi Arabia*. LAP LAMBERT Academic Publishing, 2016.

Thompson, Andrew. *Origins of Arabia*. Fitzroy Dearbourn, 2000.

Vincent, Peter J. *Saudi Arabia: An Environmental Overview*. Taylor & Francis, 2008.

Asir

The mountainous region of Asir, which literally means "Difficult Country" in Arabic, lies in the southwest of Saudi Arabia, between the Hijaz in the north and Yemen in the south. Saudi Arabia gained control of Asir as a result of the Treaty of Taif, signed to end the Saudi-Yemeni War in 1934. As the mountains increase in elevation southward, the region resembles Yemen more than the rest of the kingdom. Its highest peak is Jabal Sawda, the "Black Mountain," which exceeds 9,800 feet. Further south, the eastern side of the mountains border the Rub al-Khali Desert. Seasonal monsoon rains in higher elevations provide sufficient water for farming. Asir receives more rain than other parts of the country—up to 20 inches of rain annually—and is an important agricultural region, which produces wheat, coffee, cotton, indigo, ginger, fruits, and vegetables. The area's geography and climate also create favorable conditions for raising different kinds of livestock. Asir's topography, with its rocky slopes and isolated plates, historically provided protection for local tribes from invaders.

This region contains four Saudi provinces, among which the Asir Province is the largest. Its capital, Abha, located to the southeast of the Black Mountain, was the

The mountains of Asir. (Giuseppemasci/Dreamstime.com)

pre-Saudi administrative center of Asir and remains the largest and most important city in the region. Asir has an important strategic location, serving as a political buffer and the main ground transportation route between the Hijaz and Yemen. A thriving tourist industry grew under the former Saudi provincial amir, Khalid al-Faysal. Abha and the surrounding mountains have been transformed into a regional summer resort where Saudi families can escape the excruciating desert heat and enjoy a milder climate. Abha has many upscale hotels and a hotel management institute.

Al-Baha, the smallest of Saudi provinces, is located to the north of the Asir Province. It extends from the mountains down to the coastal Tihamah. Like Asir, it has a mild summer climate and picturesque mountainous landscapes with natural forests and streams. Its proximity to the Hijaz makes it a convenient tourist destination. Al-Baha was among the most isolated places in the country until all-weather roads were constructed in the 1960s and 1970s.

The other two provinces in Asir are Najran and Jizan. Najran is located in the southeast, near the Yemeni border. Most of its arable land lies in a valley that regularly fills with a large seasonal river flowing from the Yemeni highlands. This river is the main, albeit inconsistent, resource for irrigation in the area, and the Saudi government built a dam in 1981 to conserve its water supply. As for Jizan, it has long been the main seaport for the southern part of Saudi Arabia. This area has a long history of trade and cultural interactions with both the nearby Yemen and the Horn of Africa. The surrounding countryside is one of the most fertile agricultural areas in the country, producing various crops, coffee beans, and tropical fruit. The Jizan Valley Dam, built in a similar manner as the Najran Dam, was completed in 1970.

See also: Chapter 4: Agriculture; Tourism.

Further Reading

Abdulfattah, Kamal. *Mountain Farmer and Fellah in Asir—Southwest Saudi Arabia: The Conditions of Agriculture in a Traditional Society*. Erlangen, 1981.

Antar, Ziad, et al. *After Images: Stories from the Mountains of Asir*. Art Books from the Middle East, 2016.

Mauger, Thierry. *Impressions of Arabia: Architecture and Frescoes of the Asir Region*. Flammarion, 1996.

Border Demarcations and Disputes

Unlike in Europe, clearly demarcated boundaries were historically meaningless in the Arabian Peninsula where territorial ownership was fluid and based on the allegiance of tribes that moved over large areas in search for water and pasture for livestock. However, things have changed radically with the discovery of oil throughout the Persian Gulf region. Boundaries became strategically, economically, and politically important. After decades of complicated border negotiations with the neighboring countries, the Saudi government currently has most of its land and offshore boundaries officially defined, albeit not without controversy.

In the 1920s, the British as the mandatory power of Jordan (called Transjordan at the time) and Iraq and protecting power of Kuwait, pressured the Saudi government to accept land borders with the three countries. But with the discovery of oil, various border disputes have transpired among the neighbors. The frontier with Jordan was adjusted in 1965 when the two countries exchanged small territories, giving Jordanians the much-needed footage near their one and only seaport in Aqaba. Saudi Arabia's border with Iraq was settled in 1922 when the British, representing Baghdad, and King Abd al-Aziz signed the Treaty of Muhammarah. Subsequently, Kuwait lost some of its territory, as its border with the kingdom shifted northward when Saudi Arabia was compensated for the territorial concessions to Iraq. The kingdom also used to share two Neutral Zones with Kuwait and Iraq. The one with Kuwait was evenly divided in 1966, with each country agreeing to share its oil resources. The Neutral Zone with Iraq was evenly divided as well, following agreements reached in 1975 and 1981.

Saudi Arabia's eastern and southern boundaries are even more troublesome. The country's border with the fellow Gulf Cooperation Council (GCC) member, Qatar, was the scene of clashes in the fall of 1991 and again in 1992 when Saudi troops reportedly attacked the Qatari outpost at al-Khufus. Peace was restored only when an agreement, mediated by the Egyptian government, was signed in Medina. Both sides promised to respect the existing 1965 border demarcation. Saudi Arabia recognized Qatari control of al-Khufus, and in return, Qatar acknowledged Saudi sovereignty over the territory that separates it from the United Arab Emirates (UAE). Saudi Arabia also has longstanding border disputes with two other GCC members, Oman and the UAE. The fluidity of these boundaries is the legacy of the British control over Oman and the Trucial States (a group of tribal confederations in the southeast of the Persian Gulf that upon gaining independence formed the UAE), as well as centuries of conflicting tribal claims. One of the most prominent conflicts in this context was the continuous fighting over the al-Buraimi Oasis in the late 1940s and early 1950s between the Saudis and the British and their allies, but was not resolved at the time. Saudi Arabia and the UAE reached a settlement in 1974, when the latter received control of several villages in the oasis in return for a piece of territory along its Qatari border. Oman and Saudi Arabia were able to resolve their border disputes in a bilateral agreement in 1990. However, despite the formal settlements, all sides continue to publish conflicting maps of the area. With the ongoing political instability in the region and without historical borders to reference, the drawing up of modern clearly defined borders will likely remain problematic.

Saudi Arabia's southern border with Yemen remains its most challenging border-related issue, especially in light of the ongoing Saudi-Yemeni conflict that began in 2015. In 1934, the newly formed Kingdom of Saudi Arabia and Yemen signed the Treaty of Taif, which brought an end to a violent war between the two countries. The treaty essentially established a common border between the two nations, but in reality, the border issue has not been resolved definitively. The 1934 war cost Yemen the Asir region and Najran Oasis, and Yemenis have never reconciled with this loss. In the late 1980s, after a long bloody civil war, Southern Yemen united with the North. Subsequently, the new Yemeni state sided with Iraq in the Gulf War (1990–1991), which essentially meant going against the Saudis and further complicated the already tense relations between the two countries. In 1992, the Saudi and Yemeni governments renewed intermittent talks to settle their border issues. However, the hostilities restarted when Saudi Arabia backed southern rebellious factions against the central government in the Yemeni Civil War in 1994. In June 1995, the Treaty of Taif was officially renewed, remarking the western boundary and establishing a framework to settle the disputed area on their eastern border. Regardless, disputes continued to flare up, the most significant of which took place in May 1998 over the ownership of several islands on the Red Sea. In 2000, the Jeddah Border Treaty was bilaterally signed by Yemen and Saudi Arabia, signaling an agreement on border demarcations between the two countries—which has proven to be short-lived.

In September 2003, Saudi Arabia began the construction a physical barrier along a section of its 1,100-mile border with Yemen. This structure is made of 10-feet-high pipeline, filled with concrete, and contains electronic detection equipment. Saudi Arabia called it a "security barrier" and claimed that this construction project is meant to protect the kingdom against border infiltrations and terrorist activities. The Yemeni government strongly objected to the construction of the 47-mile barrier, arguing that it was a blunt violation of the 2000 Border Treaty. The Saudi government sought to deescalate the situation and agreed to halt construction in February 2004. During the Saudi Arabia–led military intervention into the Yemeni civil conflict, which started in 2015, it has been reported that Saudi Arabia began removing sections of its border wall with Yemeni governorates of Sa'dah and Hajjah.

The issue of Saudi Arabia's offshore boundaries is a similarly complicated one. The Saudi government claims a 12-nautical-mile limit offshore as well as a number of islands in the Persian Gulf and the Red Sea. With the discovery of vast oil reservoirs in the Gulf, it became imperative to establish a median line between Saudi Arabia and Iran. But it was only in the 1970s that such a line was finally negotiated and established, following a number of incidents between the Aramco offshore oil rigs and the Iranian navy.

See also: Chapter 2: Third Saudi State: Saudi Arabia in the 20th Century. Chapter 3: Gulf Cooperation Council. Chapter 4: Oil Industry and Aramco; OPEC and OAPEC.

Further Reading

Al-Enazy, Askar. *The Long Road from Taif to Jeddah: Resolution of a Saudi-Yemeni Boundary Dispute*. Emirates Center for Strategic Studies and Research, 2005.

Al-Mazrouei, Noura Saber. *The UAE and Saudi Arabia: Border Disputes and International Relations in the Gulf*. I. B. Tauris, 2016.

Morton, Michael Quentin. *Buraimi: The Struggle for Power, Influence and Oil in Arabia*. I. B. Tauris, 2013.

Climate

Saudi Arabia is located in one of the harshest natural environments on Earth. However, for millennia the Arabian Peninsula was home to a much more favorable climate. In prehistoric times, the peninsula looked very different: it was a green savanna with ample rainfall and diverse wildlife, crossed by large river systems. Over time, several factors played their roles in radically changing the area's climate. With the ending of the last Ice Age about 15,000 years ago, the retreat of the glaciers led to a prolonged drought. Gradually, its rivers evaporated, and the once fertile land turned to desert. The formation of various mountain ranges in the Middle East, as well as changes in ocean currents and monsoon patterns, have contributed to gradual desertification of the region.

Currently, most of Saudi Arabia has a very hot climate that one associates with deserts, but there are important variations that influence the country's development projects. The kingdom can be divided into three main climate zones: (1) desert environment in various parts of the country; (2) steppe environment along the western highlands, forming a long strip between 100 and 300 miles wide; and (3) an area of balmy and humid climate in the mountains near Yemen.

In the interior region, the lack of humidity causes temperatures to rise sharply during the day, registering temperatures as high as 130 degrees Fahrenheit in the summer. The same lack of humidity causes temperatures to drop drastically after sunset, sometimes as sharply as by 70 degrees in less than three hours. Subfreezing temperatures are common in winter. Strong desert winds, such as the southern Kauf and the northwestern Shamal, create major dust storms.

The climate in the coastal areas combines heat and high humidity. Summer months here are steamy, with temperatures usually lower than in the desert—usually around 105°F–113°F—but not dropping more than just a few degrees at night. Winters, however, are warmer and milder than they are in the interior, with occasional rainfall. The mountain areas are cooler, particularly in the Asir, where it can get quite cold at night. The Asir also receives monsoon winds from the south in winter, which brings most of its annual rain—usually about 20 inches yearly.

The Arabian Peninsula is known for its torrential rains that can create floods in one area while keeping another area—just a couple of miles away—completely dry. At other times, the same area can go without rain for 5 to 10 years. The sporadic nature of rains largely defined the life of nomadic communities who had to move around wide areas in search of pasture for their livestock. In modern times, the Saudi government built several dams in wadis that are most frequently flooded, in order to conserve water and use it for agricultural purposes.

See also: Chapter 1: Asir; Great Deserts. Chapter 4: Agriculture.

Further Reading

Al Zawad, Faisal. *Climate Change in Saudi Arabia on a Regional Scale: Impacts on Evaporation, Surface Runoff and Soil Moisture.* VDM Verlag Dr. Müller, 2009.

Eastern Arabia: Al-Hasa

Historically, al-Hasa Oasis has been the most strategically important area in the eastern part of the country. In local Arabic, al-Hasa (also called al-Ahsa) means "sandy ground with water close to the surface," which accurately describes the area between the ad-Dahna Desert and the Gulf coast. Administratively, this area is designated as the Eastern Province. Al-Hasa is one of the most important regions for the Saudi economy: in addition to containing the bulk of Saudi oil reserves, it also has a large and prosperous oases system with substantial water supplies.

Al-Hasa Oasis, located inland from the coast, is one of the largest natural palm oases in the world. Hufuf is the largest and most populated town, which serves as both the local agricultural center and a residence area for oil field workers. A smaller oasis, Watif, is located to the north of al-Hasa on the Gulf coast. The two oases are home to the Saudi Shiite community. Historically, many members of this community worked for Aramco since the early days of the oil boom. Due to its abundance of water, this area has been inhabited since prehistoric times.

Eastern Arabia has been autonomous for most of its history and was ruled by both the Ottomans and the Saudis. In the past, the primary occupations of the local population were agriculture in the oases, maritime trading, fishing, and pearling in the Gulf. All this changed drastically with the discovery of oil in Dhahran in 1938. Subsequently, the area experienced an unprecedented population boom, as hundreds of thousands of Saudis from all over the country and numerous foreign workers came here for employment. Because of its highly diverse population, including a large number of Western employees and their families, the Eastern Province is arguably the most Westernized region in the country.

The region contains enormous reservoirs of oil beneath it. The Ghawar field, stretching for more than 124 miles from north to south, is the largest single oil field in the world. Unsurprisingly, the economy of the Eastern Province almost entirely relies on oil and petroleum-based industries. Oil facilities are concentrated in the north of the region, near the Kuwaiti border. These include Ras Tanura, the main Saudi Aramco terminal that extends to Khafji in what was once part of the Saudi-Kuwaiti Neutral Zone but was divided between the two countries in 1966. North of Ras Tanura is Jubail—the site of the first disembarkation of American oilmen in 1933 to what was then a small village. In the course of only a few decades, this village has grown into an important industrial center in the Middle East, serving both as the principal site of Saudi Arabia's petrochemical industry and the main Saudi naval base on the Persian Gulf coast.

The city of Dammam is the capital of the Eastern Province and its largest urban center. Like Jubail, not so long ago it was a small pearling port, but the oil boom quickly transformed it into a busy metropolis. Dhahran, located to the south of Dammam, is another major administrative center of the Eastern Province. Dhahran is home to Saudi Aramco headquarters, King Faysal University, and the U.S. Consulate General. The city of Khobar is yet another urban center that rapidly grew from a seaside village into one of the biggest cities in the Gulf Cooperation Council (GCC). Dammam, Dhahran, and Khobar constitute the Dammam metropolitan area, sometimes referred to as the "Triplet Cities."

See also: Chapter 4: Agriculture; Oil Industry and Aramco. Chapter 5: Shia Community. Chapter 6: Urbanization.

Further Reading

Jones, Toby Craig. *Desert Kingdom: How Oil and Water Forged Modern Saudi Arabia*. Harvard University Press, 2010.

Mandaville, James. *Flora of Eastern Saudi Arabia*. Taylor & Francis, 2013.

Nicholson, Eleanor. *In the Footsteps of the Camel: A Portrait of the Bedouins of Eastern Saudi Arabia in Mid-Century*. Transworld Arabian Library, 1983.

Pampanini, Andrea. *Cities from the Arabian Desert: The Building of Jubail and Yanbu in Saudi Arabia*. Praeger, 1997.

Environmental Issues after the Gulf War

The First Gulf War (1990–1991) brought about a serious environmental crisis after the largest oil spill in history occurred in the Persian Gulf. The volume of the spill was about 240 million gallons, and the maximum size of the oil slick was 100 miles by 42 miles, in some areas as deep as 5 inches. This environmental catastrophe had a devastating impact on the Saudi Arabian shoreline, in addition to the Kuwaiti and Iranian coasts, causing long-term damage to the shallow waters, plants, and wildlife. In some sections of the coast that were most impacted, sediments were found to contain as much as 7 percent of oil. Since these shallow areas serve as the feeding grounds for birds, fish, and shrimp, the spill produced highly negative consequences for the ecosystem and devastated the Saudi fishing industry.

The most severely affected Saudi coast was Jubail and the surrounding area. The spill threatened industrial facilities, which rely on a seawater cooling system, as well as the city's desalination plans. Jubail harbor and Abu Ali Island, located north of Jubail, experienced the greatest level of pollution. Marine birds died in great numbers as a result of oil coating their plumage. The beaches around Jubail were covered in oil and tar and completely destroyed.

The oil spill was not the only environmental disaster caused by the First Gulf War. The explosions and burning of over 700 oil wells in Kuwait also generated massive atmospheric pollution. Over 300 oil lakes appeared in the Kuwaiti desert as a result of this catastrophe. For comparison, the combined volume of desert oil spills was 20 times larger than the Persian Gulf oil spill. The soot from the oil fires traveled far from the region and was found in the snow covering the Himalayas and in rainfall over Iran, Oman, and Turkey. The pollution particles moved as far south as Riyadh, where residents reported that their outdoor belongings were covered with soot on a daily basis. The full effects of this airborne pollution on people's health and the environment are yet to be observed, but samples of soil and vegetation in Northern Saudi Arabia show that oily soot particles have become an integral part of the local desert ecology. The United Nations Environment Programme issued a warning that consuming livestock that grazed within an area of 2,700 square miles of the fires, which includes most of Northern Saudi Arabia, would pose danger to human health.

Undoubtedly, this environmental disaster—both oil spills and fires—has had far-reaching and highly damaging consequences to the region's wildlife, flora, human health, and water quality. In addition to these two major sources of environmental damage, one must also consider the impact of large quantities of waste and toxic materials left behind by military forces.

See also: Chapter 2: Third Saudi State: Saudi Arabia in the 20th Century. Chapter 4: Oil Industry and Aramco.

Further Reading
El-Baz, Farouk, and R. M. Makharita. *The Gulf War and the Environment*. Routledge, 2017.
Hawley, T. M. *Against the Fires of Hell: The Environmental Disaster of the Gulf War*. Harcourt Brace Jovanovich, 1992.

Fresh Water Reserves and Water Conservancy

Given the country's predominantly barren desert terrain, shortage of fresh water is one of Saudi Arabia's main resource problems. The central part of the country has large aquifers, but these are nonrenewable sources of water that have been exploited at unprecedented rates with the rapid urbanization and population growth. The type of aquifer found in Saudi Arabia contains the so-called fossil water, which remains undisturbed for millennia in a contained space underground. These aquifers have extremely slow replenishment rates and are in danger of irreversible damage from human overuse. Some scientists warn that most of these natural water resources may disappear by the middle of the 21st century. The crisis comes as a result of the government's aggressive agricultural policies, which overstretched the already scarce water resources. In the past, various agricultural projects were created in order to support Bedouin settlements, which were growing at rapid rates. This growth produced additional problems, such as improperly drilled wells that leached the lands they were meant to irrigate.

Despite its primarily arid climate, Saudi Arabia experiences sporadic torrential rains, as well as occasional snowfall in the mountainous area. To help retain and utilize this rainwater, as well as to control flooding, dams have been built in different parts of the country, including King Fahad Dam, Baysh Dam, Jizan Dam, Wahi Rabigh Dam, Hali Dam, and several others. Numerous drainage systems were created of intersecting wadis, which can become temporary water reservoirs. Some of the biggest wadi drainage systems in the country are Wadi Sirhan near the Saudi-Jordanian frontier; Wadi al-Batin in the northeast; Wadi Rimah near the Hijaz Mountains; and Wadi Dawasir and Wadi Bishah near the Asir Mountains.

In recent years, new technology allowed to identify new possible sources of underground water. Saudi Aramco scientists discovered a number of super deep aquifers in Northern and Eastern Arabia. Additionally, the scientific exploration showed that the largest Saudi aquifer, Wasia, has larger amounts of underground water than the Persian Gulf. In recent years, various initiatives by the Saudi government, Aramco, and the United Nations Food and Agriculture Organization continue to explore the country's underground water resources.

WHAT IS A WADI?

Wadi literally means "valley" in Arabic and is an important part of the Arabian landscape. In some instances, especially in the context of desert topography and climate, the term may refer to an ephemeral (dried up) riverbed that fills up with water only at times of heavy rain. In English, this term is also used and suggests its distinction from canyons, river valleys, and gullies by the action of water. In the wadi's case, water supply is intermittent. Infrequent but sudden and heavy rainfall, typical of the desert environment, often results in flash floods. Crossing wadis at certain times of the year can be very dangerous. But flash floods also serve as a much-needed water supply, which can transform a barren and stony ground into a lush grassy landscape overnight. Historically, wadis have been central to the Arabian nomadic civilization as they provided pasture for livestock and often contained subsurface water. The term "wadi" is widely used in Arabic topography.

The kingdom has also created a massive water desalination system. To help meet the constantly increasing water consumption, the Saudi government plans to further expand its desalination operations and build new projects. The unprecedented rate of urbanization created a need for a large-scale investment—an estimated $30 billion—into the desalination industry over the next 15 years. A large number of desalination plants are currently under construction, and many more will be built in the next decade. If all planned projects are completed, they will add nearly 3 million cubic meters per day to the country's capacity. However, the desalination industry does have a negative side in its impact on local environment. The plants located on the Red Sea coast discharge large amounts of brine and various chemicals, including chlorine, which have highly negative impact on the unique coral flora and fauna of the Red Sea. Although currently this remains a localized problem, the planned growth of the Saudi desalination industry will almost certainly expand environmental issues and profoundly impact the fishing industry.

See also: Chapter 1: Climate; The Red Sea. Chapter 4: Science and Technology.

Further Reading

Alsharhan, A. S. *Hydrogeology of an Arid Region: The Arabian Gulf and Adjoining Areas.* Elsevier, 2001.

DeNicola, Erica. "Climate Change and Water Scarcity: The Case of Saudi Arabia." *Annals of Global Health*, vol. 81, no. 3, 2015, pp. 342–353.

Multsch, S. "Water-Saving Strategies for Irrigation Agriculture in Saudi Arabia." *International Journal of Water Resources Development*, vol. 33, no. 2, 2017, pp. 292–309.

Great Deserts

Although the majority of Saudi Arabia's territory is dry and barren, only part of it consists of real sand desert. There are three such deserts in the kingdom. The Rub al-Khali Desert, which means the "empty quarter" in Arabic, stretches along the entire southern frontier. The Nafud, sometimes called the Great Nafud, is located in the north. "Nafud" is one of several Arabic words meaning "desert." The long and narrow ad-Dahna Desert curves in a large arc from the Nafud westward and then south until its joining point with Rub al-Khali. The sand in all three deserts contains iron oxide, giving it a pink color that turns to beautiful deep red in sunset.

The Rub al-Khali Desert covers over 210,000 square miles and is the largest quartz sand desert in the world. The local tribes also call it *al-rumal*, which means "the sands." Apart from a few Bedouin tribes, most of this area is uninhabited and remained largely unexplored until the 1960s, when Aramco teams began searching for oil in the region. Much of the Rub al-Khali is hard-packed sand and salt flats, with sand mountains rising as high as 1,000 feet. Some of these giant sand dunes form long ridges that extend for up to 25 miles.

The dunes of the Rub al-Khali Desert. (Samir Shaji/Dreamstime.com)

The Nafud Desert, occupying about 21,000 square miles, is made up of similar but much smaller sand ridges, which reach about 295 meters in elevation and are divided by flats. Its dunes are shaped like giant horseshoes, for scientifically unknown reasons. Occasional winter rains transform the Nafud valleys into lush grazing areas in the spring. The ad-Dahna Desert stretches for more than 125 kilometers south from the Nafud. It is mainly made of a narrow strip of sand mountains and is often called the "river of sand." Its sands are similar to those of the Nafud deserts and are reddish in color, particularly in its northern part. Winter rains in the ad-Dahna also provide the Bedouins with spring pasture, although here water is even more scarce than in the Nafud Desert. The ad-Dahna is particularly famous for its high sand dunes, which are called "veins" in Arabic, *'uruq*.

See also: Chapter 4: Oil Industry and Aramco. Chapter 6: Bedouins and Nomadism. Chapter 11: Poetry.

Further Reading

Al Obaida, Abdulaziz, et al. *Rub Al Khali: Empty Quarter*. Desert, 2009.

Edgell, H. Stewart. *Arabian Deserts: Nature, Origin and Evolution*. Springer, 2006.

Kelly, Kathleen, and R. T Schnadelbach. *Landscaping the Saudi Arabian Desert*. Delancey Press, 1976.

Kirkby, Bruce. *Sand Dance: By Camel across Arabia's Great Southern Desert*. McClelland & Stewart, 2000.

Steinmetz, George. *Empty Quarter: A Photographic Journey to the Heart of the Arabian Desert*. Abrams, 2009.

Hijaz and Tihamah

The Hijaz region, which means "barrier" or "boundary" in Arabic, is situated in the western part of the country and covers an area of 58,000 square miles. Geographically, the Hijaz consists of the Red Sea coastal strip and the highland above it. This region contains some of the oldest and most important urban centers in the country: the holy cities of Mecca and Medina, the Red Sea port city of Jeddah, Taif, and the industrial city of Yanbu. About 35 percent of the Saudi population live in the Hijaz, which is divided into three provinces: the Mecca Province in the south, the Medina Province in the center, and the Tabuk Province in the north.

The escarpment highlands of the region are called the Hijaz Mountains. They do not exceed 6,400 feet and become lower as one travels north. The eastern side of the mountains borders the Najdi plateau and has several large lava fields (*harrat*), where the terrain resembles lunar landscape. The largest of them, Harrat Khaybar, is situated north of Medina. As for the highlands, due to their mild climate they have long been favored by the kingdom's elite as a summer resort. The city of Taif, located in the Mecca Province, is considered the country's unofficial summer capital.

Tihamah, the long coastal strip of the Hijaz, is characterized by high heat and humidity, and sparse rainfall. The name "Tihamah," used for the whole plain, is sometimes divided into Tihamat Al-Hijaz and Tihamat Asir, indicating the areas of the strip closer to the Hijaz or the Asir Mountains, respectively. The coast has numerous coral reefs and small islands, especially in its southern part where the Farasan Archipelago lies. Prior to the oil boom, the primary occupations of the Tihamah residents were herding, subsistence farming, and pilgrim trade. Even today, Tihamah remains noticeably underdeveloped in comparison to the rest of Saudi Arabia, and its population is among the poorest in the country.

For most of its history, the Hijaz was an independent state until it was conquered by Ibn Saud in 1924 and annexed in 1926. The Hijaz is perhaps the most cosmopolitan section of Saudi Arabia, given the high numbers of foreign visitors to the two holy cities, Mecca and Medina. One of the five basic pillars (tenets) of Islam is the Hajj, or great pilgrimage to Mecca, and the pilgrim service industry has always been the backbone of the Hijazi economy. Even before Islam, this area had important trade routes, such as caravan routes to Yemen for frankincense trade. Although non-Muslims are banned from entering both cities, for centuries Muslims from every corner on earth have been coming to this area and bringing with them elements of their cultures and traditions, with some of these pilgrims even settling down and mixing with the local population.

Most pilgrims came by land and later by sea, especially following the construction of the Suez Canal. The Hijaz Railway, which was built in 1908 and connected Damascus in the north and Medina in the south, was also a major means of pilgrim travel. It also served as an important military route for the Ottoman troops in World War I, fighting against the British advancing from Egypt, and it was made famous by guerilla attacks to disrupt it by Colonel T. E. Lawrence, better known as Lawrence of Arabia. However, in the past 30 years, Muslim pilgrims have been increasingly coming to the country by air.

See also: Chapter 1: Mecca; Medina. Chapter 2: Arab Revolt (1916–1918); Ibn Saud; Third Saudi State: Saudi Arabia in the 20th Century. Chapter 5: Five Pillars or the Tenets of Islam; Hajj. Chapter 9: Dialect of Hijaz.

Further Reading

Durrani, Nadia. *The Tihamah Coastal Plain of South-West Arabia in Its Regional Context, 6000 B.C.–600 A.D.* Archaeopress, 2005.

Great Britain, Naval Intelligence Division. *Western Arabia and the Red Sea.* Kegan Paul, 2005.

Ochsenwald, William. *The Hijaz Railroad.* University Press of Virginia, 1980.

Yamani, Mai. *Cradle of Islam: The Hijaz and the Quest for an Arabian Identity.* I. B. Tauris, 2004.

Jeddah

The city of Jeddah on the Red Sea coast, which historically served as an entry point for the pilgrims, is often called the Bride of the Red Sea. There are several theories about the etymology of the name "Jeddah." The most common of them traces its origins to the Arabic word "grandmother" or "ancestress," which has an identical spelling, in reference to the tomb of Eve located in the city. In the past, the tomb was visited by many pilgrims, until the religious authorities under King Abd al-Aziz labeled it a heretical site and had it sealed with concrete in 1975. Some archaeological studies suggest the existence of human settlement in this location since the Stone Age. According to a number of historical accounts, both Arabs and Persians were the main residents of Jeddah. After the emergence of Islam, the city was ruled by numerous Islamic dynasties and empires, including the Umayyads, the Abbasids, the Fatimids, the Ottomans, and the Wahhabis.

Jeddah was the largest city in the kingdom before Riyadh had undergone a rapid expansion and was opened to foreigners in the 1970s. Although Riyadh has overshadowed Jeddah as the country's financial and diplomatic center, the latter remains a major seaport, a commercial hub, and the gates to the Hajj and the Hijaz in general. By 2009 its estimated population exceeded 3.5 million. The city continues to expand and diversify

The Red Sea coastline at the city of Jeddah. (Sosroner/Dreamstime.com)

its economy, with rising skyscrapers, urban renewal projects, and the growth of new industries, such as desalination plants, steel-rolling mills, and manufacturing of cement, clothing, and pottery. To accommodate the enormous and constantly increasing numbers of travelers, a large international airport was built in Jeddah in 1981. It is famous for its special terminal for pilgrims, called the Hajj Terminal, which is the world's largest structure under a single roof and can accommodate 80,000 travelers at the same time. A major airport expansion is scheduled to open in 2018 and is projected to increase the airport's capacity from 13 to 80 million. Many expect that the new airport will offer a large number of diverse employment opportunities for women—yet another testimony to the city's more liberal social norms than the rest of the country.

See also: Chapter 1: The Red Sea. Chapter 5: Hajj. Chapter 6: Urbanization.

Further Reading

Al-Ziad Aseeri, Ahmed Mater. *Sculptures of Jeddah: Twentieth-Century Sculpture in the Arabian Peninsula*. Booth-Clibborn Editions, 2015.

Buchan, James, et al. *Jeddah: Old and New*. Stacey International, 1996.

Danforth, Loring M. *Crossing the Kingdom: Portraits of Saudi Arabia*. University of California Press, 2016.

Farsi, Hani M. S. *Jeddah, City of Art: The Sculptures and Monuments*. Stacey International, 1991.

Mecca

The city of Mecca, located on the Tihamah plain, is the capital and administrative headquarters of the Mecca Province. It is located 43 miles inland from Jeddah and the Red Sea and 210 miles south of Medina, in a narrow valley at the altitude of 900 feet above sea level. Mecca is surrounded by the Sirat Mountains. These include Mount Hira that rises to 2,080 feet on the northeast and is famous for its cave in which Muhammad, the founder of Islam, saw visions before becoming the prophet. According to the Muslim tradition, this cave was also the site where he received the first verse ("*ayah*") of the Quran, Islam's holy book. The city's center is the area of Masjid al-Haram, the Great Mosque, which is situated at a lower altitude than the rest of the city.

The full official name of the city is "al-Makkah al-Mukarramah," which means "Mecca, the Honored." The ancient name of this location was Bakkah, and the origins of both words remain unclear. Most think that Bakkah is merely a synonym for Mecca, but many Muslim scholars attribute it to the most sacred center of the city—the Kaaba and the area that surrounds it. According to Islamic sources, the Kaaba, located in ancient Mecca, was a place of idol worshipping for pagan Bedouin tribes long before Islam. At that time, it was a small square building containing various idols (the Arabic word *kaabah* means a "cube"). As any nomadic society surviving a harsh environment, the local tribes were in near-constant state of conflict. However, once a year all tribes declared a truce and came to Mecca for a pilgrimage. They paid respects to their idols' shrines by walking around the Kaaba and drinking water from the sacred Zamzam Well. It was also the time when debts would be settled, disputes arbitrated, trade agreements made, and when tribal poets would have public competitions. These annual events made Mecca an important economic and spiritual center of the peninsula.

With the rise of Islam, Mecca—the birthplace of Muhammad and the site of the first revelation of the Quran, in addition to being home to the Kaaba—became the holiest city of the Muslim world and the direction of Muslim prayer. In Islam, performing a pilgrimage, or the Hajj, at least once in a lifetime is a religious obligation for all able Muslims. In 2012, Mecca's resident population was about 2 million, but pilgrims from all over the world more than triple this number during the Hajj. There are two types of Islamic pilgrimage: the Hajj and the Umrah. The Hajj, or the "greater" pilgrimage, is performed annually in Mecca and nearby sites, and this takes place during specific days of the 12th month of the Islamic lunar calendar, Dhu al-Hijjah. Umrah, the "minor" pilgrimage, is not mandatory but is recommended in the Quran and can be performed at any time during the year.

In modern times, Mecca has undergone a remarkable expansion in size and infrastructure. Many ultramodern construction projects were initiated by the Saudi government, which have drastically changed Mecca's cityscape. These structures include the Abraj al-Bayt ("The Towers of the House"), also known as the Mecca Royal Clock Tower, one of the world's tallest buildings. However, the radical remodeling of the city came at a high cost. It is estimated that since 1985 almost all of Mecca's historical buildings and structures, most over a thousand years old, have been destroyed. The important historical sites demolished during the remodeling of the city include five of the renowned Seven Mosques built by Muhammad's daughter and four of his greatest companions; the Ottoman-era Ajyad Fortress, leveled to make room for the aforementioned Abraj al-Bayt; the house of Khadijah, the first wife of Muhammad; and many more.

See also: Chapter 1: Hijaz and Tihamah; Medina. Chapter 2: Muhammad, Prophet of Islam; Pre-Islamic Arabia; The Rise of Islam; Sharifs of Mecca. Chapter 5: Five Pillars or the Tenets of Islam; Hajj; Quran. Chapter 12: Great Mosque of Mecca; Modernization of Saudi Architecture.

Further Reading

Bianchi, Robert. *Guests of God: Pilgrimage and Politics in the Islamic World.* Oxford University Press, 2004.

Hammoudi, Abdellah, and Pascale Ghazaleh. *A Season in Mecca: Narrative of a Pilgrimage.* Hill & Wang, 2006.

Sardar, Ziauddin. *Mecca: The Sacred City.* Bloomsbury, 2014.

Wolfe, Michael. *One Thousand Roads to Mecca: Ten Centuries of Travelers Writing about the Muslim Pilgrimage.* Grove Press, 1997.

Medina

Like Mecca, Medina also has a formal name with an epithet: "Al-Madinah al-Munawwarah," which means the "The Luminous City." It is located in the Hijaz, the western part of Saudi Arabia, about 100 miles inland from the Red Sea and 275 miles from Mecca. Along with Mecca, Medina is one of the two holiest cities in Islam. Only Muslims are allowed to enter it. Its spiritual and cultural importance goes back to the time when Muhammad left Mecca for Medina in 622 AD, and it became the center from which the Muslim conquest of Arabia took place.

Medina is situated in an oasis at the elevation of 2,050 feet above sea level. It is surrounded by several mountains: al-Hujaj, or the "Pilgrims' Mount," to the west; Salaa is in the northwest; al-Ayr in the south; and Uhud, the highest of them, to the north. Medina sits on a flat plateau at the intersection of three valleys, which create natural green areas in the middle of the otherwise dry region. To the east of the city, there is a large lava field, which can be traced back to the volcanic eruption in the 13th century AD. About 18 miles to the northwest of Medina, there is Wadi al-Jinn, or the Jinn Valley, which attracts thousands of locals and visitors. It is famous for the curious natural phenomenon that makes cars accelerate uphill on their own, sometimes at the astounding speeds of 75 miles per hour—with engines turned off. Local legends attribute this curious phenomenon to the Jinn powers, hence the name of the place, but most scientists agree that this is a so-called gravity hill where a downhill slope looks like it is uphill, due to the optical illusion created by the surrounding landscape.

The early history of Medina is unclear, though it is known that a community of Jewish settlers lived here in pre-Christian times. On September 20, 622, the arrival of Muhammad and his closest followers to Medina turned it into one of the most prominent cities of the Arab and Muslim world. This relocation, *Hijrah*, which means "emigration," marks the beginning of the Islamic calendar. Medina quickly became the administrative center of the expanding Islamic state, until it was overshadowed by Damascus as the new capital of the Umayyad caliphs.

The religious center of the city is al-Masjid al-Nabawy, "the Prophet's Mosque," where Muhammad is buried. Medina has many other sites that hold utmost importance in Islam. Among these is the mosque of Quba—the very first mosque in history, built by Muhammad and his followers. Among other historically and religiously significant sites are the Mosque of the Two Qiblahs, which commemorates the change of the prayer direction from Jerusalem to Mecca; the tomb of Hamza, Muhammad's uncle and one of his closest allies who was killed in the Battle of Uhud in 625; and the cave at the Uhud Mount where a wounded Muhammad took refuge after the battle. The modernization of Medina was less drastic than that of Mecca, Jeddah, and Riyadh. However, new construction has completely dismantled the old city wall, among other historical neighborhoods.

The bulk of the city's income comes from the tourist industry serving the pilgrims, but its economy is diversified and also includes well-developed agriculture, focusing on fruits, vegetables, and grains. Medina is especially known for its date palms and has a thriving export industry of date fruits. Some traditions even attribute the first human cultivation of palm to this area.

See also: Chapter 1: Hijaz and Tihamah; Mecca. Chapter 2: Muhammad, Prophet of Islam; Pre-Islamic Arabia; The Rise of Islam. Chapter 5: Five Pillars or the Tenets of Islam; Hajj; Quran.

Further Reading

Ismail Muhammad Kamal, and Damluji Salma Samar. *The Architecture of the Prophet's Holy Mosque, Al Madinah*. Hazar, 1998.

Makki, M. S. *Medina, Saudi Arabia: A Geographic Analysis of the City and Region*. Bucks, Avebury, 1982.

Munt, Harry. *The Holy City of Medina: Sacred Space in Early Islamic Arabia*. Cambridge University Press, 2014.

Nasr, Seyyed Hossein, and Kazuyoshi Nomachi. *Mecca the Blessed, Medina the Radiant: The Holiest Cities of Islam*. Turtle Publishing, 2017.

Najd: Central Arabia

Central Saudi Arabia, or Najd, which means "highlands" in Arabic, is the geographical and political heart of the country. This region is where the current Saudi state emerged, as the ruling Al Saud dynasty has its roots in Najd. It occupies about one-third of Saudi Arabia or 270,000 square miles—an area almost as big as France. Geographically, four natural barriers isolate Najd from the rest of the country: the three great deserts, ad-Dahna, Nafud, and Rub al-Khali, and the fourth barrier is made of the Hijaz Mountains stretching along the Red Sea. Najd is a great rocky plateau, which includes several ranges extending from north to south, including al-Khuff, Jilh al-Ishar, and the Tuwayq Mountains, the latter the longest and highest of them. Stretching for over 800 miles, the Tuwayq Mountains stretch through the most densely populated part of Najd, which also incorporates the city of Riyadh.

Najd is among the driest areas on earth and receives an average of only 4 inches of rain per year. Summer temperatures are very severe, with highs often exceeding 129°F, but as is typical of a desert climate, winter temperatures sometimes drop below freezing, with occasional snow and sleet. In contrast with the rest of the country, Najd has low humidity.

The unique location, harsh climate, and topography of Najd, which was one of the last regions to open up to the rest of the world, shaped the lives, culture, and social norms of its inhabitants. For many centuries, this region belonged to the Bedouin nomadic tribes, although there were also sedentary families in small oases, where farming was the primary occupation. Local Bedouins and farmers had a mutually beneficial relationship where the former protected the latter from the hostile raiding tribes in exchange for agricultural products, metals, and cloth.

Historically, Najd consisted of small autonomous townships, but now it is divided into three large provinces: the Riyadh Province, the Qassim Province, and the Hail Province. Najd has numerous cities and towns, the largest of which is the country's capital, Riyadh. Having undergone an unprecedented economic, political, and cultural development in the past 60 years, Riyadh is not the only city in Najd that was completely transformed. The Qassim Province, which lies between Riyadh and Hail, is known for its neighboring and rival cities of Buraydah, which is the capital of the province, and Unayzah. Qassim's community is considered the most conservative in Saudi Arabia. Despite the area's traditionalism, the oil boom and subsequent modernization projects have changed it as much as they have Riyadh. Currently, Qassim is the richest region per capita in Saudi Arabia. In the last decades, it has become a major agricultural center because of heavy investment in modern large-scale irrigated farming. For instance, Qassim hosts over 8 million date palm trees, making this area one of the biggest producers and exporters of dates in the Middle East. However, the large-scale agricultural projects have at the same time created environmental concerns because irrigation is supplied by nonrenewable aquifers that are rapidly drying up.

See also: Chapter 2: Emirate of Diriyah: The First Saudi State (1744–1818); Emirate of Najd: The Second Saudi State (1824–1891); Ibn Saud; Ikhwan; Muhammad ibn Abd al-Wahhab; Third Saudi State: Saudi Arabia in the 20th Century. Chapter 3: Wahhabi Ideology. Chapter 6: Bedouins and Nomadism; House of Saud. Chapter 9: Dialect of Najdi.

Further Reading

Al-Juhany, Uwidah Metaireek, and Darat al-Malik Abd al-Aziz. *Najd before the Salafi Reform Movement: Social, Political, and Religious Conditions during the Three Centuries Preceding the Rise of the Saudi State.* Ithaca Press, 2002.

AlOboudi, Sharifah M. "Najd, the Heart of Arabia." *Arab Studies Quarterly*, vol. 37, no. 3, 2015, pp. 282–299.

Steinberg, Guido. "Ecology, Knowledge, and Trade in Central Arabia (Najd) during the Nineteenth and Early Twentieth Centuries." *Counter-Narratives: History, Contemporary Society, and Politics in Saudi Arabia and Yemen.* Edited by Madawi Al-Rasheed and Robert Vitalis. Palgrave Macmillan, 2004, pp. 77–102.

Northern Arabia

Al-Jawf and al-Hudud al-Shimaliyyah, the latter meaning "Northern Frontiers" in Arabic, are the two provinces that constitute the northern region of Saudi Arabia, separated from the rest of the country by the Nafud Desert. Topographically, the northern region is a part of the Syrian Desert, and the local tribes have centuries-long close relations with fellow tribes in neighboring Jordan, Iraq, and Syria. Al-Hudud al-Shimaliyyah is the least populated area in Saudi Arabia. Its capital is the city of Arar, surrounded by picturesque wadis. It is a local center for hunting with hawks and falcons.

Al-Jawf is among the lesser-known Saudi regions, but it has a rich ancient history. The two biggest towns are the provincial capital Sakaka and Dumat al-Jandal. There is evidence of prehistoric human habitation in the desert north of Sakaka—the Neolithic stone megaliths, al-Rajajil. Further west is Dumat al-Jandal, which in ancient times was the capital of the earliest known Arabian state, dating back to the 8th century BC. It was ruled by a succession of queens who controlled the tribes as far north as Syria. In the 3rd century AD, the legendary Arabian queen Zenobia attempted to conquer Dumat al-Jandal but failed. The town Dumat al-Jandal is famous for its ancient fortress, Qasr al-Marid, and one of the oldest mosques in Saudi Arabia, Masjid al-Omar, is thought to be a Christian church in pre-Islamic times. In 630 AD, the al-Jawf community were among the earliest converts to Islam.

In ancient times, Northern Arabia was an important area for trade since the main east-west caravan route from the Mediterranean to the Far East passed through the region. However, in 762 AD, the Abbasids moved this trade route north after declaring Baghdad the capital of the Abbasid caliphate. Since then, Northern Arabia has lost its strategic importance. In modern times, since the discovery of oil, this area regained some of its economic significance with the installation of the Trans-Arabian Pipeline (Tapline), which transferred crude oil from Saudi Arabia's Eastern Province to the Lebanese port of Sidon. But after the 1967 Arab-Israeli War, the Tapline lost much of its importance due to Israeli occupation of Syria's Golan Heights, although it is still used to send oil to Jordan.

See also: Chapter 2: Nabateans. Chapter 6: Major Tribes; Sulubbah.

Further Reading

Ingham, Bruce. *Bedouin of Northern Arabia: Traditions of the Al-Dhafir.* KPI, 1986.

Muaikil, Khalil Ibrahim. *Study of the Archaeology of the Jawf Region, Saudi Arabia.* King Fahd National Library, 1994.

Sudayri, Abd al-Rahman. *The Desert Frontier of Arabia: Al-Jawf through the Ages.* Stacey International, 1995.

The Persian Gulf

The Persian Gulf is an inland sea that occupies the area of 97,000 square miles and extends from northwest to southeast for 615 miles. Most of its northern, northeastern, and eastern coasts are occupied by Iran. On the southwest and south, it is bordered by the United Arab Emirates (UAE) and Oman. Southwestern and western coasts are occupied by Saudi Arabia, Qatar, and Bahrain, whereas Iraq and Kuwait are situated on its northwestern shores. The Strait of Hormuz connects the Persian Gulf to the Gulf of Oman in the southeast. The northwestern part of the Persian Gulf is marked by the Shatt al-Arab—a massive river delta that connects the waters of the Euphrates and the Tigris—the two largest rivers in Western Asia. The Persian Gulf is about 35 miles wide at its narrowest point, in the Strait of Hormuz. Its waters are very shallow, with the maximum depth of 295 feet and the average depth of 164 feet.

The controversy behind the dual naming of the Persian Gulf highlights its strategic importance, as well as the complex political situation in this region. On nearly all maps published before 1960, as well as the absolute majority of modern international agreements, proceedings, maps, and geographical references, this sea is identified by the name "Persian Gulf." This represents the convention introduced by ancient Greek geographers. The first attempt to change its name to the Arabian Gulf goes back to the 1950s and was proposed by Sir Charles Belgrave, then the British adviser to the ruler of Bahrain. With the rise of Arab nationalism in the 1960s, a number of Arab countries, including the ones situated along the Persian Gulf, introduced and promoted the term "Arab Gulf" or "Arabian Gulf" (al-Khalij al-Arabi). Saudi Arabia has been one of the most enthusiastic proponents of the Arabian Gulf cause, especially as frictions continued to escalate with Iran. Nowadays, members of the Arab League, a regional union of 22 member-states with the shared goal of promoting the affairs and interests of Arab countries, have adopted the term "Arabian Gulf." Sometimes neutral terms like "The Gulf" or the "Arabo-Persian Gulf" are used in international contexts. Iran uses the term "Persian Gulf" exclusively and does not recognize any alternative forms. Foreign airlines that do not utilize the term "Persian Gulf" are even banned from Iranian airspace. In 2004, Iran initiated the National Persian Gulf Day, which has been celebrated yearly ever since on April 30, coinciding with the anniversary of Shah Abbas—a successful military campaign that drove the Portuguese Navy from

An aerial view of Dammam on the Persian Gulf coast in Saudi Arabia. (Attila Jandi/Dreamstime.com)

the Strait of Hormuz in the 17th century. The matter of competing naming conventions of the Persian Gulf remains highly contentious and underscores the political and economic confrontations between Iran and its Arab neighbors. Google Maps shows both terms, with Arabian Gulf in parentheses. But it also shows either Arabian or Persian Gulf to local Google users, depending on geolocation and language settings.

The Persian Gulf has highly diverse and largely unique wildlife due to its geographic location and its almost complete isolation from external waters—apart from the narrow Strait of Hormuz. From corals to fish to marine animals, the Persian Gulf is home to many species who depend on each other for survival. Unfortunately, the rapid industrialization of the region put a substantial portion of its fauna and flora at serious environmental risk. The Persian Gulf has many islands, including Bahrain Island, which is an independent Arab state. In recent years, some Gulf states, particularly the UAE, have been creating various artificial islands for commercial reasons. Although very small, these islands are negatively impacting the marine environment upon which they are built.

The Persian Gulf was home to Sumer, the world's oldest known civilization. In prehistoric times, the Gulf's shallow basin was made of river valleys and wetlands, which early humans used as an environmental refuge. Nowadays, the Gulf's economic and political importance stems from its being the world's largest single source of crude oil. It also contains extensive reservoirs of natural gas. Safaniya, the world's largest offshore oil field and owned by Saudi Aramco, is located in the Gulf.

See also: Chapter 1: Fresh Water Reserves and Water Conservancy; The Red Sea. Chapter 3: Gulf Cooperation Council. Chapter 4: Oil Industry and Aramco; Petrochemical Industry.

Further Reading

Abu-Zinada, A. H. *Protecting the Gulf's Marine Ecosystems from Pollution.* Birkhauser, 2008.

Al-Azab, M., et al. *Oil Pollution and Its Environmental Impact in the Arabian Gulf Region.* Elsevier, 2005.

Rice, Michael. *The Archaeology of the Arabian Gulf, c. 5000–323 B.C.* Routledge, 1994.

Soucek, Svatopluk. *The Persian Gulf: Its Past and Present.* Mazda, 2008.

Population

According to the 2012 census, Saudi Arabia's population was estimated to be 29,195,895 persons—the 43rd largest in the world. However, more recent estimates produced in 2016 indicate that it has grown to exceed 31 million since then. Although these numbers are relatively small in comparison to the country's great wealth, the population growth in the last 40 years has been very rapid: from 5 million in 1973 to 13 million in 1990 to 22.5 million in 2003 and expected to reach 33 million in 2018.

The birth rate in Saudi Arabia is well above the world average, due to the government policy promoting large families and substantial investments in health care. The latter also helps to keep the death rate significantly below the world standard. As a result, Saudi Arabia's overall rate of natural population growth is more than twice the world average. The country has a high ratio of young population, with over half of the total population under 30 years old and about one-fourth below the age of 15.

The population includes approximately 9 million non-nationals, most of whom come to Saudi Arabia for work. However, it is very difficult to estimate the real number of foreigners, given the large number of illegal workers that some sources estimate at 2 million but is likely significantly higher. The Kingdom of Saudi Arabia has some of the strictest citizenship and naturalization laws and does not provide permanent residency to foreigners.

One of the most important aspects of contemporary Saudi society is its rapid large-scale urbanization, stemming both from the oil boom and from consistent political and administrative centralization. The urban share of the total population rose from 16 percent in 1950 to 48 percent in 1970 to 77 percent in 1990 and to 85 percent in 2000, making Saudi Arabia one of the most urbanized countries in the Arab world and comparable with urbanization levels in Western Europe. The unprecedented development of oil-based industries has encouraged a rapid growth of cities from Dammam-Dhahran-Khobar in the east through Riyadh and Jeddah in the west, gradually absorbing the great majority of Saudi Arabia's population. Riyadh is currently the largest city in the country, home to over 7 million people.

Although the government does not hold census on religion, the country's population is evidently close to being 100 percent Muslim. The majority of 85 to 90 percent belong to the Sunni branch of Islam, and the Shiites comprise the remaining 10 to 15 percent.

The indigenous Saudi population is among the most homogeneous in the Middle East. Genealogy, not geography, determines nationality, and being born in Saudi Arabia does not automatically entitle a person to citizenship. The importance of bloodlines is a manifestation of the essentially tribal nature of Saudi society. With genealogy so important, there is relatively little social mobility in Saudi Arabia. Najd is seen as having the purest bloodlines as the result of their geographical isolation. Being the center of Saudi political power, it is also regarded for the most prestigious tribal affiliations on the Arabian Peninsula. Hijaz is ethnographically the most diverse region because of the thousands of pilgrims who have settled there, mixing with the local population. Another contributing factor was the area's developed economy, which had been attracting traders and merchants from different parts of the Arab world centuries before the oil boom. In the Asir, much of the population have Yemeni background. In al-Hasa, the growth of the oil industry attracted diverse and polyglot population that now rivals that of the Hijaz.

Based on UNESCO data, 94.41 percent of adult Saudi population aged 15 years and above are literate. The literacy rate for the adult male population is 97 percent, and 91 percent for the adult female population. Youth literacy rates, covering the population between the ages of 15 and 24 years, are even higher and constitute 99.38 percent and 99.29 percent for males and females accordingly. The overall youth literacy rate is 99.34 percent.

See also: Chapter 5: Shia Community. Chapter 6: Bedouins and Nomadism; Ethnic Composition; Settled Population: *Hadar*; Urbanization.

Further Reading

Al Mogren, Faisal bin Ayyaf. "Reprioritizing the Human Factor in Building Gulf Cities." *International Journal of Middle East Studies*, vol. 50, no. 3, Aug. 2018, pp. 568–572.

Hoyland, Robert G. *Arabia and the Arabs: From the Bronze Age to the Coming of Islam*. Routledge, 2001.

Matthiesen, Toby. *Sectarian Gulf: Bahrain, Saudi Arabia, and the Arab Spring That Wasn't*. Stanford Briefs, an Imprint of Stanford University Press, 2013.

Menoret, Pascal. "The Suburbanization of Islamic Activism in Saudi Arabia." *City & Society*, vol. 29, no. 1, 2017, pp. 162–186.

Petraglia, M. D., and Jeffrey I. Rose. *The Evolution of Human Populations in Arabia: Paleoenvironments, Prehistory and Genetics*. Springer, 2009.

The Red Sea

The Red Sea is a body of water that separates the continents of Africa and Asia and covers the area of about 174,000 square miles. In the south, it connects to the Indian

Ocean through the Bab Al-Mandab Strait and the Gulf of Aden. On its northern end are the Sinai Peninsula, the Gulf of Aqaba, and the Gulf of Suez leading to the Suez Canal. The Red Sea is bordered by six countries: Saudi Arabia and Yemen on the eastern shore; and Egypt, Sudan, Eritrea, and Djibouti on the western shore. Its maximum width is 190 miles, and its greatest depth is 9,974 feet. The Red Sea's ecosystem is rich and diverse. It is home to more than 1,000 invertebrates and 200 kinds of soft and hard corals. More than 1,200 species of fish have been recorded in the Red Sea, including 42 species of deep-water fish. About 10 percent of these species are unique to the Red Sea. This great diversity of sea life is in part due to the long coral reef extending for 1,240 miles along its coastline. The Red Sea is the world's northernmost tropical sea and contains some of the warmest and saltiest seawater. No rivers enter the Red Sea, and rainfall in this region is scarce. However, the high evaporation loss of over 80 inches per year is compensated by consistent inflow from the Gulf of Aden through the Bab el-Mandab Strait.

The Red Sea received its name from the drastic variations in color of its waters. Usually, its surface has a rich turquoise color, but during the blooming season of its algae *Trichodesmium erythraeum*, it turns the water into a reddish-brown color. There are other theories on the origin of its name. Some scholars connect the name "red" to the sea's southern location, just as the Black Sea's name may refer to the north. The theory is rooted in a particular feature of some old Asiatic languages that used color words to indicate cardinal directions. For instance, Herodotus used the terms "Red Sea" and "Southern Sea" interchangeably.

The Red Sea is one of the most heavily traveled waterways in the world, as it is connected to the Mediterranean Sea via the Suez Canal and carries traffic between Europe and Asia. The Red Sea was one of the first bodies of water mentioned in recorded history. Ancient Egyptians used it for maritime commerce as early as 2000 BC, and it became a water route to India by about 1000 BC. Historical records indicate that it was accurately mapped as early as 1500 BC, given that the Egyptian queen Hatshepsut sailed its length around that time. In later times, the Red Sea became an important part of the spice trade route.

Saudi Arabia initiated a number of large development projects of the Red Sea area. In addition to increasing the already high number of desalination plants, it intends to turn its coastline into a global tourism destination, in an effort to diversify the country's economy and reduce its reliance on oil per Saudi Vision 2030.

See also: Chapter 1: Fresh Water Reserves and Water Conservancy; The Persian Gulf. Chapter 4: Tourism; Transportation.

Further Reading
Bemert, Gunnar, and Rupert Ormond. *Red Sea Coral Reefs*. Kegan Paul International, 1981.
Coleman, Robert Griffin. *Geologic Evolution of the Red Sea*. Oxford University Press, 1993
Power, Timothy. *The Red Sea from Byzantium to the Caliphate: A.D. 500–1000*. American University in Cairo Press, 2012.

Wick, Alexis. *The Red Sea: In Search of Lost Space.* University of California Press, 2016.

Zahran, M. A., and Francis S. Gilbert. *Climate—Vegetation: Afro-Asian Mediterranean and Red Sea Coastal Lands.* Springer, 2010.

Riyadh

Riyadh is the capital of the Kingdom of Saudi Arabia and its largest city. Its name comes from the plural form of *rawdah*, Arabic for "garden" or "meadow," in reference to the numerous gardens and date groves located in the area. Until the 16th century, the city was known by the name "Hajr" and was an important center in Central Arabia dating from at least the 3rd century AD. In the Middle Ages, Hajr was the capital of the al-Yamamah region, whose rulers controlled most of Central and Eastern Arabia. In recent centuries, al-Yamamah was gradually subsumed under the name "Najd."

The city is situated in eastern Najd at the elevation of approximately 1,950 feet, although the landscape of Riyadh itself is relatively flat. Summers are extremely hot in this area, with average temperatures around 100°F, while winters are cool, with lows averaging in the 50s°F. There are large fluctuations between daytime and nighttime temperatures, which is typical of the desert climate.

In modern times, Riyadh has grown from a small oasis town of about 7,500 people at the turn of the century into a major metropolis with a population of over 7 million. But the most incredible changes took place in the last 50 years. Reluctant to introduce rapid modernization to the conservative Najd, King Abd al-Aziz had initially severely limited non-Saudi residence in the city. Even in the 1960s, Riyadh was still virtually closed to Westerners. During King Abd al-Aziz's rule, foreign diplomats had to make the long trip to Riyadh for a royal audience and were required to wear local Arab dress. But with the oil boom of the 1970s the city was opened up: by 1975 the Western population numbered more than 100,000 and continued to grow ever since.

Facing an inevitable rapid expansion of Riyadh with the oil boom, the government contracted a European city-planning company in the 1960s to develop a comprehensive master plan for the city. This plan introduced a concept of linear architectural development and proposed a strictly defined street pattern of 1.25-mile square blocks. As a result, most of the city's neighborhoods and communities are situated along this flat and repetitive grid pattern. The city blocks are mainly made up of typical two-story villas, surrounded by high walls for privacy. Since the 1970s, Riyadh has undergone astonishing changes in its physical appearance. New buildings are constructed as fast as old ones can be torn down, and what was formerly open desert is quickly becoming suburbs and modern shopping centers. The pace of urban growth has been so rapid that the city has absorbed the ruins of Al Saud ancestral home, al-Diriyyah, which was previously located about 11 miles north of Riyadh. The continuous growth of the city's area and its population puts increasing pressure on Riyadh's infrastructure, resources, and spatial capacity. Facing these challenges, the comprehensive Metropolitan Development Strategy was developed in 2002, offering a long-term vision for the future growth of Riyadh. As the city continues to quickly grow and expand with the turn of the 21st century, in 2007 King Abdallah initiated a new series of development plans for Riyadh, consisting of about 2,000 projects designed to improve the city's infrastructure.

See also: Chapter 1: Najd: Central Arabia. Chapter 2: Ibn Saud; Third Saudi State: Saudi Arabia in the 20th Century. Chapter 6: Urbanization. Chapter 12: Modernization of Saudi Architecture.

Further Reading

Facey, William. *Riyadh, the Old City: From Its Origins until the 1950s*. IMMEL, 1992.

Ménoret, Pascal. *Joyriding in Riyadh: Oil, Urbanism, and Road Revolt*. Cambridge University Press, 2014.

CHAPTER 2

HISTORY

OVERVIEW

In modern times, Saudi Arabia has primarily been known as the birthplace of Islam and Muslim civilization, but several cultures and civilizations flourished on the Arabian Peninsula in ancient times, and some of the earliest traces of human habitation in the world were found on the territory of modern Saudi Arabia. In the 7th century, after the rapid unification of the Arabian population under the banner of Islam, the followers of the new religion quickly expanded their territory far beyond Arabia, conquering numerous regions stretching from India in the east to Spain in the west in less than a century—an unprecedented conquest in both its scale and pace. The subsequent great Arab dynasties, including the Rashidun (632–661), the Umayyad (661–750), the Abbasid (750–1517), and the Fatimid (909–1171) caliphates, had their roots in the Arabian Peninsula.

Whereas the coastal areas of what became contemporary Saudi Arabia and the Hijaz actively participated in the Arabian history in the Islamic period, Central Arabia for centuries remained isolated from main political and military events because of its remoteness, although it was linked with Western Arabia and the Fertile Crescent through trade. But in the 18th century in the Najd region of Central Arabia, a historic alliance of Wahhabi religious reformers and the Al Saud family began to change the balance of power on the peninsula. As a result of this alliance three successive Saudi states were created, including the modern Kingdom of Saudi Arabia, which was officially founded in 1932. Even today—three centuries later—numerous traces of the Wahhabi–Al Saud alliance are present in the contemporary Saudi governance system, its political institutions, and its social norms.

In the past, Saudi Arabia consisted of four regions with distinct geographical locations, cultures, and societies: the Hijaz, the Najd, parts of Eastern Arabia (Al-Ahsa) and Southern Arabia (Asir). In the early 20th century, all four regions had been conquered and united into a single state under the banner of Ibn Saud. The series of conquests began in 1902 with the capture of Riyadh by Ibn Saud's armies and culminated in the establishment of the current state 30 years later. Since then, Saudi Arabia has been an absolute monarchy of the Al Saud dynasty, while the ultraconservative Wahhabi ideology continues to play a key role in various aspects of Saudi culture and society.

After the discovery of petroleum in 1938 and subsequent discoveries of other valuable natural resources, Saudi Arabia has become one of world's most important producers and exporters of oil and gas. The World Bank categorizes the kingdom as a high-income economy, and it is the only Arab country included in the G-20 major economies. For decades, Saudi Arabia has been criticized for its treatment of women and minorities and use of capital and corporal punishment, although a number of reforms that began after 2010 created opportunities for change.

Further Reading

Bowen, Wayne H. *The History of Saudi Arabia*. Greenwood, 2015.

Nicolle, David. *Historical Atlas of the Islamic World*. Mercury Books, 2004.

Vasil'ev, A. M. *The History of Saudi Arabia*. Saqi Books, 1998.

Weston, Mark. *Prophets and Princes: Saudi Arabia from Muhammad to the Present*. Wiley, 2008.

Wynbrandt, James. *A Brief History of Saudi Arabia*. Facts on File, 2010.

TIMELINE

c. 100,000–75,000 BC	First humans migrate from Africa to the Arabian Peninsula, living a hunter-gatherer lifestyle.
c. 6000–3200 BC	Permanent settlements appear on the Arabian Peninsula and trade routes develop with Mesopotamia.
c. 3000–1000 BC	The first great civilization, Dilmun, develops on the eastern side of the peninsula (current Bahrain, Kuwait, and Oman).
c. 3000–2500 BC	Domestication of the dromedary camel.
c. 1000 BC–275 AD	Sabaean Kingdom comes to prominence in Southern Arabia.
853 BC	The first historical record of the Arabs as a distinct group in an inscription of the Assyrian Shalmaneser III.
c. 400 BC–106 AD	Nabatean Kingdom comes to prominence in Northern Arabia.
c. 300	Independent towns and settlements develop throughout the Arabian Peninsula, sustained by the incense trade and agriculture.
c. 550–575	The great Marib Dam, having served the Sabaean Kingdom for many centuries, breaks, forcing over 50,000 people to migrate from Southern Arabia to other areas of the peninsula. The event will be later mentioned in the Quran.
c. 570	Muhammad is born near Mecca in the Quraysh tribe.
610	Muhammad receives his first divine revelation at Mount Hira.
c. 613	Muhammad begins preaching, and the first community of Muslims establishes in Mecca.
619	Death of Muhammad's first wife Khadijah and his uncle Abu Talib—his two biggest supporters.
622	Muhammad and his followers flee from Mecca to Yathrib (later renamed Medina) to escape prosecution by the Quraysh. This

	event received the name of al-Hijrah ("migration" or "emigration" in Arabic) and marked the beginning of the Islamic calendar. The Muslim community quickly grows.
624	The Muslim army is victorious at the Battle of Badr and establishes itself as a serious force on the peninsula.
625	The Battle of Uhud—the second battle between Muslims and Meccans. The Muslims are defeated and forced to retreat, but the Meccan armies do not pursue them and return to their base in Mecca, declaring victory. Muhammad suffers a serious injury and loses his uncle Hamza ibn Abd al-Muttalib, who was one of his closest companions, in battle.
627	The Battle of the Trench. Muslims are able to withstand a 30-day siege of Yathrib.
628	Muhammad agrees to enter a truce with the Meccans, known as Truce of Hudaybiya.
630	Muhammad, his army, and many of his followers return to Mecca and take the city peacefully. Muhammad orders the cleansing of the Kaaba from pagan idols and the Meccan pilgrimage is Islamicized. Eventually, all of the citizens of Mecca accept Islam. Most tribes of the region vow allegiance to Muhammad.
632	Muhammad dies of an illness. Abu Bakr becomes the first caliph, marking the beginning of the reign of the four Righteous Caliphs, or the Rashidun caliphate.
632–634	Caliphate is led by Abu Bakr. Muslim conquests begin.
634–644	Caliphate is led by Omar ibn al-Khattab. Under his rule, the Islamic Empire expands at an unprecedented rate, annexing the Levant, Egypt, North African coast, and virtually the whole Sassanid Persian Empire, including Persia, Azerbaijan, and the Caucasus.
636	The Battle of Yarmuk, where Muslims defeat Byzantines.
644–656	Caliphate is led by Uthman.
c. 653	Caliph Uthman codifies the Quran.
656–661	Caliphate is led by Ali—the last of the Rashidun caliphs and Muhammad's cousin and son-in-law.
656	Beginning of the first Muslim civil war, the First Fitna. The Battle of the Camel takes place between the forces of Caliph Ali and Aishah—one of Muhammad's wives. Muawiyya, the governor of Syria, makes claims on the caliphate.
657	The Battle of Siffin takes place between Caliph Ali and Muawiyya. Ali relocates the caliphate to Kufa.
661	Ali is assassinated.
661–750	The Umayyad caliphate, reigning from Damascus.
680	The martyrdom of Ali's son Hussein, marking the official split of the Shia sect. Muawiyya dies.

680–692	The second Muslim civil war, the Second Fitna.
750–1258	The Abbasid caliphate, reigning from Baghdad. This period is considered the Golden Age of the Islamic Empire and is characterized by unprecedented development of sciences, arts, philosophy, and literature.
930	Qarmathians (a sect of Sevener Ismaili Shia Islam) attack Mecca and steal the sacred black stone from the Kaaba.
c. 967	The institution of the Sharifate of Mecca is established.
969	The Fatimid dynasty gains control over Cairo and thus becomes the authority in the Hijaz.
1258	The Mongol armies sack Baghdad, putting an end to the Abbasid caliphate.
1260	The Mamluks defeat the Mongols.
1425	The Mamluks establish control over Meccan sharifs.
c. 1446	Ancestors of the House of Saud establish Diriyah, which later became the capital of the First Saudi State.
1517	The Ottomans defeat the Mamluks and establish control over the Hijaz.
1744	Muhammad ibn Saud and Muhammad Abd al-Wahhab form a historic alliance. The First Saudi State is established.
1744–1818	The First Saudi State—the Emirate of Diriyah.
1794	Al Saud forces conquer al-Hasa.
1798	The Ottomans launch an offensive against Al Saud's forces.
1801	The Karbala massacre. The Saudi-Wahhabi forces sack the city of Karbala, killing 2,000–5,000 of the Shia population and destroying the tomb of Hussein ibn Ali—the grandson of Muhammad.
1802	The Emirate of Diriyah expands to the Hijaz.
1811	The Egyptian forces led by Muhammad Ali enter the Hijaz on the Ottoman orders to subdue Al Saud.
1813–1814	The Egyptian army ends the rule of Al Saud in the Hijaz.
1818	The Egyptian forces sack Diriyah and put an end to the First Saudi State.
1820	The Egyptian forces arrive to Najd to suppress the renewed attempts by Al Saud to regain their regional power.
1824	Turki ibn Abdullah ibn Muhammad, the grandson of the first Saudi ruler Muhammad ibn Saud, reestablishes the Saudi state with the capital in Riyadh.
1824–1891	The Second Saudi State—the Emirate of Najd.
1830	The Saudi forces retake al-Hasa.
1834	Turki is killed, and his son Faisal becomes the Saudi imam in Riyadh.
1837–1838	Faisal is captured by the Egyptian forces and sent to Cairo.

1843	Upon his release, Faisal returns to Riyadh and regains control of the region.
1864–1865	Upon Faisal's death, his sons fight for power.
1871	Muhammad ibn Rashid, from Al Saud's rival clan, takes control over al-Hasa from Al Saud.
1889	Abd al-Rahman ibn Faisal becomes the Saudi ruler and retakes Riyadh from Al Rashid.
1891	The Rashids defeat the Saudi forces and expel them from Riyadh, marking the end of the Second Saudi State.
1893	The Saudis find asylum in Kuwait.
1902	The new Saudi leader, Ibn Saud, retakes Riyadh.
1906	Ibn Saud's forces conquer Qasim.
1912	The Ikhwan movement is created in Arabia. Ibn Saud establishes the first Ikhwan settlement, *hijrah*.
1913	Ibn Saud's forces, joined by the Ikhwan, capture al-Hasa.
1915	Ibn Saud is formally recognized by Great Britain as the ruler of Najd and al-Hasa, under Anglo-Saudi Treaty.
1916–1918	The Arab Revolt is led by the Sharif of Mecca Hussein against the Ottomans and their German allies.
1918	The forces of Ibn Saud and Sharif Hussein clash at Khurmah, which became known as the First Saudi-Hashemite War or the First Najd-Hijaz War.
1924	The Second Saudi Hashemite War takes place, ending with Ibn Saud's conquest of the Hijaz, including Mecca, and its annexation into his territories.
1926	Ibn Saud proclaims himself the King of Hijaz and Sultan of Najd and Its Dependencies.
1927	The Ikhwan revolt against Ibn Saud.
1929–1930	The relationship between Al Saud and the Ikhwan further deteriorates, culminating in the Battle of Sabilla. The Ikhwan forces are defeated.
1932	The Kingdom of Saudi Arabia is established under the authority of Ibn Saud, who becomes the new state's first king.
1933	Saudi Arabia and the United States establish diplomatic relations. Oil concession is signed with SOCAL (Standard Oil of California).
1934	Border war with Yemen, which ended with Treaty of Taif.
1938	Saudi oil industry is established and mass production of oil begins.
1939	The first tanker of oil is sent to the United States, marking the beginning of oil exports.
1944	California Araba Standard Oil Co. is renamed Arabian American Oil Company, or Aramco.

1945	The League of Arab States is formed. Ibn Saud meets with President Franklin D. Roosevelt on a ship in the Suez Canal.
1946	Ibn Saud visits Egypt. The U.S. military air base is opened in Dhahran.
1948	The declaration of the State of Israel. The First Arab-Israeli War begins.
1953	Ibn Saud dies. His son Saud ascends the throne.
1956	Riots by Aramco workers take place in the Eastern Province. In the meantime, Egyptian president Gamal Abdel Nasser nationalizes the Suez Canal.
1957	The first university opens in Saudi Arabia, King Saud University in Riyadh. King Saud visits the United States.
1958	King Saud is pressured to appoint Crown Prince Faisal as prime minister with substantial executive powers.
1960	OPEC (Organization of the Petroleum Exporting Countries) is established in Baghdad, Iraq. Since 1965, its headquarters have been located to Vienna, Austria.
1964	King Saud abdicates in favor of Faisal who becomes king.
1968	OAPEC (Organization of Arab Petroleum Exporting Countries) is established in Beirut, Lebanon, at the initiative of Saudi Arabia, Kuwait, and Libya. Its headquarters are in Kuwait.
1973	Oil Embargo targeting Western countries is led by Saudi Arabia, in protest of their support of Israel in the Arab-Israeli War. Oil prices quadruple.
1975	King Faisal is assassinated by his nephew Faisal bin Musaid. Khaled takes the throne.
1979	Siege of the Grand Mosque in Mecca by the fundamentalist insurgents that results in over 250 casualties, most of whom are pilgrims taken hostage.
1979–1980	Shia unrest in the Eastern Province.
1980	Complete nationalization of Aramco.
1981	Gulf Cooperation Council (GCC) is formed.
1982	King Khalid dies. King Fahd ascends the throne.
1987	Iranian pilgrims and riot police clash in Mecca during Hajj, resulting in over 400 deaths.
	Saudi Arabia resumes diplomatic relations with Egypt, which were severed since 1979.
1990	Some 1,402 pilgrims are killed in a stampede inside a pedestrian pass to Mecca.
1990–1991	Persian Gulf War. When Saddam Hussein's army invades Kuwait, King Fahd requests help from the United States, and the U.S. and Allied Forces launch Operation Desert Storm.
	A group of Saudi women drive the streets of Riyadh in protest of the government ban on women drivers.

1992	Introduction of the Basic Law of Saudi Arabia, which serves as a constitution of the Saudi state.
1994	Dissident Osama bin Laden is stripped of his Saudi citizenship.
1995	King Fahd suffers a stroke, and Crown Prince Abdullah becomes a de facto ruler of the country.
September 11, 2001	Hijacked airplanes are used in suicide attacks in the United States. Fifteen out of 19 terrorists are Saudi nationals.
	Saudi government issues ID cards to women for the first time.
2002	King Abdallah meets with President Bush in Crawford, Texas.
2003	Saudi police break up a rally in Riyadh demanding political reform.
2003–2004	Sporadic attacks by al-Qaeda in various parts of Saudi Arabia, including bombings in Riyadh and attacks in Yanbu, Khobar, and the U.S. consulate in Jeddah.
2005	Nationwide municipal elections take place. Women are not allowed to vote amid protests from women activists.
2005	King Fahd dies and is succeeded by King Abdallah.
	Saudi Arabia is accepted into World Trade Organization.
2008	Saudi Arabia and Qatar agree on the final demarcation of their borders.
2011	Saudi government announces increased welfare spending and subsidies, in an effort to prevent the spread of the Arab Spring unrest into the country. Saudi troops participate in crackdown on civil unrest in Bahrain.
	King Abdallah announces that women would be allowed to vote and run as candidates in the upcoming municipal elections. Women would also be appointed to the Shura Council.
2015	King Abdullah dies and King Salman ascends the throne.
	Saudi Arabia launches air strikes against Houthis in Yemen.
	Women vote and participate as candidates in the municipal elections for the first time in the country's history. Twenty women are elected.
2016	The government announces a wide-scale development plan to reduce the country's dependence on oil and diversify economy, labeled Saudi Vision 2030.
2017	Saudi Arabia leads a number of Arab countries on an air, land, and sea blockade of Qatar.
	King Salman names his son Muhammad bin Salman as crown prince.
	The ban on women driving is lifted by the government.
2018	Public cinemas are allowed to open, after an almost 40-year-long ban.
	The killing of Saudi journalist Jamal Khashoggi in the Saudi consulate in Istanbul sparks international outcry.

2019   Two major oil-processing Aramco facilities in Abqaiq and Khurais in Eastern Arabia are attacked by drones and suffer extensive damages, cutting Saudi oil production by half. The Yemeni Houthis claim responsibility for the attack.

The Abbasids

The Abbasid dynasty was one of the great dynasties of the Muslim Empire. Having defeated the Umayyads in 750 AD, they established the Abbasid caliphate and ruled the Islamic world until its destruction by the Mongols in 1258. The name of the dynasty comes from prophet Muhammad's uncle, al-Abbas of the Hashimite branch within the Quraysh tribe in Mecca. From the early 8th century, the Abbasid family worked against the Umayyads in their efforts to take over the empire and gradually won substantial support. An open revolt in 747 resulted in the defeat of the last Umayyad caliph Marwan II at the Battle of the Great Zab River. Immediately following these events the first Abbasid caliph, Abu al-Abbas al-Saffah, was proclaimed.

Under the Abbasid rule, the caliphate entered a new era. In contrast with the Umayyads and their focus on the western parts of the empire (North Africa and the Mediterranean), the caliphate now turned eastward, especially with the symbolic move of the capital to the new city of Baghdad. The Abbasid phase is also marked by the increasingly cosmopolitan character of the Muslim Empire. Because of the rapid territorial expansion of the empire, which absorbed many diverse cultures and societies, one's membership and influence in the Muslim community became more important than their Arabian origins. For instance, the Abbasids received a great deal of support from Persian converts and, consequently, adopted various features of the Persian governance system. In the period between 750 and 833, the political capital of the Abbasids grew substantially. At the same time, they were promoting sciences and arts, trade, and various industries, especially during the reigns of Caliphs al-Mansur, al-Ma'mun, and the legendary Harun al-Rashid. The political center of the caliphate was moved to Baghdad in 762, during the reign of the second Abbasid caliph Abdullah Abu al-Abbas (r. 754–775), who ordered the building of the new capital.

When the Iranian Buyids (a Shia Iranian dynasty) entered Baghdad in 945 and demanded from the Abbasids political recognition as the sole rulers of their territory, the Muslim Empire entered a new period when it was ruled by local dynasties. Consequently, the empire was significantly weakened over the next hundred years. In 1055 the Abbasids were overpowered by the Seljuq dynasty (Oghuz Turk Sunni Muslim dynasty), who took temporary power but respected the caliph's status as the titular leader. In what followed, the authority and influence of the caliphate were gradually restored, in particular during the reigns of Caliphs al-Mustarshid (1118–1135), al-Muqtafi (1136–1160), and al-Nasir (1180–1225), who was the last effective Abbasid caliph. In 1258, the Abbasids were crushed by the Mongol armies, following a siege of Baghdad.

The reign of the Abbasids, who were even more secular than the preceding Umayyad dynasty, and the historic relocation of the empire's capital from Damascus to Baghdad, symbolized its further physical and spiritual distancing from its birthplace in the Arabian Peninsula. The Islamic community continued to expand and incorporate the customs and traditions of the conquered lands and their diverse peoples. Most of the achievements of the Golden Age under the Abbasids took place outside of the peninsula, and many of the era's greatest figures were not Arabs by origin.

See also: Chapter 2: The Golden Age of Islam in Arabia; Rashidun: The Righteous Caliphs; The Rise of Islam.

Further Reading

Bennison, Amira K. *The Great Caliphs: The Golden Age of the Abbasid Empire*. Yale University Press, 2009.

Bobrick, Benson. *The Caliph's Splendor: Islam and the West in the Golden Age of Baghdad*. Simon & Schuster, 2012.

Kennedy, Hugh. *When Baghdad Ruled the Muslim World: The Rise and Fall of Islam's Greatest Dynasty*. Da Capo Press, 2005.

Turner, John P. *Inquisition in Early Islam: The Competition for Political and Religious Authority in the Abbasid Empire*. I. B. Tauris, 2013.

Arab Revolt (1916–1918)

The Arab Revolt began in 1916 with an uprising by the Bedouin tribes from the Hijaz and the neighboring areas against the Ottomans and their German allies. The son of the Sharif of Mecca, Faysal bin Hussein, was the leader of the uprising. Faysal and his brother Abdullah received military and strategic assistance from the British agent Thomas E. Lawrence—a historical figure well known in the West because of the famous 1962 film *Lawrence of Arabia*, based on his life story.

The Arab Revolt continued to spread, and other areas of the Arab Middle East quickly joined the cause. A number of factors contributed to the virtually universal support of the revolt among Arab populations, regardless of their ethnic and religious affiliations. The internal tensions within the Ottoman Empire were brewing even before World War I. Ottoman domestic policies heavily favored Turks over other citizens of the empire, most notably Arabs who constantly demanded either an increased political participation or autonomy. These policies became even more pronounced with the rise of Young Turks. The traditionally cosmopolitan and tolerant pan-Islamic structure of the Ottoman Empire, which allowed them to rule in the Middle East for centuries, was abandoned in favor of a radical secular Turkey-focused nationalism. With the outbreak of World War I, numerous alienated Arab groups in Syria, Iraq, and the Arabian Peninsula were naturally drawn to the side of the Allies (Britain, Russia, France, Italy, and the United States), who in turn were looking for reliable regional partners against the Ottomans.

Sharif of Mecca Hussein bin Ali (of the Hashemites) saw an opportunity to liberate the region from the Turks. The British promised him that after defeating the Ottomans he would be able to form an independent Arab state, and he led the Hijaz in an open rebellion against the Ottoman forces. Hussein's goal was to unify the Arab peoples into a single state stretching from Aleppo in the north to Aden in the south. On June 5, 1916, Bedouin tribes, led by Hussein's two sons Faysal and Abdullah, attacked Turkish positions along the Hijaz Railway, which was the main supply route for the Ottoman troops. Sharif Hussein proclaimed himself King of the Arabs. Meanwhile, the British representative body in Cairo, the Arab Bureau, delegated Lieutenant Thomas Lawrence to provide financial, military, and strategic support to Hussein's campaign. Lawrence quickly became a trusted peer to Faysal (the acknowledged leader of the revolt) and Abdullah and assisted their cause through skillful guerilla warfare.

From the military point of view, the Arab Revolt was a successful campaign marked by several important victories, including the Battle of Aqaba (1917). With large support from the local population, Faysal's army liberated Damascus from Ottoman rule on September 30, 1918. By the end of the war, the Arab forces controlled most of the peninsula, the territory of what is now Jordan, and most of southern Syria. The Arab Revolt also provided significant help to the Allies in World War I in defeating the Ottomans. However, after the conclusion of the war, the colonial interests took precedence over Britain's previous agreements with the Arabs. The Ottoman territories were divided through the Sykes-Picot Agreement into mandates and protectorates under the permanent colonial rule. But despite its ultimate failure to create a united state, the Arab Revolt was effective in that it proved the ability of dispersed Arab groups to come together in the fight for liberation, and it also inspired future nationalist movements in the region.

Sharif Hussein maintained his throne in the Hijaz and in 1924 proclaimed himself the new caliph, but was quickly challenged and ousted by Abd al-Aziz ibn Saud. Arab nationalists expected that Faysal would become the ruler of the united Arab kingdom with the center in Damascus, but Greater Syria had been promised to France, who forced him out after the Battle of Maysalun in 1920. Britain made him king in the newly established Iraq. Faysal's brother Abdullah became the king of Transjordan (subsequently Jordan) and started the dynasty of Hashemite rulers in the country, who remain in power today.

See also: Chapter 1: Hijaz and Tihamah. Chapter 2: The Mamluks and the Ottomans in Arabia; Sharifs of Mecca; Third Saudi State: Saudi Arabia in the 20th Century.

Further Reading

Lawrence, T. E. *Revolt in the Desert.* Garden City Pub, 1927.

McMurray, David A., and Amanda Ufheil-Somers, eds. *The Arab Revolts: Dispatches on Militant Democracy in the Middle East.* Indiana University Press, 2013.

Walker, Philip. *Behind the Lawrence Legend: The Forgotten Few Who Shaped the Arab Revolt.* Oxford University Press, 2018.

Discovery of Oil

Since the discovery of oil in the first half of the 20th century, Saudi Arabia has gone through a series of rapid transformations—economic, political, and social. Bahrain was the first Gulf country where oil was first found and developed, soon after the discoveries followed in Iran, Iraq, Kuwait, and Saudi Arabia. When in the 1920s American and British oil companies started a large-scale campaign in search for new oil fields in Africa and the Middle East, the prospect of finding oil in Saudi Arabia made Abd al-Aziz ibn Saud, then the ruler of Najd, personally involved in these efforts. He recruited a number of American geologists to explore the area and identify specific locations that were likely to have large quantities of fossil fuel resources. These early oil explorations marked the beginning of Saudi oil industry, which quickly developed in the following decades.

In the 1930s the new era of the Saudi state began, when the American mining engineer Karl Twitchell identified large oil reserves in eastern regions of the country. In May 1933, Ibn Saud finalized the oil concession agreement with the U.S. company Standard Oil of California (SOCAL), in exchange for monetary compensations and loans. These agreements prompted the establishment of the California Arab Standard Oil Company (CASOC), the predecessor of Aramco. In September 1933, the first oil-seeking team of Americans stepped ashore in Jubayl—a coastal village that later turned into a major petrochemical center and a Saudi navy base. Drilling began on April 30, 1935. In three more years, commercial production took off when the Dammam 7 oil well began producing over 1,500 barrels daily, in contrast with most American oil wells, which produced on average 5–10 barrels per day.

However, the Saudi oil industry was not able to grow in the 1930s due to the world economic depression and the deteriorating political situation that ultimately led to World War II. After the war, Saudi oil finally entered the world market in large quantities, and in 1950 Saudi Arabia bargained with the United States over the distribution of oil revenues. Following intense negotiations, the two sides reached an agreement that divided Aramco revenues equally between the American companies (50 percent total) and the Saudi government (50 percent). In the next several decades Saudi Arabia continued to gradually increase its share of Aramco holdings, which culminated in the nationalization of the firm outright by the 1980s. Aramco's nationalization was among the series of measures implemented by Saudi Arabia to gradually replace foreign management with Saudis. These were the beginning of the so-called Saudization policy. However, even before the official takeover by the Saudis, Aramco had long been under Saudi authority. The kingdom gained control over the company's policy as early as 1972, when it acquired 25 percent of its ownership. In 1974 the Saudi share increased to 60 percent and, finally, to 100 percent in 1980.

Oil has always been and still is the cornerstone of the Saudi economy and its political bargain chip, but with the turn of the 21st century the country began a series of policies and economic measures to diversify and modernize its economy. The most recent and significant of these is the statewide plan called Vision 2030, initiated by King Salman and crown prince Muhammad bin Salman, with the goal to substantially reduce the country's dependence on oil, diversify its economy, modernize the infrastructure, invest in education, and develop other public sectors, including health care, sports, and tourism.

See also: Chapter 1: Eastern Arabia: Al-Hasa; Environmental Issues after the Gulf War; The Persian Gulf. Chapter 3: Gulf Cooperation Council; Saudi–U.S. Relations. Chapter 4: Diversification and Development Plans; Oil Industry and Aramco; OPEC and OAPEC; Petrochemical Industry.

Further Reading

Cooper, Andrew Scott. *The Oil Kings: How the U.S., Iran, and Saudi Arabia Changed the Balance of Power in the Middle East.* Simon & Schuster, 2011.

Hertog, Steffen. *Princes, Brokers, and Bureaucrats: Oil and the State in Saudi Arabia.* Cornell University Press, 2010.

Simmons, Matthew R. *Twilight in the Desert: The Coming Saudi Oil Shock and the World Economy.* John Wiley & Sons, 2005.

Emirate of Diriyah: The First Saudi State (1744–1818)

The first Saudi state was the Emirate of Diriyah, established in 1744. Its creation and political success resulted from a historic alliance between Muhammad bin Saud (1710–1765), the head of the House of Saud, and the conservative Islamic reformist and preacher Muhammad ibn Abd al-Wahhab (1703–1792). A subsequent marriage between Ibn Saud's son and Abd al-Wahhab's daughter reinforced the pact that survived several centuries and remains relevant in Saudi Arabia today. Combining their political and ideological talents, Ibn Saud and Abd al-Wahhab created a powerful movement whose goal was to unify the fragmented regional powers and free the peninsula from the Ottoman rule.

Prior to forging this partnership, Ibn Saud was a respected tribal leader, although his dynasty was indistinguishable from many similar small fiefdoms scattered throughout Central Arabia. He lived in the village of Diriyah, which gave the name to the First Saudi State as the Emirate of Diriyah. At the time, the reformist cleric Abd al-Wahhab was not a particularly popular figure either, but his conservative teachings found a receptive audience in the Najd, who were outraged at the spread of secularism and what they considered un-Islamic practices in the Hijaz.

The domination of the Al Saud family and their allies in Arabia began with the politically crucial conquest of the Najd. In what followed, they expanded their influence over Eastern Arabia, taking over territories from Kuwait to the northern borders of Oman, as well as the highlands of Asir. In the meantime, Abd al-Wahhab continued to spread his message, which entirely rejected any and all modifications of the orthodox Islamic beliefs and practices. He continued to recruit new followers, many of whom simultaneously joined Al Saud's campaign.

One of the core principles propagated by Abd al-Wahhab was the need for jihad. In its primary religious and ethical meaning, jihad refers to one's personal struggle to do the right thing and to prevent the wrong thing from happening. However, Abd al-Wahhab's teachings focused on a different interpretation of jihad—as a holy war with the goal of defeating the infidels, either by conversion or death. It is this very narrow definition that dominates the current political discourse. Abd al-Wahhab's view on jihad found many supporters in the tribal communities who practiced raiding (*ghazu*) since ancient times, long before the arrival of Islam. Abd al-Wahhab's jihad was essentially indistinguishable from the *ghazu* practice. Any tribe or settlement that refused to accept the rule of Diriyah and the religious dogmas of Abd al-Wahhab were raided and robbed of their possessions.

Muhammad ibn Saud died in 1765, and his son Abd al-Aziz took over the leadership of the House of Saud. At that time, Diriyah was the most powerful of all Arabian states. Abd al-Aziz continued to build on his father's military successes and expanded the territory to include the Washm and Sudair areas. In 1773, Riyadh was taken by the Diriyah forces. Meanwhile, Abd al-Wahhab's doctrine was acknowledged by the religious scholars of Mecca. In 1801, Al Saud forces reached the Shia holy city of Karbala, where they killed thousands of Shia Muslims and destroyed the shrines. In revenge, Abd al-Aziz was killed in 1803. Following his assassination, Abd al-Aziz's son and successor in power, Saud, set out to conquer the Hijaz. In 1805, Saud's forces captured both holy cities—first Mecca and shortly after Medina. This bold campaign was seen as a major challenge to the Ottoman authority in the region, especially after Saud expelled all Ottoman *qadis* and other official representatives from the Hijaz. Consequently, the Ottomans instructed Egyptians, commanded by the powerful Muhammad Ali Pasha, to drive Al Saud out of the area, which led to the Ottoman-Saudi War (1811–1818). Muhammad Ali's troops, led by his son Ibrahim Pasha, entered Najd and gradually captured the whole region. Saud's successor, his son Abdullah bin Saud, did not have enough power to stop the progress of Ottoman forces when the latter reached Diriyah and placed it under siege for several months. Al-Saud's capital finally surrendered in the winter of 1818. Many members of the Al Saud family were captured and sent to Egypt and Istanbul. Abdullah bin Saud was executed in Istanbul, marking the end of the First Saudi State. However, despite their defeat, the remaining members of Al Saud family and their Wahhabi allies were able to establish the Second Saudi State only a few years later, and it lasted until 1891.

See also: Chapter 2: Ibn Saud; Ikhwan; Muhammad ibn Abd al-Wahhab. Chapter 3: Wahhabi Ideology. Chapter 6: House of Saud.

Further Reading

Facey, William, and Philip Hawkins. *Dirʿiyyah and the First Saudi State*. Stacey International, 1997.

al-Juhany, Uwidah Metaireek, and Darat al-Malik Abd al-Aziiz. *Najd before the Salafi Reform Movement: Social, Political, and Religious Conditions during the Three Centuries Preceding the Rise of the Saudi State*. Ithaca Press, 2002.

Emirate of Najd: The Second Saudi State (1824–1891)

The Second Saudi State existed between 1824 and 1891 and was called the Emirate of Najd. It included Ha'il and the area surrounding Riyadh. Although the Ottomans were able to defeat the First Saudi State in the Ottoman-Wahhabi War (1811–1818), the House of Al Saud was able in a short time to restore its rule in Central and Eastern Arabia. In 1818, Mishari ibn Saud—the brother of Abdullah ibn Saud Al Saud, the last ruler of Diriyah—attempted to regain power, but he was quickly captured and killed by the Egyptians. In 1824, Turki ibn Abdullah ibn Muhammad, a grandson of the first Saudi ruler Muhammad ibn Saud, succeeded in expelling the Ottoman forces from Riyadh and the nearby area. Turki ibn Abdullah is considered the founder of the second Saudi dynasty and the forefather of the current Saudi royals. He established the capital in Riyadh. Turki's reign was marked by a balanced governance and limited territorial expansion.

Turki ibn Abdullah was assassinated in 1834 by his relative Mishari ibn Abdul-Rahman, but the latter was shortly captured in Riyadh and executed by Turki's son Faisal, who became the most prominent ruler of Al Saud's second state. The dynasty continued to be challenged by the Ottoman forces, and Faisal faced another invasion by the Egyptians in 1838. Exhausted from constant military conflicts, the local population was difficult to mobilize, and Faisal was ultimately defeated, captured, and taken to Egypt. The Egyptians appointed the great grandson of Muhammad bin Saud, Khalid ibn Saud, to rule in Riyadh. Khalid had spent many years in the Egyptian court and was seen by the locals as the Egyptian vassal. When in 1840 the Egyptian forces had to leave the region, Khalid was quickly ousted by Abdullah ibn Thunayan.

In the meantime, following his release from Egyptian captivity, Faisal ibn Turki Al Saud returned to the peninsula, retook Riyadh, and resumed his rule. He appointed his son Abdallah ibn Faisal as heir but divided the territories and powers between all of his three sons—Abdullah, Saud, and Muhammad—a decision that later caused a great deal of internal conflict in the family and ultimately brought down the Second Saudi State. Upon Faisal's death in 1865, Abdullah became the formal ruler of Riyadh, but his authority was challenged by his brother Saud, and a long civil war between the brothers and their allies followed. The head of another influential regional family, Muhammad ibn Abdallah ibn Rashid of Ha'il, took the opportunity to increase his own power during the time of instability within the Al Saud family. Ibn Rashid was able to gradually expand his rule over most of Najd and even Al Saud's home base, Riyadh. The continuing internal conflicts within Al Saud led to the dynasty's defeat at the Battle of Mulayda, which took place in 1891 between the Al Saud and the Al Rashid forces.

See also: Chapter 1: Najd: Central Arabia; Riyadh. Chapter 2: The Mamluks and the Ottomans in Arabia. Chapter 6: House of Saud.

Further Reading

Long, David E., and Sebastian Maisel. *The Kingdom of Saudi Arabia*. University Press of Florida, 2010.

Vasil'ev, A. M. *The History of Saudi Arabia*. Saqi Books, 1998.

The Golden Age of Islam in Arabia

By the end of the Muslim conquest, Islam became the dominant religion from North Africa and Spain in the west to India and China in the east. By the 9th century, the empire brought stability to the whole region. This stability and the remarkable diversity of cultures incorporated into the vast empire created favorable conditions for an unprecedented development of arts, literature, philosophy, and sciences. The intellectual and artistic accomplishments of the Islamic Empire are as astounding as were its previous military and political conquests. This was the beginning of the Golden Age of Islam, which not only predated the European Renaissance by 500 years but made the latter possible. At its peak, the society and culture under the Abbasids reached a level of sophistication and enlightenment that would be unmatched for almost a thousand years.

As the empire continued to move away from the peninsula, Arabia's contribution to the Golden Age was mainly in the area of religious scholarship. The most prominent accomplishment of the time was the codification of Islamic jurisprudence (*fiqh*) through the four schools of legal thought (*madhhab*), known as Hanafi, Maliki, Shafi'i, and Hanbali. But even though Medina was an important center for the development of religious thought in the 8th and 9th centuries, once the rules had been established, the city lost its intellectual edge. As for Mecca, although it always maintained its spiritual significance, it never became a political power center. The future birthplace of contemporary Saudi Arabia, Najd, was barely inhabited during that time. When the caliphate began to decline, the route from the Abbasid capital Baghdad to Mecca became less secure, forcing pilgrims and other travelers to find alternative routes, further isolating Central Arabia. In a later period, the increased navigation of the Red Sea contributed to the continuous isolation of Najd.

In contrast, Mecca and the Hijaz, which received pilgrims from all regions of the empire on an annual basis, were exposed to the cultural and economic developments of the Golden Age. The pilgrimage became a ceremonial occasion and an opportunity for the caliph to showcase his wealth and influence. In turn, the Hajj gradually turned away from its ascetic and spiritual codes of behavior, which eventually divided Arabia. The growing conservative population of Najd perceived the secular customs of the Hijaz as a disgrace. These internal tensions on the peninsula would continue to deepen in subsequent centuries and planted the seeds of the conservative reform movement, Wahhabism, which emerged in the 18th century.

See also: Chapter 1: Najd: Central Arabia. Chapter 2: The Abbasids; The Rise of Islam. Chapter 5: Sunni Islam and Jurisprudence.

Further Reading

Bennison, Amira K. *The Great Caliphs: The Golden Age of the Abbasid Empire*. Yale University Press, 2009.

al-Khalili, Jim. *Pathfinders: The Golden Age of Arabic Science*. Allen Lane, 2010.

Langermann, Y. Tzvi. *Avicenna and His Legacy: A Golden Age of Science and Philosophy*. Brepols, 2009.

Ibn Saud

Abd al-Aziz ibn Abd al-Rahman ibn Faisal ibn Turki ibn Abdallah ibn Muhammad Al Saud (1876–1953) was the historical figure whose highly successful political and military strategies united different parts of the Arabian Peninsula and in 1932 brought about the establishment of the current Kingdom of Saudi Arabia, or the Third Saudi State. He was the first monarch of the newly established kingdom. In the West, he is usually referred to as Ibn Saud, whereas the Arabic-speaking world usually calls him Abd al-Aziz.

Born in 1876 in Riyadh, Ibn Saud was the son of Abd al-Rahman Al Saud—then the head of the House of Saud who had taken over large parts of Central Arabia in the course of the 19th century. However, in 1891 Al Saud's biggest political rivals from Ha'il, Al Rashid family, forced the former out of Riyadh, Al Saud's ancestral home. They went into exile in Kuwait where Ibn Saud grew up. His mission to restore the family's power began with the successful attack on Riyadh in 1902. His troops pushed Al Rashid out of the city, which was reinstated as the center of Al Saud's rule. In 1913, Ibn Saud led another successful military campaign, which allowed him to take al-Hasa region from the Ottoman control. He continued to use various political and military strategies in this mission to take over Arabia. Among his many political achievements was his ability to gain British support without becoming completely dependent on them. He did so by exploiting the rivalry among other Arab leaders who fought for British funding and political support. At the same time, Ibn Saud utilized the Ikhwan, who were a powerful military force composed of recently settled Bedouins, to continue his conquests, and gradually all strategically important regions of the peninsula fell under his rule, including Ha'il in 1921 and the Hijaz in 1925. In addition to his political and military talents, Ibn Saud was also an influential spiritual leader of the Wahhabi reform movement. This combination of political might and religious influence allowed his rise as the uncontested leader of the Najd and secured the success of his task to unite the majority of the Arabian Peninsula. Ibn Saud's mission concluded in 1932 when he proclaimed the foundation of the Kingdom of Saudi Arabia.

With regard to Ibn Saud's relationship with the West, his forward-thinking strategies played a role here as well. Using his personal relations with many influential figures of the time, including Charles Crane, Ameen Rihani, Harry St. John Philby, Gertrude Bell, and many others, Ibn Saud was able to achieve unprecedented political recognition and considerable independence in a time when the rest of the Middle East was being divided by the colonial powers. With the discovery of oil in Saudi Arabia in the 1930s, Ibn Saud negotiated concessions with U.S. oil developing companies, brought the first revenues to his underdeveloped country, and opened the new era in the country's history. At the same time, he was adamant about preserving the special character of Saudi Arabia by reinforcing Islamic practices and Arabian traditions in the face of rapid technological transformations in the country. While focusing on enriching and enhancing his country with oil revenues, Ibn Saud chose a relatively simple lifestyle for himself, in line with the orthodox Islamic teachings he was preaching throughout his life. He died on November 9, 1953, in Ta'if and was succeeded by his eldest surviving son Saud.

Abd al-Aziz al-Saud (Ibn Saud), the founder and first king of Saudi Arabia. (Library of Congress)

See also: Chapter 2: Arab Revolt (1916–1918); Discovery of Oil; Ikhwan; Third Saudi State: Saudi Arabia in the 20th Century. Chapter 3: Saudi Monarchy and Branches of the Government; Saudi–U.S. Relations. Chapter 4: Oil industry and Aramco. Chapter 6: House of Saud.

Further Reading

Alangari, Haifa. *The Struggle for Power in Arabia: Ibn Saud, Hussein and Great Britain, 1914–1924*. Ithaca Press, 1998.

McLoughlin, Leslie J. *Ibn Saud: Founder of a Kingdom*. St. Martin's Press, 1993.

Ikhwan

Ikhwan (which means "brothers" or "brotherhood" in Arabic) is a name of the military and religious organization that emerged in the early 20th century and consisted of the recently settled Bedouin population. They formed a dominant military force in Central Arabia under the leadership of Abd al-Aziz ibn Saud and served as a powerful tool in consolidating his control of the region.

The Ikhwan were a tribal population who were encouraged to abandon their nomadic lifestyle and take up farming instead. Many were inspired by the Salafi (Wahhabi) preachers to join their reformist movement, which originated in the middle of the 18th century under the spiritual leadership of Muhammad bin Abd al-Wahhab. This movement called for the purification of Islam and return to the lifestyle of the early Islamic community at the time of Muhammad and his early followers. In imitation of the prophet's immigration (*hijrah*) from Mecca to Medina, the Ikhwan left their tribes and immigrated to new settlements, which were also called *hijrah*. Members of all major tribes gradually joined the organization, and by 1912 over 11,000 Ikhwan were living in the newly established agricultural colonies, called *hijrahs*—the same name as Muhammad's *hijrah*, a starting point of the Islamic calendar. Although it was based on the concept of unity among its members, the settlement structure still obeyed the tribal tradition where each colony was assigned to one particular tribe, since members of different tribes preferred not to cohabitate with each other. Farming, however, was always a challenge because of the difficult climatic conditions and the new settlers' lack of experience with the agricultural trade. Thus, they had to rely on subsidies from Ibn Saud.

With the turn of the 20th century, the majority of Arabian Bedouin tribes were weak and lacking military leadership. Ibn Saud's powerful new army gave him a substantial advantage and allowed him to quickly conquer large areas. Ikhwan participated in all major battles during the war of unification, beginning with the game-changing conquest of al-Hasa in 1913. They defeated the Al Rashid clan and the Shammar in 1921, as well as the Hijazi Hashemites, taking over the cities of Ta'if, Mecca, and Jeddah during 1924–1925. They were also instrumental in the Asir in the south (1920). In sum, Ikhwan brought a significant improvement and strengthening of Abd al-Aziz ibn Saud's political and military standing on the peninsula.

For many years, the alliances between the Ikhwan, Ibn Saud, and the Wahhabi religious establishment continued to define Arabian regional politics. Success was achieved through the regular raiding of the enemy areas—a well-known military strategy of the Ikhwan, perfected by their generations of nomads. However, an important aspect of the Ikhwan ideology is that they were motivated by their religious doctrine and its idealist worldview, not loyalty to Ibn Saud personally.

With the establishment of permanent borders and regional divisions, certain restrictions and regulations were imposed on Ikhwan, which caused their growing frustration with Ibn Saud. In addition to that, they objected to the latter's friendly relations with the British, who were considered infidels and colonizers. The Ikhwan leadership did not understand Ibn Saud's political pragmatism and were not willing to accept it. These tensions ended in an open revolt in 1929 by several sections of the Ikhwan under Faysal al-Duwaysh, Ibn Bijad, and Ibn Hithlayn, and the rebels were ultimately defeated in the Battle of Sibilla. The Ikhwan rebellion was simultaneously a protest against a "sold-out" Muslim leader and a tribal opposition to the claims of hegemony by the Al Saud. Defeating the Ikhwan was a major step in completing the process of unification and the formation of a centralized state in 1932. The official organization of Ikhwan was disbanded, but they continued living in agricultural communities and took jobs in the new administration, primarily in the military. In 1956, tribal forces were again revived and organized into a paramilitary unit called the Saudi Arabian National Guard. Tribal groups who seized the Grand Mosque in Mecca in 1979 claimed to be the descendants of the original Ikhwan movement.

See also: Chapter 2: Arab Revolt (1916–1918); Ibn Saud; Muhammad ibn Abd al-Wahhab; Third Saudi State: Saudi Arabia in the 20th Century. Chapter 3: Saudi Monarchy and Branches of the Government; Wahhabi Ideology. Chapter 5: Five Pillars or the Tenets of Islam; Jihad. Chapter 6: House of Saud.

Further Reading

Habib, John S. *Ibn Sa'ud's Warriors of Islam: The Ikhwan of Najd and Their Role in the Creation of the Sa'udi Kingdom, 1910–1930*. Brill, 1978.

Trofimov, Yaroslav. *The Siege of Mecca: The 1979 Uprising at Islam's Holiest Shrine*. Anchor Books, 2008.

King Abdullah

Abdullah bin Abd al-Aziz Al Saud was King of Saudi Arabia from 2005 to 2015, but he was also the de facto ruler of Saudi Arabia for 10 years prior to his ascension to the throne—since the previous king and his half-brother Fahd suffered a stroke in 1995. Before becoming the king, Abdallah held various important political positions, including his post as the mayor of Mecca, the commander of the Saudi National Guard, and the deputy defense minister.

During his reign, Abdullah focused on further strengthening Saudi Arabia's relations with the United States and the United Kingdom. He also had a long-standing close relationship with Pakistan, when the latter was led by Prime Minister Nawaz Sharif. Following the 1999 coup in Pakistan, the Saudi government brokered a deal between General Pervez Musharraf and the ousted Nawaz Sharif, where the latter would be exiled to Saudi Arabia for 10 years.

Abdullah's reign is characterized by attempts to implement modernizing reforms in various areas of Saudi society. He initiated a large-scale restructuring of the country's judicial structure, which introduced the system of evaluation of judicial decisions and professional training for Sharia judges. He also introduced various policies that streamlined the country's business networks. An ardent promoter of Saudi Arabia's post-oil development, he focused on education and various scientific initiatives. In 2010, a quarter of the country's budget was devoted to education. One of Abdullah's most important achievements in promoting education was the construction of the King Abdullah University of Science and Technology (KAUST). Founded in 2009, it was the country's new flagship for advanced scientific research with the first coed university campus in Saudi Arabia. KAUST's profile is quickly rising among other world universities that are known for innovative research.

King Abdullah's government stimulated the development of nonhydrocarbon sectors, including solar energy. He dedicated much effort to the extensive modernization of religious tourism in Saudi Arabia. In 2009 he made radical changes to the Ministry of Education by appointing his progressive and pro-reform U.S.-educated son-in-law, Faisal bin Abdullah Al Saud, as the new minister. Additionally, in an unprecedented move to appoint a woman to the cabinet-level position—for the first time in Saudi Arabia's history—a U.S.-educated Nora Al Fayez took the post of deputy minister, in charge of a new department dedicated to the education of women.

Abdullah substantially increased international education. In 2005 he initiated a scholarship program, which sends young Saudi men and women to receive undergraduate and postgraduate education in top-ranked universities abroad. The students have their tuition fully covered for four years, in addition to receiving living expenses. As a result of this initiative, the number of Saudi students in U.S. universities alone grew from 11,000 in 2005 to over 71,000 in 2011.

In July 2012, under mounting international pressure and an ultimatum from the Olympic Committee, the Saudi government announced that women athletes will compete and represent the country in the Olympics—for the first time in the country's history. In January 2013, Abdullah made another historic decision when 30 women were appointed to the Shura Council—the formal advisory body of Saudi Arabia. Moreover, a special law was issued mandating that from there on, no less than 20 percent of the council's 150 members would be women. Many of King Abdallah's political decisions, especially those related to gender equality, as limited as they were in the context of Saudi Arabia, were strongly opposed by the conservative clerics. Among other important programs initiated by Abdullah's government were those related to public health, such as a breast cancer awareness program and a cooperation with the Centers for Disease Control to set up an advanced epidemic screening network for the Hajj pilgrims who come to the country every year in millions.

Abdallah is known for his strong hand in fighting homegrown terrorism. His security forces made a series of major crackdowns that resulted in arrests and public beheadings, and there were reports that detainees were tortured. However, Abdallah's administration eventually developed a different strategy by focusing on the roots of the extremism. Efforts were made to promote education and implement judicial reforms that would weaken the influence of al-Qaeda on Saudi religious establishment. In November 2007, King Abdullah's historic visit of Pope Benedict XVI took place in the Apostolic Palace. Abdullah was the first Saudi monarch to visit the Pope.

See also: Chapter 3: Political Reform and Modernization; Saudi–U.S. Relations. Chapter 6: House of Saud. Chapter 7: Women in Public Office. Chapter 8: Higher Education.

Further Reading

Lacey, Robert. *Inside the Kingdom: Kings, Clerics, Modernists, Terrorists, and the Struggle for Saudi Arabia.* Viking, 2009.

Moser, Sarah, et al. "King Abdullah Economic City: Engineering Saudi Arabia's Post-Oil Future." *Cities*, vol. 45, 2015, pp. 71–80.

The Mamluks and the Ottomans in Arabia

The Mamluks had first appeared in the Abbasid caliphate in the 9th century. The word "Mamluk" means "owned" or "owned property" in Arabic and points to their origins as slave soldiers. They were not native to Egypt but were mainly from among the Qipchak Turks from Central Asia. The Mamluk dynasty ruled Egypt and Syria from 1250 until 1517, when it fell to the Ottomans. But even after the fall, they continued to form an influential group in Egyptian Islamic circles through the 19th century. The rule of the dynasty had two main periods. One lasted from 1250 to 1381 and was the time of the Bahri Mamluk sultans, and the second period, from 1382 until 1517, was dominated by the Burgi Mamluks.

The Mamluk military dynasty destroyed the crusader states, and they also saved Syria, Egypt, and the holy places of Islam from the Mongols. They established Cairo as the dominant city of the Islamic world and promoted the development of architecture and various craftsmanship. The Hijaz was under the control of the Abbasid caliphate when the Mongols invaded Baghdad in 1258. The shift from the Abbasid to the Mamluk rule was relatively smooth, as the new Sharif of Mecca Muhammad Abu Numayy (1254–1301) was able to end the long period of instability that the Hijaz experienced in the late Abbasid era. Before his death, Abu Numayy abdicated in favor of two of his sons (he reportedly had over 30)—Humayda and Rumaytha—whom he designated as successors. Shortly after, the sons began fighting for power, failing to uphold their responsibilities as caretakers of the holy sites. Sultan al-Nasir Muhammad, who was the Mamluk ruler at the time, attempted to settle the conflict and summoned both to Cairo. However, in response to the sultan's demands, the brothers reconciled and joined together in defiance of the Egyptian ruler. The sultan was about to send his army to expel both Humayda, Rumaytha, and the whole Hashemite clan from Mecca, but was ultimately convinced by the advisers against military intervention. Finally, he formally recognized Rumaytha as the Sharif of Mecca. This story highlights the difficulties that the empire had in their attempts to control Arabia. Throughout history, the Sharifs of Mecca continued to resist the central power, demonstrating over and over again how little choice the empire's rulers had in maintaining regional stability and proving the legitimacy of their regime on the peninsula, as well as having access to the holy sites.

The Ottomans were ethnic Turks and Sunni Muslims, who began expanding their territory in Anatolia soon after the Abbasids fell to the Mongols. In 1453, they captured

Constantinople and made it their capital. The Ottoman era on the Arabian Peninsula lasted from 1517 to 1918. Over the four centuries, the degree of their control over the region fluctuated and depended on strength of the central authority. When the Mamluk armies were defeated by the Ottomans in the Ottoman-Mamluk War of 1516–1517, the latter seized Cairo and, consequently, gained formal control over the Hijaz. Sultan Selim I (r. 1512–1520), who was responsible for the remarkable and quick expansion of the empire, was named Protector of the Holy Sites, that is, Mecca and Medina. In contrast to the laidback approach practiced by the Mamluks in ruling Arabia, the Ottomans launched various campaigns to subjugate the area. Gradually, the Ottomans took over Asir and al-Hasa and claimed their rule over the interior.

When the Ottomans came to power in 1517, the sultan's main objectives in the Hijaz were to assert authority over the holy cities of Mecca and Medina and to provide safe passage for the many Muslim pilgrims from various regions. Since Ottoman rulers could not claim the prophet's lineage, they promoted the image of power through financial support and numerous construction projects. In the meantime, the local administration of Mecca and Medina remained in the hands of the sharifs, as was the case since the early days of the Abbasid caliphate. The Sultan also sent the *qadis* (judges) and other officials to participate in the local governance. The Hijaz population did not pay taxes to the empire, aside from customs collected in Jeddah, as an acknowledgment of the special status and religious significance of Mecca and Medina. The central Ottoman government provided safe passage and provisions for all pilgrims coming to the holy sites. In addition to providing food and water to the travelers, the Ottomans issued special subsidies to the local Bedouin tribes, whose limited resources were used by pilgrims along the major routes from Damascus and Cairo.

The Ottomans took on various construction projects both in Mecca and Medina, most prominently the extensive repairs of the holy sites. Despite their high cost due to the holy cities' remoteness from the imperial center, these projects were necessary as a symbol of the sultan's power and generosity. Among these projects were the extensive repairs to the Kaaba site, which suffered significant damages from floods in 1630. Although the repairs focused on preserving the structural integrity of the site, the project still generated controversy among local religious scholars.

The attempts of the local population to gain independence began in the 18th century, when the First Saudi State was created in 1744, stemming from the alliance between the Al Saud family and the religious leader Muhammad ibn Abd al-Wahhab. This first state was destroyed by 1818 by Mohammed Ali Pasha's forces, but the Second Saudi State quickly regained control of the area in 1824. Throughout the rest of the 19th century, Al Saud continued to fight for control of the interior with another influential Arabian family, the Al Rashid.

In the early 20th century, the Ottoman Empire remained in control—although only nominal by then—over most of the Arabian Peninsula. The actual power was at the hands of the numerous tribal rulers, whereas the Sharif of Mecca ruled the Hijaz. Ibn Saud's victorious campaign to establish the Third (and final) Saudi State gave a major blow to the Ottoman rule when in 1913 it removed them from al-Hasa. In 1916, with the support of the British, who were fighting the Ottomans in World War I, the Sharif of

Mecca led a pan-Arab revolt against the Ottoman Empire, with the goal of liberating and unifying the Arab nations ruled by the Ottomans and creating a united Arab state. Despite the ultimate failure of the Arab Revolt, the Allies' victory in World War I ended the Ottoman rule in Arabia.

See also: Chapter 2: The Abbasids; Arab Revolt (1916–1918); The Rise of Islam. Chapter 12: Great Mosque of Mecca.

Further Reading

Faroqhi, Suraiya. *Pilgrims and Sultans: The Hajj under the Ottomans, 1517–1683*. I. B. Tauris, 1994.

Muslu, Cihan Yüksel. *The Ottomans and the Mamluks: Imperial Diplomacy and Warfare in the Islamic World*. I. B. Tauris, 2014.

Muhammad, Prophet of Islam

The majority of information about Muhammad's life comes from two major sources: *The Expeditions of Muhammad* by Muhammad ibn Umar al-Waqidi (d. 822) and *The Biography of the Messenger of God*, written by Muhammad ibn Ishaq ibn Yasar (d. c. 768) and edited by Ibn Hisham (d. 833). The Islamic tradition emphasizes Muhammad's humanity as the greatest and last of the prophets and does not see him as a divine being. Muhammad ibn Abdallah, the Prophet of Islam, was born in Mecca sometime around the year 570 AD. His father, Abdallah, died before his birth, and his mother, Aminah, died while he was a young child, leaving him to be raised with paternal relatives of the Bani Hashim branch of Mecca's ruling Quraysh tribe. Muhammad worked for his merchant uncle Abd Manaf, known as Abu Talib, and went on several trips to Syria with him. According to the legend, it is during these trips that Muhammad was recognized as a prophet by two Christian Syrian monks, Bahirah and Nastur. Later, Muhammad began working for a wealthy older widow, Khadijah, whom he eventually married. He was in his early twenties, and she was 15 years his senior. Several daughters were born in this marriage and came to play important roles in the early days of Islam. None of the sons born to Khadijah or the wives he would marry after Khadijah's death lived beyond infancy. Even before proclaiming his new faith, Muhammad was very religious and often took journeys to sacred sites near Mecca. According to tradition, during one of his pilgrimages in 610 when he was meditating in a cave on Mount Jabal al-Nour, he received the first revelation, which became the opening verses of Surat al-Alaq, Chapter 96 of the Quran. At the time, Muhammad was approximately 40 years old.

Muhammad's mission as the leader of Islam had two important phases. The first one took place in Mecca, where he started his preaching and acquired the first followers. The second period was in Medina, where he became the leader of a new rapidly growing political and religious community. Islam's first believers were his wife,

Khadija, and his close friend, Abu Bakr. In Mecca, Muhammad's preaching disturbed the social order, and the leadership of the Quraysh tribe began to persecute his followers. During this period of persecution, both his uncle Abu Talib and his wife Khadijah died. In 621, a delegation from Yathrib visited Muhammad to learn about his teachings, and the following year they asked for his help in settling a tribal conflict between Khazraj and Aws. Muhammad agreed, and together with his followers relocated to Yathrib. This relocation was called the *hijrah* (immigration); it became a turning point in Islamic tradition and set the beginning of the Muslim calendar.

Yathrib later acquired the name of al-Madinah al-Munawwarah (the Enlightened City), or simply Medina. Muhammad became the leader of the new Muslim community that quickly rose to challenge Mecca's place in Arabia. The Quraysh and affiliated tribes tried to contest Muhammad's growing power, which resulted in several wars and military conflicts. But in 630, only eight years after his departure from Mecca, Muhammad and his army marched on Mecca and were able to take the city without a fight. He removed over 300 pagan idols from the Kaaba and reestablished it as a monotheistic worship place of one God, assuming the role this ancient sacred location was initially assigned when it was built by Abraham (Ibrahim, in Arabic) and his son Ishmael (Ismail).

Muhammad did not live long after his conquest of Mecca and died in 632 in his house in Medina. During his last pilgrimage to Mecca, he defined the steps that are now followed by all Muslims during the annual Hajj pilgrimage, and gave his famous last sermon from Mount Arafat. Muhammad is one of the most influential men in human history. His actions (*Sunnah*) and sayings (*Hadith*) have become the defining texts for the subsequent formation of Islamic law and governing systems.

KAABA BEFORE ISLAM

Mecca was an important center of commercial and cultural life of the Arabian Peninsula long before Islam. There was an annual tradition among the Bedouin tribes to make a pilgrimage to Mecca to worship their pagan gods, which were located at the Kaaba site—now the holiest place in Islam. At that time, Kaaba was a rectangular stone building that contained over 300 idols, representing deities of each tribe. The pre-Islamic pilgrimage took place during the month of Dhu al-Hijjah of the Arabian calendar, which was incorporated into the Islamic calendar, and the Muslim Hajj has been taking place during this month ever since. Even before Islam, Dhu al-Hijjah was a sacred month of truce, during which all tribal warfare was forbidden. This made a very positive impact on trade, as the caravans could safely travel across the peninsula during this time. The pilgrimage was also a time of the famous poetry contests among the tribes. The most prominent and eloquent poems (*qasidahs*) were hung over Kaaba and received the name of *muallaqat*, literally meaning "something that is hung." Fortunately, many of these early poetic works have survived and today represent some of the finest literary experimentations from ancient times.

See also: Chapter 1: Mecca; Medina. Chapter 2: The Rise of Islam. Chapter 5: Five Pillars or the Tenets of Islam; Hajj; Islamic Calendar; Quran. Chapter 12: Great Mosque of Mecca.

Further Reading

Armstrong, Karen. *Muhammad: A Biography of the Prophet*. Harper San Francisco, 1992.

Cook, Michael. *Muhammad*. Oxford University Press, 1983.

Kahn, Tamam. *Untold: A History of the Wives of Prophet Muhammad*. Monkfish Book Publishing, 2010.

Rodgers, Russ. *The Generalship of Muhammad: Battles and Campaigns of the Prophet of Allah*. University Press of Florida, 2012.

Watt, W. Montgomery. *Muhammad: Prophet and Statesman*. Oxford University Press, 1974.

Muhammad ibn Abd al-Wahhab

Muhammad ibn Abd al-Wahhab (1703–1792) was a religious teacher and preacher in Najd, who became the founder of the influential Islamic revivalist movement, which is often named after him, Wahhabism. Notably, the term "Wahhabism" (or Wahhabiyyah in Arabic) is very rarely used by the followers of this ideology. Instead, they refer to themselves as Ahl al-Sunnah (the People of the Sunnah or Sunni Muslims), Salaf, Muwahhidun (unitarians), or simply as Muslims.

Muhammad ibn Abd al-Wahhab was born in 1703 into the family of a local judge in the Bani Tamim. He memorized the Quran at a very young age and became an imam. Soon he went on his first pilgrimage, followed by travels to various Islamic theological centers in Medina, Baghdad, and Basra. His preachings and overall theology were strongly influenced by the orthodox Hanbali school of Islamic thought. In a practical implementation of his teachings, Abd al-Wahhab condemned the use of wine, tobacco, music, and other luxury items as being obstacles for worshipping the one God. His rigid doctrines were unpopular in Basra, and he was forced to leave the city. Upon his return to his hometown al-Uyaynah, he continued preaching his reformist messages but was also banished by a local ruler under the pressure of the ruling tribe, the Bani Khalid.

Eventually, Abd al-Wahhab found shelter in neighboring Diriyah where the local ruling family of the Al Saud, who at the time was led by Muhammad bin Saud, offered protection to him and his religious activities. In return, Abd al-Wahhab offered religious legitimacy to the House of Al Saud, thus setting the beginning of one of the most powerful alliances in Islamic history. The pact that took place in 1744 was further strengthened by marital relations between the two families, when Muhammad ibn Abd al-Wahhab married Muhammad ibn Saud's daughter. This pact marked the emergence of the first Saudi state, the Emirate of Diriyah.

In the following years, Abd al-Wahhab provided the spiritual and political support for Al Saud's campaigns against their political rivals in Central Arabia. Their movement often used accusations of infidelity as the reason to attack neighboring emirates. As the power of Al Saud's and Abd al-Wahhab's alliance grew throughout the region, many local tribes joined the cause despite their initial reluctance to accept the new ultraorthodox doctrine. However, by the late 1780s both nomadic and settled populations of Central Arabia were united under the banner of Muhammad ibn Abd al-Wahhab's new teaching.

Abd al-Wahhab authored various books and pamphlets that described the origins and promoted the principles of his teachings, as well as offering commentaries on his opponents. His most influential religious work is Kitab al-Tawhid (the Book of the Unity of God). Abd al-Wahhab's influential teachings and bold and passionate character helped him survive severe setbacks to create one of the most prominent religious legacies in Islam and achieve great political success. His descendants became known as the Al al-Shaykh (the House of the Shaykh) and are considered the religious and political elite in contemporary Saudi Arabia.

See also: Chapter 2: Emirate of Diriyah: The First Saudi State (1744–1818); Ikhwan. Chapter 3: Sharia Law and Judicial System; Wahhabi Ideology. Chapter 5: Sunni Islam and Jurisprudence.

Further Reading

DeLong-Bas, Natana J. *Wahhabi Islam: From Revival and Reform to Global Jihad*. Oxford University Press, 2004.

Mouline, Nabil. *The Clerics of Islam: Religious Authority and Political Power in Saudi Arabia*. Translated by Ethan S. Rundell. Yale University Press, 2014.

Zarabozo, Jamaal al-Din. *The Life, Teachings and Influence of Muhammad Ibn Abdul-Wahhaab*. International Islamic Publishing House, 2010.

Nabateans

The Nabateans were an ancient people who resided in the northwest of the Arabian Peninsula. In the beginning, they were nomadic tribes in the Hijaz region, but between the 6th and 4th centuries BC they migrated to the north and began to create settlements. Toward the end of the 2nd century BC, they formed an independent kingdom with a capital in Raqmu—Petra in the present-day Jordan. Under the rule of Aretas III (87–62 BC), the Nabatean Kingdom controlled a large territory stretching from the Sinai Peninsula to Damascus. Bosra (now southern Syria) and al-Hijr (currently in Saudi Arabia) were their northern and southern metropolises, respectively. Around 63 BC, the Nabateans allied with Rome and supported the latter's military expeditions into Arabia. During the siege of Jerusalem in 70 AD, the Nabateans provided supplies for the Roman troops.

Around the 2nd century AD, the kingdom was incorporated into the Roman Empire as the province of Arabia Petraea, whose inhabitants predominantly engaged in trade and agriculture. Over time, various Arabian tribes began to challenge their rule, but the Nabateans were able to maintain their position in al-Hijr until the 4th century. After converting to Christianity, their land was split among the emerging powers of the Ghassanids and Himyarites.

Besides their nomadic origins, Nabateans were farmers, craftsmen, and merchants. They served as middlemen in the Arabian caravan trade, which gave them substantial political power.

They controlled the spice trade, especially frankincense and myrrh used for Roman religious rituals, along the northern part of the caravan route that passed through their main cities. The Nabateans levied taxes and minted their own coins. As farmers, they are known for developing sophisticated irrigation techniques. Nabatean ceramics were very popular in the region due to their distinctive designs that featured intricate floral patterns. Archaeologists were able to trace the size of the Nabatean Kingdom and their trade networks by the spread of their pottery. The Nabateans had distinct architecture known for elaborate buildings carved out of large rocks.

The Nabatean language was a dialect of Aramaic—the most common language of Northern Arabia in ancient times. Their alphabet served as the basis of the modern Arabic script. The Nabatean religion was influenced by Hellenistic and Syrian doctrines. Their main deity was Dushara (or Dusares), associated with both Dionysus and Zeus, whose sanctuary was a large cubic rock shrine in Petra. Female deities Allat and Uzzah (both mentioned in the Quran) were also worshipped.

The Nabatean state declined after a series of devastating earthquakes in the 3rd century and the relocation of the main trade routes to the northern oasis city of Tadmur (Palmyra) in the Syrian Desert. The city of Petra was abandoned in the 4th century after Emperor Constantine declared Christianity the official region of the Roman Empire. Remnants of the Nabatean culture are common in Northern Arabia, and several Nabatean sites are located in contemporary Saudi Arabia, including Madain Salih (the historical al-Hijr), al-Ula, and al-Bada. In Saudi Arabia, many of their architectural facades have been defaced because they often featured living beings, which is prohibited in Islam. However, the Saudi government recently began protection and conservation efforts in Madain Salih as a historical, archaeological, and tourist site.

See also: Chapter 1: Northern Arabia. Chapter 2: Pre-Islamic Arabia.

Further Reading

Hammond, Philip C. *The Nabataeans: Their History, Culture and Archaeology*. Coronet Books, 1973.

Healey, John F. *The Religion of the Nabataeans: A Conspectus*. Brill, 2001.

Taylor, Jane. *Petra and the Lost Kingdom of the Nabataeans*. I. B. Tauris, 2001.

Najran

The area of Najran is located in southwestern Saudi Arabia. In ancient times, Najran was an important center of trade due to its favorable position on the incense route. Its first mention traces back to the 7th century BC, when it was under the influence of the

Sabaeans and other southern Arabian kingdoms. Roman troops under Aellius Gallus reached Najran in 24 AD and initiated political and cultural changes. The region has extensive pre-Islamic ruins that are indicative of the sophisticated level of craftsmanship from that time. They also contain various inscriptions, many of them in the Thamudic language.

Several historical sources confirm the existence of a Christian community in Najran, dating back to the 4th–5th centuries AD. The early Muslim historian Ibn Ishaq (704–768) reported that Najran was the first community in Southern Arabia that adopted the Christian religion. Prior to that, the people of Najran practiced polytheistic religion and worshipped a date-palm tree. During the 5th and early 6th centuries AD, a large Christian community lived in Najran, but it was almost completely destroyed in the first quarter of the 6th century by King Dhu Nuwas who converted to Judaism. When the Christian community refused to convert, they were subsequently killed while their churches were burned. The Islamic tradition says that they were killed by being thrown into a ditch (*ukhdud* in Arabic) and set on fire, which gave the area its local name, Ukhdud, still in use today. Surah 85 of the Quran, *al-Buruj*, retells this tragic episode.

In the early days of Islam, Muhammad sent official letters to the Christian communities of Najran, who responded by sending their own delegation to Medina with the goal of finding common ground between the two religions. Although the Christians did not accept Muhammad's message, they signed a treaty that regulated the relations between the two communities. The Christians were paying a tax and were considered a protected minority with regard to life, religion, and property.

In the 18th century, local tribes joined forces with the Wahhabi movement and swore allegiance to Al Saud. But the Najran area came under Saudi jurisdiction only in 1934 after the end of the Saudi-Yemeni War. In the early 1960s, the area was drawn into the Yemeni Civil War when Saudi Arabia supported the Imam of Yemen against the republican forces. In response, the Egyptian Air Force, which supported the official government, heavily bombed the city of Najran several times, as a hub of weapon supply for the royalists. Currently, the area composes an administrative province of Najran and its capital is the city of Najran.

See also: Chapter 2: Pre-Islamic Arabia. Chapter 5: Non-Muslims.

Further Reading

Fisher, Greg, ed. *Arabs and Empires before Islam*. Oxford University Press, 2015.

Keay, John. *The Spice Route: A History*. University of California Press, 2006.

Monferrer-Sala, Juan Pedro. *Redefining History on Pre-Islamic Accounts: The Arabic Recension of the Martyrs of Najrân*. Gorgias Press, 2010.

Pre-Islamic Arabia

Archaeologists estimate that first humans arrived on the Arabian Peninsula between 15,000 and 20,000 years ago. The diverse Neolithic population survived as hunters and gatherers and left behind numerous petroglyphs (drawings on rocks) throughout the Arabian Peninsula. These drawings depicted human figures, animals, and various symbols—thousands of years before the creation of writing. As the climate on the peninsula became dryer and hotter, the land could no longer support the Neolithic nomads, and they settled in the few fertile oases. They were gradually displaced by Semitic tribes who at the time were taking roots in Southern Arabia.

Although the environment became severe in the interior of the peninsula, the southern and eastern parts of the Arabian Peninsula (the present-day Yemen, Oman, and Bahrain) remained unaffected. Several civilizations flourished in these areas, most important of which were Dilmun, Magan, and Saba. At the same time, a vibrant culture developed in the interior of the peninsula, independent of the civilizations in the south and the east. The indigenous people inhabiting the central regions called their land Jazirat al-Arab (the Island of the Arabs). The oldest descriptions of this population can be found in Egyptian, Assyrian, and Babylonian historical records. The first mentioning of the word "Arab" appeared in biblical and Assyrian texts around the 9th and 10th centuries BC. These sources referred to Arabs as desert nomads, although historically they included both nomadic and settled populations. Sedentary Arabs lived in towns near oases and wells. Their main occupations were agriculture, trade, and various crafts. Nomads were primarily breeders and traders of livestock. Both settled and nomadic societies in pre-Islamic Arabia were based on the clan, which was composed of several related families. The clans defined social norms and codes of behavior for its members, while providing protection.

The domestication of the camel was a crucial factor in the development of trade throughout the Arabian Peninsula. This process began in the 3rd millennium BC. Sometime between 1500 and 800 BC the local population developed a special method for saddling camels, allowing the transport of large loads across vast territories. Until camels were used for trade, crossing more than a thousand miles of the harsh Arabian desert was impossible. The increased trans-Arabian trade and the creation of important trade routes had two historic consequences. One was the growth of cities servicing caravans. The biggest of these were Petra in modern Jordan and Palmyra in modern Syria, both located near the Mediterranean markets. Additionally, small caravan cities appeared throughout the Arabian Peninsula along the main routes. Mecca was the most significant among these smaller cities, considering its ancient regional importance as the location of pagan shrines. The second key consequence of the increased trade was the consistent contact it gave Arabs with other populations in the region and beyond.

In the 1st and 2nd centuries AD, a nomadic society was flourishing in Northern Arabia. With the gradual deterioration of the local urban centers brought about by the decline of the caravan routes, the balance of power shifted to the nomads—the Bedouins. In addition to hunting and raiding, their primary occupations were raising livestock, such as sheep, goats and camels, and breeding horses. Their lives and migration patterns were driven by the need for water, as they were moving around during different seasons in search for pastures. The remnants of Bedouin camping areas of this period are widespread throughout the peninsula, as they left behind a great number of inscriptions on rocks. Accounts of local desert tribes are found in the records dating back to the Roman Severan dynasty, who saw them as a threatening element on the frontiers. In the 3rd century AD several large tribal confederations were formed, giving substantial power to the tribal rulers. The tribes exploited the struggle between the Byzantine and Persian Empires and played a growing role in their military conflicts.

The economic growth began to decline in the 4th century AD, along with the weakening of the Sabaean Empire and its trade. Hippalus, a Greek merchant and navigator, made a historic discovery that the monsoon winds of the Indian Ocean blew eastward for six months in the year and westward for the remaining six months. This meant that the merchants were able to bypass the trading centers in Arabia altogether and reach the Far East by sea. At the same time, the frankincense and myrrh market began to collapse in the early 4th century AD, as Rome increasingly gave way to Christian beliefs and abandoned its religious rituals requiring the use of incenses. The decline in trade had a devastating impact on the Arabian population, and by the beginning of the 7th century, the peninsula was in a weak state. The economic downturn, which made survival more difficult in the severe environmental conditions, caused many communities of settled Arabs to return to nomadism, which once again became the predominant lifestyle in the peninsula. For the Bedouins, the decline led to an increase in warfare and mutual raiding. Muslims consider this period dark ages and refer to it as al-Jahiliyyah, or the Age of Ignorance. Yet, within just one generation, Islam would radically transform the Arabian Peninsula, establish social order, and unite the clashing population.

See also: Chapter 1: Mecca; Northern Arabia. Chapter 6: Bedouins and Nomadism; Settled Population: *Hadar*.

Further Reading

Fisher, Greg, ed. *Arabs and Empires before Islam*. Oxford University Press, 2015.

Peters, F. E. *The Arabs and Arabia on the Eve of Islam*. Ashgate, 1999.

Rashidun: The Righteous Caliphs

The first Islamic caliphate was established immediately after Muhammad's death in 632 and is known as the Rashidun caliphate. Sunni Islam refers to the four Rashidun caliphs as the "Righteous Caliphs," the word *rashid* means "following the right path" in Arabic. The Righteous Caliphs are celebrated in Islamic history for their personal connection to the prophet. Since Muhammad did not name a successor to lead the Muslim community after his death and did not establish a procedure for choosing one, these caliphs were chosen through the process of *shura* (consultation)—a community forum, rooted in the Quran and encouraged by Muhammad, and considered an early form of representational democracy.

Thus, following Muhammad's death, a council of Muslim leaders met in Medina to choose his successor. Four candidates were considered, all of them the prophet's trusted companions (*al-sahabah*). Ali ibn Abu Talib was Muhammad's cousin and husband of his daughter Fatima. Uthman ibn Affan was an early convert from the powerful Umayyad clan of Mecca and Muhammad's son-in-law. Omar ibn al-Khattab was one of Muhammad's closest advisers and one of the most prominent converters to Islam (he initially was very hostile to Muhammad and the new religion, and his conversion solidified Islam's growing influence). Abu Bakr al-Siddiq was Muhammad's father-in-law through his daughter Aisha. The council could not come to an agreement on a single candidate, with the majority splitting over Ali and Uthman. However, they ended up choosing Abu Bakr as the first successor, or *khalifah* (caliph). In subsequent years, each of these four original candidates would serve as caliph in succession. The first three—Abu Bakr, Omar, and Uthman—ruled from Medina, and the last, Ali, moved the capital to Kufa, which is currently located in Iraq. Shia Muslims consider Ali to be the first rightful caliph after Muhammad.

Abu Bakr was widely respected and supported for his piety and virtue. He was also a talented and formidable military leader. After Muhammad's death, several tribes renounced Islam, but Abu Bakr decisively crushed their rebellion in the Ridda Wars (Apostasy Wars). Following that, he launched expeditions into Syria and Persia. Although Abu Bakr's rein lasted only 27 months (632–634), it set the foundation for the astonishing growth of the Islamic Empire in subsequent decades. Abu Bakr appointed Omar ibn al-Khattab as the second caliph in a written statement, thus preventing uncertainty over his succession.

Due to his stunning military achievements, Omar acquired the title Amir al-Muminun, "the Commander of the Believers." His leadership lasted for 10 years (634–644), and during this time the Islamic Empire had rapidly spread across all of the Middle East. A major factor behind the success of the Islamic forces was their humane treatment of the conquered populations, especially in contrast with the Byzantines, who caused their own downfall by merciless persecution of Christian sects. Syrian Monophysites, Nestorian Christians, and Copts generally welcomed and often even assisted the invading Muslim forces. Among other historical factors that helped Omar's military accomplishments was the weakened state of both Byzantines and Persians, who had been exhausted by decades-long wars and internal tensions. Among his most celebrated victories was the defeat of the Persian Sassanid army in the Battle of Nahavand in 642, which is often referred to as the "Victory of Victories." The Islamic caliphate under Omar featured effective governance and streamlined administration. He created an effective financial infrastructure, including a tax system, and established state control over the military.

The third caliph, Uthman, was in power between 644 and 656 and continued to expand the empire. Among Uthman's accomplishments were the foundation of the port of Jeddah and the expansion of the holy shrine in Mecca and the mosque in Medina. But his greatest contribution was the codification of the Quran, which previously existed in several versions, into one uniform written text, as we know it today. Uthman's reign was marked by the first significant internal conflict in the Muslim community. Because he distributed many of the provincial governorships and the state income among members of his own family, he was often accused of nepotism and the army began to resist his authority. The growing tensions ended violently in Uthman's assassination in 656 by a group of rebels led by Muhammad ibn Abu Bakr, the son of the first caliph.

Ali ibn Abu Talib, the last of the four original companions of the prophet, was then named caliph in Medina. A growing community of Muslims believed that Ali should have been the first caliph and Uthman's assassins had been supporters of Ali. These supporters became known as *shia't Ali* ("Ali's party") or simply *shi'a*. But the majority of Muslims supported the original election process of the caliphs. They received the name of *Ahl al-Sunnah wal-Jama'ah*, "the People of Tradition and Community," where Sunnah refers to the tradition and the actions of Muhammad. Ali's rule was contested by Muawiyya, the governor of Syria and Uthman's cousin, as well as Aisha, one of Muhammad's wives and the daughter of Abu Bakr. These disagreements resulted in a civil war (*fitna*) that became the first armed conflict within the Muslim community and lasted from 656 to 661. Eventually, Ali and Aisha agreed on mediation, but the arbitration council ruled that neither of them should be appointed the leader of the Muslim community. Ali refused to accept this decision and left for Kufa—a town in Iraq and the Shia stronghold. Meanwhile, Muawiyya declared himself caliph in 661, Ali was assassinated in 662, and a new phase in the history of the Islamic Empire began.

See also: Chapter 2: The Golden Age of Islam in Arabia; Muhammad, Prophet of Islam; The Rise of Islam. Chapter 5: Shia Islam; Sunni Islam and Jurisprudence. Chapter 6: *Sharif* and *Sayyid*.

Further Reading

Crone, Patricia, and Martin Hinds. *God's Caliph: Religious Authority in the First Centuries of Islam.* Cambridge University Press, 1986.

El-Hibri, Tayeb. *Parable and Politics in Early Islamic History: The Rashidun Caliphs.* Columbia University Press, 2010.

Rogerson, Barnaby. *The Heirs of Muhammad: Islam's First Century and the Origins of the Sunni-Shia Split.* Overlook Press, 2007.

Spuler, Bertold. *The Age of the Caliphs.* Markus Wiener, 1995.

The Rise of Islam

When Muhammad began preaching in his hometown of Mecca, his teachings were initially ignored by everyone but his closest followers. But as the crowds grew and the number of converts increased, Mecca's ruling classes also became increasingly hostile toward the emerging religious leader. Islam's message of unity and the revolutionary concept of brotherhood of the believers, regardless of their social status and origins, threatened the structure of the tribal society and its established hierarchies. The same message was very attractive to the lower classes, and they comprised the majority of early converts. Additionally, by strongly condemning pagan idol worshipping, which annually brought pilgrims to Mecca, Muhammad's message posed a threat to the economic well-being of Mecca's leading citizens who received substantial profits from the annual pilgrimage. The Quraysh—Muhammad's own tribe—was the guardian of the holy site and therefore stood to lose the most.

Despite fierce opposition by the Meccan elite, Muhammad's influence continued to grow both in his hometown and beyond. In addition to converts from poor classes, he also attracted a number of prominent Meccans. Among those were Uthman ibn Affan from the powerful Umayyad clan, and Abu Bakr al-Siddiq—a respected merchant. Both of them were destined to play a prominent role in the spread of Islam and later become two of the four Righteous Caliphs. Among other early converts was Muhammad's younger cousin Ali, the son of Abu Talib—Muhammad's uncle who raised him. Shortly after, Omar ibn al-Khattab also joined their cause. His conversion was particularly significant as he had previously been among the most vocal enemies of the new religion and had vowed to kill Muhammad. This group of early followers and trusted supporters of Muhammad were called *al-Sahabah*, or the Companions of the Prophet. Their accounts of Muhammad's life are recorded in the *Hadith*, the Sayings of the Prophet, which serves as one of the foundations for Islamic law. Following Muhammad's death, Abu Bakr, Omar, Uthman, and Ali would become the four Righteous Caliphs, ruling in succession of each other.

Islam continued to gain more popularity and converts. The Meccan establishment, fearful of the growing power of the new faith, began to prosecute Muhammad's most vulnerable followers from the poor classes who did not have tribal protection. Muhammad's position in the city also became increasingly difficult after the death of his wife Khadija and especially when, shortly after in 619, his uncle Abu Talib died as well. In the meantime, the city of Yathrib—a cultural center located in the oasis northeast of Mecca—was torn apart by disputes between the Aws and the Khazraj tribes. The Khazraj representatives decided to meet with Muhammad and ask for his help in mediating the conflict, while promising allegiance and protection in return. Muhammad accepted their offer and, together with his closest followers, left Mecca for Yathrib. This journey is known as *Hijrah* (emigration) and took place in 622, which is counted as the first year in the Islamic calendar. Yathrib became known as Madinat al-Nabi' (the city of the Prophet) and al-Madinah al-Munawwarah (the Enlightened City), or simply Medina.

In Medina, Muhammad quickly became the religious and political leader of the local community. As his position grew, he set on a series of wars with the Meccans. Early in 624, a historic battle took place near Badr, a resting stop on the caravan route, where Muslim and Meccan armies clashed in an unequal fight: Muslim numbers were slightly over 300, in contrast with the Meccan 1,500. The event, which became known as the Battle of Badr, began with a series of the duels between individual Meccan and Muslim warriors, the latter led by Ali ibn Abu Talib. During the duels, all Meccans were killed by the Muslims, which demoralized the Meccan forces and led to their defeat in the subsequent fight. The Battle of Badr was a turning point in the early years of Islam. The win served as proof of divine intervention, brought many new followers, and strengthened and united the Muslim community (*al-ummah*) for the battles that followed.

In 625 the Meccans gathered a force of about 3,000 fighters who met Muhammad's force of 500 at Uhud in the outskirts of Medina. Initially, the Muslims carried a successful charge but, after the archers disobeyed Muhammad's orders and left their positions, a surprise attack by the Meccan cavalry carried the day. Many Muslims were killed, and Muhammad himself was seriously wounded. However, the Meccans did not press their victory and withdrew toward Mecca. The Battle of Uhud was a significant setback for the Muslims, but two years later the Battle of the Trench turned the tables around once again.

In 627, determined to at last defeat Muhammad and his followers, the leader of Quraysh Abu Sufyan gathered 10,000 men and marched north to attack Medina where the city defenders numbered only about 3,000. Having learned from his Persian follower Salman al-Farsi (who was the first Persian convert to Islam) about defensive fortifications, Muhammad and his troops dug a trench across the northern side of Medina, which gave this campaign its name—the Battle of the Trench. On the other three sides, mountains provided natural defenses to the city. Unable to breach the barriers, the Meccans laid a 30-day long siege to Medina. The combination of well-organized defense, poor weather conditions, and low morale among the Meccans ended in a fiasco. The Meccan forces split apart, and one by one their leaders returned home with their troops. This victory accelerated Muhammad's rise as a regional leader and caused more tribes to seek alliances with the Muslims. On the other hand, the Meccans lost much of their trade and prestige as a result of the defeat.

Muhammad had never lost the sight of his hometown and maintained the campaign to take it back. Mecca's significance to Islam was highlighted through the establishment of Muslim ritual. Whereas initially Muslims prayed in the direction of Jerusalem, in 624 the prayer direction (*qiblah*) has shifted to Mecca. In 628, negotiations between Muhammad and Abu Sufyan resulted in the Treaty of Hudaybiyah, which established a 10-year peace between the two cities and gave Muslims permission to make a peaceful pilgrimage to Mecca in the following year. However, in 630 the Meccans violated the treaty when a Quraysh-allied tribe attacked a tribe allied with Muhammad. Muslims marched on Mecca and took the city without a fight. Abu Sufyan, Muhammad's staunchest foe, gave his fealty to Muhammad and converted to Islam. Muhammad ordered the removal of the idols from Kaaba and cleansing of the sacred site. In the following two years, the Muslims continued to expand their influence throughout the peninsula, and the majority of tribes and tribal groups accepted Islam and joined the Muslim forces. At the time of his death in 632, Muhammad had control over most of the Arabian Peninsula. Within one century, the largest empire in history would rise under the banner of Islam. It would bring about the Golden Age with its unprecedented flourishing of all areas of thought and science that would transform the human civilization—all while Europe was stalled in the Dark Ages.

See also: Chapter 2: Muhammad, Prophet of Islam; Pre-Islamic Arabia; Rashidun: The Righteous Caliphs. Chapter 5: Five Pillars or the Tenets of Islam; Hajj; Islamic Calendar; Jihad; Quran.

Further Reading
Armstrong, Karen. *Islam: A Short History*. Modern Library, 2000.

Esposito, John L. *The Oxford History of Islam*. Oxford University Press, 1999.

Gordon, Matthew. *The Rise of Islam*. Greenwood Press, 2005.

Inamdar, Subhash C. *Muhammad and the Rise of Islam: The Creation of Group Identity*. Psychosocial Press, 2001.

Sharifs of Mecca

As the Islamic Empire moved away from Mecca and Arabia into Damascus and then Baghdad, the peninsula has gradually become an entity lacking a centralized power. In the 10th century, a new governing institution, Sharifat, was established to rule Mecca and Medina. The caliphate wanted to secure the holy sites, especially after both holy cities were attacked in 930 by the Qarmathian sect. The latter massacred thousands of pilgrims, desecrated the Zamzam Well with their corpses, stole the Black Stone, and extorted a large sum from the Abbasids for its return. The new leader of the two cities would carry the title of Sharif and would serve as the protector of the holy sites and the incoming pilgrims. The meaning of the word "sharif" in Arabic is "noble," referencing the fact that these were descendants of Muhammad through his grandson Hasan ibn Ali. Ironically, the first sharif of Mecca, Jafar ibn Muhammad al-Hassani, did not come from the city itself, but arrived to Mecca with a caravan from Cairo. Al-Hassani was a moderate Shia who succeeded in making the city relatively autonomous by exploiting the rivalry between the Fatimids and the Abbasids. In 1063, the Sharifat institution was taken over by the Hashemites, when the new sharif Muhammad ibn Jafaar was appointed to rule Mecca. He was a descendant of the prophet's grandson Hasan and a member of the Hashem clan of the Quraysh tribe, and thus the Hashemite dynasty had emerged.

Sharifs remained the main and most consistent source of political power on the peninsula for centuries to come. Their authority often extended beyond Mecca and the Hijaz, at times as far as the Najd in the east and to Yemen in the south. Throughout history, sharifs had to navigate the turbulent politics of the succeeding empires. Their rule was marked by constant negotiations of their authority and uneasy alliances with the long chain of caliphs and sultans in Baghdad, Cairo, Damascus, and Constantinople. On the one hand, the power of sharifs varied in different historical periods, depending on the degree of control exerted by the empire's ruler of the time. But on the other hand, the caliphs and sultans had to maintain good relations with the sharifs—both to maintain the legitimacy of their regimes and to guarantee access to the holy sites for their citizens. Therefore, the central power has often made concessions and allowed the sharifs to govern the holy cities as semiautonomous territories, especially considering the numerous difficulties of maintaining effective military control over the distant and inhospitable Hijaz. The Hajj pilgrimage became the annual ceremony of affirmation of the relationship between the sharif and the central ruler, who would often lead a procession—himself or through his representative—to the holy sites. Meanwhile, the tradition of mentioning the empire ruler's name during the Friday midday sermon became an important proclamation of his political might. The central empire also traditionally supplied the funds for renovations of the holy sites and other projects in the two cities. The Sharifat institution came to an end in 1925, when the Hijaz was overrun by Ibn Saud's forces and was eventually incorporated into the Kingdom of Saudi Arabia.

See also: Chapter 1: Mecca; Medina. Chapter 2: Third Saudi State: Saudi Arabia in the 20th Century. Chapter 6: *Sharif* and *Sayyid*.

Further Reading

Al-Amr, Saleh Muhammad. *The Hijaz under Ottoman Rule 1869–1914: Ottoman Vali, the Sharif of Mecca, and the Growth of British Influence.* University of Leeds, 1974.

Teitelbaum, Joshua. *The Rise and Fall of the Hashimite Kingdom of Arabia.* New York University Press, 2001.

Third Saudi State: Saudi Arabia in the 20th Century

In 1902, the leader of the Al Saud family, Abd al-Aziz ibn Saud, captured Riyadh and established the Third Saudi State, and went on to unify the rest of the peninsula under his family's rule. In 1913, he overthrew the Ottomans in al-Hasa. Following that, Great Britain recognized the independence of Al Saud's emirate in 1915, which was rapidly expanded six years later after the final defeat of the Al Rashid family (Al Saud's biggest rivals in the region) and the incorporation of the Emirate of Jabal Shammar, which was traditionally ruled by Al Rashid, into the new Saudi state.

In order to build an army and increase the number of loyal citizens, Abd al-Aziz ibn Saud encouraged Bedouin nomads to settle in agricultural communities, study Islam, and raid the territory of his adversaries. This prompted the rise of the Ikhwan as a radical military force, whose members strictly observed the religious revival of the Wahhabi ideology. One of their most important campaigns was against the Sharif of Mecca, following his self-proclamation in 1924 as a caliph and King of Hijaz. Following his defeat, the area was absorbed into Al Saud's territories, which included the Hijaz, the Najd, and adjunct areas, in 1926. In another treaty with the British in 1927, Ibn Saud's sovereignty was accepted, whereas he agreed to recognize British interests in Southern and Eastern Arabia. In the subsequent phase of power consolidation, Ibn Saud concentrated the entire political, military, judicial, and religious power in his and his allies' hands through a series of administrative and legal reforms. One of these measures was a significant limitation of the authority of tribal sheikhs.

On September 23, 1932, the formation of a centralized state was concluded with the official proclamation of the Kingdom of Saudi Arabia. Al Saud and his government signed initial border agreements with neighboring countries and established a unique political system based on the Quran and Shariah, administered with the help and guidance from Muslim religious scholars. The king was the head of state, governed with a cabinet primarily consisting of the Al Saud family members.

During the Great Depression, which also affected the Saudi economy, he tried to improve the country's condition by granting concessions to search for oil, for which he strategically exploited the British-American rivalry. When Ibn Saud died in 1953, his country took a considerable step from isolated desert country to a leading supplier of crude oil. Following Ibn Saud's death, one of his two oldest sons, Saud, ascended the throne and ruled until 1964, when he was forced to abdicate and his brother Faysal became king. Faysal began a large-scale modernization project of the economy and opened the country to the West, albeit without abandoning its Islamic principles and traditional character. To achieve this, he had to find a compromise that would appease the religious elite enough to support his revolutionary ideas. After his assassination in 1975 (by his nephew), his successors Khalid and Fahd bin Abd al-Aziz continued his policies and maintained close relations with the United States. However, they also sparked controversy over Islamic issues, such as the siege of the Great Mosque in Mecca in 1979 by a group of radical Muslims, or the decision to invite non-Muslim armies to protect the Holy Places from a possible Iraqi attack in 1990. Particularly difficult were the relations with Iran after the Islamic Revolution in 1979, which culminated in various clashes with Iranian pilgrims during the Hajj and uprisings among the Shiite population in the Eastern Province. In the early 2000s, the opposition to the royal regime organized a number of terrorist attacks.

King Abdullah succeeded Fahd in 2005, although he was a de facto ruler since 1995, after Fahd suffered a stroke. Abdallah's rule was marked by numerous reforms and innovations to all sectors of Saudi administrative structure and society. Following his death, his half-brother King Salman ascended to the throne in 2015.

See also: Chapter 2: Arab Revolt (1916–1918); Ibn Saud; Ikhwan. Chapter 3: Saudi Monarchy and Branches of the Government. Chapter 6: House of Saud.

Further Reading

Jones, Toby Craig. *Desert Kingdom: How Oil and Water Forged Modern Saudi Arabia*. Harvard University Press, 2010.

Kostiner, Joseph, et al. *The Making of Saudi Arabia, 1916–1936: From Chieftaincy to Monarchical State*. Oxford University Press, 1993.

Parker, Chad H. *Making the Desert Modern: Americans, Arabs, and Oil on the Saudi Frontier, 1933–1973*. University of Massachusetts Press, 2015.

al-Rasheed, Madawi, ed. *Salman's Legacy: The Dilemmas of a New Era in Saudi Arabia*. Oxford University Press, 2018.

The Umayyads

The Umayyad caliphate (661–750) was the second of the four major caliphates established after the death of Muhammad. It was ruled by the prominent Meccan clan Banu Umayya, or Umayyads. Uthman, the third of the four Righteous Caliphs, also belonged to the Umayyad family. The dynasty began ascending to power when Mu'awiyah ibn Abu

Sufyan was appointed as a governor of Syria and later, after the end of the First Muslim Civil War in 661, proclaimed himself caliph and made Damascus his capital. Mu'awiyah is considered the first Umayyad caliph.

The Umayyad caliphate brought about an important shift to the foundations of the Islamic Empire. Whereas the four Righteous Caliphs were early converts, who were directly associated with Muhammad and shared his view on the empire as a method of spreading the new faith, the Umayyads were more concerned with the secular aspects of the state. The affairs of the state and its administration took priority over religion, as the new rulers were preoccupied with establishing governance over vast territories conquered in less than 30 years. Additionally, while the Rashidun caliphate was a designated position, Mu'awiyah instituted a hereditary rule of succession. After Mu'awiyah's death in 680, his son Yazid became the successor of the dynasty.

In the meantime, the two sons of Ali, the fourth Righteous Caliph, and Muhammad's grandsons—Hasan and Husayn—were at the center of the new movement of Muslims who were Ali's supporters. When the older brother Hasan died in 669, Husayn became the leader of this group. After Mu'awiyah's death, Husayn refused to recognize Yazid and set out from Medina to Iraq to mobilize his followers. During this travel, Husayn and 70 of his family members and supporters were surrounded and slaughtered by a large Umayyad force of 4,000 at Karbala, which is currently located in southwestern Iraq. Husayn's martyrdom in 680 magnified the division between Shia and Sunni Muslims, and this date marked the emergence of Shiism as an independent sect in Islam. The annual commemoration of this tragic event, which falls on the Islamic month Muharram, is the most important religious observance in Shia Islam.

The unrest that followed Husayn's assassination is viewed as the second *fitna*, or Second Muslim Civil War, and the Umayyad leadership was eventually assumed in 684 by Marwan I from another branch of the Umayyad clan. The dynasty established the center of their governance in Syria, with the capital in Damascus. They continued the expansion of the Muslim Empire, including large territories in the west—throughout North Africa and into the Iberian Peninsula in Spain. The Umayyad caliphate is considered among the largest empires in human history, both with regard to the size of its territories and the incorporated proportion of the world's population. The Umayyads were considered quite secular, especially in the eyes of the more conservative populations of Arabia. Large portions of the empire's population were Christians, who were allowed to practice their own religion, as were Jews. However, non-Muslims had to pay a head tax from which Muslims were exempt, and this prompted large-scale conversions to Islam. During the reign of al-Walid I (705–715), Arabic was proclaimed the official language of the empire. The Umayyads initiated a number of ambitious building projects, the most prominent of which is the Umayyad Mosque in Damascus.

The Umayyad dynasty was eventually ousted by the Abbasid rebellion (746–750), which emerged from the alienated circles of Muslims who were not Arabs by origin. The Abbasid caliphate was established in 750 but, notably, the Umayyads continued to have substantial power for several more centuries in western territories—in Cordoba, where they first ruled the Emirate of Cordoba (756–929) and then the Caliphate of Cordoba (929–1031).

The Umayyads' rise to power and the caliphate's move to Damascus symbolized the breaking of ties between Arabia, the cradle of the Muslim Empire, and its center. The dynasty even laid siege to their former home city of Mecca and destroyed the holy site of Kaaba, when a Meccan ruler, Ibn al-Zubayr, proclaimed a rival caliphate and led a rebellion against the Umayyads. The next Islamic dynasty, the Abbasids, despite physically moving even further away to Baghdad, exerted more efforts to preserve connections with Islam's Arabian roots, due to their interest in the holy sites and the pilgrimage.

See also: Chapter 2: The Abbasids; Rashidun: The Righteous Caliphs.

Further Reading

Blankinship, Khalid Yahya. *The End of the Jihâd State: The Reign of Hisham Ibn abd Al-Malik and the Collapse of the Umayyads*. State University of New York Press, 1994.

Déroche, François. *Qur'ans of the Umayyads: A First Overview*. Brill, 2014.

George, Alain, and Andrew Marsham, eds. *Power, Patronage, and Memory in Early Islam: Perspectives on Umayyad Elites*. Oxford University Press, 2018.

Hawting, G. R. *The First Dynasty of Islam: The Umayyad Caliphate Ad 661–750*. Routledge, 2000.

Rihan, Mohammad. *The Politics and Culture of an Umayyad Tribe: Conflict and Factionalism in the Early Islamic Period*. I. B. Tauris, 2014.

CHAPTER 3

GOVERNMENT AND POLITICS

OVERVIEW

Saudi Arabia's political system is based on a dual authority: one belonging to its royal family of Al Saud and another—to its religious establishment. The foundation of this system goes back to the 18th century and the formation of the First Saudi State, which grew out of a strategic agreement between the House of Saud and Muhammad ibn Abd al-Wahhab and his followers—a powerful religious movement currently known as Wahhabism. The Al Saud family govern the state, whereas the Al-Shaykh family (the descendants of Ibn Abd al-Wahhab) lead the religious establishment. In Saudi Arabia there is no separation between the state and religion. In fact, they are considered one and the same, based on the following commonly accepted idea of Saudi governance: "Islam is religion and state all in one" (*Islam huwa din wa dawlah*).

The country's religious establishment has historically been an exceptionally powerful entity, whose main task is to enforce Islamic law and Wahhabi ideology, as the country's only official form of Islam. Although Wahhabism is within the Sunni Hanbali tradition, Saudi Arabia discourages the propagation of all other forms of Islam domestically, even those within the Sunni denomination. The Saudi state does not extend the full benefits of citizenship to its Shiite communities, which for many years has been the object of international scrutiny and internal tensions, especially in the Eastern Province where a significant Shia community resides.

Saudi Arabia is a monarchy, led by a king who is the authority over all three aspects of state power—legislative, executive, and judicial. Royal decrees, regularly issued by the king, can annul any other judicial or administrative decision. The king simultaneously holds the position of the prime minister, and in this role, chairs the Council of Ministers (Majlis al-Wuzara'), members of which are appointed and dismissed by the king. The council is given various executive tasks, such as foreign and domestic policies, economy, health care, education, defense, finances, and other matters pertinent to running of the state. The council supervises a number of agencies, whose job is to implement the council's decisions in all spheres of Saudi society and economy. An important quasi-legislative governing body is the Consultative Assembly (Majlis al-Shura), established in 1993. The assembly has the authority to draft legislation and present it for the king's approval. All members of the assembly are appointed by the king. In January 2013, an important change to the structure of Majlis al-Shura was

The flag of Saudi Arabia. (Steve Allen/Dreamstime.com)

made by King Abdallah, who gave women 30 seats (out of the total 150) and stated that women should always hold at least a fifth of the seats in the assembly.

The family of Al Saud is the foundation of Saudi monarchy. Technically, the choosing of the state leader takes place by means of a traditional Islamic institution of governance. A special assembly of community leaders—consisting of religious leaders, heads of influential families, and prominent businessmen, in addition to members of the royal family—regulate and finalize the succession process. However, in reality, the royal family has dominated this process from the very inception of the state. In 1933, the founder of Saudi Arabia, King Abd al-Aziz ibn Saud, formally named his oldest surviving son, Saud, as the successor of the royal power. Ibn Saud also made clear that the next in seniority son, Faysal, should be the subsequent leader. Thus, a tradition was created where the royal succession would pass down among Ibn Saud's sons. In the course of the 20th and early 21st centuries, three important aspects have been defining Al Saud family politics: seniority of birth, generation, and sibling ties. In 2015, King Salman made a crucial change to the succession tradition of Ibn Saud's sons, when he appointed his full nephew, Muhammad bin Nayef, as crown prince—the first of Ibn Saud's grandsons to be in line for the throne. In 2017, King Salman made another fundamental change when he removed Muhammad bin Nayef from the line of succession, appointing his son Muhammad bin Salman as the new crown prince.

The highest authority within the religious establishment of Saudi Arabia is the Council of Senior Scholars (Majlis Hay'at Kibar al-Ulama). The council is appointed by the king and consists of 21 senior *ulama*. Unlike most other Muslim countries, they are directly involved in the matters of the state. They advise the king on religious issues and had historically played a key role in the development and implementation of Saudi Arabia's judicial system, as well as influencing the sphere of education. For decades, the *ulama* have been instrumental in defining and regulating the position of women in the country by means of numerous *fatwas* (legal opinions). However, throughout the last decade and due to various policies instituted during King Abdullah's and King Salman's reigns, the religious establishment has been gradually losing a substantial number of its powers. For example, in 2016, the Council of Ministers greatly limited the jurisdiction of the country's religious police (Committee for the Promotion of Virtue and the Prevention of Vice, or the *Mutawwa*) and banned the members of this unit from making arrests.

Saudi Arabia does not have a written constitution in the same form as it exists in the majority of other countries. Officially, the holy texts of the Quran, the Hadith, and the Sunnah are considered the only legitimate legal texts. However, in 1992, King Fahd issued a royal decree initiating the creation of a formal legal document, known as the Basic Law of Saudi Arabia (*al-Nizam al-Asasi lil-Hukm*), which can be considered a form of constitution, as it provides guidelines for the government and defines the rights and duties of the country's citizens. The Basic Law of Saudi Arabia consists of nine chapters, divided into 83 articles.

Saudi Arabia is currently divided into 13 regional provinces or *manatiq* (singular: *mintaqah*): Riyadh, Qassim, Mecca, Medina, Tabuk, Jawf, Hail, Eastern Province, Jizan, Asir, Najran, Bahah, and Northern Borders. Each of these provinces is led by an amir, provincial governor. Historically, amirs have been members of the royal family. Each of the provinces has a capital and is further divided into smaller administrative units—governorates/*muhafazhat* (singular: *muhafazhah*). Finally, each *muhafazhah* is subdivided into several municipalities, called *amanah*. In 2005, Saudi Arabia had its first municipal elections since the 1960s. In 2015, Saudi women participated in the elections for the first time in history—both as voters and as candidates.

Further Reading

Rich, Ben. *Securitising Identity: The Case of the Saudi State*. MUP Academic, 2017.

Wald, Ellen R. *Saudi, Inc.: The Arabian Kingdom's Pursuit of Profit and Power*. Pegasus Books, 2018.

The Arab Spring

The so-called Arab Spring, which started with the 2011 Tunisian Revolution, generated a wave of protests—the biggest that Saudi Arabia had ever seen. Most dissent came, expectedly, from Shia Muslims in the Eastern Province. The consistent discrimination endured by the Saudi Shia community, which effectively makes them second-class citizens, made them more prone to protest against the government. Their rallies particularly intensified with the beginning of large-scale protests in nearby Bahrain on

> **SHEIKH NIMR**
>
> Nimr Baqir al-Nimr (1959–2016), commonly referred to as Sheikh Nimr, was a Shia Sheikh from the Eastern Province and a prominent public figure popular among Saudi youth. He was sharply critical of the government and called for free elections in Saudi Arabia. He is also known for publicly speaking against Saudi Arabia's discriminatory policies toward its Shia population, and even called for the secession of the Eastern Province if Shia conditions were not improved. An important aspect of Sheikh Nimr's activism is that he called for peaceful protests and condemned violence.
>
> On July 8, 2012, Sheikh al-Nimr was arrested by Saudi police, after being shot in the leg. When in prison, he went on a hunger strike. In 2014, he was sentenced to death by the Specialized Criminal Court, charged with "foreign meddling, disobeying its rulers and taking up arms against the security forces." Al-Nimr was executed in January 2016, along with 46 others. His execution was widely condemned by local activists, human rights organizations, and the international community.

February 14, 2011. The repression of protests led to the death of at least 15 Shia youths. Several protesters were shot dead by Saudi authorities in late 2011 and early 2012. Rallies in the Eastern Province intensified after Sheikh Nimr al-Nimr—a known Saudi activist for Shia rights—was wounded in the leg and arrested by police in July 2012.

There were also various smaller protests and petitions in other parts of the country, calling for democratic changes in the kingdom. Pro-democracy campaigners organized a "Day of Rage" on March 11, 2011, in Riyadh, but it failed to gain any significant traction because of the overwhelming presence of Saudi security forces in the capital. Just a week earlier, the government formally banned public protests—the ban came as a reaction to Shia demonstrations taking place in the Eastern Province. However, numerous protests over human rights took place in April 2011 in front of government buildings in Riyadh, Taif, and Tabuk, and continued in January 2012 in Riyadh. After activists had been detained by the police, a series of protests took place in April and May 2011, demanding that the government release the prisoners held without charge. These started in the Eastern Province and spread to Riyadh and municipal centers throughout the country.

Protests and demonstrations in support of human rights had an accelerating effect on the ongoing campaign for women's rights as well. Activists organized a Facebook campaign Baladi ("my country" in Arabic), which claimed that, theoretically, the Saudi Arabian law does provide women electoral rights and encouraged women to exercise this right in the upcoming elections. In April 2011, groups of women in Riyadh, Jeddah, and Dammam attempted to register for the municipal elections scheduled for September of that year—as an act of civil disobedience against the existing institutional discrimination. Shortly after, King Abdallah issued a decree announcing that women would be able to participate in the 2015 elections, both as voters and candidates. A number of feminist activists, including Eman al-Nafjan, Manal al-Sharif, and others, organized a right-to-drive campaign that took place on June 17, 2011. In March 2012, thousands of female students of King Khalid University demonstrated in Abha against antisanitary conditions on campus and were violently attacked by security forces, leading to injuries. Similar protests at Taibah University in Medina and Tabuk University followed shortly after.

In an attempt to subdue the protests and stop the spreading of the Arab Spring on the Arabian Peninsula, King Abdullah's government designated a $130 billion program to increase salaries, build affordable housing, and institute additional social benefits, such as unemployment benefits, a debt relief program, as well as educational subsidies. The public aid package also contained an additional two months' worth of salary to government employees and $70 billion designated to low-income housing. Using its close alliance with the country's religious establishment, the government secured complete support from the influential religious figures who unanimously condemned any form of protest. The Grand Mufti even issued a special *fatwa* that street protests are forbidden in Islam.

See also: Chapter 5: Shia Community. Chapter 6: House of Saud. Chapter 7: Women's Mobility and Driving Ban.

Further Reading

Maddy-Weitzman, Bruce. *A Century of Arab Politics: From the Arab Revolt to the Arab Spring.* Rowman & Littlefield, 2016.

Matthiesen, Toby. *Sectarian Gulf: Bahrain, Saudi Arabia, and the Arab Spring That Wasn't.* Stanford University Press, 2014.

Capital and Corporal Punishment

Saudi Arabia's judicial system allows both corporal and capital punishments. Although both of these types of punishment are included in the Sharia (Islamic law) system, in reality, the majority of Muslim countries have abandoned the practice of corporal punishment in modern times. In Sharia, offenses are organized into two main categories, based on the severity of the crime. *Hadd* offenses are serious crimes that have universally applied penalties, whereas *ta'zir* are lesser crimes where specific punishment or penalty is decided by the judge. It is noteworthy that serious criminal offenses leading to corporal or capital punishment in Saudi Arabia include apostasy, adultery, and witchcraft—in addition to the internationally recognized crimes, such as murder and sexual assault. Apostasy is a particularly controversial topic in the Muslim world, and in Saudi law it can be punished by death—despite the fact that the Quran stipulates that religion does not have compulsion (Chapter 2, Al-Baqarah, of the Quran).

Saudi Arabia is one of the few remaining countries in the world where corporal punishment remains in place (UAE, Qatar, Yemen, Sudan, Afghanistan, and Iran are among other countries in the region that also allow this form of punishment). In Saudi Arabia, it mainly takes the form of flogging—both private and public. It is frequently assigned by courts as a principal or additional punishment for a wide range of offenses. Among the cases that received a particularly strong international reaction was the punishment assigned to the famous Saudi blogger and activist Raif Badawi, who was sentenced to 1,000 lashes, in addition to a 10-year imprisonment. He was convicted on several charges, including apostasy.

Capital punishment is a legal penalty in Saudi Arabia. On average over 100 executions are performed annually for a range of crimes—from murder to terrorism charges. Although the government does not release the official data on the number of executions, they are frequently reported by the state media. In 2018, 149 executions have been carried out, in comparison to 146 executions in 2017, and 154 in 2016. As of the month of April, 104 people have been executed in 2019. This included the largest mass execution of the past three years, when 37 prisoners were executed on the grounds of terrorism-related convictions, and the majority of them belonged to the Shia community. Amnesty International reported that one of them was younger than 18 at the time of the arrest, which sparked international outrage. The previous mass execution in Saudi Arabia took place in 2016, when 47 people were executed on similar terrorism-related charges. However, charges in terrorism are a relatively new legal offense to result in a death penalty. In the past, such sentences were most frequently given for drug-related crimes.

Death sentences are usually performed by beheading with a sword—in line with the strict interpretation of the capital punishment in Sharia. Most of them are carried out in a public setting. Additionally, a death sentence may include crucifixion (a public display of the body), when the crimes are considered particularly serious. Other forms of executions may include being shot by a firing squad and stoning to death (the cases related to adultery).

See also: Chapter 3: Constitution and Legal Reform; Human Rights and Censorship; Sharia Law and Judicial System; Ulama.

Further Reading

Albakr, Mohammad A. "The Impact of Unemployment on Crime the Case of Saudi Arabia." *Journal of Social Sciences*, vol. 32, no. 2, 2004.

Duncan, M. C. "Playing by the Rules: The Death Penalty and Foreigners in Saudi Arabia." *Georgia Journal of International and Comparative Law,* vol. 27, no. 1, 1998, pp. 231–248.

Pate, Matthew, and Laurie A. Gould. *Corporal Punishment around the World.* ABC-CLIO, 2012.

Rahimi, Zaki A. "Treatment of Offenders in the Saudi Criminal Justice System." *Journal of Muslim Minority Affairs,* vol. 17, no. 1, 1997, pp. 189–193.

Ridge, Hannah. "Economic and Historical Influence on the Application of Capital Punishment in Turkey and Saudi Arabia." *Lights: The MESSA Quarterly*, vol. 3, no. 1, 2014, pp. 1–30.

Constitution and Legal Reform

Although Sharia (Islamic law) remained in practice throughout the Muslim world since the inception of Islam, in modern times, the majority of Muslim countries adapted and incorporated European codes into their legal systems, whereas classical Sharia is primarily applied in family law. The uniqueness of Saudi Arabia's legal system is Sharia, which has been utilized in an uncodified form. For decades, the country did not have a written constitution, as the Quran and the Sunnah (the deeds of Prophet Muhammad) were considered the only acceptable legal documents. This system created considerable uncertainty in the application of laws in various spheres of life. Although these religious texts contain many specific instructions on legal conduct, especially in the area of family law, still a great number of contemporary practices are not contemplated in the primary Islamic sources. Thus, a uniform modern legal document became unavoidable, as the developing economy, financial system, international relations, and various social matters required judicial clarity.

In March 1992, King Fahd issued a legal document known as the Basic Law of Saudi Arabia (al-Nizam al-Asasi lil-Hukm). The document provided guidelines for running the government and outlined rights and responsibilities of Saudi citizens. Although it

---

FIQH AND SUNNI SCHOOLS OF JURISPRUDENCE

Islamic jurisprudence, *fiqh*, is a sophisticated theological field that is based on the Quran and a number of other Islamic sources. *Fiqh* is the science of the Sharia, although sometimes the two terms are used interchangeably. *Fiqh* provides legal theory, whereas Sharia provides its practical application.

Fiqh encompasses three types of regulations: (1) worship, religious observances, and customs (*ibadat*); (2) civil law (*muamalat*); and (3) punishments (*uqubat*). Although *fiqh* is based on the Quran and Hadith (the sayings of Prophet Muhammad), these two sources could not cover all of the possible situations that needed legal resolutions. Thus, medieval legal scholars developed two new principles of Islamic jurisprudence, namely, the use of analogies (*qiyas*) and consensus of opinion (*ijma*).

Fiqh is divided into several schools or traditions (*madhahib*), which are based on various sources and principles of law. Sunni Islam has four *madhahib*, all of which were founded during the 8th century. At that time, it became critical to develop a uniform legal system that would govern the affairs of the growing Islamic Empire and to find ways to accommodate the older Roman, Persian, and Arab legal systems within Islam. These four main schools are the Hanafi, Maliki, Shafi'i, and the Hanbali—named after their founders. The Hanbali school is considered the most conservative of the four. Based on the teachings of Ahmad ibn Hanbal (780–855), it emphasizes the authority of the Hadith. The Hanbali school takes a very guarded position toward speculative legal reasoning (*ra'y*) and analogy (*qiyas*) and rejects their use to overrule Hadiths. The Hanbali school became dominant in Saudi Arabia as a result of the 18th-century reforming movement initiated by Muhammad ibn Abd al-Wahhab, whose teachings are based on Hanbali theology.

bears the form of constitution, the document itself rejects such labeling and emphasizes that the Quran and the Sunnah are the only legitimate constitution of Saudi Arabia. The very first article states: "Its [Saudi Arabia's] religion shall be Islam and its constitution shall be the Book of God and the Sunnah (Traditions) of His Messenger."

The Basic Law consists of nine chapters, subdivided into 83 articles. The nine chapters are as follows: General Principles, System of Governance, Foundations of Saudi Society, Economic Principles, Rights and Duties, Authorities of the State, Financial Affairs, Auditing Agencies, and General Provisions. The Basic Law exists in full agreement with the country's strict interpretation of Sharia and does not supersede or replace Islamic laws. Royal decrees (*nizam*) are important legal documents that are considered legal regulations, as opposed to laws, to emphasize the superiority of the Sharia as the only acceptable legal system. Royal decrees are issued to complement Sharia in the contemporary areas that have no references in the traditional religious sources, such as matters related to labor, commercial, and corporate law.

Shortly after the Basic Law was released, a new legislative body was created in 1993—the Consultative Assembly (Majlis al-Shura), whose main task is to advise the king on various national matters. In 2004, the assembly's authority was expanded to include proposing new legislation and amending existing laws. In its core, this legislative body resembles the historic tradition where leaders would regularly hold consulting meetings (*shura*) with their community. Thus, the creation of the Consultative Assembly was the government's attempt to modernize the country's legal system while maintaining its traditions.

Although the Basic Law and the Consultative Assembly provided the necessary framework to bring Saudi Arabia's legal system more on par with modern realities, the lack of Sharia's codification continued to present difficulties in the application of law. In particular, the area of contract law required transparency and improvement, as the country aimed to expand its international cooperation and increase its position on the global market. In 2007, King Abdallah issued the Law of Judiciary, initiating a number of reforms with the objective to codify Sharia and to further modernize the court system. In 2010, the country's highest religious authority—the Council of Senior Scholars (Majlis Hay'at Kibar al-Ulama)—approved the codification of Sharia. King Salman continued his predecessor's efforts in modernizing the country's judicial system.

Significant progress in the implementation of the legal reform was achieved when a sourcebook of legal principles and precedents was published in January 2018—in a remarkable transformation of the Saudi legal system that previously did not include judicial precedent. The sourcebook consists of eight volumes and includes 2,323 principles and precedents. These were defined by the Supreme court after reviewing over 20,000 court rulings issued between 1971 and 2016.

Additionally, substantial changes have been made to laws related to tax, companies, and foreign investment.

See also: Chapter 3: Capital and Corporal Punishment; Sharia Law and Judicial System; Ulama. Chapter 5: Sunni Islam and Jurisprudence.

Further Reading

Vogel, Frank E. "The Rule of Law in Saudi Arabia: Exploring Contradictions and Traditions." *The Rule of Law in the Middle East and the Islamic World: Human Rights and the Judicial Process.* Edited by Eugene Cotran and Mai Yamani. Tauris, 2000, pp. 128–136.

Vogel, Frank E. "Shari'a and the Politics of Saudi Arabia." *Islamic Law in Practice.* Edited by Mashood A. Baderin. Ashgate, 2014, pp. 67–76.

Corruption

Corruption remains a widespread problem in all administrative entities in Saudi Arabia. Most commonly, corruption takes the form of nepotism, patronage systems, and bribery—with the latter including a large network of middlemen (*wasta*). Since the country has been in the hands of the Al Saud family since its inception, the royal family has been frequently accused of corruption and blurring the lines between personal assets and those belonging to the state. However, until recently, these accusations had a very general character, lacking any documentation or repercussions. The international nongovernmental nonprofit organization, Transparency International, whose goal is to combat global corruption, gave Saudi Arabia a corruption score of 4.4 in 2012—on a scale of 0 to 10 where 0 is "highly corrupt."

A specific allegation was made in 2007, when the BBC and the *Guardian* reported that the British defense contractor BAE Systems had paid Prince Bandar (Saudi Arabia's former ambassador to the United States) £2 billion in bribes relating to the Al-Yamamah arms deal, which took place over at least 10 years in installments of £30 million. Investigations by the British authorities resulted in a plea deal in 2010, where the company agreed to pay $447 million in fines, but did not admit to bribery. Prince Bandar denied all allegations.

On November 5, 2017, an unprecedented wave of high-profile anticorruption arrests took place in Saudi Arabia. The arrests targeted the highest echelons of Saudi society and included prominent businessmen, politicians, and members of the royal family. Among the detained were those at the very top of the country's political elite, including the prominent billionaire investor Prince Al-Waleed bin Talal and Prince Miteb bin Abdullah—the son of King Abdullah and the chief of the National Guard. Most of the detainees were held and interrogated at the Ritz-Carlton hotel in Riyadh. King Salman's government reported that a thorough anticorruption investigation was initiated in 2015, immediately after he ascended to the throne. The anticorruption committee was chaired by Muhammad bin Salman, who stated that Saudi Arabia's economic development was continuously halted by the high level of corruption since the 1980s. He further reported that an estimated 10 percent of all government spending was pocketed due to widespread corruption at all levels of the government on an annual basis, which prompted the necessary drastic measures to fix the system. However, some critics suggested that the anticorruption campaign was also a power play by the new royal prince, seeking to reinforce his authority among the elite.

At the request of the government, Saudi Arabian banks froze over 2,000 domestic accounts while the investigation took place. The *Wall Street Journal* reported that the assets targeted by the government were estimated at $800 billion. The 15-month investigation concluded in January 2019, when the majority of the detainees reached financial settlements. The government announced that it retrieved about $106 billion in cash, real estate, and other assets. In an additional step to tackle the abuse of power, the Saudi government made a major amendment to the anticorruption law in September 2018, when it eliminated a 60-day statute of limitations for investigating allegations against both current and former ministers.

See also: Chapter 3: Saudi Monarchy and Branches of the Government.

Further Reading

al-Rasheed, Madawi, ed. *Salman's Legacy: The Dilemmas of a New Era in Saudi Arabia.* Oxford University Press, 2018.

Sowayan, Saad Abdullah. "Top-Down Fight against Corruption Leaves Saudis Wondering Who Will Watch the Watchdogs." *The Kingdom: Saudi Arabia and the Challenge of the 21st Century.* Edited by Joshua Craze and Mark Huband. Hurst, 2009, pp. 83–87.

Gulf Cooperation Council

The Cooperation Council for the Arab States of the Gulf, commonly known as the Gulf Cooperation Council (GCC), is a regional organization based on economic and security cooperation. GCC members include Saudi Arabia, Bahrain, Kuwait, Oman, Qatar, and the United Arab Emirates. The Cooperation Council was established on May 25, 1981, during a summit in Riyadh, amid rising concerns over the potential spread of the Iran-Iraq War into other countries around the Persian Gulf. Saudi Arabia—the largest country territorially and with the biggest (and U.S.-backed) armed forces among the group—was the main force behind the creation of the Cooperation Council.

Since its inception, the GCC membership has not expanded. Although Yemen has sought on several occasions to join the organization, its bids have been rejected due to the country's weak economy, especially when contrasted to the rapid development of the GCC economy. All of the current GCC member states are monarchies: two absolute monarchies (Saudi Arabia and Oman), three constitutional monarchies (Kuwait, Bahrain and Qatar), and a federal monarchy (UAE). The Supreme Council, consisting of the heads of the member states, is the highest decision-making body in the GCC, where each country has one vote.

In 1984, the Peninsula Shield Force was established as an integrated military unit of the GCC. Initially, the force consisted of two brigades of 5,000 troops coming from all six GCC members. The permanent force was stationed in Saudi Arabia. The GCC states hold regular military exercises and often participate in joint exercises with U.S. and U.K. military units.

In addition to establishing regional security, economic cooperation and mutual growth was another major factor for the creation of the GCC. From the very inception of the Cooperation Council, various measures were taken to enhance economic integration. In November 1982, the Gulf Standards Organization was created by the GCC, in order to establish common standards for data and measurements. In 1984, the GCC established Gulf Investment Corporation, whose main goal was to promote economic development and fund multilateral projects in the region. All GCC members also committed to the creation of a common market by removing tariffs and streamlining trade relations. In 1988, a cooperation agreement was signed between the GCC and the European Community (now the European Union).

Over the years, tensions between different GCC states emerged, stemming from differences in foreign policies, as well as economic rivalries. The tense relationship between Saudi Arabia and Qatar is particularly noteworthy in this regard. In 2014, a major rift between the two countries took place, resulting from Qatar's support for the Muslim Brotherhood and Hamas. Following a contentious meeting of GCC members in March 2014, Saudi Arabia, UAE, and Bahrain recalled their ambassadors from Qatar. Some economists saw the Saudi-Qatari confrontation as an indication of the increasing economic competition between the producers of oil and natural gas on the global market. The tensions escalated even further on June 5, 2017, when the aforementioned states, as well as Egypt, officially cut diplomatic ties with Qatar.

See also: Chapter 1: Border Demarcations and Disputes. Chapter 2: Discovery of Oil. Chapter 3: Military. Chapter 4: Oil Industry and Aramco; OPEC and OAPEC; Trade and Exports.

Further Reading

Hanieh, Adam. *Money, Markets, and Monarchies: The Gulf Cooperation Council and the Political Economy of the Contemporary Middle East.* Cambridge University Press, 2018.

Kechichian, Joseph A. *From Alliance to Union: Challenges Facing Gulf Cooperation Council States.* Sussex Academic Press, 2016.

al-Yousef, Yousef Khalifa. *The Gulf Cooperation Council States: Hereditary Succession, Oil and Foreign Powers.* Saqi, 2017.

Human Rights and Censorship

International law generally sees the protection of human rights as a legal framework that protects the basic rights of the individual, such as the freedom of expression and religion, in a given country. A set of universal legal principles in relation to human rights have been codified in the context of international relations as the International Covenant on Political and Civil Rights (ICPCR). It exists as a multilateral international treaty, approved and implemented by the United Nations Assembly. Despite the mounting international pressure, Saudi Arabia is yet to fully sign ICPCR, highlighting the systemic violations of human rights in the country. These include the frequent practice of corporal and capital punishment, virtual absence of women's rights, consistent crackdowns on dissent, absence of freedom of religion (notably, apostasy is punishable by death), discrimination of the minorities and migrant workers, and so on.

In the area of criminal justice, the absence of a formal penal code and specific regulations on offenses creates an environment where offenders are left at the mercy of judges and prosecutors, who are able to convict them on very vague charges, such as damaging the reputation of the state or breaking allegiance with the ruler. Corporal punishments, especially flogging, are frequently assigned as primary and secondary punishments, often including hundreds and, in some cases, thousands of lashes. The government and the judicial system apply a very broad definition of terrorism, where virtually any form of protest can lead to terrorism charges and can result in a death penalty. In April 2019, Saudi Arabia executed 37 people on terrorism-related charges, one of whom was under the age of 18 at the time of the arrest. In fact, the system allows for children to be tried as adults for capital crimes if they show physical signs of puberty. Long-term detention without charges is also a common practice, as is torture and intimidation by police forces. With regard to gender-related offenses, adultery is seen as a serious crime and can be punishable by death. Saudi Arabia is known for a complete absence of LGBT rights as they are not recognized either by the government or the religious authorities. Same-sex sexual activity is deemed illegal and can be punished by fines, prison time, public flogging, and even capital punishment.

In 2018, Saudi Arabia came under intense international scrutiny when a prominent Saudi journalist Jamal Khashoggi was murdered on the territory of the Saudi embassy in Istanbul. The Saudi government ended up admitting that the murder did take place at the embassy. Eighteen individuals with connection to the incident were arrested, and a number of senior officials were fired, but in June 2019, a special United Nations investigative report claimed the existence of credible evidence that the crown prince Muhammad bin Salman bears responsibility for the murder.

Women's rights are a particularly contentious topic in the context of Saudi Arabia. The system of male guardianship effectively treats women as minors throughout their whole lives. Although a number of positive changes took place in the last several years, including the lifting of the driving ban and inclusion of women in the country's political process, these changes were accompanied by a crackdown on dissent. For instance, weeks before the driving ban was lifted, many women's rights activists—in particular those who for years campaigned against the driving ban—have been detained without charge. Loujain al-Hathloul, Aziza al-Yousef, Eman al-Nafjan, Nouf Abdelaziz, Mayaa al-Zahrani, Hatoon al-Fassi, Samar Badawi, Nassema al-Sadah, and Amal al-Harbi are the nine detained activists. The male guardianship system—which is at the core of the institutional discrimination of women—also remains firmly in place as of 2019.

Freedom of religion is an inconceivable concept in a system that not only dismisses all non-Islamic faiths, but also views the Wahhabi interpretation of Muslim faith and conduct as the only acceptable form of Islam. There is a systematic discrimination of Muslim religious minorities, in particular the Twelver Shia and Ismaili communities. The discrimination is not limited to religious freedom, but also applies to employment, education, and the justice system. Apostasy, or the abandonment of the Islamic religion, can carry a death sentence.

The only human rights entity that existed in Saudi Arabia was the Saudi Civil and Political Rights Association (ACPRA), formed in 2009 by 11 academics and activists. However, in 2013 it was banned and dissolved by the government, and by 2018 nearly all ACPRA founders have been put in jail.

See also: Chapter 3: Capital and Corporal Punishment; Law Enforcement and Security; Political Dissent and Opposition; Sharia Law and Judicial System; Ulama. Chapter 6: Sulubbah. Chapter 16: Freedom of Speech; Government Censorship.

Further Reading

Almutairi, Abdullah M. "The Domestic Application of International Human Rights Conventions in Saudi Arabia and the Need to Ratify Conventions on Migrant Workers." *Middle Eastern Studies*, vol. 54, no. 1, 2018, pp. 48–67.

Cotran, Eugene, et al. *The Rule of Law in the Middle East and the Islamic World: Human Rights and the Judicial Process*. I. B. Tauris, 2000.

Ende, Werner. "A Wahhabi Inventory of Dangerous Books." *Islamica: Studies in Memory of Holger Preißler*. Edited by Andreas Christmann and Jan-Peter Hartung. Oxford University Press, 2009, pp. 89–100.

Kraidy, Marwan M. "Saudi-Islamist Rhetorics about Visual Culture." *Visual Culture in the Modern Middle East: Rhetoric of the Image*. Edited by Christiane Gruber and Sune Haugbolle. Indiana University Press, 2013, pp. 275–292.

Simons, G. L. *Saudi Arabia: The Shape of a Client Feudalism*. St. Martin's Press, 1998.

Yamani, Mai. "Muslim Women and Human Rights in Saudi Arabia." *Women and Islam. Volume I: Images and Realities*. Edited by Haideh Moghissi. Routledge, 2005, pp. 402–410.

Law Enforcement and Security

The Ministry of Interior, created in 1951, is the central authority responsible for the issues of national security, immigration, and customs. It consists of five directorates: Directorate of Public Safety, Directorate of Corrections, Directorate of Civil Defense, Directorate of Court Services, and Directorate of the Security of the Two Holy Mosques. The Directorate of Public Safety is in essence Saudi Arabia's regular police force, headed by the director of Public Safety who reports to the minister of the interior.

In addition to the regular police force, Saudi Arabia has secret police, called the *Mabahith*, and religious police—the Committee for the Promotion of Virtue and the Prevention of Vice, or as they are more commonly called, the *Mutawwa*. The members of the *Mutawwa* force are charged with ensuring that Islamic social and moral norms are practiced by all members of Saudi society. Notably, their authority has been substantially restricted over the last few years, especially with the issuance of the new law in 2016 banning the *Mutawwa* from making arrests.

The *Mabahith*, or General Investigation Directorate, is the secret police agency, whose two primary areas are domestic security and counterintelligence. In 1955, the department was created by a royal decree and had the name of General Investigations (*al-Mabahith al-Ammah*). Later, the General Intelligence was detached from Mabahith into a separate unit under the name the Department of General Intelligence (*al-Istikhbarat al-Ammah*). Currently, the *Mabahith* officers are given extensive authority that allows them to detain (often without charges) and investigate cases on issues of national security, which are very broadly defined within Saudi judicial system. These can cover a wide range of offenses, from terrorist activities to peaceful protests by activists. The *Mabahith* have been accused in numerous human rights violations, in particular in cases that involved Saudi activists and the Shia minority.

The Saudi Arabian National Guard (*al-Haras al-Watani*), or SANG, is a unique militarized force that plays an important role in the country's security. The National Guard was created as a successor to Ibn Saud's army of Ikhwan. Sometimes it is referred to as the White Army because of the white *thawbs* (traditional long flowing garments) worn by the members of the force. The unique feature of this unit is that its membership is based on the loyalty to the royal family. SANG serves simultaneously as an internal and external security force. Throughout the 1970s, they underwent intensive training by the contracted U.S. Vinnell Corporation (the training was done mainly by Vietnam veterans), with the goal of transforming the National Guard into a powerful modern counterinsurgency force. Currently, the U.S. military continues to advise and provide both combat and technical training to SANG. The National Guard consists of about 130,000 personnel, divided into 17 brigades.

See also: Chapter 3: Capital and Corporal Punishment; Sharia Law and Judicial System; Ulama; Wahhabi Ideology. Chapter 7: The *Mutawwa*: Saudi Religious Police.

Further Reading

Cordesman, Anthony H., et al. *National Security in Saudi Arabia: Threats, Responses, and Challenges.* Praeger Security International, 2005.

Gray, Matthew. *Global Security Watch—Saudi Arabia.* Praeger, 2014.

Qasem, Islam Y. *Oil and Security Policies: Saudi Arabia, 1950–2012.* Brill, 2015.

Local Government and Municipal Elections

Saudi Arabia has 13 provinces (*manatiq*): Riyadh, Mecca, Medina, the Eastern Province, Asir, Jazan, al-Qassim, Tabuk, Hail, Najran, al-Jawf, al-Baha, and the Northern Borders Province. Each province has a capital and is headed by a governor (*amir*) and a deputy, appointed by a royal decree. Traditionally, the governors are members of the Al Saud family. Although technically their reporting line is to the minister of interior, in reality they often communicate directly with the king. Each regional province is divided into governorates (*muhafazhat*) and further into municipalities (*amanah*). There are 118 governorates and 285 municipalities in Saudi Arabia. In 1975, the Ministry of Municipal and Rural Affairs was established to oversee the administrative processes in the country's municipalities. In 1992, the Law of Provinces was issued to regulate the relationship between central and local authorities, improve the overall administrative structure, and clarify the roles, duties, and reporting lines for each administrative function. Four provinces—Riyadh, Mecca, Medina, and Jeddah—have special status. The governing authorities in these provinces have substantial freedom in managing finances and have their own budgets outside of the Ministry of the Interior's jurisdiction.

In 2005, Saudi Arabia had its first municipal elections since the 1960s. One hundred seventy-eight municipalities held elections for one-half of the seats in each municipal council (the other half were appointed). The voters had to be male over the age of 21, and all candidates had to be male as well, whereas women were completely excluded from the political process. Even the eligible Saudi voters remained largely disengaged: for example, in Riyadh the number of registered voters represented only 18 percent of those eligible, constituting a mere 2 percent of the city's total population. At the same time, the Shia community of the Eastern Province demonstrated much greater interest in the electoral process. Most of the candidates running for election were local community leaders, professionals, and businessmen, but there were also a number of activists. Overall, Islamist candidates won by a landslide, as they were backed by the religious establishment.

The subsequent municipal elections were held in 2011 and once again excluded women from the electoral process. However, due to protests and petitions from Saudi women's rights activists, as well as mounting international pressure, King Abdullah announced that women would be allowed to participate in the next municipal elections in 2015—both as voters and candidates—for the first time in the country's history. However, women accounted for less than 10 percent of all registered voters due to various bureaucratic obstacles and their limited mobility, as the driving ban still remained in place at that time.

The year 2015 saw a much higher turnout in voters and an increase in registered candidates, and included 5,938 male and 978 female candidates. A number of known women activists, who attempted to run for office, were barred from registering by the authorities. Among them were Loujain al-Hathloul, famous for her protests against the driving ban, and Nassima al-Sadah, a Shia human rights activist from Qatif. Saudi Arabia's strict policies against *ikhtilat* (gender mixing) make political campaigning incredibly difficult for women candidates as they can hold meetings only with female voters. Only 17 women were reported to win the elections among the contested 2,100 municipal council seats, but the activists see this as an opportunity for political transformation. The first elected female politician in Saudi Arabia's history was Salma bint Hizab al-Oteibi, who won a seat on the Madraka council in the Mecca Province. Notably, even in Qassim—the most conservative region in Saudi Arabia—two women were elected to office.

See also: Chapter 3: Political Reform and Modernization; Saudi Monarchy and Branches of the Government. Chapter 7: Women in Public Office.

Further Reading

Kraetzschmar, Hendrik Jan. "Electoral Rules, Voter Mobilization and the Islamist Landslide in the Saudi Municipal Elections of 2005." *Contemporary Arab Affairs*, vol. 3, no. 4, 2010, pp. 515–533.

Matthiesen, Toby. "Centre-Periphery Relations and the Emergence of a Public Sphere in Saudi Arabia: The Municipal Elections in the Eastern Province, 1954–1960." *British Journal of Middle Eastern Studies*, vol. 42, no. 3, 2015, pp. 320–338.

al-Rasheed, Madawi. *Contesting the Saudi State: Islamic Voices from a New Generation*. Cambridge University Press, 2007.

al-Sulami, Mishal Fahm. "Reform in Saudi Arabia: The Case of Municipal Elections." *Journal of King Abdulaziz University: Arts and Humanities*, vol. 16, no. 2, 2008, pp. 113–135.

Military

The Saudi Arabian Armed Forces consists of five main branches: Army, Navy, Air Force, Air Defense, and Strategic Forces. The National Guard has a special status: its main task is to protect the royal family and it can participate both in internal and external operations. In 2017, the number of active personnel was estimated at about 127,000, and additional 20,000 members of the paramilitary forces. The National Guard has as many members as the regular military. Saudi Arabia has one of the best-funded militaries in the world, with a defense budget of $69 billion.

Saudi Arabia's Army of about 75,000 troops is divided into specialized units, including armored, airborne, mechanized infantry, artillery, and aviation brigade. The Navy, consisting of 15,500 troops, includes frigates, corvettes, coastal patrol boats, a mine warfare unit, in addition to a Marine infantry regiment. The Air Force (18,000 troops) is organized into 12 fighter squadrons, 3 transport squadrons, and 2 rotary wing squadrons. The Air Defense branch has 16,000 troops organized into four battalions.

The U.S. military has always had a close relationship with Saudi armed forces and consistently provided various levels of training and technical support to the latter. Until 2003, the U.S. military had a significant presence in Saudi Arabia, but it was scaled back: the Prince Sultan Air Base in Al Kharj was handed over to the Saudi military, and the base's 4,500 U.S. troops were redeployed to other countries in the Gulf. An important aspect of the U.S. military presence in Saudi Arabia is the Office of the Program Manager–Saudi Arabian National Guard (OPM-SANG), which provides combat and technical training programs to the National Guard. Throughout the 1980s, the United States built and managed several navy ports and air bases, in addition to a number of military training academies. The equipment of the Saudi Air Force mainly comes from the United States and the United Kingdom. Its inventory of more than

200 Boeing F-15s makes the Saudi Air Force the third-largest user of these planes in the world. The United States and Saudi Arabia have had a long history of large contracts in weaponry and military technical support. The arms sales to Saudi Arabia under President Obama amounted to nearly $94 billion. In May 2017, President Trump reached a significant deal with the Saudi Arabian government, where it committed to spending $110 billion on U.S. arms immediately, and another $350 billion over the next 10 years. However, the numerous civilian causalities in Yemen by Saudi airstrikes, as well as the murder of journalist Jamal Khashoggi, prompted the U.S. Congress to oppose the Trump administration's arms agreements with Saudi Arabia.

See also: Chapter 2: Ikhwan. Chapter 3: Law Enforcement and Security; Saudi–U.S. Relations.

Further Reading

Cristiani, Dario. "The Gulf Cooperation Council, Saudi Arabia and a Turbulent Region: Evolving Counterterrorism Strategies." *The Palgrave Handbook of Global Counterterrorism Policy*. Edited by Scott Nicholas Romaniuk et al. Palgrave Macmillan, 2017, pp. 809–821.

Cronin, Stephanie. "Tribes, Coups and Princes: Building a Modern Army in Saudi Arabia." *Middle Eastern Studies*, vol. 49, no. 1, Jan. 2013, pp. 2–28.

Gray, Matthew. *Global Security Watch—Saudi Arabia*. Praeger, 2014.

Hart, Parker T. *Saudi Arabia and the United States: Birth of a Security Partnership*. Indiana University Press, 1998.

Heath, Victoria. "Defense Gaps in the GCC: A Case Study of Saudi Arabia and the Royal Saudi Air Force." *The Arms Trade, Military Services and the Security Market in the Gulf States: Trends and Implications*. Edited by David B. Des Roches and Dania Thafer. Gerlach, 2016, pp. 80–98.

Safran, Nadav. *Saudi Arabia: The Ceaseless Quest for Security*. Belknap Press of Harvard University Press, 1985.

Political Dissent and Opposition

From its very inception as a state, Saudi Arabia has been ruled by the Al Saud family, the descendants of King Abd al-Aziz ibn Saud (until now, all subsequent kings have been his sons). However, throughout Saudi Arabia's history, Al Saud's grip on power has been challenged from various sources: conservative religious establishment, fundamentalist Islamic militants, long-standing tribal tensions, regional conflicts (especially with the culturally and socially different Hijaz), the discriminated Shia minority (particularly in the Eastern Province), and in more recent times, human rights activists whose numbers have been consistently growing in recent decades—despite the series of government's crackdowns. Among these very different sources of dissent, the

Islamic militants presented the most prominent threat to the regime. In 1979, the country was shaken when a large group of militants seized the Grand Mosque, which resulted in a series of conservative reforms. Since the Gulf conflict and after the events of September 11, 2001, extremism became an even more serious problem, and a number of terrorist attacks took place in the 1990s and 2000s. In response, the Saudi government initiated a number of antiterrorism laws and reforms, and at the same time significantly broadened the legal definition of terrorism, which allows the authorities to classify virtually any form of peaceful protest as a terrorist act.

Additionally, of great concern to the Saudi government is the Islamic dissident movement inside the country and in exile in London. The conservative Islamic opposition in Saudi Arabia consistently accuses the government and the royal family of having close ties with the West and caving to Western ideas. Both King Abdallah and King Salman initiated a number of reforms—from allowing women to vote and appointing female members to the king's Consultative Assembly to greatly restricting the religious police's authority—all of which are perceived by the conservatives as betraying traditional Islamic principles. The conservatives have also been opposing the increasing economic and military cooperation with the United States and the United Kingdom.

On June 21, 2017, King Salman named his son Mohammed, who was 31 years old at the time, as crown prince, removing the king's nephew Prince Mohammed bin Nayef as heir to the throne. Widely known as MbS, he went on to implement a number of drastic economic, social, and religious reforms, shaking up the conservative establishment. These included an anticorruption probe that targeted the country's political and financial elite, and the lifting of the women's driving ban. At the same time, Prince Muhammad's activities included a series of major crackdowns on liberal dissent. For example, just weeks before lifting the driving ban, the government arrested the majority of women's rights activists who championed for this cause for decades. In 2019, the 33-year-old royal prince further escalated the crackdown on even the mildest forms of dissent, while completely ignoring the international pressure that has been mounting since the murder of the Saudi journalist Jamal Khashoggi, to which MbS has been linked by a UN report. In April 2019, at least nine people were arrested—journalists, intellectuals, and activists, including two dual Saudi-American citizens and two women. They were accused of complaining to the Western press about the government's treatment of the imprisoned women activists.

See also: Chapter 3: Human Rights and Censorship; Law Enforcement and Security; Sharia Law and Judicial System; Ulama. Chapter 5: Shia Community. Chapter 16: Freedom of Speech; Government Censorship.

Further Reading

Abedin, Mahan. "Saudi Dissent More Than Just Jihadis." *The Kingdom: Saudi Arabia and the Challenge of the 21st Century*. Edited by Joshua Craze and Mark Huband. Hurst, 2009, pp. 34–40.

Fandy, Mamoun. *Saudi Arabia and the Politics of Dissent*. 1st ed. St. Martin's Press, 1999.

Lacroix, Stéphane. *Awakening Islam: The Politics of Religious Dissent in Contemporary Saudi Arabia*. Harvard University Press, 2011.

Lacroix, Stéphane. "Understanding Stability and Dissent in the Kingdom: The Double-Edged Role of the Jama'at in Saudi Politics." *Saudi Arabia in Transition: Insights on Social, Political, Economic and Religious Change*. Edited by Bernard Haykel, Thomas Hegghammer, and Stéphane Lacroix. Cambridge University Press, 2015, pp. 167–180.

Matthiesen, Toby. *The Other Saudis: Shiism, Dissent and Sectarianism*. Cambridge University Press, 2015.

Okrůhlik, Gwenn. "Networks of Dissent: Islamism and Reform in Saudi Arabia." *Current History*, vol. 101, no. 651, 2002, pp. 22–28.

al-Rasheed, Madawi. *Contesting the Saudi State: Islamic Voices from a New Generation*. Cambridge University Press, 2007.

Political Reform and Modernization

Since the events of September 11, 2001, shook the Muslim world, the royal family has been under pressure to reform and modernize the government. This was the agenda championed by King Abdallah both before and after his accession to the throne in 2005, and his government implemented a number of important changes to the administrative structure of Saudi Arabia's monarchy. When the Consultative Assembly (Majlis al-Shura) was created in the early 1990s, it was not able to provide a meaningful forum for political participation. However, King Abdullah made an important change in 2013 when 30 women were appointed to the Consultative Assembly for the first time. Moreover, another royal decree issued at that time mandated that women's representation on the assembly would constitute at least 20 percent of its members from there on.

In 2005, the first municipal elections since the 1960s were held in Saudi Arabia. As of 2015, women are able to participate in the electoral process both as voters and political candidates. The year 2007 marked the creation of the Allegiance Council (Hayat al-Bay'ah), whose task is to regulate the process of royal succession. In the same year, King Abdullah issued a royal decree aimed at a major judiciary reform and transformation of the Saudi court system. In 2009, substantial personnel changes were made to the government, when several known moderates and reformers were appointed to key positions, and Nora Al Fayez became deputy education minister—the first woman appointed to a ministerial post.

Many of the reforms initiated by King Abdullah have been continued by King Salman, who ascended to the throne in 2015. The speed of Saudi Arabia's transformation has accelerated considerably with the appointment of King Salman's son, Muhammed bin Salman (known widely as MbS), as the crown prince in 2017. Prince Muhammad quickly positioned himself as the champion of modernization and has been actively promoting the newly cosmopolitan global image of Saudi Arabia as an agent of change in the Middle East. Many political insiders interpreted MbS's political acts and cultural initiatives, including lifting the women's driving ban, reopening cinemas, and generally promoting a more moderate interpretation of Islam, as an intent to dissolve the centuries-long pact between the House of Saud and the Wahhabi religious establishment and to completely consolidate the power in the hands of the royal family.

However, despite the broad scale of modernization reforms, changes have been criticized as being too slow or superficial. The process of political and social transformation is tarnished by a series of crackdowns on dissent and measures aimed at the centralization of royal power. The expansion of women's rights is accompanied by repression and imprisonment of the very activists who have championed for this cause for many years. Whereas women were granted more mobility and ability to participate in the political process, the issue at the core of women's limited rights—the male guardianship system—remains firmly in place. When the drastic anticorruption campaign, initiated by Muhammad bin Salman, shook the local and international political circles in 2017, it was also perceived by many as a blunt attempt to reinforce the new crown prince's power within the royal family and other influential Saudi circles. Although the country's national security agencies have undergone the much-needed reorganization and the government made substantial changes to the counterterrorism laws and regulations, these reforms are being used to suppress political dissent and imprison activists. In sum, the need for political and social reform in Saudi Arabia and the current process of modernization are confronted with and limited by the foundations of the country's monarchy and the unrestrained power of its royal family.

See also: Chapter 3: Political Dissent and Opposition; Saudi Monarchy and Branches of the Government; Sharia Law and Judicial System. Chapter 4: Diversification and Development Plans; Vision 2030.

Further Reading

Alshamsi, Mansoor Jassem. *Islam and Political Reform in Saudi Arabia: The Quest for Political Change and Reform*. Routledge, 2011.

Hammond, Andrew. *The Islamic Utopia: The Illusion of Reform in Saudi Arabia*. Pluto Press, 2012.

Le Renard, Amélie. *A Society of Young Women: Opportunities of Place, Power, and Reform in Saudi Arabia*. Stanford University Press, 2014.

al-Rasheed, Madawi. *Contesting the Saudi State: Islamic Voices from a New Generation*. Cambridge University Press, 2007.

al-Rasheed, Madawi, ed. *Salman's Legacy: The Dilemmas of a New Era in Saudi Arabia*. Oxford University Press, 2018.

Saudi Monarchy and Branches of the Government

The royal family of Al Saud has complete dominance over all branches of the government. In addition to being the country's monarch, the Saudi king also holds the title of the Custodian of the Two Holy Mosques (in reference to Mecca and Medina), highlighting the status of Saudi Arabia in the Islamic world. Besides the king, who has vast powers in all spheres of Saudi Arabia's life, a number of influential members of the royal family participate in the shaping of internal and external policies, with particular prominence given to the royal prince. The country's ulema (religious scholars), led by the Council of Senior Scholars, define and maintain religious ideology and practices, and play an important role in the country's internal affairs. Regional governments are also led by the members of the royal family, as they are appointed as governors (amirs) of Saudi Arabia's 13 provinces.

Article 5 of the Basic Law of Governance (issued in 1992) states that rulers of Saudi Arabia are to be chosen from the sons and subsequent descendants of the founder of the state, King Abd al-Aziz Ibn Saud, with the order of succession following the agnatic seniority within the family. In 2007, the process of royal succession underwent an important change when the Allegiance Council (Hayat al-Bay'ah) was formed by King Abdullah. It was envisioned as an authoritative body, whose function is to appoint a crown prince once a new king ascends to the throne. Previously, the decision on succession was the sole prerogative of the king. The Allegiance Council consists primarily of the surviving sons of Ibn Saud and his grandsons in place of the sons who are deceased, incapacitated, or do not have claims to the throne. Other members include the sons of the current king and crown prince. In 2019, the council was made up of 34 members. The decisions of the Allegiance Council have been traditionally accompanied by an informal consensus among the royal family. The Allegiance Institution Law stipulates that the king presents up to three candidates for the position of crown prince to the council, who selects one of them. Theoretically, the council may reject all of the nominees from the king and nominate its own candidate decided by the vote. The creation of the council has been seen as an opportunity to reduce the domination of the Sudairi Seven (a powerful allegiance of seven full brothers, sons of Ibn Saud and Hussa Sudairi; both King Abdullah and King Salman belong to this faction). Expectedly, internal tensions between various factions of the Al Saud occasionally spill into the deliberations of the Allegiance Council.

The Royal Court or the Royal Diwan (al-Diwan al-Maliki) consists of influential members of the royal family, ministers, members of the Council of Senior Scholars, and various advisers. The court acts as the main executive office of the king and the main advisory body on domestic and international policies, and religious affairs. Saudi citizens have the right to submit appeals to the Royal Court asking for direct interference of the king on particular matters that could not be resolved in the lower administrative circles. The royal prince also has a court, which acts as his own administration.

The main executive body of Saudi Arabia's government is the Council of Ministers (Majlis al-Wuzara'), created by Ibn Saud in 1953. All appointments of ministers are done by the king, usually every four years. In 1992, King Fahd issued the Law of the Council of Ministers, which formalized the council's regulatory authority and established the king's position as the prime minister. Currently, there are 22 ministers, in addition to the first and second deputy prime ministers. The primary functions of the Council of Ministers are to draft various internal and international policies, to manage all general affairs overseen by the state, and to pass laws that are proposed by the king.

The Consultative Assembly (Majlis al-Shura), established in 1993, is an important government body that carries limited legislative authority by drafting legislation and presenting it for the king's approval. In its core, the assembly stems from the historical tradition of *shura*—the Muslim practice of consultation by the ruler. All members of the assembly are appointed by the king and it currently consist of 150 members. In addition to drafting laws, the assembly has the power to examine economic plans and policies. As a rule, the assembly's decisions and proposals are presented to the Council of Ministers for approval. If both government bodies agree on a particular decision, it is presented for the king's approval, who puts it into effect. If one of the two groups dissents, the king makes the decision. Although previously only men were able to serve on the assembly, King Abdallah made a historic change in 2013 when he appointed 30 women to the assembly, while also mandating that from there on they would hold at least a fifth of the total seats.

The Council of Senior Scholars (Majlis Hay'at Kibar al-Ulama), established in 1971, is the highest religious authority in Saudi Arabia. As is the case with all other core government bodies, the council is appointed by the king. It consists of 21 senior *ulama* (religious scholars) headed by the Grand Mufti, whose main task is to advise the king on all matters pertaining to religion. The main difference between Saudi *ulama* and *ulama* in most other Muslim countries is that the former are directly involved in the matters of the state. Historically, the *ulama* were instrumental in regulating judicial and educational matters.

Saudi Arabia's judicial system is based on Sharia—the Islamic law—and is defined by the Basic Law of Saudi Arabia as an independent authority. In theory, the only authority over the decisions made by judges is the Islamic law, as religion is seen as superseding any human authority. But in reality, the king's royal decrees have the power to affect judicial proceedings. The king also has the power to pardon.

See also: Chapter 2: Ibn Saud; Third Saudi State: Saudi Arabia in the 20th Century. Chapter 3: Sharia Law and Judicial System.

Further Reading

House, Karen Elliott. *On Saudi Arabia: Its People, Past, Religion, Fault Lines—and Future.* 1st ed. Alfred A. Knopf, 2012.

Kechichian, Joseph A. *Succession in Saudi Arabia.* Palgrave, 2001.

Lacey, Robert. *Inside the Kingdom: Kings, Clerics, Modernists, Terrorists, and the Struggle for Saudi Arabia.* Viking, 2009.

Riedel, Bruce O., and Brookings Institution. *Kings and Presidents: Saudi Arabia and the United States since FDR.* Brookings Institution Press, 2018.

Saudi–U.S. Relations

The relations between the United States and Saudi Arabia began in the 1930s, resulting from the discovery of oil and the development of oil industry in the region. At the earliest stages of the Saudi–U.S. relationship, the United States saw Saudi Arabia as a trading partner with important natural resources, but World War II added an important geostrategic aspect to this relationship, when the United States was using Saudi oil in the war with Germany. Political relations between the two countries were solidified when King Ibn Saud met with President Franklin Roosevelt aboard a ship in the Suez Canal. This meeting marked the historic beginning of a multilayered decades-long liaison between these two very different states. The basic principle between this mutually beneficial strategic relationship was the exchange of Saudi oil, as the holder of the world's largest reserves, for U.S. military support and protection.

Over the years, this alliance saw its share of crises. Saudi Arabia indicated deep reservations concerning Israel and the support Israel received from the United States. These tensions culminated in the 1973 oil embargo imposed by Saudi Arabia and other Gulf states against the United States, in retaliation for the U.S. decision to support the Israeli military. On the one hand, the embargo quadrupled the price of oil and put a significant strain on the economy, but on the other hand, it prompted Western nations to initiate the development of various conservation efforts, especially in the aftermath of the subsequent 1979 energy crisis. Nevertheless, the Saudi–U.S. relationship survived the oil embargo and continued throughout the Cold War.

Throughout the 1960s and 1970s, the rest of the Gulf states gained independence, providing Saudi Arabia with a natural alliance of countries with whom it had deep tribal and religious ties. The newly independent Gulf states broadly followed Saudi foreign policy and also established close relations with the United States. In 1981, Saudi Arabia and the Gulf states formed the Gulf Cooperation Council (GCC), which manages a wide range of common interests between the countries, from their economies to issues of military defense.

King Faisal and Henry Kissinger in 1974. (Library of Congress)

The Soviet invasion of Afghanistan in 1979 resulted in Saudi Arabia developing closer ties with the United States, especially in the area of military cooperation. Saudi Arabia, throughout the Soviet-Afghan War, provided substantial monetary support to the anti-Soviet resistance forces in Afghanistan. The Iran-Iraq War also prompted Saudi Arabia and other Gulf states to seek increased cooperation with the United States in an effort to secure regional stability and protect their borders. By the early 1980s, Saudi Arabia had become the largest purchaser of U.S. arms and weaponry outside of Western Europe.

After the end of the Cold War, the relationship between the United States and Saudi Arabia seemed secure, although it began to generate internal tensions on both sides. In the United States, liberal groups voiced discontent over Saudi Arabia's discriminatory policies toward women and religious minorities. In Saudi Arabia, the close relationship with the United States became an object of political struggle between the government and the conservative Islamic opposition that saw the Western partner as the source of moral corruption and the government's ties with the United States as a betrayal of Islamic traditions. Despite these tensions, the Iraqi invasion of Kuwait and the subsequent involvement of the U.S.-led coalition further reinforced the close relations between Washington, Riyadh, and the heads of all other Gulf states. Arms deals and military cooperation increased, leading to the expanded U.S. military presence in the region.

Despite the regional crisis following the September 11, 2001 terrorist attacks, the U.S.-Saudi relationship continued into the 21st century. Saudi Arabia implemented a range of counterterrorism measures, while increasing intelligence and law enforcement cooperation with the United States and Western Europe. Several major arms deals followed in the next 15 years, although it became increasingly difficult for the United States to navigate regional politics with the beginning of the Arab Spring. While supporting the revolutionary processes in Tunisia, Egypt, and Syria, the United States had stayed neutral when Saudi Arabia implemented measures to suppress similar processes in its society.

See also: Chapter 2: Discovery of Oil; Ibn Saud; King Abdullah; Third Saudi State: Saudi Arabia in the 20th Century. Chapter 4: Oil Industry and Aramco.

Further Reading

Bin Hethlain, Naif. *Saudi Arabia and the US since 1962: Allies in Conflict*. SAQI, 2010.

Bronson, Rachel. *Thicker Than Oil: America's Uneasy Partnership with Saudi Arabia*. Oxford University Press, 2006.

Citino, Nathan J. *From Arab Nationalism to OPEC: Eisenhower, King Saʻūd, and the Making of U.S.-Saudi Relations*. Indiana University Press, 2002.

Gause, F. Gregory. "The Future of U.S.-Saudi Relations: The Kingdom and the Power." *Foreign Affairs*, vol. 95, no. 4, 2016, pp. 114–126.

Lesch, David W., and Mark L. Haas, eds. *The Middle East and the United States: History, Politics, and Ideologies*. Routledge, 2019.

Riedel, Bruce, and Franklin D. Roosevelt. *Kings and Presidents: Saudi Arabia and the United States since FDR*. Brookings Institution Press, 2018.

Sharia Law and Judicial System

In Saudi Arabia, Islam formally represents state, religion, and law, largely informing all three branches of the government. The term "Sharia" refers to the Islamic legal system. Literally, it means "pathway to the water source." In its essence, the Sharia is meant to provide a guiding framework for Muslims for all aspects of their public and private life. The creation of the Sharia was not a linear process, and it took several centuries to complete. Until the 10th century AD, several legal schools of thought emerged in the Muslim world, presenting a number of important differences—from theoretical interpretation of law to judicial detail. The four major schools of legal thought in Sunni Islam are Maliki, Hanafi, Shafi'i, and Hanbali. The practical implementation of Sharia in state affairs has a complicated history in the Muslim world, where other legal systems consistently competed with Sharia, especially during the colonial period. In the majority of Middle Eastern countries, the state law has gradually superseded Sharia, which is now largely relegated to matters of family and inheritance law. Among the Gulf states, Sharia is acknowledged as the main source of legislation, but only in Oman and Saudi Arabia does it apply to all aspects of law.

At the beginning of the 20th century, before the country unified under the banner of Ibn Saud, the Arabian Peninsula did not have a uniform judicial system, and individual judges made their rulings depending on the legal school to which they belonged. For example, while the Shafi'i and Hanafi legal interpretations were practiced in the Hijaz, judges in the central region primarily relied on the Hanbali school. At the same time, tribal customary law was also applied widely throughout the peninsula. Even before the formal establishment of Saudi Arabia, Ibn Al Saud's government and his religious scholars created a new judiciary system with the royal decree of 1927, where rulings would be based exclusively on the Quran and the Sunnah. The decree created a three-level court system, consisting of expeditious courts, Sharia courts, and the High Commission of Judicial Supervision as the highest legal authority in the kingdom.

The current Saudi court system has four levels of courts. The Sharia courts are the most numerous, holding general jurisdiction over most civil and criminal cases. The second tier is the general courts, responsible for criminal cases and matters related to family law and real estate. Civil claims can be filed with the governorates' offices, which perform as arbitrating authority in resolving disputes, and if that fails, the cases would proceed to regular courts. The Court of Appeal is the fourth tier of the Saudi court system, where several judges are tasked with settling submitted disputes by majority decision. There is also the Board of Grievances that hears cases regarding the government. Trials in Saudi Arabia are bench trials. The judicial establishment of *ulama* primarily consists of *qadis*, judges who make binding judgments in court proceedings, and *muftis* who issue *fatwas*—the highly influential legal opinions. The judges are appointed, promoted, and transferred based on the decisions of the Supreme Council. The Grand Mufti is a position that combines both religious and judiciary authorities at the highest level, highlighting the inseparability of Islam and law in Saudi Arabia.

See also: Chapter 2: Emirate of Diriyah: The First Saudi State (1744–1818); Muhammad ibn Abd al-Wahhab; Third Saudi State: Saudi Arabia in the 20th Century. Chapter 3: Law Enforcement and Security; Ulama; Wahhabi Ideology. Chapter 5: Quran; Sunni Islam and Jurisprudence. Chapter 7: Divorce; Gender Segregation; Guardianship; Marriage Law and Tradition; The *Mutawwa*: Saudi Religious Police.

Further Reading

Arabi, Oussama. *Studies in Modern Islamic Law and Jurisprudence.* Kluwer Law International, 2001.

Hefner, Robert W. *Shari'a Politics: Islamic Law and Society in the Modern World.* Indiana University Press, 2011.

Vogel, Frank E. "Shari'a and the Politics of Saudi Arabia." *Islamic Law in Practice.* Edited by Mashood A. Baderin. Ashgate, 2014, pp. 67–76.

Ulama

The term "*ulama*" in Saudi Arabia is used in reference to Islamic religious leaders, scholars, and jurists who not only play a central role in Saudi judicial system, but are influential in virtually all areas of Saudi society. Their main role is to act as interpreters and arbiters of the core Islamic religious texts—the Quran and the Sunnah—which in Saudi Arabia also play the role of the primary legal documents. The country's highest religious body is the Council of Senior Scholars (Majlis Hay'at Kibar al-Ulama), which consists of 21 *ulama* appointed by the king. They serve as advisers to the king on all religious matters. In the past, the Saudi legal system was led by the Grand Mufti, whose full title was the Grand Mufti and Chief Qadi, where *mufti* is one who issues *fatwas* and *qadi* is the term for an Islamic judge. The council, headed by the Grand Mufti, was still in place but met informally. It has become an official body in August 1972 by King Faysal's decree, whereas the Ministry of Justice was created in 1970. Both decisions were made in an attempt to modernize the administrative infrastructure of the traditional Islamic legal system.

The political system in Saudi Arabia relies on inseparability of state and religion: Islam is seen as much more than faith, but as a system of governance and, more generally, as a set of rules that every Muslim must follow. In this context, the power of the *ulama* cannot be underestimated. The amount of authority that *ulama* have in Saudi Arabia's political life can only be compared to Iran. For example, during the First Gulf War, the king—as high an authority as he is in Saudi Arabia—had to ask the Council of Senior Scholars to issue a special *fatwa* approving the invitation of U.S. troops into the country. Another prominent example is the key role that *ulama* played in the imposition of the oil embargo in 1973. *Ulama* were given an even more substantive authority in the wake of the 1979 seizure of the Grand Mosque by Islamic militants. The government responded to the national crisis by strengthening the position of *ulama*—both institutionally and financially. They were given an almost complete control over the education system and allowed to implement a variety of measures to reinforce the conservative Wahhabi modes of behavior. These measures affected Saudi women in a particularly severe way: throughout the 1980s, the *ulama* issued a large number of *fatwas* that aimed at regulating women's conduct and stripped them of their already limited rights and freedoms. Only when King Abdallah ascended to the throne in 2005, a number of steps have been implemented to rein back the powers of the *ulama*, such as transferring the authority over women's education to the Ministry of Education. The gradual reduction of the *ulama*'s power continued under King Salman. For example, in 2016, the Council of Ministers significantly limited the jurisdiction of the country's religious police (Committee for the Promotion of Virtue and the Prevention of Vice, or the *Mutawwa*) and stripped them of the power of making arrests.

Historically, the *ulama* have been led by the Al Sheikh family—the descendants of Muhammad ibn Abd al-Wahhab, who was the founder and ideologist of Wahhabism. The family is second in prestige only to the Al Saud, with whom they formed a power-sharing pact in the 18th century. The office of Grand Mufti was created by Ibn Saud in 1953 when Muhammad ibn Ibrahim Al Sheikh was appointed to the position. Since then, this office was held by the Al Sheikh family almost exclusively. King Faisal abolished the institution of Grand Mufti when he created the Ministry of Justice in 1970 and appointed a forward-looking scholar, Sheikh Muhammad Harakan, as the first minister of justice. However, the Grand Mufti position was restored in 1993 with the appointment of Abd al-Aziz bin Abdallah bin Baz. In June 1999, Abd al-Aziz Al Sheikh was appointed to the position of Grand Mufti and currently remains in it. Although the Al Sheikh's control of the judicial system has diminished in recent decades, they continue to be highly influential and hold important religious positions in the country: they dominate both the Council of Senior Scholars and the Higher Council of Judges. Al Saud and Al Sheikh families are also closely linked through intermarriage.

See also: Chapter 2: Emirate of Diriyah: The First Saudi State (1744–1818); King Abdullah; Muhammad ibn Abd al-Wahhab; Third Saudi State: Saudi Arabia in the 20th Century. Chapter 3: Sharia Law and Judicial System; Wahhabi Ideology. Chapter 5: Quran; Sunni Islam and Jurisprudence. Chapter 7: Divorce; Gender Segregation; Guardianship; Marriage Law and Tradition; The *Mutawwa*: Saudi Religious Police; Women's Mobility and Driving Ban.

Further Reading

Hatina, Meir. *Guardians of Faith in Modern Times: 'Ulama' in the Middle East*. Brill, 2009.

Mouline, Nabil. *The Clerics of Islam: Religious Authority and Political Power in Saudi Arabia*. Translated by Ethan S. Rundell. Yale University Press, 2014.

Wahhabi Ideology

Wahhabism is a revivalist Islamic movement and ideology that emerged in the middle of the 18th century in Central Arabia. Muhammad Abd al-Wahhab (1703–1791) was its founder and spiritual leader. In Arabic, the term "Wahhabism" usually has a negative connotation, as it is pejoratively used by the opponents of the movement. Whereas its followers never refer to themselves as Wahhabis but prefer *muwahhidun* (unitarians), Salafis, or, most commonly, they simply call themselves Muslims. In its ideological core, Wahhabism strives to rid Islam of any innovations, modifications, or additional practices that deviate from the teachings and deeds of Prophet Muhammad in the 7th century. In sum, Wahhabism calls for a complete return to the fundamentals of Islam, where the only acceptable Muslim society is the one that imitates the first Muslim community.

Abd al-Wahhab rose as a popular preacher from a family of scholars in Najd. His teachings and reformist ideas relied on the Hanbali school of legal thought, which has a notoriously uncompromising position toward *bid'a*, or the so-called innovations. Abd al-Wahhab was particularly inspired by the ideas of Ahmad ibn Taymiyyah (1263–1328)—a 13th-century Hanbali scholar, who propagated against "innovative" Islamic practices, particularly Sufism, and called for a return to the foundations and puritan lifestyle of the early Islamic community. The main focus of worship should be the oneness of God, or *tawhid*. The only way of achieving communion with God is through unconditional submission to his will, as opposed to mystical or meditative practices, such as those performed in Sufism. Although Ibn Taymiyyah's teachings were unpopular among his contemporaries and in subsequent centuries, he has become an incredibly influential figure in modern Islam, in particular the contemporary forms of Salafism, Wahhabism, and Jihadism. Ibn Taymiyyah is particularly known for his controversial *fatwa* that allowed *jihad* against other Muslims.

Although worship of anything but God is strictly forbidden in Islam, the Wahhabi teachings take an even stricter position toward any object that can distract a Muslim—even unintentionally—from worshipping the one and only God. They promulgate a puritanical lifestyle and go beyond the routine Islamic prohibition of alcohol by also banning tobacco products. Some even avoid drinking coffee due to its stimulating effect on the human body. Wahhabism compels strict observation of all Islamic duties, such as the five daily prayers that are to be performed at their exact times. The dress is also regulated, especially for women who are required to wear black *abayahs* in any public setting. Many Wahhabis reject Shiism as an Islamic denomination and look at it as a form of heresy. Moreover, Wahhabism generally tends to consider anyone who does not follow the strict monotheistic principle to be a *kafir* (unbeliever) and takes a hostile stance against them. Interestingly, *kufr*, which is a concept of intentional or informed lack of belief such as atheism, is a greater offense than *shirk*, or polytheism, if the latter stems from lack of proper knowledge.

See also: Chapter 2: Emirate of Diriyah: The First Saudi State (1744–1818); King Abdullah; Muhammad ibn Abd al-Wahhab; Third Saudi State: Saudi Arabia in the 20th Century. Chapter 3: Sharia Law and Judicial System; Ulama. Chapter 5: Quran; Sunni Islam and Jurisprudence. Chapter 7: Divorce; Gender Segregation; Guardianship; The *Mutawwa*: Saudi Religious Police; Women's Mobility and Driving Ban.

Further Reading

Ayoob, Mohammed, and Hasan Kosebalaban. *Religion and Politics in Saudi Arabia: Wahhabism and the State.* Lynne Rienner, 2009.

Commins, David Dean. *The Wahhabi Mission and Saudi Arabia.* I. B. Tauris, 2006.

Davis, Rohan, ed. *Western Imaginings: The Intellectual Contest to Define Wahhabism.* American University in Cairo Press, 2018.

DeLong-Bas, Natana J. *Wahhabi Islam: From Revival and Reform to Global Jihad.* Oxford University Press, 2004.

Nahouza, Namira. *Wahhabism and the Rise of the New Salafists: Theology, Power and Sunni Islam.* I. B. Tauris, 2018.

CHAPTER 4

ECONOMY

OVERVIEW

Saudi Arabia's economy remains largely dependent on its oil reserves and oil-based industries. Since the country began receiving its oil revenues, the Saudi government used its ample oil reserves to fund the overall modernization of all sectors of the economy, including various industries, international trade, and the financial system. Although oil remains the core aspect of the Saudi economy, great efforts are being made to diversify and expand other branches. Saudi Vision 2030—a major economic plan meant to transform and modernize the country's economy and society—places particular emphasis on continuous reduction of the oil dependence and further diversification of its economy. In addition to oil and gas, Saudi Arabia's natural resources include small reserves of iron, copper, zinc, precious metals such as gold and silver, lead, sulfur, phosphate, and a number of other minerals. The government has undertaken a policy of exploration of its nonoil resources, in an attempt to further diversify its economy. As a result of geologic explorations, deposits of various metals were discovered in the western part of the country, as well as several nonmetallic resources, including limestone, gypsum, silica, and phosphorite.

The country's economic development strategy represents the level of state involvement not experienced by other capitalist free market economies. Petroleum wealth has been of great benefit to Saudi Arabia, but at the same time it enabled the state to dominate the economic and social sphere. The vast oil funds allowed the state to shape and dominate the economic structure of the region. The oil income also meant that many other industries developed through their dependence on oil. Even independent privately owned local companies developed in the shadow of the state, feeding on contracts and depending on migrant labor.

A pioneering economic approach was implemented by Saudi Arabia through its Saudi Arabian Basic Industries Corporation (SABIC), which was established in 1976. Funded and owned by the state, SABIC's initial objective was to process oil and gas by-products into various materials, such as fertilizers, plastics, and chemicals. Since then, SABIC manufacturing enterprises greatly expanded to include rolled steel, plastics, aluminum products, pipes, copper wire and cable, truck assembly, refrigeration, cement and construction materials, and other industries. This strategy made a major impact on encouraging national production of basic materials and lessened the reliance on expensive imports. SABIC industries initiated a rapid economic development of the eastern urban centers of Yanbu and Jubail. SABIC also contains various small-scale manufacturing enterprises. Other companies producing steel, cement, and construction materials have been established by the Saudi government and the country's royal family. There has also been a significant emphasis on national production of core consumer products, including dairy, tomato paste, soap, and laundry products. All these companies are often allowed to function as monopolies with substantial legal and political support provided by the state.

Whereas all Gulf states depend on foreign labor, Saudi Arabia (together with Oman and Bahrain) is at the lower end of this dependence, since foreign workers account for less than one-third of the population. However, the rate of unemployment among Saudi population is high, mainly due to the fact that many young Saudis aspire to work white-collar jobs. The government has been implementing the Saudization policy, which focuses on replacing white-collar foreign workers with Saudi nationals. In practice, this meant the departure of professionals who came from the West and the rest of the Arabic-speaking world with local personnel. Remarkably, despite the continuous growth of employment opportunities related to production of oil, the annual influx of 2 million Hajj pilgrims still employs more people than the oil industry—despite the fact that most of these jobs only last through the pilgrimage season.

Saudi Arabia has a small agricultural sector, which the government attempts to expand. Most of the agricultural lands and facilities are located in the southwest, which has the highest annual rainfall compared to the rest of the country. Despite the harsh climatic conditions, Saudi Arabia is one of the world's largest producers of dates. It also produces livestock—a remnant of the centuries-long nomadic pastoralism of its Bedouin population. The livestock population has camels, sheep, cattle, and goats. The scarcity of water resources remains one of the main issues in Saudi Arabia, which operates the world's largest desalination program. Underground aquifers are located throughout the Arabian Peninsula, but these are nonreplenishable sources of water. The government has initiated several projects for construction of dams and water-recycling plants.

Further Reading

Aarts, Paul, and Gerd Nonneman. *Saudi Arabia in the Balance: Political Economy, Society, Foreign Affairs*. New York University Press, 2005.

Ramady, M. A. *The Saudi Arabian Economy*. Springer, 2010.

Shoult, Anthony. *Doing Business with Saudi Arabia*. 2nd ed. Kogan Page, 2002.

Agriculture

Following the discovery of oil, Saudi Arabia embarked on new agricultural policies in attempts to reduce its dependency on imported food products. Many of these measures attempted to address the peninsula's perennial issue with fresh water. Government projects included drilling deep wells to tap fossil water and building water desalination plants for irrigation purposes. The latter industry has grown considerably over the years and is considered the largest in the world. Seventy percent of Saudi Arabia's available portable water comes from desalination.

The Directorate of Agriculture was created in 1948. It began providing various subsidies and loans to farmers to improve existing agricultural infrastructure, in addition to building dams and irrigation canals. In 1953, the directorate was transformed into the Ministry of Agriculture and Water. The ministry instituted various programs, offering a range of agricultural services, including technical advice, fertilization consults, veterinary services, and pest control. In 1964, the Saudi Arabian Agricultural Bank was established and has been assisting farmers with financing of various agricultural projects.

In 1972, Saudi Arabia embarked on an ambitious project to produce large amounts of wheat and barley, using large sprinkler networks as the main irrigation technique. The project involved almost 3 million hectares of land, and by 1985 the kingdom became self-sufficient, although the cost of production remained very high. During the 1980s and into the 1990s, Saudi Arabia became the sixth-largest exporter of wheat. However, by 1996 the government began discouraging large-scale wheat production because of the quickly diminishing supplies of groundwater. The latter became the main reason for the government to end its domestic program of wheat production in 2016.

An important aspect of Saudi Arabia's agricultural sector is the greenhouse production of fruits and vegetables, mainly by means of private investments. These greenhouses use various modern technologies and are among the most sophisticated in the world. Fresh produce is widely available in local markets. Some greenhouses even produce berries and flowers for import to European markets. Saudi-processed fruit juices are sold throughout African markets.

Commercial livestock production focuses on cattle, sheep, and poultry, in addition to the traditional camel. Initially, cattle were raised for their meat and hides, but in the 1960s the government brought several dairy breeds from Europe and increased domestic milk products. Dairy farms require expensive infrastructure, not only to guarantee quality, but also to maintain high levels of production during the hot months. Because European breeds of dairy cattle are not used to the heat, dairy barns are cooled either by misters or air conditioning. Most provinces now produce sufficient quantities of eggs and chicken to satisfy the needs of the local consumers, but red meat still needs to be imported. Various livestock breeds are imported from the neighboring Arab countries, as well as Australia and the United States.

New technologies are constantly implemented in all branches of the country's agricultural sector and made a particularly visible impact on the production of dates. Date groves have been improved with drip irrigation, which greatly reduces water loss to evaporation. Tree management has also been improved, which substantially increased the level of production, making Saudi Arabia among the highest producers of dates in the world. The country has over 13 million date trees, which generate over 600,000 tons of dates a year. Dates are processed and packaged locally and exported to other countries. There is a high demand for dates throughout the Muslim world, especially during the month of Ramadan, since the traditional breaking of the fast is made with dates or dates-based drinks.

See also: Chapter 1: Climate; Eastern Arabia: Al-Hasa; Fresh Water Reserves and Water Conservancy. Chapter 4: Diversification and Development Plans. Chapter 14: Islamic Dietary Laws; Traditional Foods and Regional Variations.

Further Reading

Abdulfattah, Kamal. *Mountain Farmer and Fellah in 'Asīr, Southwest Saudi Arabia: The Conditions of Agriculture in a Traditional Society.* Im Fränkischen Geographischen Gesellschaft, 1981.

Alkolibi, Fahad M. "Possible Effects of Global Warming on Agriculture and Water Resources in Saudi Arabia: Impacts and Responses." *Climatic Change*, vol. 54, no. 1–2, July 2002, pp. 225–245.

Amin, Ammar A. "The Extent of Desertification on Saudi Arabia." *Environmental Geology (Berlin)*, vol. 46, no. 1, July 2004, pp. 22–31.

Harrigan, Jane. *The Political Economy of Arab Food Sovereignty.* Palgrave Macmillan, 2014.

Lippman, Thomas W. "Saudi Arabia's Quest for 'Food Security.'" *Middle East Policy*, vol. 17, no. 1, 2010, pp. 90–98.

Multsch, S. "Water-Saving Strategies for Irrigation Agriculture in Saudi Arabia." *International Journal of Water Resources Development*, vol. 33, no. 2, 2017, pp. 292–309.

Diversification and Development Plans

For decades, Saudi Arabia allocated its petroleum income to transform itself from an undeveloped and entirely oil-based economy into a modern industrial state, while attempting to guard the country's Islamic identity and values. As a result of various measures, the economy has progressed rapidly, and the steadily increasing oil wealth improved the living conditions for most Saudis. Although the country continues to rely on its petroleum revenues, other industries, including manufacturing and agriculture, are increasing its shares of economic activity. One factor that complicates Saudi Arabia's economic development is the very high rate of population growth. Additionally, there remains to be a disparity between the job skills of Saudi graduates and the needs of the private job market. Saudi Arabia continues to employ about 5 million foreigners. However, the big investments into education, including the creation of King Abdullah University of Science and Technology (KAUST), promise to change this situation in the near future.

The first two development plans took place in the 1970s and focused on Saudi Arabia's infrastructure. Both plans made impressive changes, including a significant increase of paved highways, power plants, and seaport capacity. The third development plan of 1980–1985 had a different objective, targeting education, health care, and social services. During the same period, the expansion of the two industrial cities of Jubail and Yanbu was nearly completed, as the two centers were built to develop the oil by-product and other industries, including petrochemicals, steel, and fertilizers.

During the period of the fourth development plan (1985–1990), the government encouraged the establishment of private enterprises and increase in foreign investment, including joint ventures between Saudi and foreign companies. The government provided various financing and other incentive programs to promote private investments. As a result, the private sector of the Saudi economy rose to 70 percent of non-oil GDP by 1987. Although it continued to dominate in the areas of trade and commerce, private shares in manufacturing, agriculture, banking, and construction business markedly increased as well.

The fifth economic plan of 1990–1995 emphasized the country's defenses and military investments, especially in light of Iraq's invasion of Kuwait in 1991. During this five-year period, the country also saw the development of regional infrastructure. Among the most important initiatives undertaken by the government during this time was the Saudization program, which aimed to create greater employment opportunities for Saudis by reducing the number of foreign workers, particularly in the private sector. Among the main objectives of the sixth plan (1996–2000) was to expand the country's educational programs and to increase affordability of government services, while improving their quality. The plan continued to work on reducing the kingdom's dependence on oil and expanded the Saudization efforts—both of which were also the goals of the seventh plan (2000–2004). The current development plan, labeled Saudi Vision 2030 and spearheaded by Crown Prince Muhammad bin Salman, is perhaps the most ambitious project in the country's history, aiming not only to diversify the economy and greatly reduce the reliance on oil, but also to maximally modernize the Saudi society, while preserving its Islamic and traditional character.

See also: Chapter 3: Political Reform and Modernization. Chapter 4: Vision 2030.

Further Reading

Albassam, Bassam A. "Economic Diversification in Saudi Arabia: Myth or Reality?" *Resources Policy*, vol. 44, 2015, pp. 112–117.

al-Rasheed, Madawi. *Contesting the Saudi State: Islamic Voices from a New Generation*. Cambridge University Press, 2007.

al-Rasheed, Madawi, ed. *Salman's Legacy: The Dilemmas of a New Era in Saudi Arabia*. Oxford University Press, 2018.

Energy

The energy sector of Saudi economy is overseen by two ministries: the Ministry of Oil and the Ministry of Water and Electricity. According to 2005 global energy numbers, Saudi Arabia was the 15th-largest consumer of primary energy in the world, 60 percent of which was based on petroleum and the remainder—on natural gas. Although widely known for its overall dependence on oil, Saudi Arabia has increasingly relied on electricity and is currently the fastest-growing consumer of electricity on the Middle Eastern market.

Since the 1970s, Saudi Arabia's electrical production has grown rapidly, largely due to diverse measures initiated by the government. In its early years, the country's electrical production was highly decentralized, but it gradually came under full state control in the second half of the 20th century. With the turn of the 21st century, one central corporation—Saudi Electricity Company (SEC)—was established in 2000 and consolidated all of the electricity-producing sector, aiming to develop a uniform national grid and a comprehensive energy-development plan. SEC continues to have a monopoly on the production, transmission, and distribution of electricity throughout Saudi Arabia. It manages all of the country's 45 power plants. Over 80 percent of the company shares are owned by the Saudi government.

The development of solar power has been identified as a priority in the energy sector, as part of the government's efforts to reduce the country's consumption of oil and gas. As late as 2011, over half of the nation's electricity was still produced by burning oil. In 2010, Saudi Arabia established a government agency responsible for the development of the renewable energy sector—the King Abdullah City for Atomic and Renewable Energy (K.A.CARE). Two years after its creation, in May 2012, the agency announced a wide-scale national energy transformation plan, which would install 41 gigawatts (GW) of solar capacity by 2032. At the time of this announcement, the country had only 0.003 GW of solar energy capacity. During the 2012 United Nations Climate Change Conference in Qatar, Saudi Arabia confirmed its commitment to developing a range of alternative energy sources, with the focus on solar power production. As a result of K.A.CARE efforts and strong governmental support, Saudi Arabia's solar power achieved grid parity in 2013 and began producing electricity at costs comparable to conventional sources.

Currently, the Saudi power program is considered the second most advanced in the Arabic-speaking world, after the neighboring Gulf country, United Arab Emirates. In anticipation of the rapid growth of domestic energy consumption, especially in light of the newest national development plan, Saudi Vision 2030, the government has announced plans to create a domestic nuclear industry. The plan proposed to build as many as 16 nuclear reactors by 2030, with the goal of not only meeting the demand of the domestic market but also producing surplus energy for export.

See also: Chapter 2: Discovery of Oil. Chapter 3: Gulf Cooperation Council. Chapter 4: Oil Industry and Aramco.

Further Reading

Cordesman, Anthony H. *Saudi Arabia Enters the Twenty-First Century.* Praeger, 2003.

El Mallakh, Ragaei, and Dorothea H. El Mallakh. *Saudi Arabia, Energy, Developmental Planning, and Industrialization.* Lexington Books, 1982.

al-Rasheed, Madawi, ed. *Salman's Legacy: The Dilemmas of a New Era in Saudi Arabia.* Oxford University Press, 2018.

Financial Institutions and Saudi Riyal

Some of the earliest forms of banking in human history came from the Middle East, as historical records trace their creation back to ancient Mesopotamia, around 2000 BC. In medieval times, the prototypes of the modern form of banking came to prominence in northern Italy, which had trading relations with the Levant and Egypt. These banks were owed by either individual merchants or merchant groups.

By the mid-19th century, branches of various British and French banks were dominating the financial sphere throughout the Arab world, including the Arabian Peninsula. Many of these European banking institutions were located in Jeddah and on the Gulf coast, including al-Manamah and Kuwait, which were at the time regional economic centers. Since the establishment of the current Saudi Arabian state and the economic boom following the discovery of oil, Saudi Arabia and all other Gulf states developed their own highly sophisticated banking systems by the end of the 20th century. Many of these banks have been nationalized in light of the increasing revenues from oil exports in the 1970s, while several new banks were established as well. During the 1980s, the annual growth rate of new banks was a remarkable 30 percent. Saudi Arabia and Kuwait have become the most important banking centers in the Gulf region. Various foreign banks have regional branches, and many have formed joint ventures through minority stakes, such as the Saudi American Bank or the British Bank of the Middle East. At the present time, there are 24 banks in Saudi Arabia. They are licensed

Saudi Riyal banknotes. (Mohd Hafiez Mohd Razali/Dreamstime.com)

> **SAUDI ARABIAN MONETARY AUTHORITY (SAMA)**
>
> Since the creation of the state, Saudi Arabia had a double standard for currency, gold and silver, and the market fluctuations made it virtually impossible to keep the currency stable. There were several attempts for reform in the late 1940s with the help from American specialists. In 1948, George Eddy, a gold expert from the Treasury Department, and Raymond F. Mikesell, from the U.S. State Department, came to Saudi Arabia to study currency reform. However, their recommendations made little headway. Another U.S. mission, led by John F. Greaney, attempted to implement changes in 1950 but also without success. Only in 1951, major reforms began to take place, when a technical assistance agreement was signed between Saudi Arabia and the United States. Arthur N. Young participated in implementing an important monetary reform, with a recommendation to establish a central bank. On April 20, 1952, the Saudi Arabian Monetary Agency (SAMA) was created. The name "monetary agency" was chosen to avoid mentioning of a bank, which would carry the connotation of charging or paying interest—a commercial practice banned in Islam. In fact, charging and paying interest were specifically prohibited in the SAMA charter. In the beginning, the agency was managed by foreigners (the first two were Americans and the third—Pakistani), but thereafter the leadership has been exclusively Saudi. After a series of novel reforms, which included currency reforms and the creation of specialized government-owned banks, SAMA has gradually become one of the most powerful banking institutions in the world. In recent decades, the word "agency" in SAMA has been replaced with "authority": Saudi Arabian Monetary Authority.

by the Saudi Arabian Monetary Authority (SAMA), which functions as the central bank of Saudi Arabia, established in 1952. Twelve of these banks are local, and 12 are branches of foreign banks.

An important feature of Saudi and other regional financial institutions is that many banks have the so-called Islamic banking system. They follow the Quranic prohibition of usury and charging interest (*riba* in Arabic). Islamic banks follow the simple principle of sharing profit and loss. Loans given out by these banks, such as mortgage and car loans, are similar to leasing contracts. Other rules and principles include the prohibition of gambling and investments in the *haram* (literally meaning "unlawful" in Arabic) categories, such as alcohol, pornography, prostitution, and products containing pork. Several private Islamic banks have been very successful on both regional and global financial markets. Among these is Al-Rajhi Bank, which is the world's largest Islamic bank by capital, based on the 2015 numbers. The National Commercial Bank (NCB), also known as Al-Ahli Bank, was established in 1953 and became the first Saudi bank to be licensed. It is the biggest financial institution in Saudi Arabia and the second-largest bank by asset in the Arab world. It functions as an Islamic bank. In 1999, its majority holding was acquired by the Saudi government.

The Saudi riyal, abbreviated SAR, is the official currency of Saudi Arabia. It is divided into 100 *halalah*. Its current exchange rate with the U.S. dollar is 3.75 SAR. The riyal has been the currency of the Hijaz before the establishment of the Saudi Arabian state and was also among the main currencies of the Mediterranean region during the

Ottoman times. The Hijazi riyal was based on the Ottoman coin worth 20 *kuruş*— *kuruş* was the standard unit of currency in the Ottoman Empire until the former Ottoman gold lira was subdivided in 1844. When the Kingdom of Saudi Arabia was established in 1932, the riyal was adopted as the new state's currency. The first coins bearing Saudi Arabia's name were issued in 1935. These were three types of silver coins, including 1 riyal, a half of a riyal, and a quarter of a riyal. The riyal's subdivision, the *halalah*, which constitutes one-hundredth of a riyal, was introduced in 1963.

See also: Chapter 3: Sharia Law and Judicial System. Chapter 5: Quran.

Further Reading

Ginena, Karim, and Azhar Hamid. *Foundations of Shari'ah Governance of Islamic Banks.* John Wiley & Sons, 2015.

Hunt-Ahmed, Karen. *Contemporary Islamic Finance: Innovations, Applications, and Best Practices.* John Wiley & Sons, 2013.

Land and Household Policy

In general, only Saudis can own land in Saudi Arabia. Certain regulations also exist to allow individual citizens and companies from Gulf Cooperation Council (GCC) countries limited rights to land ownership, but properties near Mecca and Medina are completely off limits to anyone but Saudis. There are many obstacles, legal and logistical, for non-Saudi and non-GCC ownership of land in the country. In order for an expatriate to buy property in Saudi Arabia, they need to have a special letter of permission from the Ministry of Housing.

Real estate has been one of fastest-growing sectors in Saudi Arabia, playing an important role in the country's non-oil economy. The real estate market is supported by the real estate investment trusts (REITs), which have had a significant positive impact in the last several years. Experts believe that Saudi real estate will continue to steadily expand in the next decade. In contrast with the rest of the world, most Saudis do not own their homes. If the world's average of home ownership constitutes 70 percent, only about an estimated 30 to 40 percent of Saudis own their houses. This is explained by the fact that until recently mortgages virtually did not exist—until a series of mortgage laws had been proposed and implemented. Still, these are strictly governed by the Sharia.

Saudi Arabia aims to radically transform its national real estate market within the large-scale development plan, Vision 2030. The government announced a massive housing initiative, estimated at $32 billion USD and meant to boost home ownership by Saudi nationals to 70 percent by 2030. The initiative puts forward various loan and finance programs, as well as incentive programs for the private-sector participation. An impressive $3.3 billion is allocated to support down payments. Through its various programs, the government currently provides over 60 percent of all home loans. A number of important mortgage measures are implemented by the Saudi Arabian

Monetary Authority (SAMA), which functions as the country's central bank. Diverse programs were created to help consumers navigate the lending market, relieve mortgage debt, and have options of affordable housing. The latter is a particularly urgent issue for the country's growing young population.

See also: Chapter 1: Mecca; Medina. Chapter 3: Gulf Cooperation Council. Chapter 4: Financial Institutions and Saudi Riyal; Land and Household Policy; Public vs. Private Sectors. Chapter 6: Urbanization.

Further Reading

Aina, Yusuf A., et al. "Top-Down Sustainable Urban Development? Urban Governance Transformation in Saudi Arabia." *Cities*, vol. 90, July 2019, pp. 272–281.

Al Mogren, Faisal bin Ayyaf. "Reprioritizing the Human Factor in Building Gulf Cities." *International Journal of Middle East Studies*, vol. 50, no. 3, Aug. 2018, pp. 568–572.

Mubarak, Faisal A. "Urban Growth Boundary Policy and Residential Suburbanization: Riyadh, Saudi Arabia." *Habitat International*, vol. 28, no. 4, Dec. 2004, pp. 567–591.

Opoku, Robert A., and Alhassan G. Abdul-Muhmin. "Housing Preferences and Attribute Importance among Low-Income Consumers in Saudi Arabia." *Habitat International*, vol. 34, no. 2, Apr. 2010, pp. 219–227.

Struyk, Raymond J. "Housing Policy Issues in a Rich Country with High Population Growth: The Case of Riyadh, Saudi Arabia." *Review of Urban & Regional Development Studies*, vol. 17, no. 2, July 2005, pp. 140–161.

Migrant Workers and Unemployment

Foreign workers began to arrive in Saudi Arabia shortly after the discovery of oil in the late 1930s. The numbers of migrant workers continued to increase throughout the 20th and early 21st centuries and are estimated in the millions. The first wave of non-Saudi employees was composed primarily of technical and administrative personnel coming to work in the oil industry from western and other Arab nations. Initially, many of them were employed by Aramco. Gradually, as the country's economy continued to grow, greater numbers of migrant workers came to Saudi Arabia. Throughout the 1970s, the rapid development of the country's infrastructure created high demand for both skilled and unskilled workers. During this time, many expats from other Arabic-speaking countries, including Egyptians, Palestinians, and Yemenis, came to Saudi Arabia in search of various employment opportunities. A large number of professionals and workers arrived from India and Pakistan as well. As a result of this influx of the foreign workforce, the country's population almost doubled by 1985. In the early 1980s, another wave of migrant workers arrived in Saudi Arabia, primarily from South and East Asian countries, including Bangladesh, Thailand, Philippines, and Indonesia.

Saudi Arabia has become increasingly dependent on cheap foreign labor. Even with the wide-scale government efforts to reinforce the policy of Saudization (increasing the number of Saudis in the workforce, while reducing the number of foreigners), this dependency remains urgent today, especially in blue-collar and service jobs. There is a hierarchy of foreign workers in Saudi society and the job market, based on their country of origin. For example, workers from Western countries and India are often hired for high professional positions, whereas low-wage jobs are held by migrant workers from Southeast Asia.

Like all other Gulf countries, Saudi Arabia has faced criticism over systematic mistreatment of foreign workers. It has been reported that employers often withhold wages, whereas the workers have virtually no rights as noncitizens. In many cases, employers confiscate the migrant workers' passports upon the latter's arrival into the country, thus making them completely dependent and unable to leave.

The official numbers show unemployment reaching the record high in 2018 at 12.9 percent. There is a significant gender-based discrepancy in these numbers, where the rate of unemployment among women is at 23 percent. These numbers are explained by various social and legal restrictions, including male guardianship and, until very recently, a ban on driving that greatly restricted their mobility (the ban was lifted in 2018). Among men, an important factor contributing to high unemployment rates is social resistance to certain types of employment. For example, jobs in sales and in service are considered an indication of an inferior social status among Saudis. This problem is not easy to resolve, as the roots of these social attitudes can be found in the tribal culture and reflect the centuries-long relationships between nomadic and sedentary populations of the Arabian Peninsula.

Before a series of educational reforms were implemented in the latter half of the 20th century, there was a real shortage of Saudi-educated professionals. High-skill jobs were primarily occupied by employees from Western countries, professionals from other Arabic-speaking countries, and foreign-educated Saudis. However, with the growth of the educational sector, especially the establishment of modern institutions of higher education such as King Abdullah University of Science and Technology (KAUST), the numbers of professional Saudis educated in the country continue to rise every year. Since the late 1980s, the Saudi government began implementing a policy of Saudization, which aims to replace foreign workers with Saudi nationals. In 2000, a special decree required businesses with more than 20 employees to have at least 25 percent of its workforce taken by Saudi nationals. Since the beginning of 2017, a record number of foreign workers have left the country—more than 677,000—when the government imposed higher fees on expatriate workers.

See also: Chapter 2: Discovery of Oil. Chapter 3: Gulf Cooperation Council. Chapter 4: Diversification and Development Plans; Oil Industry and Aramco; Public vs. Private Sectors; Saudization.

Further Reading
Assidmi, Luay M., and Erin Wolgamuth. "Uncovering the Dynamics of the Saudi Youth Unemployment Crisis." *Systemic Practice and Action Research*, vol. 30, no. 2, 2017, pp. 173–186.

Babar, Zahra, ed. *Arab Migrant Communities in the GCC.* Oxford University Press, 2017.

Bal, C. *Production Politics and Migrant Labour Regimes: Guest Workers in Asia and the Gulf.* Palgrave Macmillan, 2016.

Bosbait, M., and R. Wilson. "Education, School to Work Transitions and Unemployment in Saudi Arabia." *Middle Eastern Studies,* vol. 41, no. 4, 2005, pp. 533–545.

Farhan, B., Brevetti, M., and D. Laditan. "Unemployment in Saudi Arabia: The Ethical and Economic Impact of Foreign Workers on the Middle East Market." *Middle East Journal of Business,* vol. 11, no. 4, 2016, pp. 21–38.

Jain, Prakash C., and Ginu Zacharia Oommen, eds. *South Asian Migration to Gulf Countries: History, Policies, Development.* Routledge, Taylor & Francis Group, 2016.

Oil Industry and Aramco

The oil industry in Saudi Arabia began to develop in the first half of the 20th century. Oil was first discovered and developed in Bahrain; then it was located in other countries near the Persian Gulf—Iran, Iraq, Kuwait, and Saudi Arabia. The Saudi Arabian Oil Company, or Saudi Aramco, is one of the biggest and most influential oil companies in the world. In 2018, its net income exceeded $111 billion. The company's headquarters and main operation terminals are located in Dhahran, in Saudi Arabia's Eastern Province. Saudi Arabia has some of the world's largest oil reserves worldwide. The third-party audit, conducted in 2019, determined that Saudi Arabia has 263.2 billion barrels of oil—not counting the country's share of oil reserves in the neutral zone shared with Kuwait. The most productive oil fields of Saudi Arabia are Ghawar and Safaniyah (also the world's largest onshore and offshore fields, respectively), in addition to Marjan, Abqaiq, Khursaniyah, Dammam, and Khurais. All of these fields are developed by Aramco. Additionally, the company is considered a global leader in the production of natural gas liquids, which are supplied both for the domestic market and for export.

The company was founded in 1933 under the name California Arabian Standard Oil Company (CASOC), as a result of a concessionary agreement between Standard Oil of California and Ibn Saud's government. The concession was given for the period of 66 years and included much of Eastern Saudi Arabia, as well as other offshore and onshore areas, totaling an area of over 900,000 square kilometers. However, several decades later—in 1973—this area was reduced to 220,000 square kilometers. In 1936, Texaco Inc. bought half of CASOC shares as the latter had troubles locating the oil. Finally, the seventh drill in Dhahran, labeled Well Number 7, brought success in 1938 as it began producing about 1,500 barrels daily. The next year, the first tanker with Saudi oil was sent to the United States, and by 1940 oil production rapidly rose to 700,000 tons yearly. In 1944, the company was renamed into Arabian-American Oil Company, and in 1988 it received its current name, Saudi Arabian Oil Company, or Aramco.

The year 1950 set a long process of Aramco's nationalization by Saudi Arabia. Being pressured by the Saudi government, Aramco began sharing its net profits at the 50-50 rate with Saudi Arabia. In 1973, the company was partially nationalized, and in 1980, it fully came into the government's custody. However, although government owned, Aramco still functions like a commercial oil company and enjoys a great deal of freedoms and flexibilities compared to other companies in Saudi Arabia and the whole region. Some even say it functions as a state within a state. For example, the notorious religious police, the *Mutawwa*, was never allowed to operate on the territory of Aramco (the *Mutawwa* lost most of its authority in the rest of the country in 2016). Since the early days of its inception, Aramco has been employing many members of the Shia community, as

An Aramco crew working on a drilling rig in the Abqaiq field, in Eastern Saudi Arabia, during the summer of 1947. (Library of Congress)

most of them live in the Eastern Province. Along with nationalizing Aramco, Saudi Arabia began implementing Saudization with the objective of replacing most of its foreign personnel with Saudi nationals. Women have been consistently employed by the company since 1964, and in the 10 years between 2008 and 2018, the number of women employees has doubled. Several new programs are also under way in Aramco within the Saudi Vision 2030 plan, aiming to significantly increase women's workforce in the company, particularly in engineering and other technical professions.

See also: Chapter 1: Border Demarcations and Disputes; Eastern Arabia: Al-Hasa. Chapter 2: Discovery of Oil; Ibn Saud; Third Saudi State: Saudi Arabia in the 20th Century. Chapter 3: Gulf Cooperation Council; Saudi–U.S. Relations. Chapter 4: OPEC and OAPEC.

Further Reading

Anderson, Irvine H. *Aramco, the United States, and Saudi Arabia: A Study of the Dynamics of Foreign Oil Policy, 1933–1950*. Princeton University Press, 1981.

Brown, Anthony Cave. *Oil, God, and Gold: The Story of Aramco and the Saudi Kings*. Houghton Mifflin, 1999.

Hertog, Steffen. *Princes, Brokers, and Bureaucrats: Oil and the State in Saudi Arabia.* Cornell University Press, 2010.

Wald, Ellen R. *Saudi, Inc.: The Arabian Kingdom's Pursuit of Profit and Power.* First Pegasus Books ed. Pegasus Books, 2018.

OPEC and OAPEC

The Organization of Petroleum Exporting Countries (OPEC) is the most influential international organization of oil producers. It was founded in 1960 in Baghdad by Iraq, Iran, Kuwait, Saudi Arabia, and Venezuela. A number of other countries joined the organization in later years: Qatar (1961), Indonesia (1962), Libya (1962), the United Arab Emirates (1967), Algeria (1969), Nigeria (1971), Ecuador (1973), Gabon (1975), Angola (2007), Equatorial Guinea (2017) and Congo (2018). Several countries exited and reentered OPEC throughout the years. Ecuador left the organization in 1992 but rejoined in 2007. Gabon exited in 1995 and reentered in 2016. Indonesia terminated its membership in 2009, rejoined in January 2016, but then terminated it once again in November of the same year. Qatar exited OPEC in January 2019 amid political tensions with Saudi Arabia and other Gulf countries, which include the nation's complete air, land, and sea blockade by Saudi Arabia, the UAE, Bahrain, and Egypt. Thus, currently OPEC consists of 14 member states.

The organization's headquarters are in Vienna, Austria. The highest executive bodies are the Council of Governors, the General Conference, the Economic Commission, and the Secretariat. OPEC has its own news agency and issues a number of scientific and other publications. A special discretionary fund, the OPEC Fund for International Development, helps to balance payment deficits, as well as finance development projects. OPEC loans are usually long-term and interest-free. Since the 1970s, OPEC members enforced several increases of oil prices. The OPEC Statute makes a distinction between the five founding members and the organization's full members.

The creation of OPEC took place during the period of oil surplus following World War II. Oil decreased significantly, and oil producers experienced a sharp dive in revenues. To avoid a complete breakdown of the industry, the main oil companies made a joint decision to reduce production. However, this also hurt the economies of those oil-producing countries who largely depended on oil exports. The establishment of OPEC was seen as a way to stabilize the market and to influence the price of oil. However, these goals were not met initially because many of the member states at the time did not have full control over their oil reserves. Almost two decades had to pass until the Gulf countries were able to take over their national oil industries.

Throughout history, the changes in political climate impacted the relationships between OPEC states. The loss of unity was particularly apparent in the early 1980s, following the Iranian Revolution. Another oil surplus led to the dramatic drop in global prices and triggered recession in many oil-producing countries, which lasted for over a decade. Several OPEC member states, including Saudi Arabia and the United Arab

Emirates, chose to continue with a national price and production policy. For example, the 1990–1991 war between Iraq and Kuwait began over allegations that Kuwait was overproducing its oil. The most recent internal conflict was triggered by the political tensions between Saudi Arabia, the UAE, and Bahrain on the one side and Qatar on the other, resulting in the latter exiting the organization.

The Organization of Arab Petroleum Exporting Countries (OAPEC) is the consortium of oil-producing Arab states. It was founded on January 9, 1968, by Kuwait, Saudi Arabia, and Libya, with the headquarters located in Kuwait. In what followed, many other Arab nations joined OAPEC, including Egypt, Algeria, Bahrain, Iraq, Qatar, Syria, Tunisia, and the United Arab Emirates. In 1986, Tunisia withdrew from the organization. OAPEC is not associated with OPEC, but several nations are members of both, including Saudi Arabia. The organization's highest executive body is the Council of Ministers, headed by the general secretary. The council meets twice a year to develop and pursue a joint energy policy. In October 1973, OAPEC initiated an oil embargo against the nations who supported Israel during the Yom Kippur War. The embargo was initially targeting the United States and the United Kingdom, in addition to Canada, Netherlands, and Japan. Shortly after, the embargo also extended to Portugal, South Africa, and Rhodesia. When it ended in March 1974, oil prices had risen from $3 to $12 globally—or nearly 400 percent, while the prices in the United States were even higher. Thus, for the first time in history, oil was successfully used as a political weapon, exploiting the world's dependency on petroleum. In recent decades, OAPEC has been focusing on regional development.

See also: Chapter 1: Border Demarcations and Disputes; Eastern Arabia: Al-Hasa. Chapter 2: Discovery of Oil; Ibn Saud; Third Saudi State: Saudi Arabia in the 20th Century. Chapter 3: Gulf Cooperation Council; Saudi–U.S. Relations. Chapter 4: Oil Industry and Aramco.

Further Reading

Bower, Tom. *The Squeeze: Oil, Money and Greed in the Twenty-First Century*. Harper, 2009.

Citino, Nathan J. *From Arab Nationalism to OPEC: Eisenhower, King Saʿūd, and the Making of U.S.-Saudi Relations*. Indiana University Press, 2002.

Cooper, Andrew Scott. *The Oil Kings: How the U.S., Iran, and Saudi Arabia Changed the Balance of Power in the Middle East*. Simon & Schuster, 2011.

McNally, Robert. *Crude Volatility: The History and the Future of Boom-Bust Oil Prices*. Columbia University Press, 2017.

Petrochemical Industry

Since the 1980s, the Saudi government has been undertaking various measures to develop its petrochemical industry and participate in the rising global demand for petrochemicals. This industry remains a lucrative venue, presenting various possibilities for Saudi Arabia's larger goals of diversifying its economy. Based on the data presented by the International Energy Agency (IEA) in 2018, it is expected that petrochemicals will be among the main sources of oil demand growth until at least 2040.

Although the chemical industry in Saudi Arabia was created later than most of its main competitors, it has been growing at a remarkably fast pace to become one of the pillars of the nation's economy. For example, in 2015, Saudi Arabia's exports of chemicals and plastics generated $30 billion, which amounts to an impressive 60 percent of non-oil exports. Between 2007 and 2015 alone, the capacity of the Saudi petrochemical industry increased from 51.2 million to 93.7 million tons a year—an 83 percent rise in just eight years.

Saudi Arabia succeeded in becoming the region's leading producer of ethylene—the main petrochemical building block. It produces over 17.2 million tons of ethylene yearly, more than double the volume of the second-biggest regional producer, Iran. Moreover, at the global level, Saudi Arabia maintains its third place in the amount of ethylene production, after the United States and China.

In 1976, the Saudi Arabian Basic Industries Corporation (SABIC) was established by a royal decree as the nation's centralized producer of chemicals, polymers, and fertilizers. By 2008, only two decades since its establishment, SABIC became the largest and most profitable non-oil company in Asia and the world's fourth-largest petrochemical company. In 2016, SABIC was the second-largest producer of ethylene globally, generating about 11 million tons on a yearly basis in its industrial facilities in Jubail and Yanbu.

A number of new projects are meant to support and further develop various branches within the petrochemical industry. The $20 billion Sadara, which means "forefront" in Arabic, was completed in 2017 and has become the world's largest chemicals complex built in a single phase. Located in Jubail and comprised of 26 plants, Sadara materialized as a result of a corporate alliance between Aramco and the U.S.-based Down Chemical Company. The complex will be generating over 3 million tons of production annually. In 2018, Saudi Arabia announced its plans to merge its oil giant Aramco with the petrochemicals conglomerate SABIC to solidify the relationship between the country's two core industries.

See also: Chapter 2: Discovery of Oil. Chapter 3: Gulf Cooperation Council. Chapter 4: Diversification and Development Plans; Oil Industry and Aramco; Vision 2030.

Further Reading

Al Zelabani, Abdulmonem, and Reji D. Nair. *Employee Empowerment and Job Satisfaction: A Case Study of Rc & Sabic.* LAP Lambert Academic Publishing, 2015.

Graves, Heather, and David E. Beard, eds. *The Rhetoric of Oil in the Twenty-First Century: Government, Corporate, and Activist Discourses.* Routledge, 2019.

Hambleton, H. G. "The Saudi Petrochemical Industry in the 1980s." *Saudi Arabia: Energy, Developmental Planning, and Industrialization.* Edited by Ragaei and D. H. El Mallakh. Lexington Books, 1982, pp. 51–75.

Pampanini, Andrea H. *Cities from the Arabian Desert: The Building of Jubail and Yanbu in Saudi Arabia*. Praeger, 1997.

Yamada, Makio. "Gulf-Asia Relations as 'Post-Rentier' Diversification? The Case of the Petrochemical Industry in Saudi Arabia." *Journal of Arabian Studies (Arabia, the Gulf, and the Red Sea)*, vol. 1, no. 1, 2011, pp. 99–116.

Public vs. Private Sectors

Saudi Arabia offers an interesting and perhaps unique case of the relationship between public and private sectors. The degree of the state involvement is unprecedented for a capitalist economy, which had both positive and negative consequences for the country's development. However, since the turn of the 21st century, there have been increased efforts to encourage the growth of the private sector. The most recent development plan, Saudi Vision 2030, emphasizes the importance of the private sector in Saudi Arabia's future.

The two largest companies and biggest contributors to the country's economy and the overall GPD are Aramco and SABIC, both owned by the Saudi government. Established in 1933, the Saudi Arabian Oil Company (Aramco) is the largest company in the kingdom and the largest oil company in the world. Although it was privately owned in the early phases of its history, it was fully nationalized in 1980. The company's headquarters are in Dhahran, as it manages over 100 oil fields throughout the country. The other national giant, the Saudi Basic Industries Corporation (SABIC), was established in 1976 and is currently a major world player in the petrochemical industry, including chemicals, industrial polymers, fertilizers, and metals. Its headquarters are in Riyadh, but most of the operations are managed from Jubail. In essence, SABIC is a diversified manufacturing company with additional holdings in hydrocarbon-based industries. Currently, it is the fourth-largest chemical producer in the world by chemical sales, which amount to over $37 million yearly, based on the 2017 numbers.

The national carrier Saudia Airlines (formerly Saudi Arabian Airlines), founded in 1945, is another important company owned by the state. The airline operates over 70 destinations worldwide, with the peak season falling on the time of the Hajj—the yearly Muslim pilgrimage to Mecca and Medina. In 2000, the government announced its plans for Saudia's privatization and in 2007, the first steps were undertaken to turn Saudia into a privatized corporation. There are plans to make several core services a part of a holding company, including cargo, ground services, catering, and the Prince Sultan Aviation Academy. In 2012, Saudia entered into the international SkyTeam airline alliance.

The Kingdom Holding Company is a semipublic holding and investment company founded in 1980, with its headquarters in the Kingdom Tower, a landmark in Riyadh. The company's chairman and CEO is Prince Walid bin al-Talal. The Kingdom Holding Company is known for its wide-scale and diverse investments in diverse areas of economy, including banking, real estate, IT, entertainment, telecommunications, tourism, and retail. In addition to being a major regional investor, the company invests in major international corporations, including eBay, Ford, Apple, and Pepsi. The Kingdom Holding Company is famous for hiring the country's first female commercial pilot, Captain Hanadi Zakaria al-Hindi, who received her training in Jordan. The Olayan Group is another major conglomerate, established in 1947. Its founder Sulaiman Olayan was considered one of the most successful Saudi executives, with private assets worth around $8 billion. The origins of this company can be traced to the General Constructing Company (GCC), which participated in the construction of the Trans-Arabian Pipeline. The Olayan Group actively invests internationally and is a major stockholder at Chase, Occidental, Saudi British Bank, and other major entities. It is also the distributer of Coca-Cola in Saudi Arabia.

Among Saudi Arabia's major construction companies, the Saudi Binladin Group (SBG) is perhaps the oldest and the most influential. It was established in 1931 by Sheikh Muhammed bin Laden, who had a close relationship with Saudi Arabia's founder, Ibn Saud. As a result of this relationship, he was able to secure a number of major government contracts, such as the renovation and expansion of the Islamic holy sites in Mecca and Medina. It is currently a multinational construction conglomerate, with headquarters in Jeddah. In 2011, the Binladen Group signed the contract to construct the world's first 1-km-tall building, Jeddah Tower in Jeddah. In 2018, the company's chairman Bakr bin Laden and his brothers transferred their stake in SBG to a holding company owned by the Ministry of Finance, which was a functional nationalization of the conglomerate.

In the agricultural sector, Almarai Company is a standout as the largest dairy company both in Saudi Arabia and the Middle East. It began its operations in 1976. The word *al-mara'i* in Arabic means "green pasture" and represents the company's vision of turning the desert into pasture. The company's headquarters are situated near the city of al-Kharj. It grew rapidly between 2006 and 2016 and currently has almost 40,000 employees. Among the main products of Almarai are milk, yogurt-like drink *laban*, sour cream *labanah*, different types of cheeses, fruit yogurts, juices, and other desserts. The company has its own fleet of refrigerated trucks that deliver to all other Gulf countries. In 2009, Almarai partnered with PepsiCo and acquired a number of large businesses in the subsequent years as a result of this partnership.

See also: Chapter 2: Discovery of Oil. Chapter 4: Diversification and Development Plans; Oil Industry and Aramco; Petrochemical Industry; Transportation; Vision 2030.

Further Reading

Abaker, Mohamed-Osman et al. "Organizational Policies and Diversity Management in Saudi Arabia." *Employee Relations*, vol. 41, no. 3, Apr. 2019, pp. 454–474.

Cowan, David. "Setting the Agenda for Global Dialogue: A Theoretical and Practical Approach to Business Ethics in Saudi Arabia." *Employment and Career Motivation in the Arab Gulf States: The Rentier Mentality Revisited*. Edited by Annika Kropf and Mohamed A. Ramady. Gerlach, 2015, pp. 264–279.

al-Hajjar, Bandar, and J. R. Presley. "Small Business in Saudi Arabia." *Business and Economic Development in Saudi Arabia: Essays with Saudi Scholars.* Edited by J. W. Wright. Macmillan, 1996, pp. 105–126.

Luciani, Giacomo. "From Private Sector to National Bourgeoisie: Saudi Arabian Business." *Saudi Arabia in the Balance: Political Economy, Society, Foreign Affairs.* Edited by Paul Aarts and Gerd Nonneman. Hurst, 2005, pp. 144–181.

Sadi, Muhammad Asad, and Basheer Mohammad al-Ghazali. "Doing Business with Impudence: A Focus on Women Entrepreneurship in Saudi Arabia." *African Journal of Business Management*, vol. 4, no. 1, 2010, pp. 1–11.

Shoult, Anthony. *Doing Business with Saudi Arabia.* 2nd ed. Kogan Page, 2002.

Saudization

Saudization is Saudi Arabia's official policy to replace foreign workers with nationals in the private sector. Currently, the country has between 5 and 6 million expatriates, many of whom are employed by private companies. Meanwhile, only about half a million of Saudis have jobs in the private sector. Since the 1980s, the government has been implementing various measures, policies, and fees to change this proportion, with mixed success. Various reasons contributed to the underemployment of Saudi nationals in private companies. Initially, there was a lack of skilled workers, which is being addressed by the massive investments in education and several educational reforms. However, there are persistent cultural stigmas and resistance to take blue-collar, service, or retail jobs, as they are considered inferior professions, especially for men. Finally, migrant workers obviously present a cheap workforce that many private companies prefer for economical reasons. Private entities often hesitate to hire Saudis because they increase the overall costs of employment due to higher wages. Additionally, in the case with female employees, the companies often have to incur additional expenses to provide gender segregation conditions at the workplace, as required by law. Under pressure from the government, some companies adapt partial Saudization, where they hire Saudis for positions in management, but some of their duties are performed by additionally hired foreign workers.

With every development plan, the Ministry of Labor continues to create new measures and issue guidelines in an attempt to increase the rate of Saudization in different industries. The current diversification and development plan, Saudi Vision 2030, which began in 2016, declared the substantial reduction of unemployment as its key objective. An important aspect of the new strategy is the creation of several important initiatives that should significantly increase the number of Saudi women in the workforce, both in private and public spheres.

Certain fields have a long-standing tradition to employ large numbers of foreigners. For example, many professional jobs, such as education, health care, and various professions in the oil industry, have always been dominated by foreigners. However, a number of recent positive developments showed that Saudization can indeed be successful. For instance, Aramco's efforts to employ larger numbers of Saudi professionals have resulted in a marked improvement of specialized higher education which, in turn, provides the industry with highly qualified workers and, increasingly, scientists and researchers. The opening of King Abdullah University of Science and Technology (KAST) promotes the idea of Saudization in the most effective way—not through the system of fees and penalties, but through providing the industries with Saudi professionals who have world-class training and abilities.

Growing numbers of Saudis are also entering the transportation industry, especially air transportation and related fields. The national carrier airline Saudia currently has an almost 100 percent Saudi workforce. Shortly after the government lifted the decades-long ban on women drivers, the Riyadh-based airline Flynas announced that it will be actively recruiting Saudi women to work as copilots and flight attendants. Additionally, increasing rates of national employment have been noted in the financial sector and tourism industry.

Nitaqat is a program introduced in 2011 within the Saudization policy, with the goal of increasing the employment of Saudis in various areas of the private sector. The program created a classification system, which divided all private companies into six categories: Platinum, High Green, Mid Green, Low Green, Yellow, and Red. The Platinum label was given to companies that had the highest numbers of employed Saudis, and the Red label was given to companies with the lowest employment rates of the nationals. The Nitaqat system imposes a number of penalties for employing foreign workers, but the severity of these sanctions is defined by the position of the company on the scale between Platinum and Red. For example, employers in the Platinum or Green zones are subject to more favorable conditions for visa requests and time frames for employing and sponsoring the expat workers. Those falling into the Yellow and Red zones have correspondingly stricter requirements and various limitations. Nitaqat requires employers of all private companies and businesses that have over 10 employees to hire a particular percentage of Saudi nationals. Specific percentages depend on the company's industry and the total number of employees in the company. In 2016, when Saudi Vision 2030 was set into motion, the government announced that a more balanced and nuanced version of Nitaqat would be implemented in the near future.

See also: Chapter 2: Discovery of Oil. Chapter 4: Migrant Workers and Unemployment; Oil Industry and Aramco; Vision 2030. Chapter 7: Gender Segregation; Women's Mobility and Driving Ban.

Further Reading

al-Asfour, A., and S. A. Khan. "Workforce Localization in the Kingdom of Saudi Arabia: Issues and Challenges." *Human Resource Development International*, vol. 17, no. 2, 2014, pp. 243–253.

Looney, Robert. "2 Saudization: A Useful Tool in the Kingdom's Battle against Unemployment?" *Journal of South Asian and Middle Eastern Studies*, vol. 27, no. 3, 2004, pp. 13–33.

Newbury-Smith, Tanya. "The Anthropological Elements of Failed Saudization: Historicism, Image, Islam and Tribe." *Employment and Career Motivation in the Arab Gulf States: The Rentier Mentality Revisited*. Edited by Annika Kropf and Mohamed A. Ramady. Gerlach, 2015, pp. 243–263.

Science and Technology

With the turn of the 21st century, Saudi Arabia established itself as one of the leading Arab countries in education, research, and technological innovation. As one of world's biggest oil producers, the country has been receiving substantial revenues from its exports, especially following the nationalization of its oil industry in the 1980s. For several decades, considerable portions of this revenue have been earmarked by the government to modernizing and improving all levels of education and, more recently, research. In the last decade, the government began investing in high-tech universities and laboratories. In recent years, the average share of the total government budget dedicated to education was 12 percent—one of the highest levels of education funding in the world. In 2019, it reached a new record when the government announced its plan to allocate 17.5 percent of its expenditure to education—the highest spending category on the national budget, exceeding the country's military spending.

Among Saudi Arabia's current objectives is to become not only a regional but a global research hub. The creation of the King Abdulaziz City for Science and Technology (KACST) has become an important milestone in this quest. KACST is an independent scientific organization that focuses on research and functions as Saudi Arabia's national science agency. Its leadership has a direct reporting line to the prime minister. KACST's main tasks are to propose and implement strategies and methods for the advancement of science and technology in Saudi Arabia. It also advises the government on various matters related to science.

King Abdullah University of Science and Technology (KAUST) is a private research university founded in 2009 in Thuwal, in the Mecca Province. Its main objective is to provide the highest level of postgraduate education and ample research opportunities for Saudi students. Among KAUST's global goals is to enter the world's top 10 science and technology universities. Its core campus—the first mixed-gender campus in the country—has various state- of-the-art facilities and labs, and some of the best faculty in the world. Among the points of interest that promote research and innovation are the fastest supercomputer in the Middle East, a marine sanctuary, and laboratories in such cutting-edge fields as nanofabrication, biotechnology, and photonics. KAUST ranks at the top of Saudi Arabia's universities and is the only one in the Arab world to be classified among the top 500 science institutions in the world.

In 2017, Nature Index published a supplement dedicated to Saudi Arabia, which highlighted the rapid ascent of the country's scientific output in the previous several years. This kind of data is collected through a special metric called weighted fractional count (WFC), which measures the level of contribution by tracking research publications in high-impact journals. In 2012, WFC measurement ranked Saudi Arabia in 39th place, but only four years later, in 2016, its ranking rose to 31, making it the most scientifically productive country in the region, after Israel. According to the WFC data, chemistry research currently takes the largest share in the country's scientific publications.

See also: Chapter 2: King Abdullah. Chapter 3: Political Reform and Modernization. Chapter 4: Diversification and Development Plans; Vision 2030. Chapter 8: Education of Women; Higher Education; Key Universities.

Further Reading

Jones, Toby Craig. "The Dogma of Development: Technopolitics and Power in Saudi Arabia." *Saudi Arabia in Transition: Insights on Social, Political, Economic and Religious Change.* Edited by Bernard Haykel, Thomas Hegghammer, and Stéphane Lacroix. Cambridge University Press, 2015, pp. 31–47.

Mansour, Nasser, and Saeed Al-Shamrani, eds. *Science Education in the Arab Gulf States: Visions, Sociocultural Contexts and Challenges.* Sense, 2015.

Ramady, M. A. *The Saudi Arabian Economy: Policies, Achievements and Challenges.* Springer, 2005.

Taxation

Saudi Arabia's tax system consists of three main categories: corporate income tax, withholding tax, and the charitable Zakat tax. The latter category is a religious tax, mandatory for all Saudi citizens, and constitutes 2.5 percent of their income and assets, except for real estate. Zakat is based on Sharia and is one of the five pillars of Islam, informed by the idea that one needs to give a portion of their wealth to charity, to support the poor and disadvantaged members of the Muslim community. Zakat is quite unique in the context of global taxation systems. Whereas in most other Muslim countries it is a voluntary contribution, Saudi Arabia is one of only few countries to make it a state-mandated withholding (other countries are Yemen, Sudan, Libya, Pakistan, and Malaysia). The overall taxation is overseen by the Department of Zakat and Income Tax.

Taxes also apply to business income. All foreigners, except for the Gulf Cooperation Council (GCC) citizens who have special privileges, pay taxes on business income that is calculated using the percentage they hold in a business. For example, in the case of a foreign-owned real estate that is rented out, the tax is calculated at 5 percent of the gross rental income. A capital gains tax on the sale of property is not collected from individuals. Corporate taxation is also based on the ownership of the entity—whether it is owned by Saudi nationals, GCC nationals, or other foreigners, as well as the corporation's profits. If a company is owned by anyone other than a Saudi citizen or a GCC national, it must pay a 25 percent tax on its profits—unless the company earns over 1 million Saudi riyals, in which case the tax rises to 30 percent. Additionally, it must pay capital gains tax. If a given corporation is based in GCC, then it pays a Zakat tax of 2.5 percent. Joint-venture companies are also subject to taxation, but they may be given a tax release by the government for up to five years. The agency responsible for promoting both foreign and domestic investments is the Saudi Arabian General Investment Authority (SAGIA). Taxes on capital gains are applied in the same manner as with all other income, at the rate of 20 percent for those individuals who are generally subject to tax in Saudi Arabia and if the gain comes from business-related activities. In 2013, the government introduced a monthly fee of 200 Saudi riyals per a foreign worker for companies that employ the higher percentage of expatriate workers than Saudi nationals.

See also: Chapter 3: Sharia Law and Judicial System. Chapter 4: Migrant Workers and Unemployment; Vision 2030. Chapter 5: Five Pillars or the Tenets of Islam.

Further Reading

Allami, Abdullah Wahib. "Zakat as Islamic Taxation and Its Application in the Contemporary Saudi Legal System." *Journal of Islamic State Practices in International Law*, vol. 5, no. 2, 2009, pp. 83–104.

Gundogdu, Ahmet Suayb. *A Modern Perspective of Islamic Economics and Finance*. Emerald Publishing Limited, 2019.

Hertog, Steffen. "Challenges to the Saudi Distributional State in the Age of Austerity." *Salman's Legacy: The Dilemmas of a New Era in Saudi Arabia*. Edited by Madawi Al-Rasheed. Oxford University Press, 2018, pp. 73–96.

Shoult, Anthony. *Doing Business with Saudi Arabia*. 2nd ed. Kogan Page, 2002.

Tourism

Saudi Arabia is the birthplace of Islam and has many other attractions—from picturesque nature habitats, including diverse desert landscapes, mountainous regions, and two coasts, to the many commercial attributes of a modern oil nation. The most unique aspect of Saudi Arabia is the cultural hybrid of the oil wealth and the vehemently preserved traditional character. Numerous restrictions make it difficult for ordinary tourists, especially women, to visit the country, but still over 6 million people come to Saudi Arabia annually. The vast majority of the visitors are pilgrims to the holy Islamic sites in Mecca and Medina.

Tourism is a very important aspect of the 21st-century Saudi economy. It currently constitutes about 20 percent of the country's non-oil GDP and 7 percent of total GDP. Experts estimate that the revenues from pilgrimage alone will reach $150 billion by 2022. Tourism constitutes 6 to 10 percent of the annual gross domestic product and generates over a million jobs. Although a substantial portion of these jobs are held by migrant workers, the government considers the tourism industry a rapidly developing sector that should help to lower unemployment and nationalize the workforce. Saudi

Arabia is a leading regional investor in tourism topping even Egypt. Pilgrimage visas have set numbers for each country that has Muslim population, totaling over 2 million visas per year. Visas of this type restrict the length of time a visitor can stay in the kingdom and the number of places one is allowed to visit. However, the Saudi Vision 2030 plan is set to dramatically increase the annual number of pilgrims to 30 million—or 15 times the current total—by 2030. Numerous projects in construction, transportation, and technology are under way to accomplish this ambitious goal.

Whereas receiving such a massive influx of visitors would present major challenges for any city, Saudi authorities are supporting pilgrimage with a solid infrastructure and numerous services. In addition to the growing number of hotels, massive tent cities are set up yearly for the pilgrims. The government also provides a number of other services, including free bottled water and special cleaning crews to keep the living areas clean. Many of the places visited by the pilgrims have been expanded and rebuilt and have new air conditioning systems. Numerous measures are taken both to provide overall security and to avoid the dangerous overcrowding and bottlenecks, which were the cause of accidents in the past. New overpasses and underpasses have been constructed, in addition to expanding popular public areas. For example, the always crowded Jamarat Bridge has been widened to 192 feet, and a second level has been added to improve the flow of foot traffic.

In addition to the booming religious tourism, Saudi Arabia receives a significant number of nonpilgrim tourists as well. These include Saudi nationals traveling and vacationing locally, visitors from the neighboring Gulf states and other Arab and non-Arab tourists and business travelers. In 1998, the Saudi government allowed foreign travel agencies to send small groups of Western tourists to Saudi Arabia. Vision 2030 plans to significantly grow the country's capacity for secular tourism by increasing the number of modern hotels, resorts, and various leisure activities, such as golf. The country aims to train a large number of specialists in the hospitality and tourism industry by creating new educational opportunities. In 2001, the Prince Sultan College for Tourism and Business opened its doors in Jeddah. Regional councils are established to promote tourism in conjunction with the central government agency, the Supreme Commission for Tourism (SCT), which was established in 2000. While Saudi government is exerting various central efforts to promote and develop tourism, it also promotes private investments, such as hotels and transportation options. Plans are under way to ease restrictions and simplify visa applications.

The growth of domestic tourism is one of the central goals of Saudi Arabia's economic development plans, highlighted in Vision 2030. Among the most popular domestic destinations are the city of Jeddah; Abha and the Asir Mountains; coastal resorts on the Red Sea and the Persian Gulf; and Nabatean ruins at Mada'in Salih. Abha alone receives half a million visitors annually, most of whom are Saudis from other regions, and earns an estimated $50 million of tourism income. The oil revenues enabled many Saudis to vacation in other countries. Still, an estimated 70 percent of the population prefer to spend their holidays within the country. In addition to the usual centers of religious tourism in Mecca and Medina, Saudi Arabia has a range of other places of interest in various parts of the country. These include the old Saudi capital Diriyah;

the city of Hufuf with its historical old wall and Ibrahim fortress; the palace and traditional towers of Najran; Dumat al-Jandal with the ancient Umar bin al-Khattab mosque; Ha'il with the old castle in the Barzan area; among others. Popular summer resorts are located in Ta'if, which is also the usual summer retreat of the royal family. Despite the common belief that Saudi Arabia's environment is limited to deserts, the country has a variety of natural sceneries, including Abha and Baha in the Asir Mountains, the picturesque coasts of the Red Sea and the Persian Gulf, as well as the stunning red sand dunes near Riyadh. Numerous sea resorts with beautiful beaches are located north of Jeddah and south of Khobar.

The booming hotel industry in the kingdom continues to expand at a stunning rate, particularly in Mecca and Medina. Traditionally, the hotels in Saudi Arabia catered to the pilgrims and business tourists, but in recent years various facilities are being built to accommodate the needs of local tourism. Most hotels are operated by international chains. Outside of Mecca and Medina, the highest concentration of hotel industry is in Abha, Khamis Mushayit, and al-Namas—all located in the Asir region, which has the mildest climate compared to the rest of the country.

Summer festivals, which combine cultural entertainment, leisure activities, shopping, and sporting events, have become a big attraction to local tourists. The largest and longest of them is the Abha Summer Festival, but many other cities have similar events, including Jeddah, Medina, Buraydah, and many locations throughout the Eastern Province. Traditional weekend-long desert trips remain popular among many families.

See also: Chapter 1: Asir; Jeddah; Mecca; Medina; The Persian Gulf; The Red Sea; Riyadh. Chapter 4: Migrant Workers and Unemployment; Transportation; Vision 2030. Chapter 5: Hajj. Chapter 6: Urbanization. Chapter 15: Popular Consumerism.

Further Reading

Jamal, Ahmad, et al., eds. *Islamic Tourism: Management of Travel Destinations.* CABI, 2018.

Korstanje, Maximiliano, ed. *Risk and Safety Challenges for Religious Tourism and Events.* CABI, 2018.

Raj, Razaq, and Kevin Griffin, eds. *Religious Tourism and Pilgrimage Management: An International Perspective.* 2nd ed. CABI, 2015.

Scott, Noel, and Jafar Jafari. *Tourism in the Muslim World.* 1st ed. Emerald, 2010.

Stephenson, Marcus L., and Ala Al-Hamarneh, eds. *International Tourism Development and the Gulf Cooperation Council States: Challenges and Opportunities.* Routledge, 2017.

Trade and Exports

In December 2005, Saudi Arabia joined the World Trade Organization, which had a positive effect on the increase of the country's exports and imports and the overall trade agreements and infrastructure. In the last two decades, the kingdom has been consistently receiving high ranking for economic development. It is the 26th-largest economy in the world. In the 2010 report issued by the International Finance Corporation, Saudi Arabia was placed 13th on the list of the most economically competitive countries globally. Saudi Arabia's trade is robust: it is estimated that in 2017 it exported over $170 billion worth of goods.

Although the country has been exerting significant efforts to diversify its economy, this process, while largely successful, will take time. Currently, Saudi Arabia remains one of the main producers and exporters of oil and petroleum products globally. It is the second-largest oil producer in the world, after Russia. Naturally, the bulk of Saudi Arabia's exports continues to focus on oil and related industries, such as petrochemicals, which account for nearly 90 percent of the total revenues from exports. All of the top 10 exports are related to petroleum and, in turn, account for almost 95 percent of the total value of the country's international shipments.

Despite the obvious dominance of the oil industry in Saudi trade, other industries are gradually picking up the pace due to the government's wide-ranging efforts to diversify the economy. The fastest-growing export product among the top 10 categories is vehicles, whereas organic chemicals is the second in export growth. Mineral fuel products occupy the third place: they were up by 26 percent in value according to the 2017 numbers.

Saudi Arabia and the United States have long-standing trade relations, with the total trade volume between the two countries estimating at over $48 billion in 2018, of which U.S. exports were $22.4 billion and imports were $25.7 billion. In that year, Saudi Arabia was the United States' 20th-largest supplier of imported goods. Historically, trade agreements between the two countries have been a politically sensitive matter, as they focused on oil from Saudi Arabia and arms and weapons from the United States. The latter category includes the historic arms deal signed in 2017 by President Trump and King Salman, which outlined Saudi Arabia's intent to purchase $110 billion worth of arms from the United States, and another $350 billion over the following 10 years. The agreement drew wide criticism, particularly due to Saudi Arabia's ongoing military aggression in Yemen and the resulting humanitarian crisis.

The top 10 export categories of Saudi products in 2017 were as follows:

- Mineral fuels including oil: US$170.2 billion (77.4 percent of total exports)
- Plastics: $17 billion (7.7 percent)
- Organic chemicals: $9.8 billion (4.4 percent)
- Ships and boats: $2.2 billion (1 percent)
- Aluminum: $2.1 billion (1 percent)
- Vehicles: $1.6 billion (0.7 percent)
- Machinery: $1.6 billion (0.7 percent)
- Dairy, eggs, and honey: $1.1 billion (0.5 percent)
- Electrical machinery and equipment: $1.1 billion (0.5 percent)
- Gems and precious metals: $934.8 million (0.4 percent)

See also: Chapter 3: Saudi–U.S. Relations. Chapter 4: Agriculture; Oil Industry and Aramco; Petrochemical Industry.

Further Reading

al-Aali, Abdurahman Yousef. "Saudi Arabian Export Strategy: A Micro-Level Analysis." *Business and Economic Development in Saudi Arabia: Essays with Saudi Scholars.* Edited by J. W. Wright. Macmillan, 1996, pp. 152–169.

Luciani, Giacomo. "From Price Taker to Price Maker? Saudi Arabia and the World Oil Market." *Saudi Arabia in Transition: Insights on Social, Political, Economic and Religious Change.* Edited by Bernard Haykel, Thomas Hegghammer, and Stéphane Lacroix. Cambridge University Press, 2015, pp. 71–96.

Transportation

The oil boom and the subsequent economic growth initiated many ambitious development projects in Saudi Arabia. Creating a modern and efficient transportation network to support the booming economy has quickly become a priority. Saudi roads range from eight-lane highways in urban centers to two-lane roads in rural areas, but all of them are well maintained. Due to environmental conditions, roads are built with materials that can resist the extreme temperatures. In 2018, a decision was made to increase the speed limit 75 to 87 miles an hour on the four main Saudi motorways—Riyadh-Dammam, Riyadh-Gassim, Riyadh-Taif, and Mecca-Medina—that connect the country's metropolises. In 2013, a group of auto enthusiasts drove around all of Saudi Arabia's major roads in search of the best driving road and ended up choosing the Jeddah-Taif-Al-Hada highway as the country's "motoring nirvana."

The General Authority of Civil Aviation (GACA) is the national organization that administrates all aviation-industry matters in the Kingdom of Saudi Arabia. GACA owns and operates domestic and international airports in Saudi Arabia and is responsible for all air traffic control, safety, IT, finance, operations, and development matters in the country. Saudi Arabia has 26 airports that offer commercial services. According to the 2017 numbers, the airports of Jeddah, Riyadh, Dammam, and Medina handled over 80 million passengers throughout the year. Jeddah Airport, the nation's busiest, reportedly handled 34 million passengers in 2017—an increase of 9 percent from the previous year. Riyadh is the largest city in Saudi Arabia but has approximately 20 percent less traffic than Jeddah due to the latter's servicing the pilgrims coming to Mecca and Medina.

Saudi Arabia currently has five airlines—Saudia, Flynas, Flyadeal, SaudiGulf, and Nesma Airlines—compared to two airlines only a few years ago. The biggest carrier, Saudia, is government-owned and was previously known as Saudi Arabian Airlines. It is based in Jeddah but has another major hub in Riyadh. Saudi Arabia's largest private airline, Flynas, is based in Riyadh and has almost as much capacity in Jeddah. Saudia and Flynas did not have any competition in Saudi Arabia until 2016, when Nesma Airlines and SaudiGulf Airlines launched operations. SaudiGulf is based in Dammam but has more capacity at Riyadh, where it operates its only international route. Flyadeal is the newest Saudi airline, which began operations in 2017 and is based in Jeddah. It

Saudi Arabian Airlines Boeing 777 landing at Washington Dulles International Airport in Virginia, USA. (Joe Ravi/Dreamstime.com)

is owned by Saudia and serves as the latter's budget alternative. Growing competition among airlines has led to a noticeable lowering of airfares.

The development of tourism and aviation are among the core components of the Vision 2030 reform plan, as Saudi Arabia aims to liberalize and diversify its economy. Airlines of all types will likely benefit as the aviation market opens up and grows rapidly over the next several years, driven by surging numbers of both pilgrims and secular tourists. Business travel to Saudi Arabia is also expected to increase, as Saudi Arabia works to diversify its economy under the government's Vision 2030 reform plan. Among current initiatives undertaken by the government to further stimulate aviation and tourism are an ambitious expansion plan at the flag carrier Saudia and the opening of a gigantic new terminal at the Jeddah Airport.

The first railway in Saudi Arabia was the historic Hejaz Railway, stretching from the border of Jordan to Medina. This railway opened in 1908 and played an important role in the Arab Revolt of 1916–1918, but it was closed down in 1920. Currently, the central company that operates the country's rail network is the Saudi Railways Organization (SRO), which is owned by the state. There are two main lines: a passenger line and a freight line, both connecting Riyadh with Dammam. However, several large-scale expansion projects are now under way, initiated by the Saudi Railway Master Plan, which aims to develop the country's rail system and train transport by 2040. The main development projects within the plan are Saudi Landbridge to connect the country's two coasts; a new line stretching from the north to the south; and the Haramain High

Speed Rail Project to build a high-speed rail line, linking Mecca and Medina with the rest of the network at Jeddah. The latter would be providing additional transportation options for the pilgrims, in line with the government's ambitious plan to increase the annual number of pilgrims from 2 to 30 million by 2030. There is also the Gulf Cooperation Council (GCC) Railway Project under construction, which would create an extensive railway network between all GCC countries.

Saudi Arabia also has a well-developed system of sea transportation, which primarily supports the transport of petrochemical freights. The country's main ports on the Persian Gulf include the King Abdul Aziz Port in Dammam and ports in Jubail, Ras Tanura, Khafji, and Khobar. The main Red Sea ports are Jeddah, Yanbu' al-Bahr, al-Lith, Duba, Rabigh, and Jizan. Ports are centrally managed by the Saudi Ports Authority.

See also: Chapter 4: Public vs. Private Sectors; Tourism; Vision 2030. Chapter 5: Hajj.

Further Reading

Covington, Richard. "Roads of Arabia." *Saudi Aramco World*, vol. 62, no. 2, 2011, pp. 24–35.

Ekiz, Erdogan H., et al. "Tourism Development in the Kingdom of Saudi Arabia: Determining the Problems and Resolving the Challenges." *International Tourism Development and the Gulf Cooperation Council States: Challenges and Opportunities*. Edited by Marcus L. Stephenson and Ala Al-Hamarneh. Routledge, 2017, pp. 124–139.

Vision 2030

Saudi Vision 2030 is Saudi Arabia's most recent development plan. It was announced on April 25, 2016, by Crown Prince Muhammad bin Salman, who is credited for conceptualizing and spearheading the initiative. The three main objectives of Vision 2030 are (1) to reduce the country's dependence on oil and oil-based industries, (2) to diversify and expand its economy, and (3) to transform the sphere of public service. The latter category includes further investments into education at all levels, to make it competitive at the global level. The health and recreation sectors are due for a major overhaul, with the goal of improving the overall well-being and the quality of life for all Saudi citizens. The development of sports is set as a priority, both to raise the country's profile in international sports competitions and to improve the physical fitness of Saudis, who currently have some of the lowest rates of physical activity compared to other countries.

The main objective of Vision 2030 remains the reduction of Saudi Arabia's dependency on oil and oil-based industries. Decreasing its dependency on oil resources has been the government's priority since the 1970s, but the actual implementation of this goal has been uneven and contingent on the constantly fluctuating global oil prices. Even after following decades-long efforts to diversify economy and invest in various non-oil sectors of the economy, oil still comprises about 40 percent of Saudi

Arabia's GDP and accounts for almost 90 percent of the country's budget revenues. Vision 2030's central priority is to create various alternative sources of revenue. The plan also aims to lower the citizens' dependency on public spending and to encourage the private sector to substantially increase employment opportunities for Saudis. Other important goals include increased spending on the military, increased non-oil trade with other countries, and the growth of manufacturing industries.

The public announcement of Vision 2030 presents three main goals that have to do with the reconceptualization of Saudi Arabia's identity and its international status. The first of these is reinforcing the country's position as "the heart of the Arab and Islamic worlds." The implementation of this goal includes continued efforts to modernize the country's society, focusing on urbanization; increased accessibility for tourists (both religious and secular) and creation of new facilities and places of interest; the improvement of the overall social infrastructure for Saudi citizens; and the growth of domestic opportunities for leisure, entertainment, recreation, and sports. The second announced concept is to transform Saudi Arabia into a global investment powerhouse. To achieve this goal, the government plans to put forward various measures to support non-oil economy, increase the participation of women in the workforce, encourage foreign direct investment, and further develop the private sector. The third and final concept behind Vision 2030 is to transform the country's location into a hub connecting the three continents of Asia, Europe, and Africa. This ambitious objective supports all of the aforementioned goals and is meant to create a sense of unity and pride within Saudi society, while encouraging all citizens to work toward achieving its goals.

Led by Crown Prince Muhammad bin Salman and his cabinet, the implementation of Vision 2030 is overseen by a special group at the National Center for Performance Measurement, the Delivery Unit, and the Project Management Office of the Council of Economic and Development Affairs. The plan is set for completion in 2030.

See also: Chapter 3: Political Reform and Modernization. Chapter 4: Diversification and Development Plans.

Further Reading

Albassam, Bassam A. "Economic Diversification in Saudi Arabia: Myth or Reality?" *Resources Policy*, vol. 44, 2015, pp. 112–117.

al-Rasheed, Madawi. *Contesting the Saudi State: Islamic Voices from a New Generation.* Cambridge University Press, 2007.

al-Rasheed, Madawi, ed. *Salman's Legacy: The Dilemmas of a New Era in Saudi Arabia.* Oxford University Press, 2018.

CHAPTER 5

RELIGION AND THOUGHT

OVERVIEW

It is impossible to talk about any aspects of Saudi society, culture, or governance without invoking the religion of Islam. Since its birth in the 7th century AD, Islam continues to have a profound impact on the lives of contemporary Saudis. To understand Saudi culture, society, and political life, one needs to understand the rudiments of the Muslim religion, its history, and its practical application in the kingdom. In Arabic, "Islam" means "submission," implying the complete submission to one and only God. This word is also closely linked to "salam," which means "peace"—"Islam" and "salam" both come from the Arabic root *sa-la-ma*. An adherent of Islam, Muslim, literally means "the one who submits to the will of God."

Despite the fact that Islam was spread by means of military campaigns, the actual teachings of the Quran were quite liberal for the time and were interpreted and practiced with great tolerance. Instead of denying the validity of other monotheistic religions, namely, Christianity and Judaism, Islam was built on them and incorporated many of their elements and practices. Abraham, Moses, and Jesus are seen as the prophets of God, with one major difference where Jesus is seen as a prophetic and not divine figure, given Islam's emphasis on oneness of God. The main Islamic prophet, Muhammad, preached that he himself was the last one of the four great prophets who were chosen to bring the divine word to humanity. Old and New Testaments of the Bible are considered divine revelations as well, where the Quran openly builds on them. Islam shares many of the Christian and Judaic concepts, such as the Judgement Day, resurrection, and heaven and hell. Thus, Christians and Jews are seen as part of the religious brotherhood and, together with Muslims, are referred to by the Quran as *ahl al-kitab*, or "People of the Book."

The Arabian Peninsula is the cradle of Islam. It is where Muhammad was born, where he received his revelations (in Mecca and Medina), and where he built a community of followers, whose numbers spread at an unprecedented rate in a matter of decades. The fact that contemporary Saudi Arabia contains the holiest sites in Islam gives it an extraordinary religious importance for Muslims across the world. The Arabian Peninsula was the birthplace of one of the greatest empires in history—the Islamic Empire—which spread through several continents and delivered Islamic teachings to many nations and communities.

The founder of the state Ibn Saud's focus on the religious teachings of Abd al-Wahhab as the official doctrine of the kingdom has uniquely shaped the development and the national character of the country. All spheres of Saudi life—the country's governance and legal system, its societal infrastructure and culture—are influenced by the Wahhabi vision of Islam. These teachings are a part of the Sunni Hanbali school of thought and its followers consider their beliefs and practices to be the single correct version of Islam, to the extreme that they exclude all other forms and denominations within the Islamic tradition. It is important to note that Islam as a whole is not represented by the Wahhabi movement, which is one of many branches of Islam. In fact, the absolute majority of Muslims worldwide do not adhere to these teachings. However, when Muslim pilgrims visit the sacred sites of Mecca and Medina, they must observe the rules of behavior as taught by Abd al-Wahhab because these sites are under Saudi guardianship.

The absolute majority of Saudi residents are Sunni Muslims, although several important Shia communities remain in Saudi Arabia; the most prominent ones are in the Eastern Province and the Hijaz. Irreligion in Saudi Arabia is difficult to measure as it is illegal to leave the Islamic faith in the country. Apostasy is punishable by death in Saudi Arabia. In March 2014, the Ministry of the Interior issued a decree branding all atheists as terrorists.

Further Reading

Ali, Kecia, and Oliver Leaman. *Islam: The Key Concepts*. Routledge, 2008.

Alshamsi, Mansoor Jassem. *Islam and Political Reform in Saudi Arabia: The Quest for Political Change and Reform*. Routledge, 2011.

Black, Antony. *The History of Islamic Political Thought: From the Prophet to the Present*. 2nd ed. Edinburgh University Press, 2011.

Commins, David Dean. *The Wahhabi Mission and Saudi Arabia*. I. B. Tauris, 2006.

Commins, David Dean, and Malise Ruthven. *Islam in Saudi Arabia*. Cornell University Press, 2015.

Five Pillars or the Tenets of Islam

Islam requires that all believers perform five major duties that demonstrate belonging to the community. These are called five pillars of faith or five tenants of Islam, and are as follows:

1. Testimony, or declaration of faith (*shahadah*)
2. Prayer (*salat*) at five prescribed times during the day
3. Almsgiving (*zakat*)
4. Fasting from dawn to dusk during the month of Ramadan (*siyam*)
5. Pilgrimage (*hajj*) to Mecca once during a lifetime, if it is possible

These are required of all Muslims no matter if they are Sunni, Shia, or Kharaji. The Declaration of Faith is comprised of the statement "there is no god but God, and

Muhammad is the Messenger of God." To say this simple phrase in front of witnesses is to declare allegiance to Islam, and this short, simple phrase delivers the two fundamental elements of Islam. Monotheism is a central concept of Islam. The Quran establishes that God has no partner and is eternal; neither begotten nor does he beget. This proclamation is particularly clear in one of the most important chapters of the Quran, Surat al-Ikhlas (Chapter 112). When Muslims make the pilgrimage to Mecca, they recite a line that says there is no god, but God and he has no partners or companions. The second part of the Declaration of Faith is to acknowledge that Muhammad is the prophet of God. Muhammad is also often referred to as the Seal of the Prophets (*Khatam al-Anbiya'*), meaning that he is the last in the long line of prophets.

Shia Muslims add another line to the Declaration of Faith, which states that Ali—one of the first caliphs and a close companion of Muhammad—is the friend of God (*wa Ali waliyu 'llah*). This addition illustrates the core difference between Sunni and Shia denominations in Islam. Sunni teachings view Ali ibn Abi Talib as an exemplary man who was among the first converts to Islam and the fourth—and last—Righteous Caliph, but he is not considered to have a separate religious significance. Shia Muslims, on the contrary, give particular prominence to Ali and emphasize his lineage from Muhammad, as Ali was his cousin and son-in-law. He was the husband of Muhammad's daughter Fatimah Zahra and the father of his grandchildren, Hasan and Hussein, who according to Shia beliefs, are the rightful heirs of the prophet's political and religious authority.

Muslims are expected to pray five times a day in the direction of Mecca, following *qiblah* (the orientation of the prayer). Originally, Muhammad instructed his followers to pray facing Jerusalem, but in a later revelation found in Surat al-Baqarah (Chapter 2 of the Quran) the direction was changed to Mecca and the Kaaba. It is believed that the first Kaaba was built by Ibrahim (Abraham) and his son Ismail (Ishmael), following God's command to sacrifice Ismail. According to the tradition, God sent an angel to stop Ibrahim's hand, and a lamb was substituted for the boy. Following the sacrifice of the lamb, the two men set about building the first house of worship to the one God. Muslims believe that God set the five times for prayer: dawn (*fajr*), noon (*dhuhr*), mid-afternoon (*'asr*), dusk (*maghrib*), and nighttime (*'asha*). Prayer times are announced by a call for prayer, *adhan*, which is announced from a minaret or from the roof of the mosque by a person, *muadhdhin*, whose job is specifically to do the call.

Each of the prayers is composed of several prostrations called *ruka'*, which vary according to the time of day. Each of these is composed of nine attitudes of prayer: from standing straight with the arms usually folded across the chest, bending at the waist, kneeling on the ground, placing the forehead on the ground with the palms of the hands flat, rising back up to the kneeling position with the feet folded underneath, and standing again. Different Sunni schools teach slightly different ways of doing these movements. As for the Shiites, they place their foreheads on a round, flat ceramic disk that contains dirt from Najaf or Karbala, where Imam Ali ibn Abi Talib and his son Hussein are buried.

> **ADHAN: MUSLIM CALL FOR PRAYER**
>
> Once the first mosque was created in Medina by Muhammad and his followers, a method of announcing prayer times needed to be developed. One of Muhammad's followers saw in a dream that the call for prayer should be vocalized by a human voice. Bilal—a former slave and one of the first Muslims—was chosen for this role due to his beautiful voice. The call for prayer was termed *adhan* (from the verb "to listen, to hear") and the person who does the calling is *muadhdhin*. The call to prayer states "God is Great. I witness that there is no god but God and I witness that Muhammad is the Messenger of God. Come to prayer. Come to success. God is Great. I witness there is no god but God."
>
> Bilal began the tradition of announcing the call to prayer from a rooftop but, as Islam spread, the number of Muslims grew and required a more effective method to assure that large numbers of people can hear adhan clearly. Thus, the idea of building a special tower appeared. The first minarets were built around 673. In modern times, large loudspeakers are usually used to announce adhan, which became a distinct feature of Muslim cities throughout the world.

Traditionally, almsgiving has taken two forms. At the end of Ramadan, those who can, are expected to give one-tenth of their wealth to the poor, called *zakat*. Anonymity is an important part of this practice, where the giver and the receiver are not known to each other, in order to preserve honor and dignity of everyone involved. Those giving should not become proud and boastful of their actions, and those receiving should not be made to feel indebted. In Saudi Arabia, *zakat* is also a mandatory tax of 2.5 percent of one's worth, collected by the government and then distributed according to the community needs. The second form of almsgiving is called *sadaqat*, which is a charitable contribution to those in need.

Fasting is done during the month of Ramadan from dawn to dusk by all Muslims that have reached a certain age and who are physically able. Pregnant women, the sick, injured, travelers, and many others are exempted from fasting, although many fast anyway. During the daytime one should not eat, drink, smoke, or allow anything to pass the lips. In Saudi Arabia, the fast is imposed on everyone in all public places. Fasting is not required of non-Muslims, but anyone not fasting should consume food and drinks in their privacy. The daytime fast breaks at the sunset, with the *maghrib* call to prayer. Traditionally, people break the fast with milk and dates or a special drink made of water, dates, dried fruit, and nuts. This is followed by a generous meal. The fast-breaking meal is called *iftar*. Another meal, *suhur*, is eaten in the night, just before the sunrise and the *fajr* prayer.

The last required practice is the pilgrimage to Mecca. Although this is seen as an obligation for Muslims, there is a provision that the pilgrims should be physically and financially able to travel to the holy sites. There are two different types of pilgrimage. The Umrah, or the so-called "lesser pilgrimage," can be done at any time of year. The Hajj, or main pilgrimage, should be performed over the first 10 days of the month Dhu al-Hijjah, or the Month of Pilgrimage, which is the last month of the Muslim calendar. Most of the steps in the Hajj take place during the first nine days and follow those first set out by the Prophet Muhammad. On the tenth day, the main Islamic holiday Eid al-Adha (Feast of Sacrifice) takes place, where Muslims follow the example of Ibrahim and sacrifice a sheep.

All Muslim males are circumcised following the example of Ibrahim and the Abrahamic traditions. Circumcision is considered an act of purification, and although *khitan* is the Arabic word for circumcision, the word *mudhahir* (literally "purified") is often used instead. It is held that for a male to open and read the Quran, he should already be circumcised. As a result, the general practice is that boys should be circumcised while they are still very young. Female circumcision seems to have been introduced to the Arabian Peninsula from the Horn of Africa or the Sudan, where the practice is widespread among all religions. Female circumcision is not part of Islamic practice and is not endorsed by Islamic scholars, yet it remains a practice perpetuated by women in some parts of the peninsula.

See also: Chapter 2: Muhammad, Prophet of Islam; The Rise of Islam. Chapter 3: Sharia Law and Judicial System. Chapter 4: Taxation; Tourism. Chapter 5: Hajj; Islamic Calendar; Quran. Chapter 10: Dress Etiquette; Workweek and Holidays. Chapter 14: Islamic Dietary Laws.

Further Reading

Dupret, Baudouin, and Aga Khan University. *Ethnographies of Islam: Ritual Performances and Everyday Practices*. Edinburgh University Press, 2012.

Farsy, Fouad. *Modernity and Tradition: The Saudi Equation*. Kegan Paul International, 1990.

Murata, Sachiko, and William Chittick. *The Vision of Islam*. Paragon House, 1994.

Hajj

The pilgrimage, or Hajj, to Mecca is one of the five main obligations of all Muslims. The Hajj takes place annually during the first weeks of Dhu al-Hijjah, the 12th month of the Islamic calendar. The form of today's pilgrimage was set in 630 by the Prophet Muhammad and revolves around several events and acts of Ibrahim (Abraham), his son Ismail (Ishmael), and his slave and Ismail's mother Hajar (Hagar).

When the pilgrims approach the *haram*, the sacred area of Mecca, they are expected to enter the state of ritual purity, which is physically marked by bathing, trimming their nails and hair, and removing all jewelry and other signs of economic or class differences. They then change into a two-piece plain, white, seamless garb called an *ihram*. One piece is wrapped around the waist and the second covers the upper body. Once this is done, the pilgrims announce their intention to make the pilgrimage by declaring the *talbiyah*—the statement *labayk Allahumma labayk* ("God, I am at your service"). They then proceed to the city of Mecca and the Great Mosque that contains the Kaaba.

A Muslim man wearing *ihram* clothes and ready to take part in the Hajj. (Hikrcn/Dreamstime.com)

Muslims believe that Ibrahim and his son Ismail built the Kaaba as the first place of worship for the one God, following Ibrahim's sacrifice. Muslims circumambulate the Kaaba seven times in a counterclockwise motion, which is called *tawaf*. Following this, they then run between al-Safa and al-Marwa in what is called *sa'y* or running in imitation of Hajar, as she ran between the two low hills looking for water for her young son Ismail. Hajar was forced to leave Ibrahim by his wife Sarah when Ismail was still a small child. Hajar and Ismail were near death from thirst, and out of despair she kept running between the two hills, until an angel came to her and opened up the spring Zamzam to save them.

The Hajj or actual act of pilgrimage begins on the eighth day of the month, when all of the people proceed from Mecca to Mina following the practice of the prophet. The pilgrims spend the night at Mina in meditation and on the next day collectively move to Arafat, located 9 miles (15 kilometers) outside of Mecca. Here they perform what is called the *wuquf*, or standing at the foot of Jabal Rahmah (the Mount of Mercy), where Muhammad gave his farewell sermon. The pilgrims remain at Arafat from noon until sunset in prayer, following the hadith of the prophet, which says "The best prayers are those said on the day of Arafat." Many are overcome by the deep spiritual feelings they have while at Arafat. After sundown, they proceed on to Muzdalifah, which is located 4 miles back along the way to Mecca, where they spend the night. The following day, they continue their way back to Mina, passing by the three columns that represent evil.

Pilgrims throw seven stones at each of the pillars, renouncing the Devil and evil with each throw.

Once back at Mina, the Feast of the Sacrifice, or Eid al-Adha, begins with slaughtering of animals such as camels, sheep, and goats, to commemorate Ibrahim's sacrifice of a lamb in place of his son Ismail, according to the Muslim tradition. The custom is that only one-third of the animal is consumed on the day, and the rest is given away to the poor who cannot afford to buy an animal. Those pilgrims who have not yet performed the *tawaf* and *sa'y,* return to Mecca and complete the required actions of the pilgrimage.

Organization of the annual Hajj is a massive undertaking that requires the management of around 2 million people. In the past, before mass transportation, the number of pilgrims was limited by the fact that the journey was long and physically exhausting. For those who could not afford the long journey to Mecca, local pilgrimages emerged to take the place of the official Hajj. With the availability of mass transportation, the number of pilgrims exploded beyond the means of the local authorities. Prompted by the need to better manage services and to reduce the accidents that still plague the Hajj, the Saudi authorities are constantly implementing new measures.

Pilgrims are encouraged to stay in national groups, so that issues of language can be addressed. The government employs a great number of crowd-control police officers and provides multilingual guides who help the pilgrims through each of the steps of a successful pilgrimage. Special services are offered to the elderly and pilgrims with disabilities, to ensure that they participate in every step of the Hajj successfully. There are 14 hospitals dedicated to serving the pilgrims.

Performing the pilgrimage to Mecca and Medina requires wearing specific ritual garments to reflect on the spiritual status of *ihram*. The pilgrim takes a bath and puts on two clean, unstitched and seamless pieces of white cloth. The upper cloth is called *rida* and is draped over the left shoulder leaving the right shoulder bare. The lower cloth is *izar* and is worn wrapped around the waist. No headgear is permitted, except an umbrella. All male Muslims are required to wear this special clothing; no other garment is worn during the Hajj. Only in very cold weather conditions, the pilgrims are allowed to cover up with a blanket. Women can dress in their regular clothes, but should not cover their faces. This type of religious dress has not changed since the implementation of the first pilgrimage rules by the Prophet Muhammad.

See also: Chapter 1: Mecca; Medina. Chapter 2: The Golden Age of Islam in Arabia; Muhammad, Prophet of Islam; Pre-Islamic Arabia; The Rise of Islam; Sharifs of Mecca. Chapter 4: Tourism; Transportation. Chapter 5: Five Pillars or the Tenets of Islam; Islamic Calendar; Quran. Chapter 6: Urbanization. Chapter 10: Dress Etiquette; Workweek and Holidays. Chapter 12: Great Mosque of Mecca; Modernization of Saudi Architecture.

Further Reading

Faroqhi, Suraiya. *Pilgrims and Sultans: The Hajj under the Ottomans, 1517–1683*. I. B. Tauris, 1994.

McMillan, M. E. *The Meaning of Mecca: The Politics of Pilgrimage in Early Islam.* Saqi Books, 2011.

Peters, F. E. *The Hajj: The Muslim Pilgrimage to Mecca and the Holy Places.* Princeton University Press, 1994.

Ryad, Umar, ed. *The Hajj and Europe in the Age of Empire.* Brill, 2017.

Islamic Calendar

The recorded history of the Arabian Peninsula is riddled with large gaps, but from an Islamic perspective, it is clearly divided into two periods. With striking similarity to the way the Christian calendar divides history into the age before Christ and the age after Christ, the Islamic, or Hijrah, calendar divides it into the period before the birth of Islam, called Jahiliyah (literally "the Age of Ignorance"), and the period after the birth of Islam. In 622 AD, Muhammad and his followers emigrated from Mecca to Medina because of the ongoing persecution of the young Muslim community. The journey is called the *hijrah* (migration) and marks the beginning of the Hijrah calendar. The Islamic calendar is a lunar calendar based on the cycles of the moon phase.

The Islamic year has 12 months: Muharram, Safar, Rabi' al-Awwal, Rabi' al-Thani, Jumada al-Awwal, Jumada al-Thani, Rajab, Sha'aban, Ramadan, Shawwal, Dhu al-Qa'idah, and Dhu al-Hijjah. The months begin when the first crescent of a new moon is sighted. Each month consists of 29 to 30 days, which makes the Islamic year 11 to 12 days shorter than the solar year. Islamic dates migrate through the year. Like solar calendars, it follows the seven-day week concept. All Islamic celebrations, such as the Hajj, or Great Pilgrimage to Mecca, and the month of Ramadan are determined by the Islamic calendar. Ramadan is the 9th and Dhu al-Hijja is the 12th month of this calendar. On the 10th of Dhu al-Hijja, Muslims celebrate their most important holiday, the Eid al-Adha.

The other major holiday is Eid al-Fitr at the end of Ramadan. The feast is actually celebrated on the first day of Shawwal. Most Islamic countries observe Mawlid al-Nabi, the birthday of the Prophet Muhammad, on the 12th day of Rabi' al-Awal as a state holiday, but Saudi clerics consider this holiday idolatrous (for it is celebrating a human being instead of God) and it is banned. Shia Muslims consider the 10th of Muharram equally important, when they commemorate Ashurah, the death of Hussein bin Ali in 680 at the Battle of Karbala, Iraq.

In pre-Islamic Arabia, an intercalary system based on seasons, particularly the rainy season, was in use, but later was prohibited by Muhammad on the basis of divine revelation. He introduced a new model that was very similar to the previous one. For example, it continued the rule of four holy months in which fighting was prohibited.

According to historical Islamic sources, it was the second caliph 'Umar bin al-Khattab who introduced the new calendar in 638. What continued in local tradition was naming a year after an important event that happened during this time, for example, the Year of the Floods or the Year of the Locusts.

Saudi Arabia is currently the only country that uses the Islamic calendar exclusively as the official calendar for governmental and business affairs. The country is also unique for the creation of official institutions to sight the lunar crescent, *hilal*, which determines the beginning of the new month. In the past, the individual observation of the *hilal* led to confusion over the dates to begin or end the pilgrimage or fasting. Other Muslim countries only observe the moon, and still others use different astronomical techniques to mark the dates of the calendar in advance. Conversion tables between the Hijri and the Gregorian dates are available on the Internet.

See also: Chapter 2: Muhammad, Prophet of Islam; Pre-Islamic Arabia; The Rise of Islam. Chapter 5: Five Pillars or the Tenets of Islam; Quran. Chapter 10: Workweek and Holidays; Chapter 14: Islamic Dietary Laws.

Further Reading

Birashk, Ahmad. *A Comparative Calendar of the Iranian, Muslim Lunar, and Christian Eras for Three Thousand Years: 1260 B.H.–2000 A.H./639 B.C.–2621 A.D.* Mazda Publishers, 1993.

al-Gailani, Noorah, and Chris Smith. *The Islamic Year: Surahs, Stories and Celebrations.* Hawthorn Press, 2002.

Maisel, Sebastian, and John A. Shoup III. *Saudi Arabia and the Gulf Arab States Today: An Encyclopedia of Life in the Arab States.* ABC-CLIO, 2009.

Jihad

Jihad has become one of the most hotly contested and controversial words in international affairs. Unlike popular belief in many non-Arabic-speaking countries, jihad does not actually mean "holy war," but the literal translation is "struggle" or "effort." In traditional forms of Islam, both Sunni and Shia, there are two main forms of Jihad: the inner Jihad that is also called the "great Jihad," and the outer form or "lesser Jihad."

The inner form of Jihad concerns the resistance believers have to put up within themselves against the temptations of life and the forces of evil. It is primarily focused on self-restraint rather than the projection of force outward. The lesser or outer forms of Jihad are not necessarily violent. Under Sunni classification schemes, the lesser Jihad is divided into three forms: tongue, hand, and sword. The Jihad of the tongue is to speak out against evil and take a clear stance in confrontation to it. The Jihad of the hand concerns acting against evil, and this need not be violent. The final form, the Jihad of the sword, is the form that has been most recently identified as Jihad writ large. Under this last form, the believer is exhorted to engage in combat to defend his religious community or country against an external attack. This military action is governed by an Islamic law of war that strictly limited the targets of military action and the consequences for civilian noncombatants, but it did allow for slave taking.

The rise of Islamism as a political force in the 20th century led to renewed emphasis on this small part of the tradition of Jihad. For some Islamist thinkers like Sayyid Qutb, Jihad was seen as warfare to establish global Muslim hegemony. Restraint for him came only as a result of tactical necessity and not principle. The Jihad of the sword came to contain the whole meaning of the word, with the other forms ignored or forgotten. Within the context of Saudi Arabia and the GCC states, this last form of Jihad historically took place between the Wahhabi community and other Muslim communities on the Arabian Peninsula, but it also was used to justify wars within the Wahhabi community. The raids conducted by Saudi forces against Ottoman-controlled cities in the Hijaz during the 19th century were justified as Jihad, as were the wars that gave the Saudi family control over most of the Arabian Peninsula in the 20th century, concluding with the conquest of the Hijaz in 1925. The Ikhwan movement, used by Abd al-Aziz ibn Saud to conquer the vast majority of the Arabian Peninsula, believed itself to be fighting a Jihad to purify Islam from negative and pagan influences. Many of the people involved in violent movements like al-Qaidah, believe themselves to be on a Jihad to protect Islam against the encroachment of infidels and against the defilement of Muslim lands by nonbelievers. Although the interpretation of Jihad as warfare is currently dominant, Islamic history has shown that the word has many different meanings.

See also: Chapter 2: The Golden Age of Islam in Arabia; Ibn Saud; Ikhwan; Muhammad ibn Abd al-Wahhab; The Rise of Islam. Chapter 3: Wahhabi Ideology. Chapter 5: Quran; Sunni Islam and Jurisprudence.

Further Reading

Bonney, Richard. *Jihād: From Qur'ān to Bin Laden*. Palgrave Macmillan, 2004.

Cook, David. *Understanding Jihad*. 2nd ed. University of California Press, 2015.

Hegghammer, Thomas. *Jihad in Saudi Arabia: Violence and Pan-Islamism since 1979*. Cambridge University Press, 2010.

Non-Muslims

Islam is the dominant religion in the Arabian Peninsula and has been since its inception in the 7th century. No country in the region is less than 85 percent Muslim, whereas most non-Muslims are migrant workers. There are, however, small populations of religious communities that predate Islam. Saudi Arabia has criminal statutes making it illegal for a Muslim to change religion or to renounce Islam, which is defined as apostasy and is punishable by death.

Judaism was the largest single non-Muslim religion on the peninsula until the 20th century and was concentrated mainly in Yemen. In the centuries before Islam, Jews were scattered in many of the oases in the Hijaz, as well as in the urban centers of Najran and Yemen. Jewish communities that had existed in the Hijaz well into the 13th century eventually moved to more important locations on the trade routes, such as Cairo or Damascus, so that by the start of the 20th century none remained.

Christianity was never widespread in the Arabian Peninsula and was concentrated near Syria and Iraq in the north, along the Gulf coast, and in Yemen. Archaeological excavations in 1986 in the Eastern Province of Saudi Arabia have uncovered the ruins of a church near Jubayl that dates from this period. With the arrival of Islam, most of the people converted to the new faith, although officially there is still a Nestorian bishopric for Bahrain.

See also: Chapter 1: Population. Chapter 2: Najran.

Further Reading

Lassner, Jacob. *Jews, Christians, and the Abode of Islam: Modern Scholarship, Medieval Realities*. University of Chicago Press, 2012.

Lecker, Michael. *Jews and Arabs in Pre- and Early Islamic Arabia*. Ashgate, 1999.

Mazuz, Haggai. *The Religious and Spiritual Life of the Jews of Medina*. Brill, 2014.

Quran

Quran—which literally means "recitation" in Arabic—is the main scripture and the book of divine revelation in Islam. The Quran is believed to be an unaltered word of God, received by the Prophet Muhammad and transmitted through him to the rest of humankind. It serves as the ultimate source of knowledge for Muslims, covering virtually all aspects of life, including specific religious conduct, the person's overall lifestyle, community governance, law, and science. The Quran functions as the spiritual and practical criterion in the Muslim community and is used to legitimize or disprove any and all ideas, actions, and material objects, whether belonging to an individual or the whole community.

The book of Quran consists of 114 chapters, called *surahs*, which are divided into verses, or *ayahs*. *Surahs* have great variation in length, ranging from 3 to 286 *ayahs*. Quranic *surahs* are arranged by length: the book begins with the longest chapters and ends with the shortest ones. Early Muslim scholars and religious commentators classified the Quranic chapters into Meccan and Medinan *surahs*. The former are the earliest *surahs* that were received by Muhammad when he was living in Mecca, while the latter are the chapters received after Muhammad and his followers had completed the Hijrah (emigration) from Mecca to Medina.

Islamic history identifies 610 AD as the year in which Muhammad began receiving the divine revelation, which came in the form of the first five verses of Surah 96. In the next two years no other revelations came, but when they restarted, they continued uninterruptedly throughout the rest of Muhammad's life, until his death in 632. The close companions of Muhammad and the earliest community of Muslims began compiling collections of *surahs*, and several versions of the text continued to circulate until the

A copy of the Quran, the holy book of Islam. (Saajid Abuluaih/Dreamstime.com)

Quran was codified under the third caliph, Uthman, around 650.

Islam is a strictly monotheistic religion. The central message of the Quran and Islam as a whole is the term *tawhid* (literally "unification"), which emphasizes the concept of one and only God as the single existing divine being. The word *islam* literally means "surrender" or "submission," implying the complete submission of a human being to God. The ideal society of Muslims is seen as replicating the pious and honorable characters of the first community, which was created by Muhammad, his closest companions, and the first followers of the new religion. Throughout Islamic history and until today, the Quran retained its spiritual value and continued to have a major impact on the development of Islamic civilization. The second in importance Islamic text is the Hadith—the collection of Muhammad's sayings that clarifies the Quran and helps to implement the religious doctrines into practical life. The importance of these texts prompted the development of a sophisticated linguistic foundation of written Arabic, including grammatical structures, lexicography, and rhetoric, which initially meant to provide an accurate understanding of the sacred text. The field of Islamic law grew out of the need to understand the legislative content of the Quran and translated it into a concrete set of legal rules and regulations. The Quran also prompted the development of historiography, whose original goal was to elucidate the course of history from the Quranic point of view. Different philosophical schools appeared throughout history, offering different takes on the divine message. In sum, the Quran was an important catalyst for the rapid development of different fields of science in the Muslim world.

See also: Chapter 1: Mecca; Medina. Chapter 2: The Golden Age of Islam in Arabia; Muhammad, Prophet of Islam; Pre-Islamic Arabia; The Rise of Islam. Chapter 3: Sharia Law and Judicial System. Chapter 5: Five Pillars or the Tenets of Islam; Hajj; Islamic Calendar. Chapter 7: Divorce; Marriage Law and Tradition. Chapter 8: Islamic

Education. Chapter 10: Dress Etiquette; Workweek and Holidays. Chapter 12: Calligraphic Art; Great Mosque of Mecca. Chapter 13: Religious Music. Chapter 14: Islamic Dietary Laws.

Further Reading

Brown, Brian A. *Three Testaments: Torah, Gospel, and Quran.* Rowman & Littlefield, 2012.

Corbin, Henry. *History of Islamic Philosophy.* Kegan Paul International, 1993.

Nigosian, S. A. *Islam: Its History, Teaching, and Practices.* Indiana University Press, 2004.

Wagner, Walter H. *Opening the Qur'an: Introducing Islam's Holy Book.* University of Notre Dame Press, 2008.

Shia Community

Despite the prevalence of Sunni Islam in every aspect of the country's ideology and infrastructure, Saudi Arabia is home to several important Shia communities. The largest of them, Ja'faris (or Twelvers), is located in the Eastern Province. There are also a number of smaller communities in other parts of the country, including the prominent Arabian tribe Banu Yam, from the Qahtanite tribal branch. Most members of this tribe belong to a small denomination of Shia Islam—the Sulaymani Ismaili branch. Banu Yam's traditional territories are in the southwest of the Arabian Peninsula.

Anti-Shiism remains very common in government and among many Saudis. This is partly due to textbooks used in schools, in which Shia and other sects and religions are decried as unbelievers, as those that reject the oneness of God (*tawhid*). The Saudi rivalry with Iran and particularly the sectarian response to the Arab Spring have exacerbated these views, making it ever more acceptable to voice derogatory remarks against Shia in public. There has never been a Shia minister, and Shia are largely barred from the foreign and security services, the military, the police, as well as sensitive positions in the oil and other key industries. They face persecution by the religious police for their religious rituals, and their mosques and prayer houses often operate in a sort of a legal gray area and can be closed anytime. Since 2003, Saudi Shia leaders have been invited to take part in the National Dialogue, initiated by Crown Prince and later King Abdullah. This was a key part of the attempt by Abdullah to present himself as the "reformist" king who would initiate political changes in the country. The National Dialogue was a series of discussions across the country, involving representatives from many different Saudi constituencies, including conservative clerics, liberals, religious minorities, and women. He introduced elections for half the seats in largely powerless municipal councils. In 2005, when Saudi Arabia held its first municipal elections since the 1960s, Shia turned out in great numbers in the Eastern Province, electing many Shia candidates to municipal councils in Qatif and al-Ahsa, because they saw this as a sign to mark their presence. To some degree, the government has begun to allow the observance of Shia holidays, such as Ashura, in majority-Shia areas. But in practice, discrimination in government jobs and schools continues, and anti-Shia sentiments thrive.

See also: Chapter 1: Population. Chapter 2: The Golden Age of Islam in Arabia; Muhammad, Prophet of Islam; Rashidun: The Righteous Caliphs; The Rise of Islam; The Umayyads. Chapter 3: Human Rights and Censorship; Political Dissent and Opposition. Chapter 5: Five Pillars or the Tenets of Islam; Shia Islam; Sunni Islam and Jurisprudence. Chapter 6: *Sharif* and *Sayyid*. Chapter 16: Freedom of Speech.

Further Reading

Ibrahim, Fouad N. *The Shi'is of Saudi Arabia*. Saqi, 2006.

Matthiesen, Toby. *Sectarian Gulf: Bahrain, Saudi Arabia, and the Arab Spring That Wasn't*. Stanford University Press, 2014.

Shia Islam

Shia Islam, or Shiism, takes its name from the Arabic phrase "shi'itu Ali," or Partisans of Ali ibn Abi Talib. These were a community of Muslims who supported Ali, the Prophet Muhammad's cousin and son-in-law, to the political succession of the prophet. Ali was one of the first converts to Islam and played a major role in the development of the new community both in Mecca and later in Medina. He married Fatimah Zahra, daughter of the prophet, by whom he had two sons, Hasan and Hussein. Ali was elected by the Shura council, composed of the companions of the prophet, as the fourth caliph in 656, but his election was challenged by Mu'awiyah ibn Abi Sufyan, the governor of Syria and a member of the old pre-Islamic ruling elite of Mecca. Mu'awiyah accused Ali of being an accomplice in the assassination of his kinsman and third caliph Uthman Ibn Affan and refused to recognize Ali's election. The conflict escalated, and the two parties met in battle, but eventually agreed to mediation. Ali's supporters split into two main groups: those who agreed to the mediation efforts, and those who felt Ali gave up any right to the caliphate when he agreed to the negotiations. The latter group formed the early core of the Kharaji movement, whereas those who stayed with Ali formed the core from which Shiism eventually emerged.

Shiism differs from Sunni Islam in the position of the leader of the Muslim community. For Shiites, the leader must be a direct descendant of the prophet, as noted above, and takes the title of Imam rather than Caliph. As imam he is the sole source of religious and secular authority, based on that of the prophet and the Quran; the prophet broke all connections to any pre-Islamic system of legitimacy or succession principles. The imam, although not divine himself, rules through application of divine law, which is infallible. The imamate passed down to the final 12th imam Muhammad ibn al-Hasan al-Muntazir, who disappeared in 874, most likely the victim of an Abbasid plot. Shiites believe he is in a state of suspended occultation and will return one day to reclaim his rightful place as head of the Muslim community, much like a messianic figure. Since the last imam, no government is fully legitimate because it rules in his place and will be fully replaced when the imam returns. As such, all governments need to be well advised by doctors of religious law, to make sure the community does not stray too far from divine law during the imam's absence.

Twelver Shiism became the state religion of Iran in the 16th century with the Safavid dynasty (1501–1786), but Shiism in the Arabian Peninsula predates this. The radical Ismaili Qaramitan movement was widely supported in the 9th century, and Bahrain served as its main base. Twelver Shiism spread in the eastern provinces of Saudi Arabia, Kuwait, and Bahrain from Iraq, as well as Iran, before the rise of the Safavids. Zaydi Islam became well established in Yemen, before the rise of the Qasimi imams in the 16th century.

See also: Chapter 2: The Golden Age of Islam in Arabia; Muhammad, Prophet of Islam; Rashidun: The Righteous Caliphs; The Rise of Islam; The Umayyads. Chapter 3: Political Dissent and Opposition; Sharia Law and Judicial System. Chapter 5: Five Pillars or the Tenets of Islam; Shia Community; Sunni Islam and Jurisprudence. Chapter 6: *Sharif* and *Sayyid*. Chapter 16: Freedom of Speech.

Further Reading

Bengio, Ofra, and Meir Litvak. *The Sunna and Shi'a in History: Division and Ecumenism in the Muslim Middle East*. Palgrave Macmillan, 2011.

Brunner, Rainer, and Werner Ende. *The Twelver Shia in Modern Times: Religious Culture & Political History*. Brill, 2001.

Daftary, Farhad. *A History of Shi'i Islam*. I. B. Tauris in Association with the Institute of Ismaili Studies, 2013.

Hazleton, Lesley. *After the Prophet: The Epic Story of the Shia-Sunni Split in Islam*. 1st ed. Doubleday, 2009.

Nasr, Seyyed Vali Reza. *The Shia Revival: How Conflicts within Islam Will Shape the Future*. W. W. Norton, 2007.

Sunni Islam and Jurisprudence

Sunnah refers to the traditions of the Prophet Muhammad, and the majority of Muslims belong to the mainstream division of Islam called *ahl al-sunnah*, meaning people of the sunnah, or Sunni Islam. The majority of Arabs and the majority of Muslims on the Arabian Peninsula are Sunnis, following one of the four main legal schools: Hanafi, Shafi'i, Maliki, or Hanbali. Hanbali Islam is the majority in Saudi Arabia and the United Arab Emirates, whereas Maliki is the majority school in Bahrain and Qatar. Sunnis in Yemen, Oman, and Kuwait tend to be mainly Shafi'i. Each of the four schools differ on several legal points and even on the sources of Islamic law, but historically they have been part of the general mainstream of the religion with their scholars in agreement about important aspects of government.

When the first major split in Islam took place, the nascent Sunni community agreed to the arbitration between Mu'awiyah ibn Abi Sufyan and Ali ibn Abi Talib over claims to the Muslim caliphate. Sunnis accept the validity of the succession of the first four caliphs, called the Righteous or Rightly Guided Caliphs to the Prophet, including Ali, and do not recognize Mu'awiyah as the caliph until after Ali's death in 661, because the arbitration efforts were not conclusive. Once Mu'awiyah was able to secure the sole leadership for himself, Sunnis did not dispute the legality of his claim. Sunnis accept the succession within the Umayyad family and agree to the dynasty change from the Umayyads to the Abbasids in 760 as legal, whereas Shiites do not.

Sunni jurisprudence did not fully emerge until the first century of the Abbasids. During the first centuries of Islam, there was no organized or standardized approach to law, particularly as long as Companions of the Prophet were still alive to serve as sources of information about what the prophet said or did. The Quran as the word of God was seen as the only needed source of law. Individual jurists made decisions based on the Quran and on individual reasoning, once the Companions were no longer alive to be consulted. The Umayyad caliphs supported debates between Muslims and Christians over matters of faith, but had not encouraged a standardized collection of judicial decisions. Muslims in Iran, Syria, and Egypt encountered centuries-old legal traditions that needed to be reconciled with Islam and the practices of Arabia.

Starting in the 770s, two major centers of Islamic jurisprudence became established: Kufa in Iraq, and Medina on the Arabian Peninsula. Scholars in Kufa attempted to reconcile legal procedures of the former Persian and Roman Empires with the divine revelations of the Quran when possible, but the Quran did not have clear legal decisions on all matters. The *hadith* (sayings) and *sunnah* (actions) of the prophet also did not cover all possibilities, and authoritative collections of them were not made until the 9th century by al-Bukhari (d. 870) and ibn Muslim (821–875). Two other forms of legal procedures emerged, *qiyas* (analogy) and *ijma'* (consensus). *Ijtihad* (individual reasoning) remained a practice in Sunni Islam until the 13th century, when it was decided that any further use of reasoning ran the risk of diverging too much from the divine word of God and that all possibilities had already been exhausted. Following the example of the Syrian Hanbali scholar Ibn Taymiyah (1263–1328), *ijtihad* was replaced by *taqlid*—imitation (of previous scholars).

Sunni Islam was nearly swamped by a wave of popular support for Ismaili Shiism from the 10th to the 11th centuries. The power of the Abbasids, weakened by the middle of the 9th century, allowed for several local dynasties to emerge. In North Africa, the Ismailis were able to first take Tunisia and then Egypt, establishing the Fatamids (909–1171) as a rival caliphate. The Abbasids themselves became hostage to the Persian Shiite Buwayhids from 932 to 1062. Sunni scholars dealt with the political weakness of the caliphate by recognizing a division of power and authority between the caliph, as head of the Islamic community, and the sultan, who wielded actual power. Sunni jurists wrote that it was proper to obey the sultan, no matter who he was, because he ruled in the name of the caliph for the eventual good of the Muslim community. They argued that a bad Muslim sultan was better than to be ruled by a non-Muslim; stability was better than rebellion. Sunni scholars took a very realistic and pragmatic approach to government, and when Kamal Ataturk finally abolished the office of the caliph in 1924, there was little reaction from Sunnis anywhere. The recognition of sultan and the division of political power from the religious leadership of Islam in the 9th century allowed Sunnis to adjust to new political realities.

Sunni Islam was revived with the arrival of the Saljuq Turks (1037–1194), recent converts to Sunni Islam who defeated the Buwayhids and placed the Abbasid caliph under their protection. They proceeded on into Syria and Anatolia, defeating both the Shiite Fatamids and the Christian Byzantines. The Saljuqs and their successors, the Zangids (1127–1222) and the Ayyubids (1169–1260), began establishing madrasas, or religious colleges, where Sunni jurisprudence could be taught. In North Africa, the al-Murabitun (1040–1146) movement firmly established Maliki Sunni Islam, ending centuries of Kharaji and Shiite states. The madrasah system was imported from the east to help with teaching Sunni jurisprudence. Main centers of Sunni Islamic learning developed in Egypt, Syria, and North Africa, and in the 20th century Saudi Arabia established its own center in Medina.

See also: Chapter 2: The Golden Age of Islam in Arabia; Muhammad, Prophet of Islam; Rashidun: The Righteous Caliphs; The Rise of Islam; The Umayyads. Chapter 3: Sharia Law and Judicial System; Ulama. Chapter 5: Five Pillars or the Tenets of Islam; Quran; Shia Islam.

Further Reading

Bengio, Ofra, and Meir Litvak. *The Sunna and Shi'a in History: Division and Ecumenism in the Muslim Middle East.* Palgrave Macmillan, 2011.

Hazleton, Lesley. *After the Prophet: The Epic Story of the Shia-Sunni Split in Islam.* 1st ed. Doubleday, 2009.

Heer, Nicholas, and Farhat Jacob Ziadeh. *Islamic Law and Jurisprudence.* University of Washington Press, 1990.

Nahouza, Namira. *Wahhabism and the Rise of the New Salafists: Theology, Power and Sunni Islam.* I. B. Tauris, 2018.

CHAPTER 6

SOCIAL CLASSES AND ETHNICITY

OVERVIEW

The population of Saudi Arabia exceeds 32 million. The absolute majority of the population are Sunni Arab, but the country has several ethnic and religious minorities. About 10 percent of Saudis are of African origin, most of them being descendants of former slaves. The main religious minority are Shia Muslims (or Shiites) of two denominations: Twelver Shiites, who are primarily located in the Eastern Province, and Ismaili Shiites, who are concentrated in the Najran area. The annual population growth of 3.8 percent is one of the highest in the world. Saudi Arabia has a very young population, with over 50 percent below the age of 18. Having gone through a process of rapid and radical urbanization, the absolute majority of Saudi population—about 83 percent—currently live in cities.

More than 5 million foreigners reside in Saudi Arabia for work and religious reasons. About 1 million of workers came from Yemen alone—prior to the Saudi-Yemeni War of 2015. Many expatriates from Egypt, Sudan, Lebanon, and Palestine work in the education sector. Despite the consistent government efforts to promote Saudization (employment of Saudis to all sectors of the economy), migrant workers from Southeast Asia are widely employed in manual labor, construction, and service industries, while Western expats have various management and technical positions. During the annual Muslim pilgrimage, another 2 or 3 million visitors visit the western part of the country, the Hijaz, home to Mecca and Medina, where the most important and sacred Islamic sites are located. Islam continues to dominate both private and public life in Saudi Arabia. It is a key component of the country's identity and a foundation of its political, legal, and social systems and institutions.

Since the 1960s, the effects of the oil wealth are noticeable in the social and economic infrastructure of the country. For many, it is impossible to imagine how their ancestors lived only a few decades ago. Some look at it from an angle of romanticism and nostalgia, whereas others connect this to an era of underdevelopment. The rapid social and economic change continued during the 1970s and reached its climax during the oil crises of 1973. It brought with it a major demographic change: the population exploded, the elder generations lived longer, infant mortality decreased, and the population became younger and younger. Today, more than half of Saudi population are under the age of 18. Additionally, rapid and often radical urbanization caused major population shifts and internal migrations. The influx of foreign workers continues to cause various challenges and conflicts, both economically and socially.

The concept of descent is particularly important in Saudi Arabia and the rest of the Arabian Peninsula. Tribal affiliation considers two main origins: Adnan, referring to northern Arabian tribes, and Qahtan, referring to southern Arabian tribes. Adnani Arabs trace their origin back to Ismail (Ishmael), son of Ibrahim (Abraham). Tribes descending from Adnan include Bani Tamim, Hudayl, Qays, Rabi'a, Bakr, Taghlib, and the Quraysh of Mecca. Qahtan is the Arabic name of the biblical Joktan, son of Noah, whom the tribal culture considers the forefather of the tribes coming from the mountains of Southern Arabia. Some of these tribes relocated to the north and achieved prominent social status. Among the tribes of Qahtani origin are al-Murrah, Shammar, Ajman, Harb, and Dawasir. Being able to trace one's ancestry back to either Adnan or Qahtan is essential in the social hierarchy of Saudi Arabia. Those who cannot produce a clear and pure pedigree are often considered inferior, even if they are wealthy and well connected. In the past, one's social status was closely linked to their occupation. Traditionally, the main occupation of Bedouins, nomadic pastoralism, was regarded the most noble. The notion of descent remains relevant in the distinction between nomadic Bedouins, *badu*, from different tribal affiliations and sedentary people, *hadar*. One's origin is at the core of the kingdom's social hierarchy. At the top of it are the noble tribes of pure descent, who cannot have marital relations with representatives from non-noble tribes or *hadar*—even if both groups reside in the same area and have friendly and mutually respectful relations. At the bottom of the social ladder are those with no kinship ties, descendants of historically inferior tribes and slaves, and foreigners.

The most important form of social organization in Saudi Arabia and its core unit is the extended family. As with tribal affiliations, origins are the core of a Saudi family and determine its status within the society. Families are defined and organized by ancestry, whereas tribes are essentially an alliance of families who share common descent. Usually, a family is organized into a strong unit with a set of functions, duties, and rights. The Saudi extended family is patriarchal (elder males have the utmost authority), patrilocal (relatives tend to live closely), patrilineal (descent is measured along the father's side of the family), and endogamous (marital relations are maintained within the group). Although relations with maternal relatives are sustained, they are considered secondary. The kinship-based society has clearly defined rules and norms, which center around the concepts of honor and shame. Some of tribal customs and norms were incorporated into Islamic traditions and codes of behavior, others function outside of Islam and even in contradiction with it, but nevertheless continue to define all aspects of Saudi society. For instance, the very concept of descent stands in sharp contrast with the Islamic idea of unity, where the community of believers is based in faith and completely disregards one's origins, either noble or modest.

Honor and shame form the basis for many of the daily interactions between all parts of the society that are regulated by customary law (*'uf*) and traditions (*adat*). The concept of family honor is articulated through various rules and responsibilities for both the individual member of the family and the whole group. Loyalty to one's kin is closely connected to the concept of honor. Members of the family constantly work to maintain and strengthen the bond through mutual visits, patronage, and marital arrangements. In times of hardship, the family network can provide various forms of support, both material and emotional. Family support is not seen as a favor, but something completely expected according to the local social norms. Although each kinship network has leadership—exercised by influential and reputable male members, usually senior in age—they still rule by consensus and continuous consultation with the rest of the group.

Further Reading

Exell, Karen, and Trinidad Rico. *Cultural Heritage in the Arabian Peninsula: Debates, Discourses and Practices*. Ashgate, 2014.

House, Karen Elliott. *On Saudi Arabia: Its People, Past, Religion, Fault Lines—and Future*. 1st ed. Alfred A. Knopf, 2012.

Izraeli, S. *Politics and Society in Saudi Arabia: The Crucial Years of Development, 1960–1982*. C. Hurst, 2012.

Samin, Nadav. *Of Sand or Soil: Genealogy and Tribal Belonging in Saudi Arabia*. Princeton University Press, 2015.

Bedouins and Nomadism

The term "Bedouins," stemming from the Arabic word *badu*, is used to refer to the tribally organized nomadic groups of Arab origin that live throughout the Middle East and North Africa. Outside of the Arabian Peninsula, Bedouin tribes reside on the territories of Egypt, Jordan, Israel and Palestine, Syria, Iraq, and North Africa. In a general sense, Bedouins are pastoral nomads who share a common sense of tribal origin, social values, and cultural customs. It is difficult to clearly connect particular Bedouin tribes to particular countries: nation states do not play a defining role in the self-identification of this nomadic people, and they associate their belonging with tribes, and only then with their country. Descendants of many Arabian tribes are scattered through more than one country on the Arabian Peninsula. The most prominent tribes of the Peninsula include Shammar, Mutayr, Ajman, al-Murrah, Qahtan, Amarat, Ruwalah, Huwaytat, Utaybah, Dawasir, Manahil, and others. A classification system within the tribal group identified the following hierarchy: the tribe (*qabilah*), the tribal section (*'ashirah*), the clan (*fakhd*), the lineage (*hamulah*), and the extended family (*bayt*). Every tribal section traced their descent to a common ancestor and shared a territory with water and pasture grounds. Each group was headed by the most prominent and reputable member who had the title of *shaykh*. The leaders of large tribal confederations were called *shaykh al-shuyukh* (literally "the shaykh or shaykhs").

Only a limited number of Bedouin groups had the status of *asil*, indicating their recognized noble origins. These included Shammar, Anizah, Dhafir, and Harb, among others. Other tribes, who were unable to trace their lineage to the two main ancestors,

Bedouin women weaving, circa 1940s. (Library of Congress)

Adnan and Qahtan (northern and southern Arabs, respectively), were considered secondary. Among them are the Shararat, Hawazim, and Hutaym. Consequently, the tribes with less noble descent were engaged in less prestigious professions, such as sheep breeding or farming, and they could not have marital relations with the noble tribes. However, both tribal groups had various mutually beneficial economic and cultural ties. At the bottom of the Bedouin hierarchy were the Sulubbah—hunters and artisans without a tribal origin.

A major event in the development of the nomadic civilization was the domestication of the camel around 1500 BC, whereas their superior skills with horses—including the legendary breed of the Arabian horse—assured their military supremacy over the whole region. Bedouins usually lived in small camping units of closely related families called *khamsah*, but joined with other families for political, economic, and military purposes. Historically, Bedouins always emphasized their distinction from the sedentary population (*hadar*), stressing the different identities of the two groups and the superiority of the tribal population over the settlers.

Material possessions of Bedouins were traditionally very modest and were limited to essential items that were easy to transport. The main dwelling was a tent made from camel and goat hair. It was divided into two sections: one for the family and the other for the guests. The family quarters were reserved for women and children. Men spent most of their time in the guest section, where they received visitors, drank tea and coffee, and exchanged the news. This ancient division of the dwelling is still very much in practice in contemporary Saudi Arabia, including the most modern and wealthiest houses. A Bedouin tent was always open for any guests and visitors—hospitality remains a fundamental feature of the Bedouin culture and an important survival tool. Guests have almost unlimited rights, and the host is expected to do everything to assure a comfortable and safe stay for them. The Bedouin code of behavior guaranteed generous reception even to the host's sworn enemies—if they came as guests. The tradition of hospitality, which was incorporated into Islamic culture, remains prevalent in Saudi Arabia and other Arab nations. Bedouin culture is also known for its great tradition of poetry. Poets were highly regarded and respected members of the tribe.

Raising livestock was the main occupation and included camels, goats, and sheep. The migration patterns of the tribes were dictated by the search for grazing grounds and water, which changed depending on season. Meat, milk, and hides provided by livestock helped the Bedouins survive the difficult natural conditions of the Arabian Peninsula. There was ongoing contestation and intertribal fighting over the ownership of wells and pasture, but over time, most tribal territories (called *dirah* in Arabic) were clearly established and recognized. According to the tribal ownership system, animals belonged to individual families, while water and pasture were the shared property of the tribe. When Ibn Saud conquered and united different regions of the peninsula, he abolished the system of tribal territories and privileges, and nationalized the land.

The practice of raiding (*ghazu* in Arabic)—of both *hadar* and other tribes—was an important economic and social institution in pre-Islamic Arabia. Raids were seen as a method of increasing the collective wealth, weakening rival groups, and increasing the tribe's reputation. Each raid had an assigned leader (*qa'id*), who would take the biggest share if the campaign was successful. Customary law prohibited raids from turning into massacres, and the adherence to those rules was strongly enforced by all tribes. Because every raid would almost certainly cause retaliation, the tribes were in a constant state of warfare. Other Bedouin activities included hunting with falcons and dogs, as well as gathering truffles and other desert goods in the spring. Women were responsible for all chores including cooking, cleaning, and weaving. Children were spared from work until they reached the age of 5 or 6.

Before the arrival of Islam, most Bedouin tribes practiced paganism, while some converted to Christianity and Judaism. Tribal gods were worshipped as idols, and the ancient Kaaba in pre-Islamic Mecca was the main regional holy site containing the idols. Once in a lunar year, the tribes would enter the period of truce and make a pilgrimage to Mecca. When Islam arrived on the peninsula, it had the most impact on the community's moral values. At the same time, many pre-Islamic tribal concepts, such as honor and shame, remained important and became part of the collective identity of the local people, equally regarded by Bedouins and other populations.

In modern times, the Bedouin culture faces enormous challenges. As the Arabian Peninsula underwent a series of economic, political, and cultural transformations, generated by the oil boom, the Bedouins could no longer maintain their nomadic lifestyle and practice most of their centuries-old customs. The introduction of cars and the drawing of political borders were arguably the two biggest factors that forever changed their world. Since the establishment of the Saudi state, the government undertook various measures to subdue and control the country's nomadic population, whose way of life was incompatible with the principles of the nation-state and modern economy. In the 1960s, as the region began to undergo significant social and economic changes, including a process of rapid urbanization, nomads made up about 20 percent of the country's population. Since then, they experienced a constant decline in numbers, resulting from government settlement programs and other factors. Nevertheless, the impact of the Bedouin culture on the larger Saudi society is undeniable. Their codes of behavior, moral values, and customs are largely accepted in the entire Saudi culture and constitute an important aspect of the national identity. Among these features are kin-based networks, social importance of descent, the concepts of honor and shame, and the high cultural value of hospitality.

See also: Chapter 1: Population. Chapter 2: Arab Revolt (1916–1918); Ikhwan; Muhammad, Prophet of Islam; Pre-Islamic Arabia; The Rise of Islam; Third Saudi State: Saudi Arabia in the 20th Century. Chapter 6: Major Tribes; Settled Population: *Hadar*; Sulubbah; Urbanization. Chapter 10: Honor; *Majlis*. Chapter 11: Poetry. Chapter 12: Bedouin Jewelry; Sadu Weaving; Traditional Garments. Chapter 13: *Ardha* Dance; Bedouin Music.

Further Reading

Abd al-Jabbar Falih, and Hosham Dawod. *Tribes and Power: Nationalism and Ethnicity in the Middle East*. Saqi, 2001.

Abu-Lughod, Lila. *Veiled Sentiments: Honor and Poetry in a Bedouin Society*. University of California Press, 1999.

Ginat, J., and Anatoly M. Khazanov. *Changing Nomads in a Changing World*. Sussex Academic Press, 1998.

Jabbur, Jibrail Sulayman, et al. *The Bedouins and the Desert: Aspects of Nomadic Life in the Arab East*. State University of New York Press, 1995.

Kurpershoek, P. M. *Arabia of the Bedouins*. Saqi, 2001.

Maisel, Sebastian. "The New Rise of Tribalism in Saudi Arabia." *Nomadic Peoples*, vol. 18, no. 2, 2014, pp. 100–122.

Ethnic Composition

Saudi Arabia has a markedly homogenous population, excluding the guest workers that make up about 20 percent of the overall population. Almost all Saudis are ethnic Arabs. African Saudis constitute a small ethnic minority as well. They are primarily the descendants of former slaves. Another distinct ethnic minority comes from Central Asia, whose ancestors are pilgrims settled in the Hijaz. There are also various Arabic-speaking communities, originating from Egypt, Yemen, and Sudan, but they do not have Saudi citizenship. The largest non-Arab communities are from Southeast Asia, Pakistan, India, Sri Lanka, and the Philippines.

An important aspect of citizenship in Saudi Arabia, as well as other Gulf states, is that it is based on the concept of ethnicity and descent. A major criterion for defining citizenship is a proof of belonging to one of the recognized ethnic groups. Being born in Saudi Arabia does not guarantee citizenship. Originally, the population of the Arabian Peninsula was Arab, with a number of small Persian, Turkish, and Indian communities. When nation-states were established and the whole region began to rapidly transform in the wake of the oil boom, new ethnic groups migrated to the region and a clear differentiation between citizens and residents were made. Only citizens fully enjoy the whole spectrum of social and economic benefits in Saudi Arabia.

In pre-Islamic times, the Arabian Peninsula was mainly inhabited by the Arab people, but also had significant numbers of non-Arabs who had lived here for many centuries. Several non-Arab communities have settled in the region in more recent times and retained their original identity, including language. These groups should not be confused with migrant populations of guest workers who came to the region as a result of the oil boom and who usually cannot become citizens. The Bukhari people are one of these groups who came into the peninsula prior to the discovery of oil. They are Turkish-speaking people, most of whom are Uzbeks from Central Asia. The general term "Bukhari" comes from the fact that many of them have the last name al-Bukhari (literally "from Bukhara" or "of Bukharian origin"), although al-Andajani and al-Samarqandi family names are also common. The Bukhari are Sunni Muslims, and most of them came to the Arabian Peninsula following the 1918 Bolshevik Revolution, when Muslim religious leaders and scholars were being persecuted. They have scattered through various towns and cities, but the majority came to Mecca and Medina. The Bukhari were able to preserve their language at home, allowing younger generations to study at Turkish universities. Currently, the Bukhari are an educated urban population who work in various occupations. They are also famous for their skills in fine crafts. For example, the Bukhari artisans created the gold thread used for embroidery pieces in the cover (*kiswah*) of the Kaaba.

See also: Chapter 1: Population. Chapter 2: Pre-Islamic Arabia. Chapter 4: Migrant Workers and Unemployment. Chapter 5: Hajj. Chapter 6: Bedouins and Nomadism; Settled Population: *Hadar.*

Further Reading

Abd al-Jabbar Falih, and Hosham Dawod. *Tribes and Power: Nationalism and Ethnicity in the Middle East.* Saqi, 2001.

Exell, Karen, and Trinidad Rico. *Cultural Heritage in the Arabian Peninsula: Debates, Discourses and Practices.* Ashgate, 2014.

Health and Welfare

In Saudi Arabia, health care is considered a citizen's right and is guaranteed free of charge to all citizens and those expatriates who work in the public sector. With regard to expatriate workers employed in private companies, the government mandates their employers to provide them with health care coverage. Saudi health care is funded through two main sources: public, which constitutes 75 percent, and out-of-pocket expenditures, estimated at about 25 percent. An important aspect of the Saudi system is the low level of private insurance in the provision of health care. Nearly all private expenditures are actually out-of-pocket expenses for care provided by private hospitals and clinics. The government provides an annual budget to the Ministry of Health and its many programs. Additionally, royal decrees may be issued to allocate supplementary funding for special health programs and projects.

Saudi Arabia is divided into 13 provinces and 20 health directorates. The government gives each directorate considerable autonomy in administering health care, while providing general guidelines set by the Ministry of Health. Provinces are assigned budgets provided in lump sums, which are then allocated to regional hospitals. The Ministry of Health places particular emphasis on primary care and prevention, maintaining over 3,300 health centers nationally. A unique aspect of Saudi health care is that in addition to the native population, the country annually received over 5 million pilgrims and visitors. The government provides free health services to pilgrims through the Ministry of Health facilities.

There are three main types of health care facilities: (1) a national network of hospitals and clinics administered by the Ministry of Health, (2) other government-sponsored facilities, and (3) private hospitals and clinics. The Ministry of Health is the largest provider of health care in the country, including preventive, curative, and rehabilitative services and support. Over 60 percent of inpatient care is provided by the ministry. The rest of the inpatient care is provided by other public and private facilities (around 20 percent and 17 percent, respectively), which are outside of the ministry's jurisdiction, although the ministry generally oversees the private sector as well. Saudi Arabia has over 200 general and specialized hospitals.

The government has been making substantial investments to modernize the country's infrastructure and social services, and much progress has been made in the last two decades. But despite many positive developments, the need to increase and diversify medical research remains urgent. The only long-established medical scientific research center is located at the King Faisal Specialist Hospital and Research Center and is funded by the government. Currently, the main areas of research are oncological diseases, cardiovascular health, genetics, infectious diseases, and environmental health. Because for several decades the country's economic development prioritized oil industries, Saudi Arabia was until recently lacking an educational infrastructure to produce an adequate number of doctors, nurses, and health care technicians for the rapidly growing population. Although the educational capacity has drastically increased in the last decade, the majority of health care professionals continue to be foreigners or foreign-educated Saudis.

See also: Chapter 4: Diversification and Development Plans; Public vs. Private Sectors; Science and Technology. Chapter 5: Hajj. Chapter 8: Higher Education.

Further Reading

Alkhamis, Abdulwahab, et al. "Financing Healthcare in Gulf Cooperation Council Countries: A Focus on Saudi Arabia." *The International Journal of Health Planning and Management*, vol. 29, no. 1, 2014, pp. 64–82.

Almalki, M., et al. "Health Care System in Saudi Arabia: An Overview." *Eastern Mediterranean Health Journal*, vol. 17, no. 10, 2011, pp. 784–793.

Petraglia, M. D., and Jeffrey I. Rose. *The Evolution of Human Populations in Arabia: Paleoenvironments, Prehistory and Genetics*. Springer, 2009.

House of Saud

The ruling family of Saudi Arabia is Al Saud, or the House of Saud, who date their origins to the 15th century AD. The oldest ancestor is considered Mani al-Muraydi from Qatif who was awarded two villages in Najd, where he founded the city of Diriyah in 1446. Soon after, al-Muraydi and his allies gained control over Wadi Hanifah as well. Al-Muraydi's descendants reappeared in the area in the early 17th century, where they continued to control Diriyyah and its vicinity.

The name "Al Saud" comes from the father of the dynasty's founder, Abd al-Aziz bin Muhammad bin Saud, who died in 1725. In 1744, Muhammad bin Saud signed the historic treaty with Muhammad ibn Abd al-Wahhab, a religious scholar and reformer. By collaborating with the emerging Islamic revivalist movement led by Muhammad ibn Abd al-Wahhab, the Al Saud gained the religious legitimacy to conquer the surrounding areas. In return, they promised to support his interpretation of the Quran and Sunnah, which was based on the teachings of the Hanbali school of thought and their most influential scholar, Ibn Taymiyah. Their first state, the Emirate of Diriyah, was destroyed in 1818 by Egyptian Ottoman forces. The Ottomans were continuously provoked by Al Saud's military and political victories, which posed a real threat to the Ottoman hegemony over the area, including the two holy cities of Mecca and Medina.

In the following decades, under the leadership of Turki ibn Abdallah Al Saud, the Al Saud were able to regroup after their losses and establish yet another state on the same territory. With this second attempt at an organized state, they moved the capital from the still devastated Diriyah to Riyadh. However, another tribal dynasty and their allies, the Al Rashid and the Shammar tribe, were able to oust them from power as a result of internal conflicts within Al Saud. In the last decade of the 19th century, the Al Saud were forced to live in exile in Kuwait and other places throughout the region.

In 1902, Abd al-Aziz ibn Saud reconquered Riyadh and later Najd. When the British government recognized his rule, he was able to unite many tribal groups, both sedentary and nomadic, under his authority. In 1921, Ibn Saud defeated his biggest rivals—the Al Rashid in the Jabal Shammar region, and in 1925 the Hashemites in the Hijaz. Additional campaigns led to the inclusion of the Asir and Najran areas in the south. On September 23, 1932, Ibn Saud proclaimed the Kingdom of Saudi Arabia, which became the only country in the world named after its ruling family.

After the discovery of oil in 1938, Ibn Saud put all his efforts into his country's economy. His successor and oldest son, Saud ibn Abd al-Aziz Al Saud, was lacking the same visionary style of leadership and succumbed to his more able brother Faysal. The latter was known for his ability to modernize the kingdom without secularizing it. In the 1960s, the country was drawn into the regional conflicts over pan-Arabism, when Saudi Arabia and Egypt provided support to the opposite sides in the Yemeni Civil War. The Al Saud have always seen themselves as guardians of that country that contains within its borders the holiest places in Islam and the world's largest oil reserves. Throughout the whole history of the current Saudi state, their main challenge has been to balance the Islamic traditions with the ambitions to become a major global economy. Among these balancing measures was the initiative to create the Organization of Petroleum Exporting Countries (OPEC) in 1960, while also joining the Organisation of Islamic Cooperation (OIC) in 1969.

When King Faysal was assassinated by his own nephew in 1975, another brother, King Khalid, assumed the throne and ruled the country until his death from a heart attack in 1982. The next Saudi king was Fahd bin Abd al-Aziz, whose reign was characterized by several economic reforms, including attempts to diversify the Saudi economy and develop closer ties with Western nations. After several strokes in the mid-1990s, Fahd's half-brother Abdallah began to manage most of the state affairs and became king in 2005, following Fahd's death. King Abdullah's reign lasted until his death in 2015. In these 10 years, he implemented a number of important reforms, including giving women the right to vote. He maintained and further strengthened Saudi Arabia's relationship with the United States and the United Kingdom. He was succeeded by his half-brother Salman bin Abd al-Aziz, who is the current king of Saudi Arabia.

The Al Saud rule over Central Arabia for over 250 years brought a sense of political stability and continuity to the region. The system of succession after Ibn Saud is simple: the oldest brother of Ibn Saud's male offspring is selected as the new crown prince. However, in present times, younger generations of Al Saud princes have been challenging the system and asking for more participation in defining the country's vision and development. In 2017, in a historic political move, King Salman named his 34-year-old son Muhammad bin Salman the crown prince. The latter is playing an increasingly important role in the domestic and international affairs of Saudi Arabia.

Often labeled a state within a state, the Al Saud continue to maintain the dominant position in all aspects of life in the kingdom. They control the central government and local administration with over 150 members in high-ranking positions, including ministers, provincial governors, and military leaders. The family is divided into several branches: Al Thunayan, Ibn Jiluwi, Saud al-Kabir, and the dominating branch, Faysal bin Turki. Important decisions are made either by the family council or the inner circle of the family council, which includes only senior members of Al Saud.

See also: Chapter 2: Arab Revolt (1916–1918); Discovery of Oil; Emirate of Diriyah: The First Saudi State (1744–1818); Emirate of Najd: The Second Saudi State (1824–1891);

Ibn Saud; King Abdullah; Third Saudi State: Saudi Arabia in the 20th Century. Chapter 3: Saudi Monarchy and Branches of the Government.

Further Reading

Bowen, Wayne H. *The History of Saudi Arabia*. 2nd ed. Greenwood, 2015.

Kechichian, Joseph A. *Succession in Saudi Arabia*. Palgrave, 2001.

McLoughlin, Leslie J. *Ibn Saud: Founder of a Kingdom*. St. Martin's Press, 1993.

Wald, Ellen R. *Saudi, Inc.: The Arabian Kingdom's Pursuit of Profit and Power*. Pegasus Books, 2018.

Major Tribes

The most prominent of the Arabian tribes are the Anizah, Shammar, Harb, Mutayr, Dhafir, Banu Khalid, Ajman, Banu Hajir, al-Murrah, Qahtan, Utayba, Dawasir, Sahul, Manasir, Banu Yas, Sibay, Qawasim, Banu Yam, Za'ab, and Banu Tamim. There is also a secondary set of tribes, whose origins are considered less noble than the aforementioned group. The main tribes of this group are the Awazim, Rashayda, Hutaym, Aqayl, and Sulubbah. The Sulubbah, the nomadic hunters also known for their skillful metalwork, were inferior to the more affluent Bedouin and are considered to have the lowest position on the tribal social scale. Bedouin groups are further divided into southern and northern congregations. The first group are called Ahl al-Janub (People of the South) and includes Harb, Utaybah, and Ajman tribes. Historically, they grazed their flock in the areas of Najd and al-Hasa. Ahl al-Shimal (People of the North) includes the tribes of Anizah, Shammar, and Dhafir, and they used to move around the Syrian steppes.

Shammar is one of the largest and most prestigious Arab tribes. It is a part of the Arab Qahtanite confederation and traces its origin to the ancient tribe of Tayy. The historical geographical center of the tribe is the current city of Ha'il—previously the Emirate of Jabal Shammar. The peak of Shammar's dominance on the peninsula fell on the middle of the 19th century, when it controlled almost the entire Central and Northern Arabia—a vast territory stretching from Riyadh to the Syrian and Iraqi regions. Historically, the Shammar tribal group had three main branches: the Abdah, the Aslam, and the Zoba. A significant number of the Shammar left their home base Jabal Shammar in the 17th century and relocated to the north of Iraq, with Mosul being their current center. The Shammar remain one of Iraq's largest and most influential tribes. The remaining population of the Shammar, who stayed on the Arabian Peninsula, owned large tribal territories in the central and northern regions of the peninsula. The Shammar and the Anizah tribal group, who inhabited the same area, had a notoriously long rivalry with each other. Al Rashid, or the House of Rasheed, is one of the most well-known dynasties coming from the Shammar. Historically, Al Rashid were the most formidable rivals of Al Saud. Among other historical figures belonging to this tribe is the legendary Hatim Al-Tai (d. 578)—an early Arab poet, renowned for his generosity and hospitality and mentioned in the Arabian Nights.

Anizah is another large tribal group, whose origins predate Islam—as is the case with the most prominent Arabian tribes. It belongs to the Adnan (or northern) tribes. Anizah had two main branches—nomadic and sedentary. The nomadic section of the tribe inhabited Northern Arabia near the Syrian and Mesopotamian borders. The settled population, known as Bani Hizzan, occupied the wadis of eastern Najd. The Anizah tribe was known for their superior breed of horses. They had the most influence on the peninsula during the Ottoman times, when they ruled the entire northwestern Arabia. Today, Anizah remains a prominent tribe in the north of Saudi Arabia, but large communities belonging to this tribe also live in Riyadh, Medina, and the Eastern Province.

Harb is a Qahtanite Arabian tribe, whose members are predominantly Sunni. In Arabic the word *harb* means "war," and this tribe is known for its raids on caravans and pilgrimage. Their tribal lands stretch from the Red Sea coast in Tihamah to Najd, and from Medina in the north to al-Qunfudhah in the south. Harb's influence extends beyond Saudi Arabia and includes Iraq, Kuwait, Bahrain, and UAE. Their origins can be traced to the 9th century AD. Historically, Harb had the most dominance in the Hijaz, with the center in the city of Medina. Like many other prominent Arab tribes, Harb is a confederation of various smaller tribes and clans. In the 20th century, many of its members migrated to several major metropolitan areas of Saudi Arabia—Riyadh, Jeddah, and Dammam—in search of education and employment opportunities. Bedouins from Harb are famous for their various forms of traditional music and dancing.

Mutayr is an important tribal confederation located in northeastern Saudi Arabia between Qasim and Kuwait. The center of their influence is in the areas of Hafr al-Batin, the Tapline, and al-Artawiyah. The tribe has been almost exclusively nomadic, with only a few settled communities in Najd. First historical records of the tribe go back to the beginning of the 14th century in eastern Hijaz, but some historians associate Harb with the pre-Islamic tribe of Ghatban, who fought Muhammad and his forces in the Battle of the Trench in 627. Since the discovery of oil and the consequent rapid urbanization, most branches of Mutayr settled around the cities of Buraydah and Unayzah, gave up their nomadic lifestyle, and took on various agricultural occupations. Mutayr's various branches include both of the two main tribal origins—Adnan and Qahtan. The two biggest branches are Alwah and Bureyh. In modern times, Mutayr participated in the power struggle between the rival Houses of Saud and Rashid, eventually siding with Ibn Saud.

Banu Tamim is a tribal group living in Central Arabia and is considered one of the oldest tribes on the Arabian Peninsula. It traces its lineage to Adnan and considers Tamim ibn Murr, who lived around the 1st century AD, its main ancestor. In Arabic, the word *tamim* means "strong" or "solid." In pre-Islamic times, the Banu Tamim dominated other Arab tribes due to its numbers and vast territories. However, gradually they went into decline, which is attributed to the fragmentation of their settlement pattern. They often share their tribal territory with other groups, mainly from the larger Shammar tribe, but these two confederations have very different tribal cultures and traditions. In contrast to the predominantly nomadic Shammar, the Bani Tamim were sedentary farmers who owned the land in the oases that they cultivated.

> ## BANU AL-NADIR
>
> Large Jewish communities were well established in the Hijaz about two centuries before the arrival of Islam. Their settlements spread over a large area in oases, and they were particularly prominent around Yatrib—which later received the name of Medina. Shortly before Muhammad and his followers came to the city from Mecca, the Jewish population of Yatrib was around eight or ten thousand. Various traditions have conflicting views on the origins of these communities, but it is known that there were over 20 Jewish clans, of which the three biggest tribes were Banu al-Nadir, Banu Qaynuqa, and Banu Qurayza. Members of the Banu al-Nadir were successful both in agriculture and trade. They cultivated date palms and traded textiles and weapons, in addition to agricultural products.
>
> Upon Muhammad's arrival to Medina in 622, the Banu al-Nadir leadership signed a treaty with him, but it only lasted for three years. The leader of the Banu al-Nadir, Ka'b ibn al-Ashraf, who was also a gifted poet, was assassinated (historical records do not have consensus on who killed him), and some members of the tribe were plotting to kill Muhammad in retaliation. The conflict escalated into a siege of Banu al-Nadir by the Muslims. After their palm trees were destroyed, Banu al-Nadir capitulated. The conditions of their surrender were to leave Medina and take with them only what they could carry on camels. The whole tribe left on a caravan of 600 camels, and their land was divided between Muhammad's companions who immigrated with him from Mecca. Most of Banu al-Nadir relocated to the Jewish community of Khaybar, and others went further north to Syria. The expulsion of the Banu al-Nadir is reflected in the Surah al-Hashr, the 59th surah/chapter of the Quran.

See also: Chapter 1: Population. Chapter 2: Arab Revolt (1916–1918); Ikhwan; Muhammad, Prophet of Islam; Pre-Islamic Arabia; The Rise of Islam; Third Saudi State: Saudi Arabia in the 20th Century. Chapter 6: Bedouins and Nomadism; Settled Population: *Hadar*; Sulubbah; Urbanization. Chapter 10: Honor; *Majlis*. Chapter 11: Poetry. Chapter 12: Bedouin Jewelry; Sadu Weaving; Traditional Garments. Chapter 13: *Ardha* Dance; Bedouin Music.

Further Reading

Crone, Patricia. *From Arabian Tribes to Islamic Empire: Army, State and Society in the Near East, c. 600–850*. Ashgate, 2008.

Eickelman, Dale F. "Tribes and Tribal Identity in the Arab Gulf States." *The Emergence of the Gulf States: Studies in Modern History*. Edited by J. E. Peterson. Bloomsbury, 2016, pp. 223–240.

al-Fahad, Abdulaziz H.. "Rootless Trees: Genealogical Politics in Saudi Arabia." *Saudi Arabia in Transition: Insights on Social, Political, Economic and Religious Change*. Edited by Bernard Haykel, Thomas Hegghammer, and Stéphane Lacroix. Cambridge University Press, 2015, pp. 263–291.

al-Juhany, Uwidah M. *Najd before the Salafi Reform Movement*. Ithaca Press, 2002.

Kurpershoek, P. M. *Arabia of the Bedouins*. Saqi, 2001.

Lecker, Michael. *People, Tribes, and Society in Arabia around the Time of Muhammad*. Ashgate, 2005.

al-Rasheed, Madawi. *Politics in an Arabian Oasis: Rashidis of Saudi Arabia*. I. B. Tauris, 1992.

Samin, Nadav. "Kafā'a Fī l-Nasab in Saudi Arabia: Islamic Law, Tribal Custom, and Social Change." *Journal of Arabian Studies (Arabia, the Gulf, and the Red Sea)*, vol. 2, no. 2, 2012, pp. 109–126.

Settled Population: *Hadar*

In Saudi Arabia, *hadar* refers to settled populations in towns and oases throughout the Arabian Peninsula who were primarily farmers and merchants. In the case with settlers living along the coasts, they would frequently engage in various maritime occupations. The Bedouin population usually looked down at *hadar* and considered them of inferior status, mainly because the latter were lacking tribal origin or could not keep their tribal lineage pure due to external marriages. *Hadar* remained outside of the Bedouin value system because they could not defend themselves or participate in warfare or raiding. Nevertheless, the societies and economies of tribal pastoralists and settled agriculturalists were historically closely linked, as they depended on each other for survival in the harsh environment of the Arabian Peninsula. *Hadar* received various animal products from the nomads, such as meat, milk, and wool, while providing the tribes with various agricultural products and metalwork.

An important distinction between the two groups of population was the question of descent—which remains a defining feature of contemporary Arabian society. The term "Bedouin" did not simply refer to their trade of pastoral nomadism, but it indicated one's noble tribal origins. Throughout history, many tribal families settled into oases for various reasons, but they were still considered to have Bedouin identity and continued to be distinguished from *hadar*.

The *hadar* population was not uniform and showed significant sociocultural differences, depending on particular geographical areas and types of settlements. Before the oil boom, the most popular occupations among the *hadar* were farming, trade, and a great variety of crafts. In recent times, Saudi Arabia's rapid urbanization radically changed traditional settlement patterns throughout the peninsula and made the distinctions among the Bedouin and *hadar* less obvious. However, traditional tribal culture continues to play an important role in all spheres of Saudi society, including the issues of lineage, ethnicity, and descent. Therefore, marital ties between *hadar* and Bedouin remain problematic.

See also: Chapter 1: Population. Chapter 2: Pre-Islamic Arabia. Chapter 4: Agriculture. Chapter 6: Bedouins and Nomadism; Sulubbah; Urbanization.

Further Reading

Galaty, John G., and Philip Carl Salzman. *Change and Development in Nomadic and Pastoral Societies*. Brill, 1981.

Metz, Helen Chapin, and Library of Congress. Federal Research Division. *Saudi Arabia: A Country Study*. 5th ed. Federal Research Division, Library of Congress, 1993.

Sharif and *Sayyid*

The title *sharif* in pre-Islamic times among the nomadic and settled population of Arabia was given to people of noble descent and disposition. It was often used to refer to tribal leaders. In Arabic, the word *sharif* means "to be noble" or "to be highborn," usually in reference to an honorable and well-respected man. Even today, some leading tribal families continue to use the title *sharif* or *ashraf* (the latter is a superlative form of *sharif*), in addition to their family name.

In the days of the Islamic caliphate, this title was used specifically for members of the Hashemite family, as well as the Fatimid dynasty starting in the 10th century, and the descendants of Hasan ibn Ali, the grandson of Muhammad. In contrast, those descending from his brother Hussein were called *sayyid*. Occasionally, all descendants of the prophet were called *sharif* and formed an elite social group, led by the *naqib*, who acted as a supervisor of the group's noble lineage and reinforced appropriate codes of behavior among its members. In the early 14th century, the *sharifs* began to be visually recognized by wearing a green turban, which indicated their high social status. A high status, however, did not automatically imply the person's wealth.

Various regions of the Islamic world were led either by families of *sharifs* or *sayyids*, depending on the political powers at play. For example, the current royal family of Morocco claim lineage from the *sharifs*. Among other important *sharif* families are the descendants of the Grand Sharif of Mecca, the Hashemites. In the past, they ruled over Syria and Iraq, and are currently the royal family of Jordan, which takes the name of the Hashemite Kingdom. The Sharifs of Mecca were governors of the Hijaz and guardians of the two holy cities of Mecca and Medina, starting from the 10th century. Under various Muslim rulers, including the Ayyubids, Mamluks, and Ottomans, it was their obligation to protect those important places and guarantee the safety of the annual pilgrimage to them. In 1925, Ibn Saud conquered Mecca, banished the last Grand Sharif from the city, and eliminated the sharifate institution.

See also: Chapter 1: Mecca; Medina. Chapter 2: Third Saudi State: Saudi Arabia in the 20th Century.

Further Reading

al-Amr, Saleh Muhammad. "The Hijaz under Ottoman Rule 1869–1914: Ottoman Vali, the Sharif of Mecca, and the Growth of British Influence." University of Leeds, 1974.

Teitelbaum, Joshua. *The Rise and Fall of the Hashimite Kingdom of Arabia*. New York University Press, 2001.

Sulubbah

The Sulubbah are a nomadic people who lived throughout the northern region of the Arabian Peninsula. They were primarily hunters and gatherers. The Sulubbah are considered a pariah group within Saudi society and occupy the lowest position in the country's complex social hierarchy. Other Saudis see them as outsiders, which makes intermarriages incredibly difficult and rare. Bedouins from tribes of noble descent normally avoided close contact with the Sulubbah. They have a distinct culture and customs and speak a dialect of Arabic. Although they are technically Muslims, the remnants of ancient pagan traditions can still be found in their rituals and doctrines.

The Sulubbah are considered of non-Arab origins, but there is no definitive historical evidence about their ancient history. This lack of information led to various misinterpretations of their descent, further reinforcing their inferior position within the larger society—given the importance of descent among Saudi population. Many consider them the descendants of the crusaders who were captured and enslaved, and then mixed with nomadic gypsy communities. But some anthropological evidence suggests that they might be the last survivals of Paleolithic hunters—the most ancient regional population who once dominated the peninsula. The Sulubbah have a tribal social structure, although the clans within the tribe are usually unrelated and live separately. An important difference between their social organization and that of the rest of Arabian communities is the elevated position of women, who can openly socialize with men, participate in public occasions, and choose their spouse.

Historically, the Sulubbah were primarily nomadic hunters, but some were practicing various crafts and worked as wage laborers and entertainers—the professions that were greatly despised by the dominant Bedouin society. Due to their occupations, the Sulubbah tend to live close to large tribes and seek the latter's protection, in exchange for a variety of artisan production, especially metalwork. They also had to pay a protection tax, called *khuwah*. If the increasing urbanization minimized the distinction between Bedouins and *hadar*, it did not have any noticeable impact on the social inferiority of the Sulubbah. This population continues to be marginalized due to the stigma of "unpure" descent—despite the fact that the term "Sulubbah," or "Sulayb," has been abandoned in Saudi Arabia.

See also: Chapter 1: Northern Arabia; Population. Chapter 2: Pre-Islamic Arabia. Chapter 3: Human Rights and Censorship. Chapter 6: Bedouins and Nomadism; Major Tribes; Settled Population: *Hadar*; Urbanization.

Further Reading

Bamyeh, Mohammed A. "The Nomads of Pre-Islamic Arabia." *Nomadic Societies in the Middle East and North Africa: Entering the 21st Century*. Edited by Dawn Chatty. Brill, 2006, pp. 33–48.

Betts, Alison. "The Solubba: Nonpastoral Nomads in Arabia." *Bulletin of the American Schools of Oriental Research*, no. 274, May 1989, pp. 61–69.

Galaty, John G., and Philip Carl Salzman. *Change and Development in Nomadic and Pastoral Societies*. Brill, 1981.

Ingham, Bruce. *Bedouin of Northern Arabia: Traditions of the Al-Dhafir*. KPI, 1986.

MacDonald, M. C. A., and Werner Caskel. "Was There a 'Bedouinization of Arabia'?" *Der Islam*, vol. 92, no. 1, 2015, pp. 42–84.

Urbanization

A number of urban centers in Saudi Arabia date back to the premodern and pre-Islamic periods, most prominent of which are Jeddah, Riyadh, Mecca, and Medina. The ancient Arabian cities were situated along the caravan and sea trade routes. With the discovery of oil, new cities and towns were established to support the quickly developing oil and petrochemical industries, particularly in the Eastern Province. New employment opportunities and social infrastructure attracted many communities to settle and relocate to these areas. Foreign workers also arrived in big numbers. The growth of the oil industry in the 1950s and the 1970s prompted a fast rate of urbanization—much more rapid in Saudi Arabia than in other comparable areas of the Middle East. Virtually all Saudi cities expanded both in population and size. For example, if Riyadh occupied 110 square kilometers in 1968, by 1990 it increased to 1,600 square kilometers. Over the same period, the capital's population grew from 160,000 to over 2 million. On average, Saudi Arabia has an 83 percent ratio of urbanization. The social and cultural impact of this process was particularly severe along the coast of the Persian Gulf. The rapid growth of areas that were small fishermen villages into oil metropolises dramatically transformed the lives of the local population in just a few decades, prompting clashes between traditional and modern, local and foreign cultures and communities. Social hierarchy, gender roles, the relationship between nomadic and settled populations, codes of behavior, dietary customs, and many other societal aspects changed almost overnight and required the local community to quickly adapt.

Following the investments in the eastern oil cities, Saudi government established planning commissions to oversee the transformation of other cities into administrative centers. Oil revenues enabled the government to initiate various ambitious construction projects—from wide-scale building of administrative and residential areas to completely reconfiguring the areas surrounding the Muslim holy sites in Mecca and Medina. In most cases, Western concepts of city planning were used that radically changed the landscape of many local historical cities. However, some core aspects of traditional settlements remained, such as architectural designs that supported gender segregation and the preference of extended families to live in each other's vicinity. These traditional notions of social interaction continue to define even the most modern urban developments. Saudi Arabia's high birthrate and overall demographics support the trend of urbanization. Currently, there are several urban conglomerations in the country. The western urban center, which is also the oldest, is comprised of Jeddah, Mecca, Medina, and Ta'if. Saudi Arabia's capital Riyadh is the main urban center in Central

An urban area in Saudi Arabia. (Think Design Manage/Dreamstime.com)

Arabia. The eastern region is the heart of the oil industry and includes the cities of Dammam, Khobar, and Dhahran. The two main cities in the Asir Mountains are Abha and Khamis Mushait.

See also: Chapter 1: Jeddah; Mecca; Medina; Population. Chapter 2: Third Saudi State: Saudi Arabia in the 20th Century. Chapter 4: Diversification and Development Plans. Chapter 6: Bedouins and Nomadism; Major Tribes; Settled Population: *Hadar*. Chapter 12: Modernization of Saudi Architecture.

Further Reading

Abou-Korin, Antar A., and Faez Saad al-Shihri. "Rapid Urbanization and Sustainability in Saudi Arabia: The Case of Dammam Metropolitan Area." *Journal of Sustainable Development*, vol. 8, no. ix, 2015, pp. 52–65.

Benna, Umar G., and Shaibu Bala Garba. *Population Growth and Rapid Urbanization in the Developing World*. Information Science Reference, 2016.

Ménoret, Pascal. *Joyriding in Riyadh: Oil, Urbanism, and Road Revolt*. Cambridge University Press, 2014.

Pampanini, Andrea H. *Cities from the Arabian Desert: The Building of Jubail and Yanbu in Saudi Arabia*. Praeger, 1997.

CHAPTER 7

GENDER, MARRIAGE, AND SEXUALITY

OVERVIEW

Women's rights have always been a controversial issue in Saudi Arabia. The country is widely known for its repressive policies and gender inequality issues that perpetuate all levels of Saudi social and political life, despite the fact that recent years saw a number of historic changes under way. The 2018 Global Gender Gap Report demonstrates that Saudi women remain excluded from full participation in society and politics. The report ranks the country at 141 out of 149 countries, while noting certain improvements in wage equality and women's labor force participation compared to previous years. Currently, female university graduates outnumber males: in 2016, over 105,000 women graduated from Saudi universities and 98,000 men. But it is much more difficult for women to find employment, even when they are highly qualified for the positions. The problems with employment faced by Saudi women are rooted in the country's highly conservative culture and a number of laws that greatly restrict women's mobility and independence. For decades, Saudi Arabia was the only country that legally forbid women to drive, until the ban was lifted in September 2017. The absolute majority of public spaces, including work spaces, are segregated, and companies often have cultural resistance to employing women. In these circumstances, it is not surprising that a third of working-age Saudi women are unemployed, a rate nearly five times higher than men.

Unlike other Muslim countries, Saudi Arabia applies the strictest interpretation of the highly conservative Wahhabi religious doctrine, which is carried out by the Saudi *ulama* (religious leaders) and their many *fatwas* (legal opinions) on various aspects of women's lives—from marital laws to dress codes. The doctrine and the legal system around it are held responsible for the many restrictions imposed on Saudi women and for their institutionalized exclusion from the society. Even compared with similarly conservative Gulf countries, Saudi Arabia stands out with its broadest policies of gender segregation. In most other Muslim countries, the system of coed institutions prevails. Women and men attend school together, and the majority of work spaces are also mixed. But the most striking difference is the overall legal status of women, or rather lack thereof. Whereas other Muslim women are treated as legal persons, Saudi women remain under male guardianship from birth to death, where men control their marriage, work, mobility, and education. In other words, the women remain minors throughout their whole lives. In court, the testimony of one man equals that of two women. For decades, all judges were male, and only in 2010 women lawyers were allowed to represent other women in court. Family law itself is discriminatory against women. For example, daughters receive only half the inheritance of sons, and a woman cannot marry without permission of her male guardian (*mahram* or *wali*). A wife cannot divorce her husband without his permission, unless she is able to provide a clearly defined legal justification, such as proof of harm. At the same time, a man can divorce his wife without any legal grounds at all. In the case of divorce, courts generally grant custody of children to their father and his side of the family in the case of his death.

Despite a persistent and wide-ranging exclusion of women being attributed to the religious ideology of Wahhabism, there were numerous other scholars and teachings promoting similar conservative opinions throughout Islamic history. In fact, the Islamic tradition is not dissimilar from other orthodox traditions, where patriarchy and misogyny have been essential practices throughout history, including Christianity and Judaism. Like these two other monotheistic traditions, Islam took different forms and practical applications in different historical moments and cultural contexts, in addition to showing a great deal of regional variety. Thus, Wahhabi doctrine alone cannot be the only explanation for obstacles preventing the emancipation of Saudi women. One should also consider a traditional regional culture that, along with a particularly strict

---

LOUJAIN AL-HATHLOUL

Loujain al-Hathloul (b. 1989) is a Saudi women's rights and human rights activist, a social media figure, and currently a political prisoner. She is known for defying the ban on women driving on numerous occasions, for which she was arrested and harassed by the authorities. In 2015, she was ranked third on the list of Top Most Powerful Arab Women. In 2019, she was on the Time 100—the magazine's annual list of 100 most influential people in the world.

A graduate of the University of British Columbia, al-Hathloul was married to the well-known Saudi stand-up comedian Fahad Albutairi—until the Saudi authorities allegedly forced them to divorce in 2018. Al-Hathloul has been an ardent opponent of the male guardianship system in Saudi Arabia. In September 2016, al-Hathloul was one of the 14,000 Saudi citizens who signed a petition asking King Salman to abolish the guardianship system. In June 2017, she was arrested and detained at King Fahad International Airport in Dammam. Finally, in May 2018, she was once again arrested in a crackdown on Saudi women's rights activists, along with Aziza al-Yousef, Eman al-Nafjan, Nouf Abdelaziz, Mayaa al-Zahrani, Samar Badawi, Nassima al-Saada, Hatoon al-Fassi, Shadan al-Onezi, Amal al-Harbi, Aisha al-Mana, and Madeha al-Ajroush, as well as a number of men who participated in the movement, including Mohammed Rabea. As of April 2019, al-Hathloul and most of the other activists remain in prison. There have also been reports of torture that several of these women were subjected to. In March 2019, the activists were charged under the country's cyber-crimes law and put on trial. Foreign journalists and diplomats were barred from attending the closed session.

religious teaching, dictated the establishment of the legal and government systems currently in place.

Although discrimination against women and the great limitations they face are common features in all areas of Saudi society and governance, the women's status and rights on the Arabian Peninsula have greatly varied both geographically and historically. For example, the women of Riyadh and the conservative Najd historically experienced many more restrictions than those residing in the cosmopolitan Red Sea coastal area of Hijaz, especially the port city of Jeddah. It is important to note that many of the current legal and sociocultural restrictions were imposed on women after the national crisis of 1979, when the Holy Mosque in Mecca was seized by the extremists and many worshippers were taken hostage. As a result of this crisis, which claimed hundreds of lives, both the state and the religious establishment felt the threat of internal Islamist forces and responded by fighting against the alleged "moral corruption" of the nation. The conservative circles promoted the view of the Holy Mosque siege as a punishment for opening up Saudi society. In what followed, many *fatwas* on women were issued throughout the 1980s to regulate and significantly restrict their lives. Many working women were fired, and the number of government scholarships for women sharply declined. Women could not conduct business or travel abroad without a male relative or their written permission. These measures were accompanied by other restrictions such as banning Western music from public places. Additionally, women anchors stopped appearing on television.

Since King Abdullah (r. 2005–2015) assumed the throne in 2005, a number of reforms have been initiated to gradually improve the position of Saudi women, who began to play a more visible role in various sectors of Saudi society, although the legal restrictions have not been lifted or modified. In 2008, two women were elected to the board of the Jeddah Chamber of Commerce and Industry, which drew a great deal of attention and inspired other businesswomen. There has been an increased participation in charitable foundations, community groups, and voluntary and professional associations, but this activity was limited to nongovernmental organizations, as women remained excluded from legal and government institutions. However, an important milestone was achieved in 2009 when a woman was named a deputy minister for education—the highest official position ever held by a woman in Saudi Arabia. In 2013, another significant event took place when King Abdullah appointed 30 women to serve for the first time in his Shura Council, or the Consultative Assembly, which is the formal advisory body to the king, consisting of 150 members. Although women campaigned unsuccessfully for the right to vote in the 2011 municipal elections, Abdullah announced that they would be eligible to vote and run for office in the country's 2015 municipal elections. In the field of family law, women have also made progress. In 2005, forced marriage was banned, and in 2013, the King Abdulaziz Center for National Dialogue organized a campaign entitled "No More Abuse" to combat domestic violence. In 2017, the driving ban for women was officially lifted, despite objections from the most conservative groups of Saudi society.

Changing the gender status quo has been pronounced as one of the core objectives of the most recent reform plan, led by Crown Prince Muhammad bin Salman and dubbed Saudi Vision 2030, which aims to transform the economy to reduce its dependence on oil and to modernize all Saudi social and cultural spheres. With regard to women's employment, the ambitious plan intends to increase their participation in the workforce from 22 percent to 30 percent by 2030. But even with these signs of progress, Saudi women continue to face significant challenges—both legal and cultural—in their pursuit of full rights as Saudi citizens.

Further Reading

Almunajjed, Mona. *Women in Saudi Arabia Today.* St. Martin's Press, 1997.

Bernardi, Chiara L. *Women and the Digitally-Mediated Revolution in the Middle East: Applying Digital Methods.* Routledge, 2019.

Galán, Susana. "Cautious Enactments: Interstitial Spaces of Gender Politics in Saudi Arabia." *Freedom without Permission: Bodies and Space in the Arab Revolutions.* Edited by Frances S. Hasso and Zakia Salime. Duke University Press, 2016, pp. 166–195.

Joseph, Suad, and Susan Slyomovics, eds. *Women and Power in the Middle East.* University of Pennsylvania Press, 2001.

Le Renard, Amélie. *A Society of Young Women: Opportunities of Place, Power, and Reform in Saudi Arabia.* Stanford University Press, 2014.

al-Rasheed, Madawi. *A Most Masculine State: Gender, Politics and Religion in Saudi Arabia.* Cambridge University Press, 2013.

Tsujigami, Namie. "Stealth Revolution: Saudi Women's Ongoing Social Battles." *Arab Women's Activism and Socio-Political Transformation: Unfinished Gendered Revolutions.* Edited by Sahar Khamis and Amel Mili. Palgrave Macmillan, 2018, pp. 149–166.

Yamani, Maha A. Z. *Polygamy and Law in Contemporary Saudi Arabia.* 1st ed. Ithaca Press, 2008.

Divorce

Divorce is an important aspect of family law and social norms, governed by Islamic and cultural traditions. The general idea is that marriage is sacred in Islam, and therefore divorce is strongly discouraged. Paradoxically, divorce in Saudi Arabia is common and straightforward socially, but complex legally. This institution is based on ancient tribal traditions, in which divorce was an easy affair due to the requirements of nomadic lifestyle and the historically challenging environment. The current complexities are a relatively recent historical development and reflect Sharia law. The Islamic law contains explicit procedures on the dissolution of a marriage, such as the disposal of property, the custody of children, and the mandatory restrictions on the timeline given to women wishing to remarry (with the goal of establishing clear paternity). There are two legal categories of divorce: repudiation (*talaq*) and the mutual dissolution of marriage (*khul*). Repudiation, as a one-sided form of divorce by the husband, is an essential principle of Islamic family law in many Muslim countries, including Saudi Arabia. The divorcing man is recommended to say the statement "I repudiate you" to his wife three times.

After the first two announcements, he should wait and reflect before issuing his third and final statement, after which a divorce is irreconcilable. If the husband announces the three statements altogether, reconciliation is legally impossible—unless the woman marries another man, consumes the marriage, and then divorces from him.

In theory, women may seek divorce too, but the procedures are much more complicated and, in many cases, an impossible undertaking. First of all, she needs the support of her legal guardian who, in the case of the married woman, is almost always her husband. The process is usually based on the inclusion of a divorce formula in the marriage contract or the husband's failure to fulfill the terms of this contract. Another method for a woman to divorce her husband is to buy her way out of the wedding contract. This can be done by returning the dowry or paying him a certain amount of money, and this is the form of divorce that is practiced by women relatively frequently, as it has the least legal ramifications. Otherwise, the other legal reasons for a woman to seek divorce, as defined by Sharia, are the husband's impotence, insanity, abuse, or neglect. In these cases, she has to go to court and rely on the verdict of the judge.

Islam does not have unilateral provisions for alimony. The general custom is that the woman can keep the dowry but does not receive other forms of compensation. She is also required to return to her own family. The father is wholly responsible for the support of all his minor children, although they generally remain with their mother until the age of 5 or 6. After that, boys come to live with their father to begin their formal education, whereas the girls often remain with their mother. After the official divorce, women are required to wait for a specific period of time (usually three menstrual cycles) before getting remarried, so that in the case of pregnancy, the child's paternity can be established without ambiguity.

Thus, even with the turn of the 21st century, historical Arabian rites of passage continue to reflect the patriarchal and patrilineal nature of Saudi society. The institutions of marriage and divorce, having incorporated both ancient tribal structures and Islamic societal innovations, emphasize the importance of bloodlines, the division of labor by gender, and the role of family and the larger community in defining a person's life. At the same time, the conservative traditions are beginning to slowly but steadily change under the influence of modernity—both from within the Saudi society and from the outside.

See also: Chapter 3: Sharia Law and Judicial System; Ulama. Chapter 5: Sunni Islam and Jurisprudence. Chapter 7: Guardianship; Marriage Law and Tradition; Parents and Children.

Further Reading

Rapoport, Yossef. *Marriage, Money and Divorce in Medieval Islamic Society*. Cambridge University Press, 2005.

Sawaf, Zina. "Encountering the State: Women and Divorce in Riyadh, Saudi Arabia." *Arabian Humanities*, vol. 10, 2018.

Sonbol, Amira El Azhary. *Women, the Family, and Divorce Laws in Islamic History*. 1st ed. Syracuse University Press, 1996.

Domestic Violence

Domestic violence remains a major problem in Saudi Arabia, although in recent years the society and the government began addressing this issue. The male guardianship system enables an environment where, for decades, the great majority of such cases either went unreported or were ignored by the authorities. According to Saudi laws, fleeing a home—even an abusive one—is a crime for women. Under the guardianship system, male relatives have vast powers over women. Women are not legally allowed to run away from male guardians, including fathers and husbands. The guardians have complete control over the women's mobility, such as permission to travel and the issuance of passports. If runaways are caught, they can be jailed until their guardian asks for their release. It is therefore unsurprising that the exact figures on domestic violence in Saudi Arabia are difficult to estimate. Various reports indicate that between 16 percent and 50 percent of married women suffer from at least one form of spousal abuse. Others speculate that around 35 percent of all Saudi women experience at least one form of violence in their lifetime. Until recent changes, for decades domestic violence and spousal rape were not crimes according to Saudi law. Additionally, social and cultural consequences of reporting violence of any kind made it very difficult for women to come forward.

The explosive topic of domestic violence captured the attention of the public in 2004, when a well-known Saudi television presenter, Rania al-Baz, was physically abused by her husband. Graphic images of her injuries appeared in the press and generated a powerful movement both inside and outside the country. In 2008, a special decree was issued by the prime minister, ordering the creation of the so-called social protection units in several large cities—a version of women's shelters. In the same year, the government began drafting a national strategy to address domestic violence. Several royal foundations, including the King Abdulaziz Center for National Dialogue and the King Khalid Foundation, initiated various education and awareness efforts.

However, only in 2013, violence against women and children was formally recognized as a crime. In August 2013, the Saudi cabinet approved a domestic violence law, which established a system of punishment of up to a year in prison and a fine of up to 50,000 Saudi riyals (approximately 13,000 USD). Repeat offenders may receive a double of the maximum punishment. An important aspect of this law is that it criminalizes not only physical violence, but also psychological and sexual abuse. It also includes a provision obliging employees to report workplace abuse to their superiors. Saudi women's rights activists welcomed the new legal measures, although concerns remained about successful implementation of the laws, which would require extensive training of judges. Additionally, male guardianship, which remains firmly in place despite a number of recent reforms, will always present an obstacle for prosecutions.

In 2013, Saudi Arabia initiated its first major public and media effort against domestic violence. The "No More Abuse" campaign ads showed a veiled woman with one black eye. The English version was accompanied by the statement "some things can't be covered." The campaign website included a report on reducing domestic violence and emergency resources for victims. The efforts against domestic violence continue both in the form of grassroot movements and campaigns led by women from the royal family, who use their social status and visibility to promote the cause.

See also: Chapter 3: Sharia Law and Judicial System; Ulama. Chapter 5: Sunni Islam and Jurisprudence. Chapter 7: Divorce; Guardianship; Marriage Law and Tradition; Parents and Children.

Further Reading

Cochran, Cybèle. "Women and the Law in Islamic Societies: Legal Responses to Domestic Violence in Saudi Arabia and Morocco." *Al Nakhlah*, Spring 2009, pp. 1–11.

al-Rasheed, Madawi. *A Most Masculine State: Gender, Politics and Religion in Saudi Arabia*. Cambridge University Press, 2013.

Gender Segregation

The prohibition against *ikhtilat* (gender mixing) is strictly enforced throughout the country, requiring unrelated men and women to not interact socially or be in physical proximity to each other in public spaces. Saudi clerics believe that this system is required by the Sharia law and ultimately by the Quran. Gender segregation is maintained in schools, places of work, restaurants, parks, and shopping centers, which generally have separate areas for men and women. Even hospitals are required to respect segregation, where it is preferable for patients to be treated by medical professionals of the same sex.

The system of gender segregation throughout Saudi Arabia has a particularly dramatic effect on education and employment. None of the educational institutions of any level, including universities, are coed. A rare exception is the King Abdullah University of Science and Technology—a graduate-level research university, founded in 2009, where women are allowed to attend class without covering, work together with men, and drive cars on campus (even before the driving ban was lifted). But despite the great limitations imposed on women by this system, the women's literacy rate is over 80 percent and close to that of men, and more than a half of Saudi university students are women. Saudi Arabia is also home to Princess Nourah Bint Abdulrahman University, the world's largest university for women, located in Riyadh.

In much contrast to women's remarkable progress in education, they continue to suffer discrimination in employment as a direct result of the prohibition against *ikhtilat*. With some exceptions, including hospitals, a number of newspapers and advertising agencies, and international corporations such as Saudi Aramco, where men and women are allowed to work together on private compounds, most Saudi companies adhere to policies that require the separation of their male and female employees. In some professions, women are not hired at all, and in others they must telework from home. The Ministry of Labor encourages the employment of women in specific sectors of the economy, such as medicine and energy, but women who want to start their own business still need the permission of their male guardian. In 2011, the ministry announced a widely publicized and controversial decision to require that all stores selling women's cosmetics and underwear must be staffed exclusively by women.

See also: Chapter 3: Sharia Law and Judicial System; Ulama; Wahhabi Ideology. Chapter 5: Sunni Islam and Jurisprudence. Chapter 7: Guardianship; Marriage Law and Tradition; *Mutawwa*: The Saudi Religious Police; Social Life, Kinship, and Friendships; Women's Mobility and Driving Ban. Chapter 8: Education of Women. Chapter 10: Dress Etiquette; Social Life. Chapter 15: Women in Sports.

Further Reading

Le Renard, Amélie. "'Only for Women:' Women, the State, and Reform in Saudi Arabia." *Middle East Journal*, vol. 62, no. 4, Sept. 2008, pp. 610–629.

Le Renard, Amélie. "From Qur'ānic Circles to the Internet: Gender Segregation and the Rise of Female Preachers in Saudi Arabia." *Women, Leadership, and Mosques: Changes in Contemporary Islamic Authority*. Edited by Masooda Bano and Hilary Kalmbach. Brill, 2012, pp. 105–126.

Meijer, Roel. "The Gender Segregation (Ikhtilāṭ) Debate in Saudi Arabia: Reform and the Clash between 'Ulamā' and Liberals." *Journal for Islamic Studies*, vol. 30, 2010, pp. 2–32.

Guardianship

The system of male guardianship severely limits both the legal rights and the social roles of Saudi women. It mandates that every Saudi woman of any age have a guardian, whose Arabic term is *mahram* or *wali*, depending on the legal context. This role could be performed by the father or another male relative such as an uncle, the husband, and even by her son. The Arabic word *mahram* means "taboo," combining the connotations of "sacred" and "forbidden." For a married woman, her husband automatically becomes her guardian. If she is single, one of her male relatives acts as a *mahram*—her father, an uncle, a brother, or a son. The system of male guardianship is derived from Saudi clerics' interpretation of the following Quranic verse in the *Surat al-Nisa'* (titled *The Women*): "Men are the protectors and maintainers of women, because God has given the one more (strength) than the other, and because they support them from their means. Therefore, the righteous women are devoutly obedient, and guard in (the husband's) absence what God would have them guard" (Quran 4:34).

A Saudi woman legally must obtain her guardian's permission in order to engage in virtually any economic, political, or legal activity. These include permissions to marry or divorce, seek employment or take a job, open a bank account, start a business, obtain health care, register at a hotel, rent an apartment, attend a university, or travel abroad. In sum, any Saudi woman remains a minor throughout her whole life, stripped even of the limited rights of Saudi men. Although they are legally entitled to own property and receive financial support from their guardians, many are not well-informed of their legal rights and do not to take advantage of them because of informal cultural practices. One of the very few exceptions to the guardian rule is the *umrah* pilgrimage (the so-called minor pilgrimage, in comparison with the annual Hajj pilgrimage), which women have been performing on their own, without a male guardian, since the late 1970s. In April 2017, an important change was made by King Salman's government that ordered all agencies to allow women access to any government service without consent from their male guardian. But despite the recent loosening of the *mahram* system and a number of reforms such as the lifting of a ban on female drivers, the guardianship law remains firmly in place.

A powerful campaign against the male guardianship was initiated by the activists under the hashtag *#IAmMyOwnGuardian*. The protest movement grew out of an online campaign that began in July 2016, when Human Rights Watch published a report on the male guardianship system and its great limitations. Nearly 15,000 Saudi women signed an online petition demanding the abolishment of this legally abusive system. In September 2016, the petition was handed to the Saudi government and additionally reinforced by over 2,500 direct telegrams sent to the king's office by women of all ages, urging the change.

See also: Chapter 3: Sharia Law and Judicial System; Ulama; Wahhabi Ideology. Chapter 5: Sunni Islam and Jurisprudence. Chapter 7: Gender Segregation; Marriage Law and Tradition; The *Mutawwa*: Saudi Religious Police; Social Life, Kinship, and Friendships; Women's Mobility and Driving Ban. Chapter 8: Education of Women. Chapter 10: Dress Etiquette; Social Life. Chapter 15: Women in Sports.

Further Reading

Alshahrani, Bandar. "A Critical Legal Analysis of the Impact of Male Guardianship System on Women's Rights in Saudi Arabia." *Journal of Islamic State Practices in International Law*, vol. 12, no. 2, 2016, pp. 31–70.

Hassanein, Saffaa. "I Am My Own Guardian: Reflections on Resistance Art." *JMEWS: Journal of Middle East Women's Studies*, vol. 14, no. 2, 2018, pp. 234–241.

Tønnessen, Liv. *Women's Activism in Saudi Arabia: Male Guardianship and Sexual Violence*. Chr. Michelsen Institute, 2016.

Hijab and Dress Code

The conservative clerics see the female body as a source of *fitna* (chaos, dissent). The total veiling of the body is seen as a requirement in public life, excluding the context of prayer and pilgrimage. The most ubiquitous symbol of a Saudi woman's required modesty is the black *abayah*—an outer garment in the form of a cloak—which she must wear whenever leaving the confines of the home. The *abayah* covers the clothing and may be decorated with embroidery, satin, or sequins. It is accompanied by a black head covering called *shayla*.

When in public, women should never wear white clothes since such attire is the prerogative of the men. Such visual regulation of color in clothes helps reinforce gender segregation. This explains the persistence of the black *abayah,* which is not only a cultural code of dress but has also attained a religious significance. Although the Islamic sources do not specify any particular required colors for female clothes, Saudi scholars have elevated black to the rank of a religious obligation, reinforcing the notion of female modesty. The colors black and white in the public sphere have become informal national symbols. In their simplicity, they represent the piety of the state and the nation. Another important aspect of color-based segregation is that women in black distinguish Saudis from non-Saudis. They serve as visible signs of being part of the nation, defining membership by means of clothes at a time when many foreign women arrived in the country.

In the 1980s, distinguishing Saudi women from Western women became extremely important. Drawing the boundaries between the pious Saudi women and the "morally corrupt" Westerners was done by means of rejecting the lifestyles of the latter. The country experienced a surge in expatriate labor, which included both wives of expatriates and single women who worked in hospitals as doctors and nurses. Therefore, contact with foreigners became an everyday possibility. The religious establishment reacted to this threat by issuing a large number of *fatwas* (legal opinions by clerics), with the goal of regulating the moral and physical boundaries of Saudi women. Various prohibitions and limitations were centered on all aspects of the female body and its appearance. Along with the use of dress as a marker of national identity, the *fatwas* went into such specific matters as banning high heels, coloring of hair, perfuming the body, eliminating excessive facial hair, and tattooing the skin for decoration or tribal belonging. The body was supposed to be the medium for expressing only one form of identity—Islamic. Moreover, this Islamic identity was not a matter of interpretation, but should be defined exclusively through specific guidelines from the *ulama* (religious scholars), whose main concern was to shield Saudi women from external influences and foreign lifestyles.

See also: Chapter 3: Sharia Law and Judicial System; Ulama; Wahhabi Ideology. Chapter 5: Sunni Islam and Jurisprudence. Chapter 7: Gender Segregation; Guardianship; The *Mutawwa*: Saudi Religious Police; Women's Mobility and Driving Ban. Chapter 8: Education of Women. Chapter 10: Dress Etiquette. Chapter 12: Traditional Garments. Chapter 15: Women in Sports.

Further Reading

Commins, David Dean, and Malise Ruthven. *Islam in Saudi Arabia*. Cornell University Press, 2015.

Mernissi, Fatima. *The Veil and the Male Elite: A Feminist Interpretation of Women's Rights in Islam*. Addison-Wesley Publishing, 1991.

Mouline, Nabil. *The Clerics of Islam: Religious Authority and Political Power in Saudi Arabia*. Translated by Ethan S. Rundell. Yale University Press, 2014.

Quamar, Md. Muddassir. "Sociology of the Veil in Saudi Arabia: Dress Code, Individual Choices, and Questions on Women's Empowerment." *Digest of Middle East Studies*, vol. 25, no. 2, 2016, pp. 315–337.

Identity Cards

The National Identification Card of Saudi Arabia is the official identity-verification document and proof of Saudi citizenship. It is often commonly referred to by its colloquial name *bitaqat al-ahwal*. It has the size of a credit card and contains a 2.86-megabyte optical strip, which stores data and the owner's photograph. The Saudi ID also serves as a travel document to any of the countries that are members of the Gulf Cooperation Council (GCC).

When a Saudi male becomes 1 year old, he is issued an identity card, and in adulthood is required to carry it with him at all times. In the past, women did not have a right for ID cards, but were instead named as dependents on their male guardian's card, reinforcing the rule that women could not be in public places without their guardians. In addition to the prohibitions by the religious clerks (*ulama*), the particularly conservative groups within Saudi society fervently opposed the issuance of ID cards to women because they contain a picture of the woman's unveiled face which, they argue, can only be seen by the woman's husband and her family. The lack of a personal ID card also made it challenging for a Saudi woman to prove her identity in court. She would have to produce two male relatives as witnesses to confirm her identity. This made women extremely vulnerable to violations and abuse by male relatives, including inheritance rights, claims to property, and many other issues. In sum, if a woman had a family dispute with a male relative, the legal system automatically put her at a significant disadvantage.

In 2001, the Saudi government began to issue separate identity cards for women for the first time. In order to qualify for an ID card, a woman had to be 22 years of age and needed a written consent of her male guardian. The picture's requirements included covered hair, and no makeup could be used on the woman's face. In 2008, women were given official permission to enter hotels and furnished apartments without their guardian if they had their identity cards with them. In April 2010, ID cards of the new format were issued for women, allowing them to travel to and from other GCC countries. The permission of the male guardian was required to obtain the card, but not to travel. A new law was issued in 2003, making identity cards a requirement for all women, starting with the age of 15.

See also: Chapter 7: Guardianship; Gender Segregation; Women's Mobility and Driving Ban. Chapter 8: Education of Women.

Further Reading
Joseph, Suad. *Gender and Citizenship in the Middle East*. Syracuse University Press, 2000.
Meijer, Roel. "Citizenship in Saudi Arabia." *Middle East Journal*, vol. 70, no. 4, 2016, pp. 667–673.

Marriage Law and Tradition

In the Muslim tradition, marriage is an essential component of one's life and a source of empowerment. Both the law and the cultural tradition assign particular obligations, responsibilities, and rights to husbands and wives. The marital division of labor requires from the husband to provide for the material welfare and security of the family outside the home, while the wife is expected to raise the children and manage the home internally. These customs serve as the basis of Islamic family law. The Sharia defines marriage as a legal contract (*nikah*), where the formal responsibilities of men are greater than those of women. This status difference is also reflected in the marriage contract, in which husband and wife are not considered fully equal. A Saudi woman is required to be represented by her legal guardian, often her father, who negotiates and signs the contract. She cannot marry without permission from her guardian.

Endogamy (marriage between cousins, close relatives, or members from the same tribe, region, or town) continues to be common in Saudi Arabia. However, rapid urbanization, increasing mobility, the ongoing population growth, and in more recent times Internet networks and social media, prompted the increase in marriages between unrelated spouses. In the past, marriages were usually arranged by the two families and were based social and economic matching of the families, whereby personal compatibility between the prospective spouses was not important. Today, because of higher standards of education and additional leisure time to spend, spousal compatibility is given attention.

Polygamy is formally allowed in Islam, where a man can have up to four wives and is required to treat them all and provide for them equally. However, in modern times marriage has increasingly become monogamous. There are various factor contributing to this trend: in addition to the obvious economic constraints, mutual compatibility is playing an increasingly important role, particularly among highly educated couples. Additionally, many women include specific paragraphs in their marriage contract prohibiting the husband from taking a second wife.

Structurally, the procedure for choosing a spouse has not changed significantly throughout the centuries. It is customary for the women of both families to work together on finding the right match. The first step in the marriage process is the formal proposal (*taqdim*) from the prospective groom's family. The female elder, typically his grandmother, conveys the man's intentions to the mother of the prospective bride. After that, both families determine the suitability of the marriage. In recent times, the service of a marriage broker (*khatib*) is becoming increasingly common in determining and arranging the match. When the initial agreement is met, the ceremony of *shawfa* (the viewing) follows, where the bride is formally allowed to unveil in the presence of her future husband. However, among the more conservative Saudi communities, particularly in the Najd, the viewing only takes place at the wedding party.

Upon reaching the general agreement, the groom and the bride's legal guardian work out the specific terms of the contract, including the dowry and many other details. The amount of the dowry usually goes through long negotiations. It is still customary to ask the groom and his family for large sums, in addition to jewelry, residence, and a car. The formal meeting of the families (*shabkah*) of the bride and the groom consists of a gala party hosted by the bride's family, at which time the groom presents the dowry and an engagement ring to the bride, along with other gifts and jewelry. The bride must consent to the marriage and cannot be married against her will. But she also cannot marry without a formal agreement from her legal guardian.

The execution of the contract is called *nikah* or *milkah* and has to be formalized and witnessed by an Islamic official (usually a judge) and two male relatives. Female relatives can also serve as witnesses, but there should be two of them in place of one man. When the marriage is recorded by the judge, it becomes a legally binding contract. In Najd, the *milkah* takes place just before the wedding celebration, which is an important public recognition of the marriage. The traditional customs and the complex process of marriage agreement conclude with the wedding celebration (*irs* or *zaffaf*).

Saudi marital law also allows a controversial form of marriage called *misyar*, or traveler's marriage. Unlike a regular marriage, *misyar* does not obligate men to provide their wives with a residence or to support them financially. Often, this form of marriage is used to evade objections from the first wife, because *misyar* can remain a secret—at least until children are born. In theory, a man can legitimately have up to three *misyar* marriages, in addition to the first "formal" marriage. In *misyar*, the wife usually remains in her family household, whereas the relationship with the husband is maintained through occasional visitation, without any financial responsibility toward her livelihood. As is the case with *milkah*, the woman's male guardian has to issue permission for it to happen, in addition to having two witnesses. Shiite communities have a similarly controversial form of temporary marriage called *mut'ah*, which is practiced in Iran.

Saudi women face numerous restrictions while choosing their husbands, which include their religion, ethnic origin, socioeconomic status, and tribal affiliation. Although Muslim men are allowed to marry non-Muslim women, such as Christians and Jews, Muslim women can only marry Muslims. The issue of the prospective spouse's origins can be a legitimate obstacle for marriage. There are instances when the Saudi Sharia court forcibly divorced a couple over allegations that the husband was of a lower tribal descent than his wife.

See also: Chapter 3: Sharia Law and Judicial System; Ulama. Chapter 5: Sunni Islam and Jurisprudence. Chapter 7: Divorce; Guardianship; Parents and Children; Traditional Wedding. Chapter 13: Wedding Music and Dance.

Further Reading

Mallat, Chibli. "The Normalization of Saudi Family Law." *EJIMEL: Electronic Journal of Islamic and Middle Eastern Law,* vol. 5, 2017, pp. 1–27.

Osmani, Noor Mohammad. "Misyar Marriage between Shari'ah Texts, Realities and Scholars' Fatawa': An Analysis." *IIUC Studies (Research Journal of the International Islamic University Chittagong (IIUC)),* vol. 7, 2011, pp. 297–320.

Quraishi, Asifa, and Frank E. Vogel. *The Islamic Marriage Contract: Case Studies in Islamic Family Law.* Islamic Legal Studies Program, Harvard Law School, 2008.

The *Mutawwa:* Saudi Religious Police

The *Mutawwa* is a special police force whose role is to enforce the moral aspects of Sharia law under the authority of the Saudi government. Saudi clerics justify the existence of this special force by the need to promote and protect virtuous lifestyles for all Saudi citizens. The formal name of this unit is the Committee for the Promotion of Virtue and the Prevention of Vice, and it was created in 1940. Locally they are more commonly called the *mutawwa* (which could mean both "the pious" and "volunteer") or *hayaa* (simply "the committee"). The members of the force are called *mutawwiyun*, since they, in fact, join the organization voluntarily.

Approximately 5,000 members are employed in the organization, and the unit's director reports directly to the minister of interior. In the past, they would often patrol the streets together with members of the regular police force. The *mutawwa*'s main task is to inspect and regulate public behavior and appearance, where the main objective is to prevent *ikhtilat*—so-called gender mixing of men and women who are not married or closely related, which is banned by law. *Mutawwiyun* often check on couples in public places to verify their legal status. Among other tasks they perform is searching for and confiscating the products that are considered un-Islamic, such as Western music and films, and merchandise for non-Islamic holidays, such as Christmas or Valentine's Day. The *mutawwa* also reinforce the compliance with Islamic dietary regulations, such as the prohibition of sales and consumption of pork and alcohol. Other tasks include the prevention of *irtidad* (apostasy), which is considered a crime punishable by death for the converts and the missionary, as well the prosecution of homosexuality, which is deemed illegal in Saudi Arabia. They also reinforce the observance of prayer times and ensure that shops are closed during these times. *Mutawwa* track down and prosecute all non-Islamic folk traditions such as witchcraft, sorcery, and the production and sale of traditional medicine. *Mutawwiyun* used to have great authority almost everywhere in Saudi Arabia, with the exception of the territory of Saudi Aramco, King Abdullah University of Science and Technology, which is a coed institution, and foreign embassies, all of which are off limits to the religious police. Until recently, they even had the authority to arrest the suspects.

The committee and its actions have increasingly been viewed negatively in contemporary Saudi society. The tragic event of March 11, 2002, was particularly damaging for their reputation and caused wide public outrage. On that day, 15 schoolgirls died in a school fire in Mecca and 50 others were severely injured. *Mutawwiyun* were ultimately responsible for the fatalities as they prevented the victims from leaving the burning building because they were not wearing appropriate body coverings. This and a number of other incidents led to public criticism and sometimes even violent attacks against the committee and its members. In response to the growing public discontent with *mutawwa*, the government reacted by putting the committee through an administrative reform. However, the small-scale changes did little to subdue the *mutawwa*'s zealous behavior. The historic change came only in April 2016, when the Saudi government took away the religious police's power to make arrests and detaining people when carrying out duties and enforcing Islamic law. Currently, the legal extent of their power is reporting the observed or suspected "misbehaviors" of people to the regular police, who are the only force with the authority to follow, stop, question, verify identification, and arrest any suspects.

See also: Chapter 3: Sharia Law and Judicial System; Ulama. Chapter 5: Sunni Islam and Jurisprudence. Chapter 7: Gender Segregation; Marriage Law and Tradition; Social Life, Kinship, and Friendships; Women's Mobility and Driving Ban. Chapter 8: Education of Women. Chapter 10: Dress Etiquette; Social Life. Chapter 15: Women in Sports.

Further Reading

Moaddel, Mansoor. "The Saudi Public Speaks: Religion, Gender, and Politics." *International Journal of Middle East Studies*, vol. 38, no. 1, Feb. 2006, pp. 79–108.

Pietenpol, Annelise M., et al. "The Enforcement of Crime and Virtue: Predictors of Police and Mutaween Encounters in a Saudi Arabian Sample of Youth." *Journal of Criminal Justice*, vol. 59, 2018, pp. 110–121.

Truszkowska, Natalia. "Irreligious Police: Women's Rights in Saudi Arabia." *Harvard International Review*, vol. 23, no. 2, Summer 2001.

Parents and Children

Children's behavior inside and outside the house is regulated by the rules that protect the family's reputation and honor. Both male and female children are expected to recognize parental authority and obey their parents' wishes in virtually every aspect of life. Parents have almost an unlimited authority, extending from approval of a spouse to selection of a major in college. One's refusal to follow parental orders is seen as a serious sin in Islam. Showing any form of disrespect to one's parents is strongly condemned by both religious and societal norms.

These traditional expectations have been increasingly creating generational conflicts. The rapid development of Saudi society and the economy, especially in the last 30 years, created marked differences between different age groups who have different worldviews. Complete submission to parental authority is increasingly seen as problematic, especially among the highly educated youth, who wish to shape their own future while avoiding sinful disrespect of their parents. Thus, modern relationships between parents and children in Saudi Arabia are often a process of constant negotiation of change and avoiding the parents' wrath, or *ghadab*. The concept of *ghadab* refers to a variety of responses and reactions to disrespectful acts and disobedience from the children. The forms of parental *ghadab* can range from a momentary anger to a longer-lasting discontent and, in extreme cases, to rejection and even expulsion from the household. *Ghadab*, however, cannot result in disinheritance, according to Islamic law.

Islamic tradition stipulates that adult children must care for their aging parents both financially and, if necessary, physically. According to the values of the community, this kind of provision goes far beyond the basic necessities. It is expected that those who are considerably wealthier than their parents, assure that the living conditions of the latter are more comfortable than their own. The expectations of providing care apply to both male and female children, but a daughter's support is secondary to that of a son and becomes essential only when she does not have brothers. A son, who can afford to provide luxuries but does not go beyond necessities, is not respected and often condemned by the community. Daughters are expected to physically take care of the parents, especially in cases of illness. Children who support their parents win parental contentment or *rida*—the opposite of *ghadab*. The concept of *rida* also implies the divine satisfaction with one's deeds and lifestyle. An important note is that children are expected not only to treat their parents with kindness and respect, but also show the same attitude to their siblings. A child may lose their parent's *rida* as a result of one's bad treatment of their sibling.

Although the daily interactions between parents and children have become more flexible in recent times, many families still maintain considerable social distance between generations. In these families, the youth continue to observe traditional rituals of respect, such as standing up when a parent or an elderly relative enters the room, kissing their hands, exercising respectful body language, etc. They also abstain from smoking in their presence, from excessive laughing, and from raising the voice in conversation. Generally, this distance is more strictly kept with the father than the mother. The ideal family environment stipulates loving care from the mother, firm discipline and unlimited support from the father, and gratitude and obedience from the children. The two parents are expected to receive equal support and respect from all children. Although according to the famous *hadith*, the Islamic tradition prioritizes the needs of the mother over the father's, in reality, the father is usually given more formal respect, whereas the mother is seen as a source of unconditional love and compassion.

See also: Chapter 5: Five Pillars or the Tenets of Islam; Quran. Chapter 10: Honor; Social Life.

Further Reading

Fadaak, Talha H., and Kenneth Roberts. *Youth in Saudi Arabia*. Palgrave Macmillan, 2019.

Yamani, Mai. *Changed Identities: The Challenge of the New Generation in Saudi Arabia*. Royal Institute of International Affairs, 2000.

Social Life, Kinship, and Friendships

The separation of the sexes in Saudi Arabia results in a radical exclusion of women from public life and the larger community. This legal and cultural obstacle emphasizes the importance of formal and informal networks of kin and friendship. Whereas both men and women actively participate in these networks, they are particularly significant for women as they often constitute the only manifestation of Saudi women's social life. In a society where women's mobility is restricted—even after the lifting of the driving ban—social visits are often the main means of contact with other households and the community at large.

Visiting patterns of men differ from those of women and take place in separate settings, although it is becoming more common among younger couples to visit their friends and extended families together. As a rule, men of middle and younger ages frequently participate in social gathering—commonly referred to as *majlis*—which brings together friends, relatives and colleagues. These gatherings take place at one of the participants' houses, usually in the homes of wealthier and socially influential men among the group. The common time for these meetings is either in the late afternoon, ending at the evening prayer time (*asha'*), or they start after the sunset prayer (*maghrib*) and extend long after the evening prayer. In these circles, coffee, tea, and sometimes dinner are served.

Although friends and social networks are very important for men, they play a more significant role in women's lives as they come to constitute a network of support similar to kinship ties. There is a special term, *wafa'*, which refers to the pattern of social visits among women and the ensuing connections and mutual support. This concept also includes a tradition of the reciprocal gifts and favors that highlight and reinforce these relationships. Very often, social visits are the only means for women to develop and sustain relationships with friends and relatives, especially for women who do not work and therefore do not have regular access to the outside world. The frequency of mutual visits indicates the level of closeness and also signals one's commitment to help in times of need.

The most important communal occasions that require social visitation from both men and women are marriage, the naming of children, death, and serious illness. But if men's failure to pay a visit could be excused on almost all occasions, except paying respect to the deceased and their family, women are expected to be present at each and every one of these events, as their social networks are often seen as a glue holding the family and even large tribal connections together. Although there is certainly an expectation for social visits on occasions of marriage, birth, and naming, the highest cultural importance is given to being there for your relatives and friends in times of crisis. For instance, failure to visit someone and pay condolences in the event of death in the family would likely result in a complete disintegration of relations. Failure to visit during celebrations and festive occasions may affect one's friendship negatively, but normally does not completely suspend relations between friends or families. The principle of reciprocity underlies all kinds of social visiting.

Visitations can be of a formal or informal kind. Formal visits, which are called *wu'ud*, are usually arranged by appointment among several friends of the hostess. These gatherings are highly ritualized and often include formal guests. It is expected that both the hostess and her guests dress up for the occasion, whereas the guests are received in a special room in the house. Refreshments and snacks are also offered in a formal manner. As a rule, formal visits take place in the late afternoon or just before the sunset prayer (*maghrib*), and rarely extend into dinner time.

See also: Chapter 6: Bedouins and Nomadism; Urbanization. Chapter 7: Gender Segregation; Traditional Wedding; Women's Mobility and Driving Ban. Chapter 10: Death Rites; Honor; *Majlis*; Social Life.

Further Reading

Almunajjed, Mona. *Women in Saudi Arabia Today*. St. Martin's Press, 1997.

Altorki, Soraya. "Sisterhood and Stewardship in Sister-Brother Relations in Saudi Arabia." *The New Arab Family/Al-Usra Al-'Arabīya Al-Jadīda*. Edited by Nicholas S. Hopkins. American University in Cairo Press, 2003, pp. 180–200.

al-Khateeb, Salwa. "The Oil Boom and Its Impact on Women and Families in Saudi Arabia." *The Gulf Family: Kinship Policies and Modernity*. Edited by Alanoud Alsharekh. Saqi & London Middle East Institute, 2007, pp. 83–108.

London Middle East Institute, and Gulf Cooperation Council. *The Gulf Family: Kinship Policies and Modernity*. Saqi in Association with London Middle East Institute, SOAS, 2007.

Smith, W. Robertson. *Kinship and Marriage in Early Arabia*. University Press of the Pacific, 2001.

Thompson, Mark C. *Being Young, Male and Saudi: Identity and Politics in a Globalized Kingdom*. Cambridge University Press, 2020.

Yamani, Mai. *Changed Identities: The Challenge of the New Generation in Saudi Arabia*. Royal Institute of International Affairs, 2000.

Traditional Wedding

The culmination of the marriage rites consists of separate wedding celebrations (*irs* or *zaffaf*) for men and women. Weddings are very important social events in the local tradition and are usually heavily attended. In the past, wedding parties were generally held in homes, but in more recent times, there is a growing tendency to rent luxurious lounges in hotels or special halls built specifically for holding weddings. Although separated by gender, both male and female relatives, friends, and guests of honor gather to socially recognize and celebrate the new family. Tribal traditions see attendance of a wedding as a social duty. Thus, large crowds of guests are expected on both sides of the family.

The men's party takes the form of a large gathering around a large meal that begins after the evening prayer (*'asha*). It consists of a traditional festive meal of lamb or baby camel over rice or cracked wheat, side dishes, and desserts placed on tablecloths laid on the carpeted floor with 10–12 men in each sitting. Upon arrival, a guest first congratulates the groom and then finds a place at one of the sittings. A traditional tribal congratulatory phrase says, "From you the money; from her the children" (*Mink al-mal, minha al-a'yal*).

Then the male members of the groom's and the bride's immediate family relocate to the women's section, where a lively celebration takes place. Here, the guests eat, dance, and enjoy various forms of entertainment. The women's wedding party is much more elaborate and usually takes place in a hall decorated around a particular theme. Guests are seated on each side of a central aisle. Traditional wedding gowns on the Arabian Peninsula are colorful, but the Western style of wearing white is becoming increasingly popular as well. In addition to food and traditional and contemporary music, singing and dancing are part of the entertainment. Women from the bride's family also participate in the dancing. Often professional musicians are hired to perform at the wedding.

If the bride arrives first, she and her party walk down the center aisle to a raised podium where closest family and friends are seated. Around midnight, the groom arrives with the male members from the two families. Sometimes the bride, the groom, and their parties arrive together. They are announced and enter the hall amid the traditional celebratory ululation of women (*zagharit*). The groom sits beside his bride on the podium. Afterward, the male family members depart, leaving the groom with the women's party. After the celebrations, the couple is escorted to their new house. Some wedding celebrations last for several days, but the groom only needs to attend the first night. There are often women's parties on at least two succeeding nights hosted by the grandmothers.

The wedding is usually preceded by the henna party (*haflat al-hennah*) for the women—a custom throughout the Arabian Peninsula and in many other regions of the Middle East. Henna painting on the body is the art of decorating the hands and feet with a paste made from the henna plant. Traditionally, the women from the bride's family would beautify the bride with henna in preparation for wedding ceremonies. More recently, specially trained professional beauticians are hired for the party. The "Night of the Henna" has become a form of a prenuptial party for the bride.

See also: Chapter 3: Sharia Law and Judicial System. Chapter 7: Parents and Children; Social Life, Kinship, and Friendships. Chapter 13: Wedding Music and Dance.

Further Reading
Cuddihy, Kathy. *Saudi Customs and Etiquette*. Stacey International, 2002.
London Middle East Institute, and Gulf Cooperation Council. *The Gulf Family: Kinship Policies and Modernity*. Saqi in Association with London Middle East Institute, SOAS, 2007.
Long, David E. *Culture and Customs of Saudi Arabia*. Greenwood Press, 2005.

Women in Public Office

In the 1980s, Saudi *ulama* strongly rejected any form of female political participation in all three branches of government: political leadership (*imarah*), religious leadership (*imamah*), and justice (*adalah*). In the 1970s, it was common for Saudi clerics to theorize about women's inadequacies on the basis of biology. Even with the turn of the 21st century, they continue to enforce a very strict and particular interpretation of religious texts, where women are seen as essentially unsuitable for positions of leadership—in much contrast with contemporary theological debates elsewhere in the Arabic-speaking world. As the rest of Saudi society is becoming more open to new ideas about women's rights, the majority of *ulama* are adamant to change their position, which only acknowledges the rights that Islam offered women.

From the judicial point of view, women are designated as half-witnesses in court: in other words, a male witness equals two female witnesses. In the public sphere, if women attend a sermon or a lecture, they should be seated in the back rows because *sadara* (priority in seating arrangements) is the men's prerogative. A proper Muslim woman is the one who willingly and eagerly occupies the very last set of rows. Her subordinate legal, religious, and social status must be reinforced in physical space. The *ulama* insist that it is the men's responsibility to provide financial support for their families, despite the fact that many women have been employed as teachers. All these various factors make women's participation in political life an extremely difficult, almost impossible undertaking.

However, this situation has begun to gradually improve in the last 20 years—resulting from a combination of grassroot activism and progressive reforms coming from the new generation of Saudi leadership, striving to bring Saudi social norms closer to those of other countries in the region and beyond. One noticeable group of women received greater visibility in Saudi society in the aftermath of September 11, 2001: highly educated women who are vocally critical of religious restrictions. In the last two decades, this group has become a marked category in Saudi society and is comprised of women educated in the sciences and humanities, many of whom have completed graduate degrees abroad. A high proportion of these activists come from Wasim, al-Hasa, and the Hijaz, where social norms have historically been much more liberal than in Najd. As a cohort, these women began to enjoy both media attention and state recognition. As Saudi Arabia increasingly fell under international pressure, this group of women proved to be useful in countering images of Saudi Arabia as a source of radicalism. From 2000 onward, Saudi media employed women in highly visible positions as presenters and celebrated the achievements of the first female eye surgeon, chief executive, pilot, and deputy minister—thus offering a stark contrast to the country's restrictive laws. Royal princesses have increasingly been given international visibility in representing the state. They often appear in various international forums and initiatives on various economic, educational, and cultural matters, as patrons who play leading roles in society. Among the most known women from the royal family and the country's elite are Loulwa al-Faisal, Adila bint Abdulla Al Saud, and al-Walid bin Talal's wife Amira.

A small but visible group of women among the educated elite has become prominent in the field of commerce. Elected women members of the Jeddah Chamber of Commerce and Industry (JCCI) have emerged as the new face of Saudi entrepreneurial culture. Their mission is centered on lifting restrictions on businesses owned by women, especially with regard to allowing women to obtain their own commercial licenses, to hire male colleagues to all-female businesses, and increasing women's mobility without their guardians.

Traditionally, only men were able to serve as members of Majlis al-Shura, or Consultative Assembly of Saudi Arabia, which is a formal advisory body to the king and has a limited legislative power. In September 2011, King Abdullah announced that women would be able to hold appointments in Majlis al-Shura, which was formally confirmed in the royal decree in 2013, which granted women 30 seats at the assembly. Additionally, the decree stated that from now on, women should hold at least a fifth of the seats in Majlis al-Shura. In the same year, three women were named deputy chairs of three important committees. Thoraya Obeid became the deputy chairwoman of the Human Rights and Petitions Committee, Zainab Abu Talib became the head of the Information and Cultural Committee, and Lubna Al Ansari was appointed the chair of the Health Affairs and Environment Committee. A year earlier, in 2012, another important appointment took place at the Ministry of Health, when Muneera bint Hamdan al-Osaimi became the assistant undersecretary of the Department of Medical Services.

In 2005, Saudi Arabia ran its first municipal elections since the 1960s, but women were completely left out of this renewed political process, as they were not allowed to vote or run for office. However, the number of activists continued to grow and campaign for the voting right in the 2011 municipal elections. Although they were not successful in that election cycle, King Abdullah issued a decree allowing women to both vote and run for office in the subsequent 2015 municipal elections. As a result of this historic change, 978 women registered as candidates to 2,100 contested seats in 2015. Twenty-one of them were elected to office. The first elected Saudi female politician was Salma bint Hizab al-Oteibi, who won a seat on the council of Madrakah, a region in Mecca—beating seven men and two women to the spot. Early 2019 saw the most significant step yet in the increasing political visibility of Saudi women, when Princess Reema bint Bandar Al Saud was appointed the ambassador of Saudi Arabia to the United States. She became the first female envoy in the history of the kingdom.

Despite these many positive developments, women still do not have representation at the High Court or on the Supreme Judicial Council. In 2010, the government formally allowed female lawyers to represent women in family cases. In May 2013, Saudi Arabia registered its first female trainee lawyer, Arwa al-Hujaili, after she petitioned the Ministry of Justice for three years. In November of the same year, Bayan Mahmoud al-Zahran became the first woman attorney in the country's history.

See also: Chapter 2: King Abdullah. Chapter 3: Local Government and Municipal Elections; Political Reform and Modernization; Sharia Law and Judicial System; Ulama. Chapter 7: Gender Segregation; Guardianship; Women's Mobility and Driving Ban. Chapter 8: Education of Women.

Further Reading

Kraetzschmar, Hendrik Jan. "Empowerment through the Ballot Box? Women's Suffrage and Electoral Participation in the Saudi Chambers of Commerce and Industry." *Journal of Arabian Studies (Arabia, the Gulf, and the Red Sea)*, vol. 3, no. 1, 2013, pp. 102–119.

Le Renard, Amélie. "'Only for Women': Women, the State, and Reform in Saudi Arabia." *Middle East Journal*, vol. 62, no. 4, 2008, pp. 610–629.

Sakr, Naomi. "Women and Media in Saudi Arabia: Rhetoric, Reductionism and Realities." *Gender and Diversity in the Middle East and North Africa.* Edited by Zahia Smail Salhi. Routledge, 2010, pp. 93–112.

Women's Mobility and Driving Ban

The great restrictions that women faced with mobility and travel have been and remain a highly controversial issue in Saudi Arabia. The *ulama* saw any form of women's independent movement as a threat to traditional gender roles and a source of *fitna* (dissent). As a result, for many decades they regulated women's travel for education and work through legal restrictions that obliged the traveling woman to be accompanied by her male guardian. One of the guardian's main tasks was to ensure that while in a foreign country, the woman maintains her pious lifestyle and appropriate behavior, according to Saudi religious and cultural norms. Similarly, the debate about women driving, which started in the late 1980s, culminated in the infamous prohibition of 1991, when Abd al-Aziz Ibn Baz, the Grant Mufti of the time, and the influential cleric Muhammad al-Uthaymin issued *fatwas* (legal opinions) that forbade women from driving. This is considered the most controversial *fatwa* of Ibn Baz's career. The ban was a consequence of a daring driving incident that became an important milestone in the history of the Saudi feminist movement. The incident took place in Riyadh at the time when Saudi Arabia invited foreign troops to defend the country against Iraq's invasion of Kuwait. A group of educated women, mainly university professors and other professionals, drove their cars around Riyadh. As a result, they were arrested and removed from their jobs. The Grant Mufti ruled that the already existing ban against women driving should remain and be reinforced. Driving was compared to other temptations of corrupt lifestyle brought from the West. The clerics argued that if women were allowed to drive, they may next remove their veils, violate the ban on gender mixing, commit adultery, and engage in other forbidden acts. Until the lifting of the ban in 2017, Saudi Arabia was the only country in the world that prohibited women from driving.

Saudi Arabian society is split on the issue of women's driving. Some argue that the ban is mainly a symbolic problem, a lightning rod that only diverts attention from the core problem, which is the guardianship system. Others point out the serious economic impact of the ban at both the national and the household level. Since there is virtually no public transportation in Saudi cities, driving is the only viable means of travel. Working women were forced to hire drivers, most of whom were non-Saudis, and it was not unusual for a single woman to spend half of her salary on paying the driver to take her to work and back. Unsurprisingly, the inability to drive had been one of the major obstacles to women's full participation in the workforce.

However, while women were technically not allowed to drive and the presence of the religious police in Saudi cities made such attempts very difficult, Bedouin women in rural areas had, in fact, driven for decades. Driving was an essential part of their lives, necessary to support their families. They would regularly drive to transport water tanks,

A Saudi woman at the wheel after the lifting of the driving ban. (Korrawin Khanta/Dreamstime.com)

camels, and other goods between settlements, often carrying a gun to protect themselves. There was an incident when Saudi religious police, *mutawwa*, requested from the local authorities in Hail to arrest a number of women for driving, but the local officials, much more attuned to the realities of rural life, simply ignored the request.

In September 2007, the Association for the Protection and Defense of Women's Rights in Saudi Arabia, cofounded by activists Wajeha al-Huwaider and Fawzia al-Uyyouni, submitted a petition with over a thousand signatures to King Abdullah, asking to lift the driving ban. The following year, al-Huwaider drove and filmed herself, and consequently received wide international media attention after posting the video on YouTube. In early 2011, another Saudi women's rights activist Manal al-Sharif launched a social media campaign #Women2Drive, which quickly drew tens of thousands of followers on Facebook and Twitter. The campaign urged Saudi women to come out and drive on June 17, 2011. In May 2011 al-Sharif decided to do a "test-drive" to see how the police would react. She asked al-Huwaider to videotape the experience on her phone. After driving around for about an hour, al-Sherif was arrested, then released, then rearrested. On June 17, 2011, about 50 women took to the streets in various Saudi cities, including Riyadh, Dammam, and Jeddah. Protest drives by women continued consistently from there on, despite arrests, intimidation by the religious police, and serious consequences that these women faced at work as a result of their activism. In November 2014, Saudi activist Loujain al-Hathloul attempted to cross the Saudi border by car with her Emirati driver's license, after which she was arrested.

On September 26, 2017, King Salman issued an official statement, where the right of women to drive was acknowledged and confirmed as a legitimate activity from the Sharia point of view. On June 24, 2018, the Saudi government began issuing licenses to Saudi women. But despite these positive developments, in May 2018, the police arrested a number of prominent activists who campaigned both for women-to-drive campaigns and for ending the male guardianship system. Among them were Loujain al-Hathloul, Eman al-Nafjan, Aisha al-Mana, Aziza Yousef, Madeha al-Ajroush, and others. According to the Human Rights Watch, the detainees have been tortured. As of February 2019, the activists remained in prison and have not been presented with any charges.

See also: Chapter 2: King Abdullah. Chapter 3: Local Government and Municipal Elections; Political Reform and Modernization; Sharia Law and Judicial System; Ulama. Chapter 7: Gender Segregation; Guardianship. The *Mutawwa*: Saudi Religious Police. Chapter 8: Education of Women. Chapter 16: Internet and Social Media.

Further Reading

Altoaimy, Lama. "Driving Change on Twitter: A Corpus-Assisted Discourse Analysis of the Twitter Debates on the Saudi Ban on Women Driving." *Social Sciences (Basel)*, vol. 7, no. 5, 2018.

Danforth, Loring M. *Crossing the Kingdom: Portraits of Saudi Arabia*. University of California Press, 2016.

al-Sharif, M. "Driving My Own Destiny Defying the Ban on Female Drivers in Saudi Arabia." *Virginia Quarterly Review*, vol. 88, no. 4, 2012, pp. 96–101.

CHAPTER 8

EDUCATION

OVERVIEW

Saudi Arabia's public education did not exist as a system until the 1960s. Prior to that, only 2 percent of girls and 22 percent of boys attended any kind of school. In the decades that followed, the country spent billions of dollars on education and educational facilities. At present, every Saudi citizen has the right to free education at all levels, from preschool through the end of university studies. The government has mostly replaced the traditional Islamic madrasah with modern schools. Although the curriculum remains rooted in Islam, it also provides education in a variety of fields, including sciences and arts. The state places a great emphasis on the value of education as the foundation of Saudi Arabia's future and continues to invest a substantial part of its budget to promote education at all levels, for both male and female members of Saudi society.

Education for boys was established even before the formal creation of the Saudi state. In 1901, the private but tuition-free Falah schools were established by Hajj Abdullah Alireza. By 1915, 78 public elementary schools had already been in operation throughout the Hijaz region. The first noteworthy government school was founded in 1925 under the authority of Al Saud. In the subsequent decades, the demand for education quickly rose, and by 1949, the number of (male) students increased to over 20,000. The debates about women's education resembled the disputes in Europe and the United States before governments formally established schools for girls. Women were seen first and foremost as mothers and wives, whose morals could be corrupted by education. When the Saudi Ministry of Education was created in 1954 under the leadership of Prince Fahad, it was not concerned with the education of women at the time. Schools for girls were finally introduced in 1960, but they remained outside the jurisdiction of the ministry. A separate administrative body was established to oversee female education and was supervised by the highest religious authority in the country, Shaykh Muhammad ibn Ibrahim. Thus, the education of men was the prerogative of the state, whereas women's education was under strict control of the religious establishment.

Secondary public education typically includes the following levels: kindergarten; elementary school, consisting of six years; middle school, consisting of three years; and three years of high school, vocational school, or religious high school. Before starting their high school education, students choose between vocational or academic programs.

National standards determined by the government are assigned to each phase of schooling.

Saudi Arabia heavily subsidizes all levels of public education. For example, textbooks are provided by schools free of charge. In higher education, unmarried college and university students are given stipends, which allow them to focus exclusively on their studies. When King Abdullah came to power in 2005, he took on reforming education as one of his main objectives and announced a $2.5 billion initiative to transform the country's educational system, in the so-called *tatwir* ("reform, development") project. By 2010, 29 universities were operating in Saudi Arabia. In addition to that, the country has 24 colleges, the Faculty of Medicine at King Fahd Medical City, the Institute of Public Administration, and the Prince Sultan Aviation School.

In 2007, the Department of Statistics and Information conducted a thorough demographic survey, which determined the overall illiteracy level of the Saudi population at 13.7 percent. However, there was a remarkable disparity in illiteracy levels among different generational groups, reflecting the rapid transformation the country went through in the course of mere decades. For example, for the group between 10 and 14 years of age, the illiteracy rate was only at 1.4 percent, while for those over the age of 65, the rate was almost 74 percent. Additionally, the report showed significant regional disparity. The lowest level of illiteracy among both genders was in the Riyadh region, at a little under 10 percent, and the highest, in Jizan, at 23.5 percent.

With regard to the educational infrastructure, several government bodies define and supervise educational policy and administration. The Education Policy Document, issued in 1969, serves at the foundation of the Saudi educational system. The Ministry of Education (which was merged with the Ministry of Higher Education) and the Technical and Vocational Training Corporation are responsible for creating and reinforcing laws pertaining to education, monitoring and regulating their implementation, and creating curricular standards, delivery, and assessment. Educational policy is developed and supervised by the Supreme Committee for Educational Policy, which was created in 1963. Formerly, women's education was overseen by the General Presidency for Girls' Education, which was an independent authority. But in 2003, the supervision of women's education came under the jurisdiction of the Ministry of Education.

Saudi Arabia has always experienced a lack of qualified teachers and heavily depended on expatriate teachers from other Arab countries. In the 1960s, King Faisal initiated recruitment of Muslim Arab teachers, primarily from Egypt and Jordan. However, in recent times, the state has taken various measures to increase the number of Saudi educators. Teacher-training institutes have been created throughout the country for both women and men, and the ratio of Saudi versus foreign faculty has slowly begun to change.

Further Reading

Aljaber, Abdullah. "E-Learning Policy in Saudi Arabia: Challenges and Successes." *Research in Comparative and International Education,* vol. 13, no. 1, 2018, pp. 176–194.

Mansour, Nasser, and Saeed Al-Shamrani, eds. *Science Education in the Arab Gulf States: Visions, Sociocultural Contexts and Challenges.* Sense, 2015.

Martin, Rose, et al. "Reflections on Contemporary Arts Education in Egypt, Lebanon and Saudi Arabia." *The Palgrave Handbook of Global Arts Education*. Edited by Georgina Barton and Margaret Baguley. Palgrave Macmillan, 2017, pp. 171–185.

Education of Women

Public education became available to women only in the early 1960s, when the first public school was established in 1964. Since then, women's education has grown rapidly and has become one of Saudi Arabia's most publicized achievements. The official narrative of the state's remarkable progress in this area focuses on the role of two kings: King Saud, who reigned between 1952 and 1964, and King Faisal, who ruled from 1964 to 1975. Although many important reforms were initiated during that time by the government, one cannot underestimate the powerful voices of the opposition, which included writers and other prominent intellectuals. They began advocating for the girls' schooling as early as the 1920s. These intellectuals were particularly active in the Hijaz, with the two Hijazi writers standing out in that respect: Muhammad Awad (1906–1980) and Ahmad Sibai (1905–1984). Awad argued that women's education is in line with Islamic tradition and that the emancipation of women would inevitably lead to the revival of the Arab nation (*ummah*). Similarly, Sibai emphasized the importance of education for both Muslim men and women and highlighted the role that educated women played in Islamic history.

In the absence of formal government schools, Saudi girls had very limited opportunities for education in the first half of the 20th century. In the Hijaz, two schools were available: al-Sawlatiyyah and al-Hazaziyyah. As limited as the educational opportunities were in the Hijaz, girls living in Najd did not have access to anything similar. Even in the 1950s, only women who belonged to the royal family and the elite classes were exposed to regular education within their homes—by teachers who were hired by their families. During that time, many upper-class families in Riyadh employed local religious scholars, preferably blind, to visit their homes and teach the women in the rudimentary knowledge of the Quran, recitation of the *hadith*, and basic literacy. The tradition of the visiting blind scholar continued through the 1970s, even when public education became commonly available for women. Only a small number of young women, primarily from among the urbanites of Riyadh and the Hijaz, were sent to boarding schools abroad. Few families dared to send their daughters away from home, as the risks and social stigma were too great. One enclave of limited education for girls was available in the Eastern Province—in the headquarters of Aramco, where schools for the western expatriate community flourished behind the walls of the compound.

The idea of formal education of girls in public schools gained traction in the late 1950s and culminated in the opening of the first private school in Jeddah, Dar al-Hanan, in 1957. In Riyadh, the first school, Kuliyat al-Banat (literally "the girls' college"), opened in 1960. These two schools operated under the patronage of Iffat, King Faisal's wife, and were available to a small number of girls. Women teachers from other Arab countries, primarily Egypt, Lebanon, and Syria, were brought to build the curriculum in these schools. The beginnings of girls' education in Saudi Arabia remains a matter of controversy. The initiative is widely attributed to King Faisal and especially his progressive wife Iffat. But in more recent years, in an effort to rehabilitate the deposed King Saud, some emphasize his role as well. Initially, schools were not made compulsory for girls, in the face of the heated debates—which continued for years—on whether or not women should be educated outside of their homes. The process of convincing the conservative layers of Saudi society was slow, as well as the process of reconciliation of women's right for education with the religious dogmas. As late as the 1970s, the literacy rate among women remained extremely low—2 percent, compared to the 15 percent of literate men.

In the last decades, remarkable changes in women's education have taken place in Saudi Arabia. The transformation was particularly notable with the turn of the 21st century, when the numbers of male and female students have matched in all stages of education. By 2006, girls made up over 50 percent of all Saudi students. Despite the many positive changes, the conservative religious views and the law against *ikhtilat* (gender mixing) are reflected in the segregation of schools. Female higher education is separate, both physically and administratively. At all stages in the educational system, classes and schools are segregated in different buildings. Boys and girls also have different curricula. This continues at the university level, where specialized women's colleges were founded to offer undergraduate education and bachelor's degrees.

See also: Chapter 7: Gender Segregation; Guardianship; Hijab and Dress Code; Women in Public Office; Women's Mobility and Driving Ban. Chapter 8: Higher Education; Key Universities; Princess Nourah Bint Abdulrahman University; Secondary Education.

Further Reading

Doaiji, Nora. "From Hasm to Hazm: Saudi Feminism beyond Patriarchal Bargaining." *Salman's Legacy: The Dilemmas of a New Era in Saudi Arabia*. Edited by Madawi Al-Rasheed. Oxford University Press, 2018, pp. 117–144.

Hamdan, Amani. "Saudi Arabia: Higher Education Reform since 2005 and the Implications for Women." *Education in the Arab World*. Edited by Serra Kirdar. Bloomsbury Academic, 2017, pp. 197–216.

Koyame-Marsh, Rita O. "The Dichotomy between the Saudi Women's Education and Economic Participation." *Journal of Developing Areas*, vol. 51, no. 1, 2017, pp. 431–441.

Higher Education

After completing their high school education—either in general high schools or specialized arts and sciences high schools—students may pursue higher education in a range of institutions, which include universities, teacher-training colleges, and women's colleges. Despite its short history, Saudi higher education plays an extremely important role in constructing the country's identity, especially with the turn of the 21st century. When King Faysal served as the country's Prime Minister in the 1960s, Saudi Arabia had only a dozen holders of a doctorate degree. At that time, any kind of scholarly degree guaranteed a high-ranking position. Today the situation is quite the opposite, and large numbers of university graduates cannot find appropriate jobs. The ambitious 10-year strategic plan, implemented by the Ministry of Education between 2004 and 2014, had a very positive effect on the country's education at all levels. Saudi students quickly became competitive internationally. For the last several years, Saudi Arabia's institutions have been topping university rankings in the Arab world. In 2019, the list compiled by Times Higher Education (THE), placed King Abd al-Aziz University at the top, with another Saudi higher education institution, Al-Faisal University, occupying the third place.

In recent decades, the Saudi government significantly expanded its system of higher education, and with the growing population, hundreds of thousands of high school graduates seek to enter one of the country's public or private universities. The Saudi student population has grown from 33,000 in 1953 to 2.65 million by the early 2000s. In order to be admitted to institutions of higher education, students must take the General Secondary Education Certificate Examination, a nationwide simultaneous test. Those who receive the highest scores have more choices in disciplines to study. Architecture, medicine, and computer science are currently the most popular fields among Saudi students.

The big advantage of public education in Saudi Arabia is that it is free at all levels. Until 2003, all Saudi universities were public. However, a number of private colleges and universities appeared since then, and several more are undergoing the accreditation process, challenging the state's educational monopoly. The largest and most important among private institutions is the Prince Sultan College for Tourism and Hotel Management. The public university sector has two main areas: secular and religious education. The most important universities from the secular branch include the King Fahd University for Petroleum and Minerals (KFUPM), founded by Aramco in 1963 in Dhahran; the King Saud University (KSU), the oldest Saudi university, founded in 1957; King Abd al-Aziz University (KAU) in Jeddah; and the King Faysal University in Hufuf and Dammam. These institutions are fully funded by the government, and students receive a monthly stipend, allowing them to concentrate on their studies without a need to find a job. The language of instruction is Arabic, except for the King Fahd University, where English prevails. Three Islamic universities offer various religious subjects, including Quranic studies, Islamic law, Arabic, and social sciences. This branch of higher education is primarily represented by the Islamic University in Medina, the Imam Muhammad Bin Saud University in Riyadh, and the Umm al-Qura University located in Mecca. Among the seven Islamic universities, the Ministry of Higher Education operates six, whereas the Islamic University in Medina is under the supervision of the Council of Ministers.

The core difference between Saudi academia and its counterparts in other countries is that it does not guarantee academic freedom. Although peer committees are incorporated into the university structure, seniority usually trumps peer governance. Political science, contemporary history, and sociology are among the new areas of study, but Saudi academics, understandably, cannot engage in the kind of criticism that many university members across the world traditionally launch against their governments.

See also: Chapter 4: Diversification and Development Plans; Migrant Workers and Unemployment; Petrochemical Industry; Science and Technology; Vision 2030. Chapter 6: Urbanization. Chapter 7: Gender Segregation; Guardianship; Parents and Children. Chapter 8: Education of Women; Key Universities; Princess Nourah Bint Abdulrahman University.

Further Reading

Hamdan, Amani, ed. *Teaching and Learning in Saudi Arabia: Perspectives from Higher Education*. Sense, 2015.

Profanter, Annemarie. "University Is a Private Matter: Higher Education in Saudi Arabia." *Rethinking Private Higher Education: Ethnographic Perspectives*. Edited by Daniele Cantini. Brill, 2017, pp. 158–192.

International Schools

For decades, Saudi Arabia has had a considerable number of international schools attended by children of expatriates brought by the oil boom. As of January 2015, 203 international schools were operating in Saudi Arabia. Some of these schools are owned by expatriate communities, and others are private schools owned by Saudi individuals. Community-owned international schools are not required to obey gender segregation rules on their campuses, both for classrooms and social activities. However, private international schools are mandated to follow Saudi regulations.

An interesting phenomenon in Saudi Arabian education is the presence of private Philippine schools. Currently, there are around 24 of them around the country, of which 13 are located in Riyadh and 5 are in Jeddah. The opening of these schools resulted from a large wave of Filipino workers arriving in Saudi Arabia in the 1980s. The first of these schools was established in Jeddah in 1983, due to the Philippine consulate's efforts. Afterward, more schools opened in Riyadh and other big cities throughout the country.

When Western workers began to arrive to the country with the growth of the oil industry, they were initially sending their children to study in Beirut. However, gradually, international schools have been established throughout the kingdom. One of the earliest of these schools was the Riyadh International School. Later, the British International School and King Faisal Schools were established, also in Riyadh. Saudi Aramco developed its own school system. Several international schools operate in Dhahran, including the Dhahran British Grammar School for children of foreigners. Khobar has the British International School and al-Hussan Academy. Jeddah is home to a large number of international schools, including several American, British, and Dutch schools. Additionally, the coastal city has the Continental School, Jeddah Preparatory and Grammar, and the al-Waha International School. Several international schools are located in Yanbu and Jubail. Most of these are preparatory schools, subsidized by the corporations and companies that employ the parents. Although generally these schools have not been open to Saudi students, they promoted modern cultural enclaves in contrast with the rest of the conservative country.

See also: Chapter 4: Migrant Workers and Unemployment; Oil Industry and Aramco. Chapter 8: Secondary Education.

Further Reading

Hammad, Waheed, and Saeeda Shah. "Dissonance between the 'International' and the Conservative 'National': Challenges Facing School Leaders in International Schools in Saudi Arabia." *Educational Administration Quarterly*, vol. 54, no. 5, Dec. 2018, pp. 747–780.

Islamic Education

Saudi Arabia has a much larger proportion of students specializing in Islamic studies than other countries of the region. Historically, religious knowledge was transmitted from teachers to students, where the latter would apprentice with a senior scholar and receive a special certificate (*shahadah*) at the completion of their studies. The certificate gave the right to teach that particular subject to others. The royal initiative to establish the King Abdullah University of Science and Technology and a number of other secular universities aimed to counterbalance traditional religious education that left the country's scientific and technological development at the hands of foreigners and foreign-educated Saudis.

Saudi Arabia is known for its specialized Sunni Islamic education, which is offered not only to Saudi citizens but also to many non-Saudi Muslims who come to the country for this purpose. Traditional religious education begins at home at a young age and continues through the entire educational system. Among institutions of higher education, a number of renowned Islamic programs are offered at the University of Medina, the Umm al-Qura University, Dar al-Hadith al-Khayriyyah in Mecca, and the Muhammad ibn Saud University in Riyadh, which enrolls over 24,000 students. Dar al-Hadith al-Khayriyyah is particularly known for its education in Islamic jurisprudence (*fiqh*).

The Islamic University of Medina, established in 1961, has free tuition and offers both undergraduate and graduate degrees, in addition to a certificate program. The university provides students with a stipend and pays for an annual round-trip ticket for foreign students. The Umm al-Qura University in Mecca accepts both men and women, but female students have to be approved and accompanied by their male guardian. This university also offers free tuition and free housing, in addition to sponsoring travel for

> **MADRASAH**
>
> In Arabic, madrasah literally means "school," in reference to any institution of primary or secondary education, or any educational level below college or university. However, the term is also frequently used to specifically refer to religious educational institutions, in contrast to secular ones. In the early days of Islam, madrasahs were associated with mosques, where students were taught the Quran, reading, writing, and other basic subjects. Education in a madrasah is provided for free, as they have been generally sponsored by the state or through donations that were popular among the wealthy and influential members of the society. During the time when only 5 percent of the European population were literate, madrasahs became valuable centers of learning and spread very quickly throughout the Middle East, North Africa, and as far as India, China, Mongolia, and Russia. In the 10th and 11th centuries AD, the core aspect of the madrasah curriculum became the study of Islamic law (Sharia), although a variety of other subjects—both Islamic and general—were taught as well. These include the Quran and hadith, Muslim theology, Arabic language, history, math, geometry, astronomy, and medicine. The course of study usually lasted four years, at the end of which the teacher would determine whether an individual student could be certified to teach law. The main method of teaching and learning in these schools was memorization. By the 11th century, madrasahs evolved into respectable independent centers of learning, with buildings, staff, residential areas where students and some teachers lived, libraries, and sometimes even hospitals.

single students living in the dorms. Dar al-Hadith focuses on education in Sunnah (customs and practices based on the life and deeds of the Prophet Muhammad) and Sharia (Islamic law). Specialized programs of study are offered for graduates of middle school, high school, and college.

See also: Chapter 2: Muhammad, Prophet of Islam; The Rise of Islam. Chapter 3: Sharia Law and Judicial System; Wahhabi Ideology. Chapter 5: Quran.

Further Reading

Daun, Holger, and Reza Arjmand, eds. *Handbook of Islamic Education*. Springer, 2018.

Hefner, Robert W., and Muhammad Qasim Zaman. *Schooling Islam: The Culture and Politics of Modern Muslim Education*. Princeton University Press, 2007.

Samin, Nadav. "Saudi Primary Education and the Formation of Modern Wahhabism." *Welt Des Islams*, vol. 58, no. 4, 2018, pp. 442–460.

Key Universities

King Saud University, established in 1957, is the oldest university in Saudi Arabia. It was the first secular institution of higher education. Its name was changed to the

The campus of King Abdullah University of Science and Technology (KAUST) in Thuwal. (Volodymyr Dvornyk/Dreamstime.com)

University of Riyadh in 1967, but in 1982 it went back to its original name. It has both male and female students who are taught in segregated classes. It currently enrolls over 50,000 students, of which about 7 percent are international students. Most courses are conducted in Arabic, with the exception of engineering and medical programs, which are taught in English. King Saud University has a high ranking in the Arab world and is especially noted for its medical program. The university consists of various colleges, including science, health, and humanities, as well as two community colleges. It also has 18 libraries and 14 research centers. A branch of the university that opened in Qasim has recently become an independent institution. King Saud University has faculty with both international and Saudi training, and follows the common Western model where professors combine research with teaching.

King Abd al-Aziz University in Jeddah was founded in 1967 as a private university. The well-known Saudi writer Hamzah Bogary was one of the cofounders of this institution. In the early 1970s, it was converted to a public university at King Faisal's orders. The university enrolls both men and women. In the early 2000s, King Abd al-Aziz University enrolled over 37,000 undergraduates, several thousand graduate students, and 500 doctoral candidates. King Abd al-Aziz University is ranked number one among all Arab universities by Times Higher Education.

King Fahd University of Petroleum and Minerals was established in 1963 as a college, and opened its doors in 1964 for 67 male students. In 1975, it received university status. It is located in Dhahran, close to the headquarters of Saudi Aramco. Its programs in science, engineering, and business administration are highly regarded both within in the country and in the region. With an acceptance rate of less than 10 percent, it is the most coveted university in Saudi Arabia. The current enrollment exceeds 8,000 students. King Fahd University's objective is to provide the fields of petroleum and petrochemicals with highly trained specialists.

King Abdullah University of Science and Technology opened in 2009 at Thuwal on the Red Sea coast. It is a postgraduate research university, with English being the main language of instruction. King Abdullah was personally involved in the conceptualization and establishment of this university. It has both a board of trustees and an international advisory council. The main objective of this modern university is to produce cutting-edge research and graduate highly qualified specialists in a number of scientific and technological fields. A groundbreaking aspect of this university is its coeducational campus—the first in the country. According to the Saudi Vision 2030 plan, whose goal is to modernize and diversify Saudi economy and education, King Abdullah University is set to play an important role. New initiatives include a collaboration agreement with Elm, a semiprivate digital solutions company, to facilitate research in the area of smart city technology.

For many decades, Saudi Arabians have traveled abroad to receive their higher education. Saudi students began to arrive in the United States and United Kingdom after World War II to study at the universities. The number of Saudis studying abroad continued to grow through the end of the 20th century. In addition, some studied in Egypt, Lebanon, and other universities in the region. Following the terrorist attacks of September 11, 2001, U.S. student visas to Saudis were substantially restricted. However, by 2007, the educational relationship between the two countries was reestablished. According to Saudi sources, the total number of Saudi students studying abroad reached almost 115,000 studying on government scholarships in 2007, with over 35,000 students in the United States alone. A special government scholarship for study abroad is available to both male and female students, although women are required to be accompanied by a male relative or guardian, who also receives benefits.

See also: Chapter 4: Diversification and Development Plans; Oil Industry and Aramco; Petrochemical Industry; Science and Technology; Vision 2030.

Further Reading

Alghafis, Ali N. *Universities in Saudi Arabia: Their Role in Science, Technology & Development*. University Press of America, 1992.

Corbyn, Zoë. "Oasis in the Desert." *Times Higher Education*, no. 1921, Nov. 2009, pp. 32–37.

Mansour, Nasser, and Saeed Al-Shamrani, eds. *Science Education in the Arab Gulf States: Visions, Sociocultural Contexts and Challenges*. Sense, 2015.

Mervis, Jeffrey. "The Big Gamble in the Saudi Desert." *Science*, vol. 326, no. 5951, Oct. 2009, pp. 354–357.

Thompson, Mark. "Self-Motivation, Career Aspirations and Work Responsibilities: The Perspective of Saudi Male Undergraduates at King Fahd University of Petroleum and Minerals." *Employment and Career Motivation in the Arab Gulf States: The Rentier Mentality Revisited.* Edited by Annika Kropf and Mohamed A. Ramady. Gerlach, 2015, pp. 35–55.

Princess Nourah Bint Abdulrahman University

Princess Nourah Bint Abdulrahman University is a public university and the largest university for women in the world. It has over 60,000 students and 5,000 of academic and administrative staff in 34 colleges, located in the city of Riyadh and in the neighboring cities. Princess Nourah University is famous for its architectural design that combines innovation with the features of traditional Saudi culture. It offers several graduate and postgraduate levels of education in all major academic disciplines. The university is comprised of Academic Colleges, Health and Science Colleges, a 450-bed teaching hospital, campus housing, a K–12 school, a central mosque, a library, and various sporting facilities.

The university opened in 1970 as the first College of Education for women in Saudi Arabia. In the next 25 years, over one hundred similar colleges were established in 72 cities throughout the country. Six of these colleges operated in Riyadh alone, offering degrees in education, sciences, arts, social work, and economics. In 2004, all women's colleges located in Riyadh were merged into the first women's university in the country. In what followed, many other colleges throughout Saudi Arabia have been combined into independent universities. In 2008, King Abdullah inaugurated the merged Riyadh campus, and it was formally named after Princess Nourah Bint Abdulrahman—commemorating the sister of the country's first king, Abd al-Aziz. Thereafter, the campus was expanded through a massive construction project and transformed into a modern university-city. Princess Nourah University is known for its vibrant student culture and regularly holds various events. In February 2017, it hosted the first opera performance in Saudi Arabia—the show *Antar and Alba*—produced by Opera Lebanon.

See also: Chapter 7: Gender Segregation; Women's Mobility and Driving Ban. Chapter 8: Education of Women; Higher Education; Key Universities.

Further Reading

Almansour, Sana, and Ken Kempner. "Princess Nourah Bint Abudulrhman University's Challenge: Transition from a Local to a Global Institution." *Higher Education,* vol. 70, no. 3, Sept. 2015, pp. 519–533.

Almansour, Sana, and Ken Kempner. "The Role of Arab Women Faculty in the Public Sphere." *Studies in Higher Education*, vol. 41, no. 5, May 2016, pp. 874–886.

Almansour, Sana, and H. L. Wendy Pan. "The Challenges of International Collaboration: Perspectives from Princess Nourah Bint Abdulrahman University." *Cogent Education*, vol. 2, no. 1, 2015.

Secondary Education

The academic year in Saudi Arabia consists of 153 days. It begins in September and ends in June. Children between the ages of 3 and 5 may attend kindergarten, but it is not a compulsory phase of education that begins in elementary school. In 2007, only a little over 11 percent of boys and 10 percent of girls were attending kindergarten in the kingdom. But with the expansion of women's employment, preprimary education is growing rapidly throughout the country.

Elementary schools admit children who are at least 5 years and 9 months old. The main subjects are Arabic, Islamic studies, history, geography, art, physical education, mathematics, and science. Students are granted a certificate upon graduation from elementary school. The middle school curriculum offers the same set of subjects as elementary school, but they are taught at a more advanced level. English as a foreign language begins in middle school as well.

Students attending high school that specializes in arts and sciences have a common curriculum in their first year of study. If students receive a score of at least 60 percent in every subject, they can choose between science and literature curriculum for the remaining two years of high school. Those who score less than 60 percent can only enter the literature program. Students enrolled in Islamic high schools focus on the Arabic language and literature and religious studies, in addition to history, geography, and English. In recent years, the Ministry of Education added computer training as a core subject in high school.

Various specialized vocational high schools are available to students, such as technical, commercial, and agricultural schools. These schools and their curriculum are supervised and administered by the Technical and Vocational Training Corporation. Technical schools offer a range of practical subjects, including electrical skills, machine and auto mechanics, metal mechanics, radio and television, and architectural drawing. Additionally, Arabic, English, and chemistry are taught at these schools. The curriculum in commercial schools focuses on mathematics, accounting, economics, and management skills, and also includes Arabic and English, and religious studies. The core subjects in agricultural schools include agronomy, agricultural economics, zoology, farm management, and applied biology. Vocational schools support the Saudization initiative of the government, which aims to replace foreign workers in all fields with Saudi nationals.

In addition to public education, Saudi Arabia has various private schools. Despite being private, these schools are supervised by the Ministry of Education and are subsidized by the government, as are public schools. For example, students in private schools are provided with stipends and free textbooks.

See also: Chapter 8: Education of Women; International Schools; Islamic Education.

Further Reading

Farooq, Muhammad Umar, et al. "English Language Teaching and Cultural Implications in Saudi Arabia." *International Journal of English Linguistics*, vol. 8, no. 3, 2018, pp. 177–185.

Ghalib, Thikra K. "Children, Gender and School Curricula in Saudi Arabia." *International Journal of English Linguistics*, vol. 7, no. 1, 2017, pp. 85–93.

Samin, Nadav. "Saudi Primary Education and the Formation of Modern Wahhabism." *Welt Des Islams*, vol. 58, no. 4, 2018, pp. 442–460.

CHAPTER 9

LANGUAGE

OVERVIEW

Arabic is the official language of Saudi Arabia. There are over 300 million Arabic speakers globally, which puts it among the five most spoken languages in the world. It is the most widely spoken language of Africa, with over 200 million speakers, and one of the largest languages of the Asian continent, spoken by 120 million natively. Arabic has one of the world's most remarkable distribution across national borders and is claimed as the official language in 26 African and Asian countries: Algeria, Bahrain, Comoros, Chad, Djibouti, Egypt, Eritrea, Iraq, Israel, Jordan, Kuwait, Lebanon, Libya, Mauritania, Morocco, Oman, Qatar, Saudi Arabia, Somalia, Sudan, Syria, Tunisia, United Arab Emirates, Yemen, Palestine, and Western Sahara. In 1974, Arabic became one of the six official languages of the United Nations. Additionally, its special status as the language of Islam's holy book, the Quran, gives Arabic particular importance throughout the Muslim world. Many Muslims learn Arabic to be able to read the Quran in its original form.

With regard to its origins and regional affiliation, Arabic is a Semitic language—the youngest among the group, which also includes Hebrew and Amharic (Ethiopian), as well as several ancient languages such as Akkadian, Aramaic, and Assyrian. Contemporary Arabic has three main variations that are based on social contexts and regional distribution: (1) colloquial or dialectal Arabic, (2) classical Arabic language, and (3) Modern Standard Arabic. Each of these forms is used for different purposes and in different social situations. Classical Arabic is the liturgical language of the Quran. Its roots can be traced to several regional dialects of the Arabian Peninsula, including the dialect of the Quraysh—the tribe to which Prophet Muhammad belonged. Classical Arabic is a canonized version of the Arabic language. Nowadays it is used primarily for religious purposes. Classical Arabic strictly follows the grammatical conventions defined and codified by early Arabic linguists, including Abdallah Ibn Abi Ishaq al-Hadrami (d. 735), Sibawayh (760–796), Abu Muhammad al-Hamdani (893–945), al-Mubarrad (826–898), al-Ru'asi (d. 802), and many others. The vocabulary of classical Arabic also relies on medieval lexicography, such as the famous dictionary *Lisan al-Arab* (*The Language of Arabs*) compiled in 1290 by Ibn Manzur (1233–1311/1312). Nowadays, it is very rare to find antiquated classical Arabic in writing, as most authors use an updated version of the literary language, commonly known as Modern Standard Arabic or *fusHa* (the Arabic root of this word means "pure," "clear," "proper"). While largely following the grammar of classical Arabic, *fusHa* uses simplified structures and incorporates modern vocabulary. It is the language of the Arabic media, education, contemporary literature, science, etc. *FusHa* is understood by all educated Arabic speakers. In other words, Modern Standard Arabic is a language of the written culture, designated for formal occasions. However, more recently, one may observe an increasing participation of various Arabic dialects in many of the aforementioned areas, especially in media and literature.

Arabic dialects represent the living language of the daily culture in the Arab world. Given the vast region in which these numerous dialects developed over time, they often demonstrate substantial differences. The local dialect is learned as the Arabic speaker's first language or mother tongue, while *fusHa* is subsequently learned in school. Dialects developed naturally, not adhering to a strict set of rules as exemplified by *fusHa*, and have absorbed various influences from neighboring languages, colonial languages, and local languages that were present in the area before the Arab conquests and the spread of Islam. Each dialect is governed by its own set of rules and often shows significant differences in phonetics and morphology—even with the colloquial languages of neighboring countries. For example, some Arabic dialects in North Africa are almost incomprehensible to an Arabic speaker from Egypt, Syria, or the Gulf. In addition to the geographic diversity, additional differences can be observed between Bedouin and sedentary speech, urban and rural populations, ethnic and religious minorities, social classes, generations, and gender groups.

Over centuries, Arabic has been in close contact with other languages in the region, and increased exponentially with the rise of Islam and the expansion of the Muslim Empire. Because the Quran is written in Arabic, the latter acquired the status of a sacred language and quickly became the lingua franca of the Muslim world. Millions of new converts learned Arabic and began mixing it with their native tongues. As a result, many languages in the Middle East, Africa, and Central Asia contain numerous words borrowed from Arabic. The most notable examples among these are Persian and Turkish, each exhibiting an abundance of Arabic-based vocabulary. In the case of Swahili, not only was this language greatly influenced by Arabic in both its structure and vocabulary, but the actual word "Swahili" originates from the Arabic word *sawahili*, which means "those of the coast."

The historical and cultural significance of Arabic stretches far beyond the Middle East and Africa. In the Middle Ages, Arabic played a vital role in the development of European culture—particularly during the rise of al-Andalus, also known as the Muslim Spain, which was ruled by the Islamic Empire for several centuries, from 711 to 1492. At that time, Arabic was a medium of culture and a vehicle of knowledge in Europe, and its influence spread across many fields, including sciences, mathematics, and philosophy. Unsurprisingly, various Arabic words can still be found in European languages, especially Spanish, Portuguese, Valencian, and Catalan. Spanish alone has a vocabulary of approximately 4,000 words of Arabic origin, accumulated during the eight centuries of contact between these languages on the Iberian Peninsula. Balkan languages, such as Greek and Bulgarian, also contain a significant number of Arabic words—often as secondary borrowings through Ottoman Turkish. In English, words of Arabic origin include algebra, chemistry, coffee, cotton, alcohol, and many others.

Further Reading

Beeston, A. F. L. *The Arabic Language Today.* Georgetown University Press, 2006.

Owens, Jonathan. *A Linguistic History of Arabic.* Oxford University Press, 2006.

Suleiman, Yasir. *The Arabic Language and National Identity: A Study in Ideology.* Georgetown University Press, 2003.

Arabic Alphabet and Script

The Arabic alphabet, or *al-abjadiyyah*, is simple and concise. There are 28 letters written from right to left in a cursive style, which connects letters into words. Most of these letters are consonants and three are long vowels. Many Arabic letters have similar and sometimes identical shapes, but are distinguished from one another by the number and placement of the dots. For example, the letters representing the /b/, /t/ and /th/ sounds have the same basic shape, but are set apart by the number and location of the dots: /b/ has one dot below the shape, whereas /t/ has two dots and /th/—three dots above it. In addition to the dots, Arabic has a number of diacritics, which are small symbols written above or below the consonants and carry various phonetical meanings and purposes, such as short vowels, an absence of a vowel, a doubled or emphasized pronunciation of a consonant, and so on.

SIBAWAYH (c. 760–796): THE GREAT GRAMMARIAN OF ARABIC

Sibawayh, whose full name was Abu Bishr ibn Uthman ibn Qanbar al-Basri, is considered one of the greatest grammarians of the Arabic language. Remarkably, Sibawayh was Persian and not a native speaker of Arabic. His monumental work of five volumes, titled *Al-Kitab fi al-Nahw* (*The Book on Grammar*), was the first comprehensive analysis of Arabic, having described its various linguistic features in much detail. The way he applied logic and structural analysis to the language was groundbreaking for his time. This book's magnitude remains unparalleled until today.

Sibawayh's name is also associated with the legendary battle between the rival grammarian schools of Basra and Kufa, which became known as "The Question of the Hornet." Subawayh, who represented the Basra school, had a scholarly debate in Baghdad with al-Kisa'i, the leader of the Kufa school, over a proper grammatical ending of the sentence: "I have always thought that the sting of a scorpion was more painful than that of a hornet, but then I found out that one is just like the other." The judgment was that the argument should be decided by a group of Bedouins who were standing outside the courtyard where the debate was taking place. They all sided with al-Kisa'i, and it was later reported that they were in a prior agreement with al-Kisa'i to support his version of the sentence. Sibawayh, humiliated and crushed by the defeat, returned to Shiraz and soon died at a young age of 35. The legend says that he died out of sadness over his defeat. It is said that out of respect for Sibawayh, al-Kisa'i read the former's *al-Kitab fi al-Nahw* (*The Book on Grammar*), came to appreciate Sibawayh's brilliance, and continued teaching it to his own students through the rest of his life.

Scholars still do not have a uniform theory about the precise development of the Arabic script. Some trace its origins back to the 2nd millennial BC, but the earliest archaeological evidence indicates that it emerged around the 4th century AD. Most scholars agree that the earliest Arabic script was closely related to Nabatean, which, in turn, evolved from the ancient Aramaic. With the advent of Islam, Arabic needed to be codified and standardized in order to record the Quran with utmost accuracy. During this period, the Arabic script underwent numerous revisions with the goal of defining the structure of the alphabet and its vowels. The contributions of the renowned grammarians Abu al-Aswad Al-Duali (603–688) and al-Khalil ibn Ahmad Al-Farahidi (718–791) are particularly important, as they are credited with developing and finalizing the complex system of dots and diacritical marks that is used today.

The importance of the Arabic script goes far beyond the Arabic language. In fact, this is the second most widely used writing system globally—after the Latin alphabet. Due to its spread throughout Asia and Africa with the growth of Islam, many regional languages adopted the Arabic script, including Persian, Turkish, Urdu, Pashto, Central Kurdish, Azerbaijani, Malay, and others. Until the 16th century, Spanish texts were occasionally recorded in the Arabic script. A number of West African languages began using the Arabic script as well. The term "Ajami," originating from the Arabic word "foreign," is often used in reference to Arabic-based orthographies of African languages, most prominently Hausa and Swahili.

See also: Chapter 2: Nabateans; Pre-Islamic Arabia. Chapter 5: Quran. Chapter 12: Calligraphic Art.

Further Reading

Gruendler, Beatrice. *The Development of the Arabic Scripts: From the Nabatean Era to the First Islamic Century According to Dated Texts*. Scholars Press, 1993.

Hoigilt, Jacob, and Gunvor Mejdell, eds. *The Politics of Written Language in the Arab World: Writing Change*. Brill, 2017.

Moginet, Stefan F. *Writing Arabic: From Script to Type*. American University in Cairo Press, 2009.

Arabic Calligraphy

The cultural significance of the Arabic script is much greater than simply serving as a recording system for the Arabic language. Over time, Arabic calligraphy grew into a highly elaborate form of art used in architecture and various forms of visual culture. Its evolution was stimulated by the Islamic aniconism—a prohibition to create images of humans and animals, rooted in the anti-idolatry message of Islam. Although a written form of Arabic existed in pre-Islamic times, its calligraphic scripts developed and diversified with the spread of the new religion, which assigned particular importance to the language of the Quran. In the early days of Islam, calligraphy was celebrated as an artistic recording and preservation of the sacred text. With time, the calligraphic art evolved into a prestigious profession, closely linked to science, literature, and philosophy. Its cultural and artistic significance is best described by a famous Arabic proverb which states that "calligraphy is the geometry of the soul expressed through the body." Gradually, a great diversity of Arabic scripts was created at different periods and in different parts of the Islamic Empire. The two main phases of the Arabic calligraphic tradition are associated with two highly influential schools: the early Baghdadi school (900–1300) and the later Ottoman school (1500–1900).

Musnad is considered the first Arabic script, which emerged in the south of the Arabian Peninsula, developed into its final form around 500 BC, and was used until the 6th century AD. Interestingly, it did not have the cursive aesthetic that defines the Arabic script today. Musnad featured basic shapes that looked similar to Nabatean and Canaanite letters. Al-Jazm was the first script to resemble the contemporary Arabic alphabet and was used by northern Arabian tribes. Most scholars agree that it still was closely related to the Nabatean script, but also influenced by other early scripts that originated in this area, such as Syriac and Persian. Al-Jazm continued to evolve until the early days of Islam and was particularly popular in the Hijaz. When Islam began to spread in every direction, various calligraphic styles emerged simultaneously across the vast geography of the Islamic Empire, reflecting the diverse cultures and societies that were adopting the new religion. Al-Jazm, too, developed in several ways and had four main varieties—Hiri, Anbari, Makki, and Madani—representing different regions, the last two referring to Mecca and Medina.

The next major script to make an impact on the Arabic writing system was the Kufic script—one of the oldest scripts that remained popular through the 13th century. It takes its name from the city of Kufa in Iraq where it originated, although historical records of this script were found much further south—in Medina. The Kufic script developed during the 7th century and played a key role in documenting the Quran. Unlike Musnad and al-Jazm, Kufic letter shapes look familiar to a contemporary Arabic speaker. In its early form, the Kufic letters did not have dots, which were added when the written language was codified. This script is characterized by angular shapes and long vertical lines, which made it particularly suitable for architectural design. Over time, Kufic inscriptions became a prominent element in Islamic architecture and continue to be used for architectural and decorative purposes in modern times.

The Abbasid period (750–1258) was a Golden Age for the development of sciences, arts, and literature throughout the Islamic Empire. It was during this era that calligraphy became an art form and a separate field of study. Over time, a number of rules were developed to enhance and organize the scripts from the geometrical and aesthetic points of view. Calligraphic art received the epithet that is still widely applied—"al-Khatt al-Mansub," meaning the "well-proportioned script." This period witnessed the emergence of several important Arabic scripts, including Thuluth and Naskh, which were developed by three famed calligraphers—Ibn Muqlah in the 10th century, Ibn al-Bawwab in the 11th century, and Yaqut al-Mustasimi in the 13th century. Many consider Ibn Muqlah (886–940) the father of the Arabic calligraphic art. His contributions included organizing the calligraphic proportions into six cursive styles: Thuluth,

Naskh, Muhaqqaq, Rayhani, Tawqi, and Riqa. He also invented an important element—the rhombic dot—which played a central role in subsequent developments of Arabic calligraphy. Yaqut al-Mustasimi is credited with the innovative technique of cutting the nib of the reed pen at an angle instead of a straight line, which allowed for much more variation and elegance in calligraphic writing. A famous legend about al-Mustasimi's dedication to calligraphy tells that at the time when Baghdad was ravaged by the Mongol army in 1258, he did not attempt to escape but sought refuge in a minaret at the top of a mosque in order to finish a calligraphy piece. This story illustrates the extreme level of dedication and discipline that characterizes the work of a true calligrapher.

The Thuluth script emerged during the Abbasid era and continued to be refined and widely used for centuries. The name "Thuluth" means "one-third" in Arabic—likely in reference to the technique where one-third of each letter slopes. This script is recognized for its clear structure and readability, while featuring beautiful shapes. This combination of beauty and practicality assured its longevity and made it very popular in decorative arts. Thuluth is still widely used for ornaments in mosques and textual embellishments.

Naskh was another important script that developed alongside Thuluth. The word "Naskh" comes from the Arabic root "to copy," likely referring to the fact that its structure allows for faster and easier copying of texts than most other scripts. It was extensively used to make copies of important manuscripts and books, including the Quran. Although this calligraphic style was invented and initially developed during the Abbasid era, its finalized form was refined by the famous Ottoman calligrapher Sheikh Hamdullah (1436–1520). Known for its clear and readable style, Naskh continues to be in broad use today in printed Arabic books.

Outside Baghdad, Cairo was an important center for the Arabic calligraphic art, particularly during the Mamluk period (1250–1517), given the dynasty's enthusiastic support of different forms of Islamic art. This period in the development of Arabic calligraphy is highlighted by many masterpieces made by renowned calligraphers such as Muhammad Ibn Abd al-Wahid, Muhammad Ibn Sulayman al-Muhsini, Ahmad Ibn Muhammad al-Ansari, and others. Arabic calligraphy continued to flourish under the Ottomans (1500–1923). During the four centuries of Ottoman rule in the Middle East, the art of calligraphy reached new heights at the hands of legendary masters of Istanbul and other parts of the Ottoman Empire, including Sheikh Hamadullah al-Amasi, Alhafuth Othman, Mustafa Raqim, and Shawqi Afendi. In addition to perfecting the scripts that were already in use, they invented new calligraphic styles, such as Diwani, Jeli Diwani (or "clear Diwani"), Tughra, and Siyakat.

Three distinguished scripts emerged in Persia. The elegant Taaliq, which appeared around the 10th century, had rounded forms and exaggerated horizontal strokes. Designed specifically to meet the needs of the Persian language, it was used extensively for correspondence until the 14th century when it was replaced by Nastaliq—a combination of Naskh and Taaliq. The creation of Nastaliq was attributed to Mir Ali Sultan al-Tabrizi (1360–1420), one of the most prominent Persian calligraphers. Nastaliq was the principal style of Persian calligraphy of the 15th and 16th centuries and was often incorporated into paintings. Traditionally, this script has defined Persian calligraphic tradition and continues to be popular in Iran, Afghanistan, India, and Pakistan. Other important developments of the Arabic script in the east include the Hirati script in Afghanistan, Bihari and Zulf al-Arus ("the bride's curls") in India, and Sini in China. In the western part of the Arab world, the most prominent calligraphic style is the Maghribi script, deriving its name from "Maghrib," which means "the west," and is also the Arabic name of the country Morocco. It is rooted in the early Kufic angular scripts used by the local Muslim population. Maghribi script has rounded forms, with exaggerated extension of horizontal elements, and remains prevalent throughout North Africa.

See also: Chapter 2: The Abbasids; The Golden Age of Islam in Arabia; The Rise of Islam. Chapter 3: Sharia Law and Judicial System. Chapter 5: Quran. Chapter 12: Calligraphic Art.

Further Reading

Blair, Sheila. *Islamic Calligraphy*. Edinburgh University Press, 2006.

George, Alain. *The Rise of Islamic Calligraphy*. Saqi, 2010.

Gharipour, Mohammad, and Schick Irvin Cemil. *Calligraphy and Architecture in the Muslim World*. Edinburgh University Press, 2013.

Khatibi, Abdelkebir, and Mohamed Sijelmassi. *The Splendor of Islamic Calligraphy*. Thames & Hudson, 1996.

Osborn, J. R. *Letters of Light: Arabic Script in Calligraphy, Print, and Digital Design*. Harvard University Press, 2017.

Arabic Dialects

Colloquial or dialectal Arabic refers to the wide range of national and regional variations of Arabic, which constitute the spoken language of daily life throughout the Arab world. Given the expanse of the Arabic-speaking world, colloquial Arabic illustrates a remarkable geographic diversity. Additionally, each of these regional dialects contains internal variations, such as urban and rural dialects. Throughout history, dialects were considered a "low" form of language, in contrast to the exalted and celebrated formal Arabic. Consequently, dialects did not have written forms until about a hundred years ago. However, today dialects and colloquial speech are widely used in media and popular culture, especially film, television, and music. The cultural, social, and political importance of dialects has been endorsed by various national movements, which grew in opposition to the al-Ummah al-Arabiyyah (the Arab Nation) concept that calls for a united Arab community based on common language and religion.

Arabic has always had dialects. Prophet Muhammad spoke the Meccan dialect of the Quraishi tribe, and therefore, the Quran was recorded in this particular form of Arabic. But eastern Arabian dialects of the time had more prestige, which prompted the ultimate adoption of the latter's phonology in Islam's holy book. It is this eastern Arabian pronunciation that characterizes modern formal Arabic. Therefore, classical Arabic, including its modern variety *fusHa*, is in itself a dialect that has been canonized.

The contemporary sociolinguistic situation in the Arabic-speaking world exemplifies the phenomenon of linguistic diglossia—the existence of two distinct varieties of the same language in different sociocultural situations. Educated Arabs of any nationality are expected to be fluent both in *fusHa*, which they learn through education, and their native dialects. Although some linguists claim that dialects are essentially different languages, most dialects have enough common elements to be understood by speakers from other Arab countries. Some dialects, such as Egyptian and Levantine, are more widely understood as they have been popularized throughout the Arab world by the entertainment industry. The only Arabic dialect that received the status of an official language is Maltese—spoken in Malta and transcribed in the Latin script. Maltese is a descendant of Sicilian Arabic, which over time evolved into a separate language and is viewed as such by most linguists.

Arabic dialects are usually classified into regional groups, where speakers of the same group comprehend one another with much ease and have minimal differences among colloquial languages within that group. Some regional groups consist of a single national language (Iraqi); others include several neighboring dialects (Levantine). Sometimes linguists disagree on ways of dividing national dialects into groups, but the following typology is the most commonly used:

- North African Arabic (Morocco, Algeria, Tunisia, and Libya)
- Hassaniya Arabic (Mauritania)
- Egyptian Arabic
- Levantine Arabic (Lebanon, Syria, Jordan, and Palestine)
- Iraqi Arabic
- Gulf Arabic (Kuwait, Bahrain, Qatar, the UAE, and Oman)
- Hijazi Arabic (Western Arabia)
- Najdi Arabic (Central Arabia)
- Yemeni Arabic (Yemen and Southwestern Arabia)

As the regional typology demonstrates, as many as four regional variants of Arabic are spoken in Saudi Arabia—Hijazi, Najdi, Gulf Arabic, and Yemeni—highlighting the country's linguistic and cultural diversity.

See also: Chapter 1: Eastern Arabia: Al-Hasa; Hijaz and Tihamah; Najd: Central Arabia. Chapter 2: Muhammad, Prophet of Islam; The Rise of Islam. Chapter 5: Quran. Chapter 6: Ethnic Composition. Chapter 9: Dialect of Hijaz; Dialect of Najdi; Gulf Arabic and Minority Languages.

Further Reading
Albirini, Abdulkafi. *Modern Arabic Sociolinguistics: Diglossia, Variation, Codeswitching, Attitudes and Identity.* Routledge, Taylor & Francis Group, 2016.

Embarki, Mohamed, and Moha Ennaji. *Modern Trends in Arabic Dialectology*. Red Sea Press, 2011.

Ingham, Bruce. *Arabian Diversions: Studies on the Dialects of Arabia*. Ithaca Press, 1997.

Prochazka, Theodore. *Saudi Arabian Dialects*. Kegan Paul International, 1988.

Suleiman, Yasir. *A War of Words: Language and Conflict in the Middle East*. Cambridge University Press, 2004.

Dialect of Hijaz

Hijazi, or western Arabian Arabic, is prevalent in western regions of Saudi Arabia, in particular the urban centers of Mecca, Medina, and Jeddah. Northern Hijazi has 4 geographically based varieties, whereas southern Hijazi has 16. Despite this regional diversity, the Hijazi dialect is usually divided into two main subgroups, based on the population of speakers: rural and urban. The rural form of Hijazi is spoken by the local Bedouin population, while the urban form is spoken in Mecca, Medina, Yanbu, and Jeddah. In modern times, the Hijazi dialect usually references its urban variety, given the proportional prevalence of urban population in this region. Although historically the Najdi dialect is considered the most prestigious spoken language of Saudi Arabia, Hijazi Arabic is the most widely used and most commonly understood dialect of the Arabian Peninsula. In the past, it was used as a trade language throughout much of the Red Sea region, and currently serves as the main language of communication in Saudi government and trade.

Hijazi Arabic consists of 26 to 28 consonant phonemes, the use of which depends on the speaker's background and the level of formality. It has an 8-vowel system, in contrast to the 6 vowels (3 long and 3 short) of classical Arabic. Hijazi vocabulary mainly comes from classical Arabic Semitic roots. Urban Hijazi vocabulary differs in some respect from that of other Arabian dialects, given the specific geographic and cultural features of the Hijaz. For example, there are fewer specialized words related to desert life and nomadism, and a larger variety of words on maritime and fishing. Over time, due to the cosmopolitan environment of the Hijazi urban centers and the diverse origins of their inhabitants, the Hijazi dialect absorbed many words and expressions brought to the area from other Arabic-speaking regions and non-Arab countries. Non-Arabic borrowings mainly come from Persian, Turkish, Latin, and English.

See also: Chapter 1: Hijaz and Tihamah. Chapter 2: The Rise of Islam. Chapter 6: Ethnic Composition. Chapter 9: Arabic Dialects; Dialect of Najdi; Gulf Arabic and Minority Languages.

Further Reading

Alessa, Aziza. "When Najd Meets Hijaz: Dialect Contact in Jeddah." *Between the Atlantic and Indian Oceans: Studies on Contemporary Arabic Dialects*. Edited by Stephan Procházka and Veronika Ritt-Benmimoun. Transaction Publishers, 2008, pp. 51–66.

Jarrah, Ali Saleh Ibrahim. "English Loan Words Spoken by Madinah Hijazi Arabic Speakers." *Arab World English Journal*, vol. 4, 2013, pp. 67–85.

Dialect of Najdi

Najdi Arabic is used as the first language in the central region of Saudi Arabia. This dialect is the closest ancestor of classical Arabic. The second half of the 6th century AD in Najd saw the development of a relatively homogeneous poetic lingua franca, which was used for intertribal communication and was distinct from the surrounding vernaculars. This language was rooted in the Bedouin dialects of Najd and, with the advent of Islam, was codified into what is now known as classical Arabic.

The geographical remoteness of Najd impacted its language as well. Because of the area's isolated location, for many centuries Najdi Arabic had very limited interactions with other languages. As a result, it has an archaic structure and shows very little non-Arabic influence, which, in turn, gave it the reputation of the "purest" form of Arabic and the preserver of the area's linguistic and cultural pedigree. Najdi is considered the most prestigious of the Arabian Peninsula dialects. Its noble status was further advanced by the royal family, who originate from Najd and speak this dialect as their first language. A popular myth says that although classical Arabic has long been extinct among urban populations, it remains to be spoken by the Bedouins whose community is seen as the keeper of Arabic cultural heritage. In the case of the Najdi dialect, there is actually some truth to this statement, because many of its old linguistic features remained unchanged over time.

Najdi Arabic can be divided into four subdialects. Northern Najdi is spoken in Jabal Shamaar, Zufi, and among the Shammar tribes. Central Najdi is the dialect of both sedentary and Bedouin communities in the central part of the peninsula, as well as some areas in the Syrian Desert. The urban dialect of Riyadh also belongs to this dialectal group. Southern Najdi includes the subdialects of the city of Kharj and the surrounding area. It is also spoken by the southern tribes of Najran and Gahtan and the eastern tribes of al-Murrah and Ajman. The mixed central-northern Najdi is a separate dialectal group that includes the languages of Qasim and Dhafir tribes. Overall, the speakers of Najdi subdialects believe that their differences are very minor and usually involve a particular word choice or an accent. However, from a linguistic point of view, these subdialects illustrate variations in grammar, such as differences in the future tense marker. Najdi Arabic does not have a distinct written form, unlike, for example, the Egyptian Arabic, but it plays an important literary role because most of the Bedouin oral poetry is composed in this dialect.

See also: Chapter 1: Najd: Central Arabia. Chapter 2: The Rise of Islam. Chapter 6: Ethnic Composition. Chapter 9: Arabic Dialects; Dialect of Hijaz; Gulf Arabic and Minority Languages.

Further Reading

Ingham, Bruce. "Notes on the Dialect of the Ḍhafīr of North-Eastern Arabia." *Bulletin of the School of Oriental and African Studies*, vol. 45, 1982, pp. 245–259.

Ingham, Bruce. *Najdi Arabic: Central Arabian*. J. Benjamins Publishing, 1994.

Gulf Arabic and Minority Languages

Gulf Arabic, which is also called Sharqi ("eastern") Arabic, is the dialectal group predominant in the Persian Gulf countries. This group includes the eastern Arabian dialect, as well as dialects of Kuwait, Iraq, Bahrain, the UAE, Qatar, Iran, and northern Oman. Gulf Arabic can be defined as a set of closely related varieties of Arabic, where the level of dissimilarity depends on the distance between them. The dialects within this regional group differ in vocabulary, grammar, and pronunciation. For example, Kuwaiti Arabic and the dialects of Qatar and the UAE show some significant differences, especially in pronunciation, which may even impact the level of mutual understanding between the speakers of these dialects. Gulf Arabic is not the native tongue of most Saudis, as the majority of native Saudi population comes from Najd and the Hijaz. There are only about 200,000 speakers of Gulf Arabic in Saudi Arabia, most of them residing in the coastal Eastern Province. Variants of Yemeni Arabic are spoken in the southwest, particularly the Tihamah region.

Saudi Arabia has a large expatriate population, which has been consistently increasing since the early days of the oil boom. These expatriate communities speak their own languages, the most numerous of which are Tagalog, Rohingya, Urdu, and Egyptian Arabic. Tagalog is an Austronesian language prevalent in the Philippines. Over time, large numbers of Filipino workers came to Saudi Arabia for employment opportunities, and they now constitute the largest foreign community in the country. There are currently about 700,000 speakers of Tagalog in Saudi Arabia. Rohingya is an Indo-Aryan language written in the Arabic script and spoken by the Rohingya people, who are predominantly Muslim and live in Myanmar and Bangladesh. The Rohingya-speaking community in Saudi Arabia has about 400,000 expatriates, but these numbers are expected to increase after the 2016–2017 political crisis in Myanmar. The speakers of Urdu constitute another large foreign community living and working in Saudi Arabia. Urdu emerged in the 1600s in Central Asia and is the national language of Pakistan. Its name has its origins in the Turkish word "ordu," which means "camp" or "army." It was used as a communication tool between Muslim soldiers of different backgrounds during their military campaigns in India and Eastern Persia. In Saudi Arabia, the Urdu-speaking community is estimated at 380,000 people. Egyptian Arabic is the dialect spoken by Egyptian expatriates, whose population is estimated at about 300,000. In addition to these, there are several other languages spoken by smaller minority communities and foreign worker groups within Saudi Arabia. These include Iranian Persian (102,000 speakers), Sudanese Arabic (86,000), Korean (66,000), English (60,000), Chinese (58,000), Somali (42,700), Indonesian (37,000), Italian (22,000),

French (22,000), and Bengali (15,000). There are also about 100,000 users of the Saudi Sign Language in the country.

See also: Chapter 1: Eastern Arabia: Al-Hasa; The Persian Gulf. Chapter 3: Gulf Cooperation Council. Chapter 6: Ethnic Composition. Chapter 9: Arabic Dialects; Dialect of Hijaz; Dialect of Najdi.

Further Reading

Almoaily, Mohammad. "Language Variation in Gulf Pidgin Arabic." *Pidgins and Creoles beyond Africa-Europe Encounters.* Edited by Isabelle Buchstaller et al. Benjamins, 2014, pp. 57–83.

Avram, Andrei A. "Superdiversity in the Gulf: Gulf Pidgin Arabic and Arabic Foreigner Talk." *Philologica Jassyensia*, vol. 13, no. 2 [26], 2017, pp. 175–190.

Holes, Clive. *Dialect, Culture, and Society in Eastern Arabia: Ethnographic Texts.* Brill, 2005.

Zughoul, Muhammad Raji. "Lexical Interference of English in Eastern Province Saudi Arabic." *Anthropological Linguistics*, vol. 20, no. 5, 1978, pp. 214–225.

CHAPTER 10

ETIQUETTE

OVERVIEW

For those living in the west and even the rest of the Middle East, Saudi Arabian social and cultural norms are often associated with the social codes of Bedouin tribes. Although nomadic Bedouin culture played and continues to play a very important role in the construction of the Saudi national identity, the overall culture is much more complex than the popular stereotypes may imply. Throughout history, Saudi society has been introverted and highly conservative, and this still holds true in the 21st century, as the local cultural norms have been remarkably resistant to global influences. The conservatism of Najd—the political and geographical center of the country—is particularly well known. Having been isolated from the rest of the world throughout most of its history, Najd has developed a high sense of ethnocentricity that continues to influence the social and political life of modern Saudi Arabia. Not only is Arabia seen as the cradle of Islam and thus the center of the Muslim world, but the tribes of the peninsula are perceived as forefathers of the whole Arab race. Additionally, Arabic is considered a divine language and thus occupies a special, exalted status within world languages. The fact that unlike the majority of its regional neighbors, most of the Arabian Peninsula was never conquered or colonized—even the Ottomans could not control the local rulers—added to the sense of ethnic exclusivity. One should note, however, that ethnocentrism is much less obvious in the Hijaz, which for many centuries welcomed Muslim pilgrims from all over the world and which remains the most cosmopolitan and culturally open region in Saudi Arabia.

Although Saudi culture is imbued with Islamic values, many tribal cultural codes, customs, and traditions continue to influence Saudi society. The cultural significance of kin cannot be underestimated. The social interaction between tribal members is regulated by ancient rules that go back centuries before Islam. Their main characteristic is the common responsibility and solidarity within the kin group, where one is expected to prioritize family over any other relationships throughout life. Added to that is the concept of right and wrong, honor, and shame, which also reflects on nontribal members. Other important moral and cultural values include generosity, hospitality, chivalry, and bravery. Social behavior is exercised through a set of rituals and customs, including the rites of passage, holidays, interactions between different generations, the *majlis*, and so on. Group decision-making has been among the core mechanisms of the Arabian society since ancient times. Whether in community governance or family matters, decisions have relied heavily on the concept on consensus (*ijma'*), which was, in turn, based on the consultation with the elders (*shura*). This practice was incorporated into Islamic methods of governance and still exists today. Thus, Majlis al-Shura, or the Shura Council, is an essential advisory body to the Saudi king.

The basic structural unit of Saudi society was and still is the extended family, which includes not only the parents and their direct line of descendants (children and grandchildren), but also aunts, uncles and their families, and even distant cousins. All traditional extended families were patriarchal, patrilineal (male bloodlines), patrilocal (from specific locations), endogamous (encouraging marriage ties with extended family), and polygamous. In all families, elders and generational seniority are held in great respect. Although patriarchal in structure, most families have a highly respected matriarchal figure, usually the grandmother on the father's side. Lineage is recognized through the male line, as in most Western cultures. To this day, married women keep their (maiden) last names and do not take the husband's family name. Bloodlines are also very important, with many Saudi families tracking their lineage to the early days of Islam and taking pride in it.

One important aspect of behavior that is closely related to Islamic worldview is a keen sense of inevitability of the course of history, in general, and specific life events, in particular. This fatalism is based on the core principle of Muslim belief—the omnipotence of God's will. Among other things, it is expressed in numerous linguistic expressions with the word "God" (*Allah*) in them, indicating the ultimate reliance of all things in life on the divine power. One of the most common of such phrases is *inshallah*, which literally means "God willing," which ordinarily accompanies any mentioning of the future. This reinforces the idea that even the most routine things that normally would be considered within one's personal responsibility, can happen only at the will of God.

Although rapid modernization brought about by the oil boom challenged many of the traditional aspects of Saudi society, it is remarkable how resilient the culture and social behavior remains toward secular Western values.

Further Reading

Cuddihy, Kathy. *Saudi Customs and Etiquette*. Stacey International, 2002.

Farsy, Fouad. *Modernity and Tradition: The Saudi Equation*. Kegan Paul International, 1990.

Long, David E. *Culture and Customs of Saudi Arabia*. Greenwood Press, 2005.

Death Rites

For Muslims, death is considered the return of the soul to the creator. An important aspect of Muslim philosophy is looking at the inevitability of death as something to prepare for throughout people's lives. One's deeds should be always put in perspective for the eternal life. According to the more conservative religious views in Saudi

Arabia, mourning should not be exaggerated, because the departed might join paradise soon.

A set of specific rituals is performed after death, some of which were inherited from pre-Islamic cultural practices and others regulated by Islam. If a person is nearing death, it is appropriate to place them in the director of Kaaba, which is the direction of the daily prayer. Upon hearing the news of a person's death, the customary saying is *inna lillahi wa ileyhi raji'un* ("we belong to God and to him we shall return"). Like their ancestors, Saudis bury the dead in the ground, rejecting other forms of funerals such as cremations. It is also advised that the body should be buried as soon as possible after death. According to Islamic regulations, the body of the diseased is to be washed in the ablution ceremony (*ghusl*) by the people of the same gender. It is a complex ritual that usually takes place in three phases and is accompanied by special prayers. During the last washing, scented substances may be applied, usually in the form of rose water, cedar tree oil, and camphor. After the washing, the body is wrapped in a seamless white shroud for burial called *kafan*. It is about 15 meters long and made of soft cotton. Women can then be draped with an extra cover, usually a green cloth.

Relatives and friends carry the deceased to the mosque, where an imam recites funeral prayers, and later is taken to the cemetery. Only men can escort the body to the cemetery, where it is placed in a grave facing the Kaaba. In the especially conservative Najd, the grave is simply a hole in the ground. In other Saudi areas, small stone structures may be erected. At the gravesite, people are not allowed to erect elaborate grave markers, tombstones, or mausoleums. The best grave is one that can be washed away with one hand, according to ancient Bedouin tradition. The simple rituals are also meant to discourage relatives from excessive mourning or wailing since death is perceived as one's (desired) return to God. One of the important doctrines of Muhammad ibn Abd al-Wahhab's reform was to eradicate those practices, which existed in ancient Arabia. Worshipping the dead was seen as connected to the pagan worshipping of idols and something that may distract the believers from the main task of one's lifetime, which is the worshipping God. Excessive mourning was also seen as showing discontent with God's wishes. Instead, relatives and friends are encouraged to remember the good deeds of the deceased and pray that God welcomes them in heaven.

After the burial, a three-day mourning period, *aza'*, is observed. During this time, regular visits are paid to the family of the deceased. *Aza'* visitations are considered an important social obligation. Between the two evening prayers, guests are received to offer condolences to the family. Typically, a senior family member meets the visitors, who then sit quietly together commemorating the deceased. In Hijaz and other areas, religious sheikhs read verses from the Quran during *aza'*. However, public display of grief is strongly discouraged. Widows are required to observe a mandatory "waiting period" (*'iddah*) of four lunar months and 10 days, in accordance with Quranic rules. During this time, she is not allowed to remarry or move from her home.

See also: Chapter 2: Muhammad Ibn Abd al-Wahhab. Chapter 3: Wahhabi Ideology. Chapter 5: Quran; Sunni Islam and Jurisprudence. Chapter 6: Bedouins and Nomadism. Chapter 7: Social Life, Kinship, and Friendships.

Further Reading

Halevi, Leor. *Muhammad's Grave: Death Rites and the Making of Islamic Society.* Columbia University Press, 2007.

Strathern, Andrew, and Pamela J. Stewart. *Contesting Rituals: Islam and Practices of Identity-Making.* Carolina Academic Press, 2005.

Weeks, Lloyd R., ed. *Death and Burial in Arabia and Beyond: Multidisciplinary Perspectives.* Archaeopress, 2010.

Dress Etiquette

In public, both sexes wear obligatory outer garments, which are considered part of the traditional clothing. Since the requirement is that these garments cover the entire body, they are very wide and reach down to the ankles. Unlike other Middle Eastern regions, Saudi Arabia maintained the traditional clothing style successfully even in times of dramatic socioeconomic changes, for example, after the oil boom. People wear basically the same clothes that were worn in ancient times on the Arabian Peninsula. In more recent years, Western fashions did get a significant following among women of affluent classes, but these clothes can only be worn inside the house, and when they go in public, a mandatory black *abayah* cloak has to be worn, along with the veil covering their hair. Many women also wear a facial veil (*niqab*). Although the same law does not apply to foreign women, they are required to dress modestly. Non-Saudi Muslim women usually wear a cloak and headscarf, but do not cover their faces. Expatriates are not expected nor encouraged to dress in the traditional attire, but they should wear professional clothes without exposing too much skin. For instance, shorts and T-shirts are

A young Saudi man wearing traditional clothes in travel. (Saksit Kuson/Dreamstime.com)

not allowed in public. Nevertheless, there is a distinct shift toward Westernized clothing among young generations, which can also be seen as a form of social rebellion.

For men, basic forms of outer garments have the simple shape of a wrapper or a cloak, *abayah* or *bisht,* which is worn over the traditional dress called *thawb*—a flowy long shirt. Another type is the knee-long jacket, *farwah,* worn in the winter. A belt serves as an important accessory: it simultaneously holds the overgarment in place and serves as decoration and storage for weapons and money. It is made from a variety of materials, including leather, cotton, and wool, and often shows much creativity of form.

For women, a veil is an essential and mandatory part of the clothing, regardless of one's social class or any other factors. Men frequently wear a form headgear as well: the most popular is the *ghutrah*—a *kufiyah* made of a square piece of cloth, secured with *aqal*—a special cord to keep the *ghutrah* in place. Conservatives are known to use one of the hadiths for clothing regulations banning seven luxurious items, among which are silver vessels, gold rings, silk, brocade, satin, tanned hides, and *qassi* (a striped fabric from Egypt containing silk).

Today, Western fashion is very common in many Arab countries, except on the Arabian Peninsula, where people from all social classes prefer to wear an indigenous style that includes *thawb* and *abayah,* as well as traditional headgear. This traditional attire is considered the national dress in many Arabian Gulf states; wearing Western clothing, on the other hand, is seen as a statement of modernization and belonging to the non-native section of the population.

See also: Chapter 7: Hijab and Dress Code. Chapter 12: Traditional Garments.

Further Reading

Ingham, Bruce. "Men's Dress in the Arabian Peninsula: Historical and Present Perspective." *Languages of Dress in the Middle East.* Edited by Nancy Lindisfarne-Tapper and Bruce Ingham. Curzon, 1997, pp. 40–54.

Le Renard, Amélie. "Dress Practices in the Workplace: Power Relations, Gender Norms and Professional Saudi Women's Tactics." *Al-Raida*, vol. 135, 2011, pp. 31–38.

Quamar, Mohamed Muddassir. "Sociology of the Veil in Saudi Arabia: Dress Code, Individual Choices, and Questions on Women's Empowerment/Md. Muddassir Quamar." *Domes: Digest of Middle East Studies*, vol. 25, no. 2, 2016, pp. 315–337.

Tawfiq, Wijdan A., and Jennifer Paff Ogle. "Constructing and Presenting the Self through Private Sphere Dress: An Interpretive Analysis of the Experiences of Saudi Arabian Women." *Clothing & Textiles Research Journal*, vol. 31, no. 4, Oct. 2013, pp. 275–290.

Honor

Honor has been and still is an important concept in the culture of the Arabian Peninsula since ancient times, which is arguably one of the most prominent features of the nomadic Bedouin society incorporated into Islamic culture. Honor has two related articulations—the group honor, which is called *sharaf*, and the individual honor, which is called *wajh* (meaning "face" in Arabic). The concept of honor is closely linked to the concept of shame, which is called *'ayb* or, in a religious context, *haram*. This concept implies generosity, hospitality, bravery, and respect for others. A community member who consistently shows these attributes, acquires a good reputation and common respect. Honor should be exercised in interpersonal relations between relatives, as well as other members of society, pointing to the existence of individual and collective forms of honor. One's honor, as well as good reputation and communal respect, can be lost due to behavior or a deed that is publicly considered unacceptable and shameful. To win their honor back, a person may have to submit to a socially sanctioned punishment. Reputation and status, both good and bad, are linked to wider considerations of family and can be passed on to the next generations and distant relatives. Neither honor nor reputation are measured by wealth—the only measurement is the person's behavior and the behavior of their family members. Hospitality, rooted in the traditional Bedouin culture, is considered a very important aspect of honor. It is expressed through particular codes of behavior toward not only relatives, friends, and neighbors, but also complete strangers.

In the context of collective honor, particular importance is placed on the women and strictly regulates their conduct and reputation. According to the tribal concept of collective responsibility, honor of the entire group is dependent on the chastity of its female members of childbearing age. Misconduct affects not only an individual woman, but also her female and male relatives. Women's honor has a special term in Arabic, *'irdh*, and plays an important part in the general definition of *sharaf*. To maintain honor and preserve her good reputation, a woman should avoid contact with men outside of her family and show restraint when this cannot be avoided. She is expected to dress modestly, avoid eye contact, and show utmost restraint in her body language. Sexual violation is among the most serious offenses against honor. Because every woman is a member of a larger extended kin group, the honor of the whole group is also violated and therefore requires legal actions to restore it. Honor must be defended when it is questioned or violated. It is extremely difficult to live in Saudi society with a damaged reputation or tainted honor, as one immediately becomes a social outcast.

Clan or family honor was an important aspect of tribal law, implemented by means of revenge or monetary compensation, termed *diyah* (blood payment), for example, in cases of murder or severe bodily injury. Male family members were expected to avenge crimes committed against their relatives. Payment or acts of revenge were seen as a means to avoid a prolonged feud between families. The tribal system of compensation or revenge was incorporated into Islamic law.

In Saudi Arabia, as well as many Gulf societies, the value of honor is closely mixed with religious values, although other Muslim societies interpret them more liberally. For example, modest dress is required for Muslim women, which usually includes covering the body and hair. Although Saudi clerks explain the country's much more strict requirements to women's covering with religious arguments, this practice is mainly an extension of the concept of female honor and protection from shame, as opposed to being a religious requirement. The same applies to the traditional custom of gender segregation and its application to virtually every aspect of public life.

See also: Chapter 3: Sharia Law and Judicial System; Chapter 5: Sunni Islam and Jurisprudence. Chapter 6: Bedouins and Nomadism; Major Tribes. Chapter 10: *Majlis*.

Further Reading

Abu-Lughod, Lila. "Honor and the Sentiments of Loss in a Bedouin Society." *American Ethnologist*, vol. 12, 1985, pp. 245–261.

Abu-Lughod, Lila. *Veiled Sentiments: Honor and Poetry in a Bedouin Society*. Updated ed. with new preface ed. University of California Press, 1999.

Idriss, Mohammad Mazher. "Honour, Violence, Women and Islam—An Introduction." *Honour, Violence, Women and Islam*. Edited by Mohammad Mazher Idriss and Tahir Abbas. Routledge, 2011, pp. 1–15.

Jabbur Jibra'il Sulayman, et al. *The Bedouins and the Desert: Aspects of Nomadic Life in the Arab East*. State University of New York Press, 1995.

Kurpershoek, P. M. *Arabia of the Bedouins*. Saqi, 2001.

Tønnessen, Liv. *Women's Activism in Saudi Arabia: Male Guardianship and Sexual Violence*. Chr. Michelsen Institute, 2016.

Majlis

Majlis is a formal custom for men of influence and social statue to hold a weekly assembly where family members, friends, and acquaintances can discuss various issues and make petitions. In Arabic, *majlis* literally means "a place of sitting." In a social sense, it describes a private place of getting together in the private houses of Arabia, or a tribal council under the leadership of an experienced mediator. Nowadays, formal and informal *majlis* gatherings are regularly held by family members, friends, colleagues, and acquaintances in order to discuss events, business opportunities, and do general social networking. These events are always segregated. The term *majlis* usually applies to male gatherings, while women hold their own. Hosting of *majlis* and other visitations of guests usually takes place in a separate quarter of people's private homes.

There is also a tradition of public *majlis*, where mayors, tribal and community leaders, religious scholars, and businessmen hold meetings in *majlis* that are open to the public. As a place to make decisions, the *majlis* provides direct access to the leaders and other community members who hold authority. These events are very ceremonial and give every citizen, at least in theory, the chance to bring their grievances, requests, and petitions directly to the highest authorities. The short individual conversation begins with a greeting ritual where the guest touches or kisses the host's head rope (*aqal*) and then his shoulder. Depending on the social status of the guest and the host, the greeting may involve kissing the top of the head or touching noses. In what follows, the petitioner provides a short oral report on the situation or the request, accompanied by a longer written statement, which is handed down to officials who will look into the case. Saudi kings traditionally held and continue to hold a weekly *majlis*, where the king would receive hundreds of citizens and hear their requests, which are later attended to by his administration. It was during one of such public hearings when King Faisal was killed by his own nephew, who is believed to have carried out a blood revenge for his brother, killed in demonstrations against the introduction of television in Saudi Arabia. Since then, because of high-security risks, people are not allowed to be physically close to the king. Traditionally, no one can be rejected from attending *majlis*. In other parts of the Gulf region, including Kuwait and Bahrain, the *majlis* is called *diwan* but follows the same principles.

See also: Chapter 3: Saudi Monarchy and Branches of the Government. Chapter 6: Bedouins and Nomadism; Major Tribes. Chapter 7: Social Life, Kinship, and Friendships.

Further Reading

Anderson, Glaire D. "Aristocratic Residences and the Majlis in Umayyad Córdoba." *Music, Sound, and Architecture in Islam*. Edited by Michael Frishkopf and Federico Spinetti. University of Texas Press, 2018, pp. 228–254.

Dekmejian, Hrair. "Saudi Arabia's Consultative Council." *Middle East Journal*, vol. 52, no. 2, Mar. 1998, pp. 204–218.

Dhanani, Gulshan. "Political Institutions in Saudi Arabia." *International Studies*, vol. 19, no. 1, Jan. 1980, pp. 59–69.

Social Life

Saudi social life remained quite resilient in the face of Western influences and still centers around one's home, family, and close circle of friends. The traditional daily schedule involves an afternoon nap, and social life would begin after the sunset prayers (*maghrib*), often lasting well past midnight. Despite the age of modernization, these socializing traditions remain in place in many Saudi families. There are very few outlets outside people's homes where people can socialize. Until very recently, public cinemas were banned in the country. As a result, television has taken on a role of the main source of entertainment, especially after the rapid spread of satellite television in the region. In more recent times, Internet and social media have had a major impact both on the forms of entertainment and on methods of socialization, especially among younger generations.

Saudis regularly visit family members, particularly the elders of the family. It is also customary for women—both family members and friends—to visit each other during the day, although their mobility was very limited until the recent lifting of the driving ban in 2018. Working men do most of their socializing in the evening, often in groups of men of similar age, background, and occupation. Such a group is usually called *shillah* or *majmu'ah,* and they typically gather in special quarters of each other's homes, called *diwaniyyah.* As usual, male and female gatherings are gender-segregated, even within one's extended family. One of the still popular weekly traditions among Saudis is a family picnic on a Friday—either out in the desert or along the coast, depending on the region.

In the absence of commercial entertainment, going out for meals has become a favorite pastime. With the growing mall culture, the number of new local and international restaurants are increasing almost on a daily basis, especially in larger cities. Restaurants have special secluded areas for families. Additionally, shopping has become a form of entertainment and opportunity for younger people to meet with their friends. Despite Saudi society's overall resistance toward what is perceived as modern and secular social practices, visible changes do take place. For many younger people, a parallel social life exists online—in numerous chat rooms, message boards, and social media channels. This virtual life created an opportunity for men and women to communicate with each other, overriding the rules of gender segregation.

See also: Chapter 7: Gender Segregation; Parents and Children; Social Life, Kinship, and Friendships. Chapter 10: *Majlis*; Workweek and Holidays. Chapter 15: Popular Consumerism.

Further Reading

Aldossry, Theeb, and Matthias Zick Varul. "A Time to Pray, a Time to Play? Everyday Life in the Kingdom of Saudi Arabia between the Temporalities of Religion, Tradition and Consumerism." *Time & Society,* vol. 25, no. 3, 2016, pp. 471–492.

London Middle East Institute, and Gulf Cooperation Council. *The Gulf Family: Kinship Policies and Modernity.* Saqi in Association with London Middle East Institute, SOAS, 2007.

Yamani, Mai. *Changed Identities: The Challenge of the New Generation in Saudi Arabia.* Royal Institute of International Affairs, 2000.

Workweek and Holidays

Prayer (*salat*) five times a day is the second requirement of Muslim life and is a mandatory practice among all Muslims. Interrupting the daily routine for prayers has been a common practice throughout Islamic history and remains a prevalent practice today, but Saudi Arabia enforces the prayer times through law. All businesses, schools, shops, restaurants, and virtually all public places remain closed during the prayer times at dawn (*fajr*), noon (*dhuhr*), mid-afternoon ('*asr*), sunset (*maghrib*), and evening (*asha*').

Traditionally, Saudis had a six-day workweek. The only day off was Friday, when Muslims are expected to attend mosque for a special Friday prayer ceremony. Eventually, the government added Thursday to the official weekend, but in 2013, Saudi Arabia had switched to a Friday–Saturday weekend, in an effort to better align the kingdom's working week with other countries in the region and internationally. Saudi Arabia, the biggest Arab economy, remained the only member of the Gulf Cooperation Council to have a Thursday–Friday weekend after Oman shifted to a Friday–Saturday earlier in 2013. Although some Saudi religious conservatives objected against the change and saw it as caving in to Westernization, it was widely welcomed by the country's many businesses.

Official Saudi holidays are centered on Muslim religious celebrations. The two major holidays are Eid al-Adha (Feast of the Sacrifice), which is celebrated on the 10th of the Islamic month Dhu al-Hijjah; and Eid al-Fitr (Feast of the Breaking of the Fast), which marks the end of the month of Ramadan. These are the only two religious festivals fully sanctioned in Islam. All Islamic celebrations are determined by the Hijrah calendar, the Islamic lunar calendar.

Eid al-Adha, which falls on the 10th day of the Hajj Pilgrimage, is also called al-Eid al-Kabir or the Great Festival. The holiday commemorates the sacrifice, recorded both in the Christian and Muslim traditions, of a lamb substituted by God in testing Ibrahim's (Abraham's) faith, who was asked to sacrifice his son Ismail (Ishmael). In the morning of Eid al-Adha, a lamb or sheep is slaughtered ceremoniously. A portion of the meat is left for the immediate and extended family and friends, and the rest is traditionally given away to the poor, following the example of the Prophet Muhammad, who did the same after the sacrifice.

Eid al-Fitr marks the end of the month of Ramadan and celebrates the breaking of the monthlong fast. It is also referred to as the al-Eid al-Saghir (the Lesser Festival). When the new moon of the next Islamic month is sighted, an official announcement

---

PRE-ISLAMIC ARABIAN CALENDARS

On the eve of Islam, a number of calendars were used throughout the Arabian Peninsula, as indicated by the inscriptions of ancient Southern Arabian calendars. Of these, at least some followed the lunisolar system, which has an intercalary month added (making a 13-month year) roughly every three years to reconcile months with seasons. The Jewish calendar is also lunisolar and was influenced by the Babylonian calendar. Historical evidence suggests that the Jewish calendar may be closely connected with the calendar used in pre-Islamic Mecca.

Historical records indicate that ancient Arabs of the Hijaz, Najd, and the Tihamah region differentiated between two types of months: *halal* ("permitted") months and *haram* ("forbidden") months. The latter category stipulated that fighting was forbidden during four months: Rajab, and the three months around the pilgrimage time of year—Dhu al-Qa'dah, Dhu al-Hijjah, and Muharram. The Quranic tradition connects the four *haram* months with the concept of *nasi'*, which means "postponement" in Arabic.

The names of the months have been adopted by the Islamic calendar, but it was reformed into a purely lunar calendar, changing the traditional pilgrimage, the trading system, and in a larger sense, changing the conception of time.

is made stating the beginning of the holiday. The next day, a special prayer is given at the mosque and followed by a sermon. Families prepare a special type of cookie, called *ka'k*, to be eaten on that day. Eid al-Fitr lasts for three days and is a joyful and widely celebrated time, which focuses on communal celebrations with family and friends and exchanging gifts.

The communal prayers constitute an important part of these holidays. For both Eid al-Fitr and Eid al-Adha, men gather for the morning prayer. Because the number of people on these days is usually greater than what a regular mosque can accommodate, often large outdoor places (*musallah*), marked with the direction of prayer, are installed outdoors. Men wear their best or new clothes to attend the prayer, and fathers bring their sons.

In addition to the two main holidays, the community celebrates a particularly holy time during Ramadan, Laylat al-Qadr, which is when Muhammad received the first revelation of the Quran, according to the Muslim tradition. The Mawlid al-Nabi, the Prophet's Birthday, is not an official holiday in Saudi Arabia. The celebration of the Prophet's Birthday is seen by many conservative Islamic scholars as "innovation" (*bid'*) and therefore deemed illegal. Historically, the celebration appears to have started in Egypt under the Fatimids and was later accepted by the Muslim dynasties of Egypt and Syria. The Ottoman Turks embraced it and made it an official holiday. In the past, the Gulf region celebrated Mawlid by reading and singing religious poems in praise, but little is done for it today. New Year's Day, both in the Hijrah and Western calendars, is not a holiday in Saudi Arabia, although it is celebrated in several other Gulf states and as a secular holiday. The Saudi National Day is the only nonreligious holiday in the country, which was officially proclaimed as a holiday in 2005. National Day has come to be a means by which the Saudi government promotes the notion of national unity.

See also: Chapter 2: Muhammad, Prophet of Islam; The Rise of Islam. Chapter 5: Five Pillars or the Tenets of Islam; Hajj; Islamic Calendar; Quran. Chapter 7: Social Life, Kinship, and Friendships. Chapter 10: Social Life.

Further Reading

Aldossry, Theeb, and Matthias Zick Varul. "A Time to Pray, a Time to Play? Everyday Life in the Kingdom of Saudi Arabia between the Temporalities of Religion, Tradition and Consumerism." *Time & Society*, vol. 25, no. 3, 2016, pp. 471–492.

Whitehead, Kim. "Chapter 6: Islamic Celebrations." *Islam: The Basics*. Mason Crest Publishers, 2004, pp. 22–25.

CHAPTER 11

LITERATURE

OVERVIEW

The Arabian Peninsula has a long and rich literary tradition. Long before the arrival of Islam, the codification of written Arabic, and the literary masterpieces that were created during the Golden Age of the Muslim Empire, Arabic was used to compose oral poetry that was thriving on the peninsula for centuries. Historical records trace the earliest Arabic poetic forms emerging in the tribal communities around 500 AD. In Bedouin culture, poetry was—and, in many ways, still is—the most refined form of artistic expression. Poets have always been highly regarded members of their communities, as their artistry would bring honor and prestige to their whole tribe. Poetic competitions were held during the annual pilgrimage to the pagan idols of Mecca. Moreover, poets and their oral literature served as the containers of their tribe's collective knowledge and transmitters of information. A number of distinct schools of poetry, recitation styles, and a sophisticated system of poetic meters emerged during the pre-Islamic period.

With the spread of the Islamic Empire and the relocation of its political and cultural center to Syria, Iraq, and Egypt, Arabia fell into decline and, for centuries, did not make significant contributions to the thriving tradition of Arabic written literature. After the collapse of the Abbasid Empire in 1258, the Golden Age of Arabic medieval literature came to an end, and it entered a long period of general decline (*inhitat*). The 19th century marked the beginning of the Arabic Renaissance, Nahdah, and Arabic literature entered a new and exciting phase of rapid development. In the course of a century, literary and other intellectual production was completely revived, including the emergence of new literary genres, translation of various European works into Arabic, the opening of new educational institutions, and the rapid growth of print culture and publishing houses. Although Egypt and Syria were the centers of the Nahdah culture, its ideas and influences were made available through publications and welcomed by the Hijazi intellectuals. There were also numerous direct contacts between the literati in the Hijaz and Syria. Among those who had particularly notable influence on the new literary movements of the Hijaz were the Lebanese poet and revolutionary Fuad al-Khatib and writer and intellectual Ameen Rihani. During that period, the most popular literary genres were poetry and emerging short story. The collection *The Literature of Hijaz* (1926) became the first important publication, marking the region's entry onto the Arabic literary scene of the 20th century. The collection included works of many Hijazi poets and was edited by Muhammad Surur al-Sabban—a talented and popular poet in his own right.

The 1960s marked a new period of literary development in Saudi Arabia. At that time, the country began to receive its first sizable oil revenues and invested in education. The latter had a profound impact on Saudi society: literacy levels were growing rapidly and paved the way to a new generation of writers and poets. Litterateurs also benefited from the simultaneous growth of mass media and publishing houses across the Arab world. Literary clubs appeared in all major cities and towns, but they were under the jurisdiction of the Ministry of Culture and Information and, thus, strict censorship was imposed on all activities undertaken by these clubs. Although the government was avidly encouraging literature and the arts, it was done through a very narrowly defined and sanctioned artistic expression, with the goal of promoting Islam and the Arabic language. Those intellectuals and literary figures who disagreed with such tight control and censorship often had to leave the country and work from abroad.

In modern times, Saudi Arabia's literature is known for its diversity, as its bold literary experimentations coexist with highly traditional genres. Tribal poetry remains an important literary production—not only for its aesthetic qualities, but also as a preserver of the living memory of the Bedouin identity. In contrast, it is more difficult for novelists to get public recognition, especially if they choose to write on controversial topics. Writers like Abdelrahman Munif and Turki al-Hamad paid a heavy price for

---

HWJN: SAUDI SCIENCE FICTION LITERATURE

HWJN, labeled the first Saudi science fiction novel, took Saudi Arabia by storm in 2013. It was written by Ibraheem Abbas and translated/coauthored into English by Yasser Bahjatt, quickly becoming a best seller in Saudi Arabia. Coming out of the country with some of the strictest censorship in the world, *HWJN* features a young Jinni (Jinns are angel-like figures in Islamic tradition) named Hawjan, who lives in a different dimension and communicates with our world through the Ouija board. He falls in love with a human, a young woman Sawsan, and the story of an impossible science fiction romance ensues.

The book was published simultaneously in Arabic and English through Ibraheem Abbas's and Yasser Bahjatt's own publishing company, Yatakhayaloon, and was enthusiastically promoted by the coauthors. The Arabic edition became very popular in Saudi Arabia, and the English version of the book also gained some traction, especially after Bahjatt appeared at the World Science Fiction Convention in San Antonio and gathered largely positive reviews.

HWJN also received attention from Saudi religious police, who expressed concerns that the book promotes sorcery and even "polytheistic practices," which is a grave offense in Saudi Arabia. But although the *mutawwa* confiscated the books from some of the bookstores, new copies were found available in stores shortly after. What distinguishes *HWJN* from an average teen paranormal romance is a sustained, albeit subtle, critique of the government. The novel also contains satire on affluent parts of Saudi society in its portrayal of the privileged wealthy Saudi teens.

their critical remarks with continual repressions by the state and religious authorities. However, the new generations of readers have proven to be very eager for daring and outspoken literature.

Further Reading

Alshiban, Afra S. "Saudi Arabia's Role in Advancing Comics." *International Journal of Comic Art*, vol. 19, no. 2, 2017, pp. 51–77.

al-Ghadeer, Moneera. "Saudi Arabia." *The Oxford Handbook of Arab Novelistic Traditions.* Edited by Waïl S. Hassan. Oxford University Press, 2017, pp. 397–410.

al-Hazimi, Mansour, Salma Khadra Jayyusi, and Ezzat Khattab, eds. *Beyond the Dunes: An Anthology of Modern Saudi Literature.* I. B. Tauris, 2006.

Seymour-Jorn, Caroline. "Youth Culture in the Arab World: Explorations through Literature in Translation." *Teaching Modern Arabic Literature in Translation.* Edited by Michelle Hartman. Modern Language Association of America, 2018, pp. 169–182.

Abdelrahman Munif

Abdelrahman Munif (1933–2004) was a prominent Saudi novelist, known for his politically charged novels that often contain criticism of ruling classes throughout the Middle East. Munif's most famous work is his quintet *Cities of Salt* (1984–1989), which vividly depicted the radical changes experienced by the Saudi society, resulting from the discovery of oil and the subsequent growth of the oil industry.

Munif was born in Amman, Jordan, to a Saudi father and an Iraqi mother. In 1952, he came to Baghdad to study law. He quickly joined the emerging Arab Socialist Ba'ath Party and became a political activist. His activism, in which he would persist from then on, in many ways defined the course of his life. In 1955, he was expelled from Iraq along with many other Arab nationals for participating in protests against the Baghdad Pact. Munif relocated to Egypt, which at the time was a hub of pan-Arab nationalism under Nasser. Then, in 1958, he went on to study at the University of Belgrade in Yugoslavia, where he earned a doctorate degree in oil economics in 1961. Munif continued to be politically active and to suffer consequences as a result of it. In 1963, he lost his Saudi nationality after making critical comments about the regime. When he finally came to Lebanon to work in journalism and to begin a writing career, his extensive travels across the Middle East and Europe and his nationalist ideas enabled him to produce highly creative and impactful literary works.

Although Munif began writing only when he was 40 years old, he wrote 15 novels. The first novel was *Trees and the Assassination of Marzouq* (1973), telling a story of a man who flees his homeland after being jailed and tortured. His five-part novel *The Cities of Salt* (1984–1989) is his most prominent work. It follows the evolution of the Arabian Peninsula, as its traditional Bedouin culture is being forever transformed by the oil boom. The first novel of the quintet is *Cities of Salt* (1984), which depicts the destruction of the desert oasis of Wadi al-Uyoun by the Western oilmen. Munif's work documents the economic, social, and psychological effects of radical interventions into Arabian tribal and oasis communities. The subsequent parts of the quintet are *The Trench, Variations on Night and Day, The Uprooted,* and *The Desert of Darkness.* The quintet highlights the author's conviction that Arabs have always suffered from injustice, deprivation, and oppression—at the hands of both local and foreign rulers. This subject remained the central theme of his writing, including his other famous novel *East of the Mediterranean* (1975), in which he revealed, in graphic detail, the torture and abuse suffered by the prisoners in Arab jails and detention camps.

Munif's novels have been translated into 10 languages. He is also a recipient of two distinguished awards in Arabic literature. He continued to be politically active to the end of his life and promoted a type of literary writing that actively engaged with sociopolitical and economic issues experienced by contemporary Arab societies. An avid opponent of both Gulf wars, he was writing a book on Iraq at the time of his death. Abdelrahman Munif became a highly influential literary figure in the Arab world, especially in the advancement of social realism in Arabic literature. His contributions to world literature are also evident, as he is considered among the first writers to develop the genre that is currently known as petrofiction.

See also: Chapter 2: Discovery of Oil. Chapter 3: Political Dissent and Opposition. Chapter 4: Oil Industry and Aramco. Chapter 6: Urbanization. Chapter 11: Prose.

Further Reading

Enderwitz, Susanne. "Memories for the Future: Abdelrahman Munif." *Arabic Literature: Postmodern Perspectives.* Edited by Angelika Neuwirth et al. Saqi, 2010, pp. 134–145.

Macdonald, Graeme. "'Monstrous Transformer': Petrofiction and World Literature." *Journal of Postcolonial Writing,* vol. 53, no. 3, 2017, pp. 289–302.

Munif, Abd al-Rahman, and Peter Theroux. *Cities of Salt: A Novel.* Random House, 1987.

Upchurch, Michael. "Abdelrahman Munif: Mixing It Up with Oil, Politics, and Fiction: Interview." *Glimmer Train Stories,* vol. 11, 1994, pp. 66–77.

Ghazi al-Gosaibi

Ghazi Abdul Rahman al-Gosaibi (1940–2010) was a prominent Saudi Arabian intellectual, poet, and writer. In addition to that, he played an important role in his country's political life. He was born in Hufuf into one of the oldest and richest trading families of the Arabian Peninsula and grew up in Bahrain. He lived a visibly cosmopolitan life, having studied in Egypt and the United States, and served for many years as Saudi Arabia's ambassador in London.

An Apartment Called Freedom (1994) is one of al-Gosaibi's most famous and critically acclaimed works and a best-selling novel. It tells a story of four students from Bahrain who live and study in Cairo in the tumultuous 1960s. It is the journey for self-realization and freedom in an open and intellectually stimulating environment of the revolutionary Cairo, reflecting on al-Gosaibi's own experiences as a student in Egypt. The novel contains satirical commentary on various political and social issues in the Arab world, which kept the novel censored and banned for many years. Only two weeks before al-Gosaibi's death in 2010, this ban was lifted in recognition of his numerous contributions to Saudi Arabia's cultural and political life.

Al-Gosaibi continued to frequently engage in controversial topics in his other novels. For example, *Seven* (2003) is a satirical depiction of Arab realities through the eyes of seven different characters who are interested in the same woman. *A Love Story* (2002) is about a novelist who, while on his deathbed, is consumed by memories of his past relationship with a married woman. He also authored an autobiography titled *Yes, (Saudi) Minister! A Lifetime in Administration* (1999).

As a poet, al-Gosaibi was considered a classicist, although he occasionally wrote free-verse poetry as well. His poems show a great range of subject matter and include politics, romance, and eulogies, as well as the so-called poems of the occasion. It is the latter that often got him into trouble, as he frequently used poetry as a weapon of sharp political criticism. Apart from his literary work, al-Gosaibi was known as a very vocal politician. His career consistently suffered as a result of his outspokenness, which usually took a form of critical poems. For instance, he was dismissed from the position of minister of health in 1984 after writing the poem *A Pen Bought and Sold* for King Fahd. The poem, published on the front page of Al-Jazirah, indirectly accused the ruling elites of corruption, most prominently Prince Sultan, who at the time was the minister of defense. King Fahd fired al-Gosaibi immediately after reading the poem. Twenty years later, another poem cost him his post as Saudi ambassador to the United Kingdom and Ireland. In 2002, he published a short poem "You Are the Martyrs" in Al-Hayat, where he praised a female Palestinian teenager who became a suicide bomber. The poem also attacked the U.S. and Arab political and intellectual elite, whom al-Gosaibi accused in neglecting the Palestinian suffering.

See also: Chapter 3: Political Dissent and Opposition. Chapter 11: Poetry; Prose. Chapter 16: Freedom of Speech.

Further Reading

Aboud, Ahmed Mohamed, and Mohamed Abdulmalik Ali. "Universal Elements in Saudi Novel: A Study of Al-Gosaibi's Freedom Apartment and Alem's The Dove's Necklace." *International Journal of Comparative Literature and Translation Studies*, vol. 3, no. 1, 2015, pp. 55–63.

Obank, Margaret. "Ghazi Algosaibi: 'A True Poet Has to Be Classical and Romantic and a Realist.'" *Banipal: Magazine of Modern Arab Literature*, vol. 5, 1999, pp. 16–19.

Poetry

Poetry is the oldest literary genre in the Arabic-speaking world. The *qasidah* (the ode) is the oldest and most well-known poetic form and is considered the golden standard of the genre. Each *qasidah* can include up to 100 pairs of half-lines composed in different meters. The most renowned early Arabian *qasidahs* received the title of *mu'allaqat*—literally meaning "suspended," as they were hung on the walls of the Kaaba in Mecca to celebrate their beauty and eloquence. Classical Arabian poetry showed incredible variety and addressed all aspects of the Bedouin life, including romance, battles and intertribal conflicts, travels, observations of the desert nature, and so on.

In addition to their aesthetic value, poems were also frequently used as a powerful social tool. Various poetic genres emerged to reflect different social situations and included mockery, vilification of the enemy, praise, elegy, and proclamation of love. Poetry was much more than entertainment: it was used in war times during tribal fighting as a tool to inspire one's own tribe and intimidate the enemy. *Qasidahs* and ballad-like songs about the heroes and battles of the past were often recited at public gatherings. Annual poetic competitions were also very popular, such as the ones that took place during the pilgrimage to the pagan idols in Mecca. Pre-Islamic *qasidahs* were preserved through collective memory and oral transmission, as written transcription of these poems began only 200 years later. Among the most prominent pre-Islamic poets were Imru' al-Qais, Antarah ibn Shaddad, al-Nabigha, Samaw'al ibn Adiya, Tarafa, Zuhayr bin Abi Sulma, and others. Bedouin women poets were also highly regarded. For instance, the Bedouin poetess al-Khansa was praised by the fellow poet al-Nabigha, who referred to her as "the finest poet of the jinn and the humans."

The rise of Islam and the Quran had a profound impact on the development of Arabic literature, as they did on all other aspects of Arab culture. Even the timeline of Arabic literary tradition was evaluated in parallel to the Islamic era. Poets and other litterateurs were divided into three categories: those who lived entirely in pre-Islamic times, al-Jahiliyah ("The Age of Ignorance"); those who were born during the Jahiliyah but later experienced Islam, referred to as *mukhadramun*; and those who lived during later periods—exclusively in Islamic times, *muwalladun*. In addition, the religious importance projected by the Quran and the Hadith (sayings of the prophet) served as major literary inspirations and influences, especially in the development of Arabic prose.

Two types of poetic expression remained prominent in contemporary Arabia: classical poetry and *nabati* poetry. Modern classical poetry is the descendant of the classical *qasidah*, which must adhere to the traditional style and follow its strict rules on meter and rhyme. It has to be composed in classical Arabic. Both new and old classical poetry can be heard throughout the Arabian Peninsula, especially during special occasions, such as rites of passage, holidays, and large family gatherings. Ability to recite long classical poems by heart is a source of pride and great respect in one's social circles. In contrast, *nabati* poetry is considered folk literature. It is composed in local dialects and does not follow the majority of rules required in classical Arabic poetry. As a result, some conservative scholars see *nabati* poetry as a lower form of literary expression with lesser artistic value—despite its popularity. Nevertheless, this form of literary expression plays an important role in constructing unique identities of various tribal groups, who are keen to preserve the cultural heritage of their ancestors. The opposition between classical and *nabati* poetry thus represents the cultural conflict between tribal and Islamic forms of life—the conflict that essentially defines the uniqueness of Saudi society. Arabic poetry, both classical and *nabati*, is one of the few cultural products that withstood modernization in Saudi Arabia. This form of artistic expression continues to be very popular in Bedouin and urban communities alike. Poets continue to enjoy utmost respect and play important social roles, since poetry recitations are an integral part of any official occasion. Muhammad bin Abdallah Uthaimin and Ahmad Ibrahim al-Ghazzawi are considered the two most prominent traditional Saudi poets of Saudi Arabia.

A third form of Arabic poetry, which emerged in the 1960s during the peak of pan-Arabism, is the so-called free verse. Although it was not fully embraced by the more traditional and conservative literary society of Arabia, several prominent Saudi poets contributed to the development of this genre. Among the earlier generation of authors who wrote free-verse and prose poetry are Muhammad Hassan Awwad, Ali al-Dumayni, Muhammad al-Thubayti, Khadijah al-Umari, Fatimah al-Qarni, Abdallah al-Rashid, and Abdallah al-Khashrami. Contemporary prose poets include Fawziyah Abu Khalid, Muhammad al-Dumayni, Ghassan al-Khunayzi, and Huda al-Daghfaq.

See also: Chapter 2: Pre-Islamic Arabia; The Rise of Islam. Chapter 5: Quran. Chapter 6: Bedouins and Nomadism. Chapter 9: Arabic Alphabet and Script; Arabic Dialects.

Further Reading

Frangieh, Bassam. "New Voices of Arabia—The Poetry: An Anthology from Saudi Arabia by Saad Al-Bazei (Ed.)." *Middle Eastern Literatures*, vol. 17, no. 2, May 2014, pp. 205–207.

al-Ghadeer, Moneera. *Desert Voices: Bedouin Women's Poetry in Saudi Arabia*. Tauris Academic Studies, 2009.

al-Odadi, Mohammed S. "Poetry as a Weapon: Saudi Poems on the Gulf War." *The Georgetown Journal of Languages and Linguistics*, vol. 1, no. 3–4, 1991, pp. 215–222.

Prose

Unlike the rich and diverse tradition of poetry, for centuries Arabic prose played a minor role in the development of Arabic literature. The Saudi short story and novel both emerged between World War I and II in the Hijaz—the intellectual center of Arabia. Many of these early prosaic examples first appeared in newly established newspapers and magazines. The literary magazine *al-Manbal* was founded in 1937 and played a pivotal role in promoting the new genres. The editor of *al-Manbal*, Abd al-Quddus al-Ansari, was an important short story writer in his own right. Among other short story writers of the earlier period were Ahmad Rida Huhu and Muhammad Alim al-Afghani, both non-native Hijazis. A notable feature of these prosaic works was experimentation, which combined indigenous literary traditions with influences from world-renowned short story giants such as Edgar Allen Poe, Guy de Maupassant, and Nicolai Gogol.

The 1960s saw a new phase in the development of Saudi short story. As pan-Arabism was gaining popularity, local authors benefited from the advances of the genre in other Arabic-speaking countries. Some of the well-known representatives of this group include Ibrahim al-Nasr, Saʿad al-Bawaridi, Luqman Yunis, and Najjat Khayyat, who were influenced by the works of their Egyptian counterparts Yusuf Idris, Yahya Haqqi, and Nagib Mahfuz. In more recent times, new original voices emerged, such Abdallah Bakhashwan and Jarallah al-Hamid, who greatly contributed to the creation of a unique Saudi short story.

The Twins (1930) by Abd al-Quddus al-Ansari is considered the first Saudi novel, followed by Muhammad al-Jawhari's *The Temperamental Revenge* (1935), Ahmad Rida Huhu's *Mecca's Maiden* (1947), and *The Resurrection* (1948) by Muhammad Ali Maghribi. These early examples of fiction are regarded primarily for their portrayal of important social issues than their literary value. In the 1950s and 1960s, along with the country's economic boom and educational reforms, the Saudi Arabian novel began to gain popularity with the emerging middle class. Hamid Damanhuri's *The Price of Sacrifice* (1959) was the first work of this period to describe the changing world of Mecca. Two conflicting trends characterize this phase of prose development: reconciliation with modernity and rebellion against it. Abdelrahman Munif was a major contributor to the development of the Saudi novel—although he lived outside of Saudi Arabia his whole life and his Saudi citizenship was revoked due to his political activism. Munif's *Cities of Salt* (1984) is considered among the most prominent Arabic-language novels—not only in Saudi literature, but in the Arabic literary tradition overall. The novel became the first part of the quintet, which vividly depicted the dramatic transformation of the Arabian Peninsula during the oil boom. The semiautobiographical genre, which combines fictional elements with the depiction of the author's own experiences, became popular among Saudi authors of the later period, including Abd al-Aziz Mishri, Abdu Khal, Turki al-Hamad, and Raja Alem.

Despite the rapid development of Saudi prose in recent decades, fiction writers face considerable competition from poets, as poetry remains a genre that is traditionally more popular and respected on the Arabian Peninsula. Additionally, the religious establishment and authorities—with the great power of censorship that they possess in Saudi Arabia—resist the development of the novel, as they are suspicious of its potential to offer social commentary and criticism. In order to make their works accessible to a larger audience, many writers resort to publishing outside of Saudi Arabia—either in the neighboring Gulf countries, or in more remote publishing centers such as Beirut or London. Despite all these obstacles, one observes a remarkable increase of novels published in Saudi Arabia with the turn of the century. Only 200 novels were published in the country throughout the 20th century (between 1930 and 1999), versus almost 600 novels published between 2000 and 2011.

See also: Chapter 1: Hijaz and Tihamah. Chapter 3: Human Rights and Censorship. Chapter 16: Government Censorship; Internet and Social Media.

Further Reading

Bagader, Abubaker, et al. *Assassination of Light: Modern Saudi Short Stories*. Three Continents, 1990.

Bagader, Abubaker, et al. *Voices of Change: Short Stories by Saudi Arabian Women Writers*. Lynne Rienner Publishers, 1998.

Khal, Abdu. "The Novel in Saudi Arabia: Establishing an Aesthetic." *Banipal: Magazine of Modern Arab Literature*, vol. 20, 2004, pp. 77–133.

Zalah, Ali. "The Progress of the Novel in Saudi Arabia." *Banipal: Magazine of Modern Arab Literature*, vol. 20, 2004, pp. 82–86.

Raja Alem

Saudi Arabian author Raja Alem was born in Mecca in 1970. She was raised in her grandfather's house near the Great Mosque, where he held the position of the Sheikh of the Water Carriers from the Well of Zamzam. Alem is a leading voice in contemporary Arabic literature and is the most extensively published Saudi woman novelist. Her literary works spread across various genres and include novels, plays, a biography, short stories, essays, literary journalism, children's literature, and collaborative creative projects with artists and photographers. She was the first woman to win the highly prestigious International Prize for Arabic Fiction (the Arabic Booker) in 2011 for her novel *The Dove's Necklace* (2010). In addition to her Arabic-language novels, Alem has coauthored two novels in English with Tom McDonough: *Fatima* (2002) and *My Thousand and One Nights* (2010). She is known for her postmodern experimentation with language and form, incorporating a rich philosophical and literary repertoire from classical Arabic sources from different historical eras. Her writing often includes philosophical reflections on various existential questions on aesthetics, gender, identity, history, and human relations. As a native of Mecca, she features this historical city prominently in her writing.

Alem's latest novel is titled *Sarab* and tackles one of the most controversial topics in Saudi Arabia's history—the 1979 siege of the Grand Mosque in Mecca by Islamic militants. The novel tells the story of a young woman, Sarab, who disguises herself as a man and takes part in the siege as one of the militants. The novel appeared first in German and then in English translations in 2018, but is yet to come out in Arabic.

In addition to her literary work, Raja Alem made other contributions to Saudi cultural life. One of her accomplishments is the creation, together with her sister and famous Saudi artist Shadia Alem, of the Cultural Club and Recreation Center for girls in Mecca. The goal of this establishment is to promote women's education, particularly in the arts. Alem is a recipient of various awards in the Arab world and in Europe, including the UNESCO award for creative achievement in 2005. She currently lives and works in Paris.

See also: Chapter 8: Education of Women. Chapter 11: Prose.

Further Reading

Aboud, Ahmed Mohamed, and Mohamed Abdulmalik Ali. "Universal Elements in Saudi Novel: A Study of Al-Gosaibi's Freedom Apartment and Alem's The Dove's Necklace." *International Journal of Comparative Literature and Translation Studies*, vol. 3, no. 1, 2015, pp. 55–63.

Temsamami, Hafsa. "Women and Words in Saudi Arabia: Unveiling the Female Identity in Rajaa Alsanea's Girls of Riyadh." *Aux Marges de La Littérature Arabe Contemporaine*. Edited by Laurence Denooz and Xavier Luffin. Academia Scientiarum Fennica, 2013, pp. 161–167.

Turki al-Hamad

Turki al-Hamad (b. 1952) is a prominent Saudi litterateur. In addition to his fiction writing and journalistic work, he is also a well-known political activist. He was born in Jordan in 1953 to Saudi parents from Buraydah. He grew up in Dammam, where he became fascinated with Ba'athist ideologies during his teenage years. These experiences were later reflected in his semiautobiographical work. Later in life, al-Hamad referred to this period as the "revolutionary romanticism" of the left—an ideology that attracted many Arab youth in the 1960s and 1970s—which he compares with the counterculture of radical Islamism that attracts some of the young people today. As a result of his political activism, al-Hamad spent a year in prison when he was 18. Following that, he studied in the United States—first in Colorado and later in California. In 1985, he received a PhD from the University of Southern California, having completed a dissertation titled "Political Order in Changing Societies: Saudi Arabia, Modernization in a Traditional Context." Al-Hamad talked about a profound ideological change he experienced while living in the United States: he came to the country, in his own words, as a "committed Marxist," but had rejected socialism as an ideology by the time he left. In 1995, he retired from King Saud University in order to fully devote his time to writing.

Al-Hamad's novels explore a myriad of issues, which are considered highly controversial in Saudi Arabia, including grassroot political opposition movements, questions of religious freedom, conflicts between religion and science, and sexuality. His most significant literary work is the semiautobiographical trilogy, *Specters in Deserted Alleys*, which tells the coming-of-age story of Hisham al-Abir—a young Saudi man from Dammam, who gets embroiled in the ideological conflicts within his native country in the late 1960s to the early 1970s. The first part of the trilogy, *Adama*, appeared in 1995. Although banned in Saudi Arabia, Bahrain, and Kuwait, the novel became an explosive best seller throughout the Middle East, selling over 20,000 copies. It focuses on Hisham's high school years when he joins the Saudi branch of the Arab Socialist Ba'ath Party. The second volume, *Shumaisi*, follows Hisham to Riyadh, where he is now a college student. The author continued to present highly contentious topics—Hisham has an affair with a married woman, drinks alcohol, and gets arrested for his political activities. The last novel of his trilogy, *Al-Karadib* (1999), was found to be particularly offensive by the conservative clerics, as the protagonist makes a suggestion that God and the devil might be two sides of the same coin. Unsurprisingly, Saudi religious clerics issued four *fatwas* against al-Hamad, in addition to a statement by al-Qaeda that proclaimed him an apostate. But despite numerous death threats that flowed thereafter, al-Hamad continues to live in Riyadh.

Throughout his life, al-Hamad's activism made him and his literature the object of fury from the conservative clerics and the religious police, but he never attempted to hide his views. He is often called a secularist and a liberal, but the author prefers to avoid these labels and describes himself as simply a citizen who cares deeply about his country. In December 2012, al-Hamad had yet another brush with the authorities, when he was arrested following a number of controversial tweets that included: "Neo-Nazism is on the rise in the Arab world under the guise of Islamism" and "Our Prophet came to rectify the faith of Abraham and now is the time when we need to rectify the faith of Muhammad." He was released in 2013 and continues to be vocal about his views.

See also: Chapter 3: Political Dissent and Opposition. Chapter 11: Prose. Chapter 16: Freedom of Speech.

Further Reading
Hamad, Turki. *Adama*. Saqi, 2003.
Hamad, Turki. *Shumaisi*. Saqi, 2005.

Women Writers

Despite being bound by religious and traditional limitations, Saudi women consistently find new ways of participating in the country's cultural life and create extraordinary pieces of literature and artwork. Saudi women began to publish in newspapers and magazines for the first time in the mid-1950s. The first article by a woman was published in *al-Manhal* in 1956. Due to a more cosmopolitan and welcoming environment, Hijazi women writers were in the forefront. Most prominent members of that generation of litterateurs were Fatna Shakir, Thuraya Qabil, Abdiyah Khayyat, and Huda Dabbagh. Shortly after, women from the central region joined the movement, including Hissa al-Fadhl and Sultanah al-Sudayri. In addition to newspaper articles, these authors wrote poetry, short stories, and novels. Samira Khashoggi, Amal Shata, Huda al-Rashid, and Hind Baghaffar were Saudi Arabia's first women novelists. Samira Khashoggi, who published several novels under the pseudonym Samira bint al-Jazira (Samira Daughter of the Arabian Peninsula), is considered the country's first woman novelist, with the publication of her novel *Farewell to My Dreams* (1958).

The first generation of women novelists focused on writing as a liberating force. In a country that has one of the most repressive systems for women, female writers have made some remarkable contributions to the Arab novel. There are three important phases highlighting the literary trajectory of women novelists. The first phase took place between 1959 and 1979: it is characterized by women authors beginning to actively participate in the literary life of their country. The second phase falls in the 1980s and 1990s and is marked by increasing experimentation. The third and current phase, which began around 2000, can be defined as the feminist novelistic revolution, increasingly claiming its own unique space—not only within Arabic-language literature but in the global literary tradition.

An interesting feature of the early novels is that they are often set outside Saudi Arabia, as exemplified by the works of Samira Khashoggi, Hind Baghaffar, and Huda al-Rashid. The events either take place overseas, or the setting remains unidentifiable as a way of averting possible criticism and censorship. Importantly, the tactic of concealing the setting was gradually replaced by an opposite trend, starting in the early 1980s, when the novel's location began to be identified and emphasized as a markedly Saudi space. During the second period, women novelists began to experiment with the genre, while participating in a fierce cultural debate between the conservatives and modernists. Raja Alem is one of the main writers in this period and is considered a pioneer of postmodernist Saudi literature. Other novels by women published since the 1980s also contributed significantly to the genre and presented provocative depictions of gender, race, and sexuality, focusing on the issues and counterculture of Saudi women. A number of writers of the later period addressed a number of shocking and previously unthinkable topics. These include a blunt representation of adultery and abortion in Laila al-Juhani's *Barren Paradise* (1998) and women in prison in Samar al-Muqrin's *Women of Vice* (2008). Following Samira Khashoggi's example, several novelists chose to publish under pseudonyms, to avoid censorship and negative attention from the conservatives. Among these writers are Warda Abd al-Malik, who wrote *The Return* (2006), and Tayfal-Hallaj, the author of *The Sacred Marriage* (2005).

With the turn of the century, a new generation of Saudi women novelists claimed their space on the cultural scene. They represent—both in their novels and their real-life personas—an image of a cosmopolitan woman, which has been actively promoted by Saudi Arabia after the events of September 11, 2001. These women belong to the affluent middle class that benefited from oil wealth, free market economy, rapid urbanization, international education, and social media. The latter was and is particularly important in this new phase of literary development, as social media and the Internet opened up completely new forms of communication—previously completely unavailable to women in this highly segregated society. These writers are urban, educated, sophisticated, and multilingual. Most of them were in their twenties when they began writing and publishing. For example, Raja al-Sani was only 24 when her first novel *Girls of Riyadh* (*Banat al-Riyadh*) came out in 2005. The heroines in *Girls of Riyadh* and similar literary works are presented as living a cosmopolitan fantasy. They are globe-trotting Starbucks drinkers, shisha smokers, and brand shoppers. They move between home, college campus, and a shopping mall as seamlessly as they move between continents—in many ways, indistinguishable from other privileged millennials anywhere else. They speak in a mixture of Arabic and English, infused with new-gen abbreviations and hashtags from social media.

In sum, these women are situated between cultures, geographies, and languages. International attention projected onto these novelists and their works highlights the familiar Orientalist fascination with Muslim women in general, and Saudi women in particular. Thus, interest in this literary production goes beyond its creative quality and involves deeper ideological and social issues.

See also: Chapter 7: Gender Segregation; Women's Mobility and Driving Ban. Chapter 8: Education of Women.

Further Reading

Arebi, Saddeka. *Women and Words in Saudi Arabia: The Politics of Literary Discourse.* Columbia University Press, 1994.

Dhahir, Sanna. "From Flat to Round Men: Male Characters in Saudi Women's Fiction." *Journal of Middle East Women's Studies*, vol. 12, no. 1, Mar. 2016, pp. 31–49.

Fassi, Hatoon Ajwad Al. "Saudi Women and Islamic Discourse: Selected Examples of Saudi Feminisms." *Hawwa: Journal of Women of the Middle East and the Islamic World*, vol. 14, no. 2, 2016, pp. 187–206.

Michalak-Pikulska, Barbara. "Girls from Riyadh by Rajaa Alsanea as a Literary Statement of Changes within Contemporary Saudi Society." *Rocznik Orientalistyczny*, vol. 66, no. 2, 2013, pp. 105–108.

al-Rasheed, Madawi. "Deconstructing Nation and Religion: Young Saudi Women Novelists." *Novel and Nation in the Muslim World: Literary Contributions and National Identities.* Edited by Elisabeth Özdalga and Daniella Kuzmanovic. Palgrave, 2015, pp. 133–151.

CHAPTER 12

ART AND ARCHITECTURE

OVERVIEW

Architectural tradition of the Arabian Peninsula offers a diversity that contrasts with the stereotypical image of Bedouin tents scattered in the desert. Although it may not have the grandeur of some other artistic forms that Arab culture is known for, such as poetry or calligraphy, a number of distinct architectural styles can be found throughout the peninsula. Arabian architecture combines both art and pragmatism, taking into consideration the requirements of everyday living and the constant battle to adapt to a harsh environment. The development of local architectural styles has been based on several important factors: climate, the availability of building material, and cultural and religious norms. Additionally, Arabian architecture is markedly different from the rest of the Middle East, which can be explained by the influence of conservative religious beliefs on all aspects of culture on the peninsula. But despite these limitations, traditional building structures still featured a great deal of creativity.

In ancient times, architecture flourished in the south of the peninsula under the Sabaean civilization and in the north under the Nabateans. Cities were usually shaped as rectangles or ovals and had large walls, intricate irrigation systems, houses of worship, and various other public buildings. Structures were built from smoothly trimmed limestone blocks and were decorated with flat ornamental reliefs. The Nabateans were particularly skilled at structural engineering and construction craftsmanship. Their architectural legacy included structures carved out of mountainsides and large rocks, such as amphitheaters and tombs.

In Central Arabia, the only important architectural site was the ancient Kaaba—a large cubic structure, which prior to the coming of Islam served as a pagan sanctuary in Mecca. The main forms of housing on the peninsula were brick houses for sedentary populations and tents for the nomadic Bedouins. Harsh regional climate was a major aspect in the architectural design of the entire region, having to develop innovative methods of controlling the extreme heat in the summer. These measures included high thick walls, covered yards, small windows, and various architectural inventions to control the direction of the wind and to cool the water. Control over the flow of air is a particularly interesting element of traditional Arabian architecture. Houses often contained special ventilation towers and roof vents that were operated and controlled from the ground level. Carefully aligned to face the prevailing winds, these mechanisms directed air into the inner sections of buildings, making living conditions comfortable during the scorching summer months.

The growth of Islamic cities brought about a new era for regional architecture. The oldest Muslim places of worship, such as the ones constructed in Medina, featured a mosque built in a simple style and surrounded by a spacious yard. These early mosques did not have minarets that appeared at a later time. With the relocation of the Muslim Empire to urban centers in the north under the Umayyads and Abbasids, the architecture of the area remained unchanged for many centuries. Only in the 18th century did the Ottoman influence become visible, but it was limited to the coastal cities of the Red Sea. Prior to the discovery of oil in 20th century, Saudi architectural style continued to feature simple forms that reflected the severe environmental conditions and poverty of the local population. Different housing designs reflected lifestyle distinction between nomadic and sedentary people. The Bedouins lived in tents made of black goat hair, while the residents of oases built their dwelling from unfired sun-dried brick or pounded earth. In the mountains, mud and stone were the main construction materials. On the coasts of the Red Sea and the Gulf, blocks made from sea coral were often used in construction. Other natural building resources included wood from tamarisk and palm trees, used for doors, windows, roof beams, and sunscreens. In hot and humid coastal areas, builders often constructed temporary shacks from reeds, palm fronds, and similar material.

The artistic expression in Saudi Arabia has been greatly limited by the Wahhabi doctrine, which reinforces the already strict Islamic prohibition of worshipping idols and inanimate objects. This belief is based on the idea that the only being to be worshipped is the one God, and no person or object may stand in the path of direct communication between the believers and God. From this point of view, memorials and monuments in commemoration of historical events and persons are often seen by Saudi clerics as heresy and thus must be destroyed. This strict ideology resulted in the annihilation of many important historical sites tracing back to the early days of Islam, particularly those that have spiritual significance to the Shia community. The policy of demolition of potential idolatry-worshipping sites affected various important tombs. The trend began in the 19th century when Saudi rulers ordered the erasure of the historical graves near the Prophet Muhammad mosque in Medina. Among other destroyed sites are the tombs of Muhammad's wives and close companions, as well as the mosque of his daughter Fatima. Mecca is the city that experienced the most severe and wide-scale demolitions of historic buildings and sites. This is an ongoing process driven by the expansion of the area surrounding Kaaba and the building of modern hotels and facilities for the incoming pilgrims. For instance, the recently constructed Abraj al-Bait Towers were built in place of the historically important 18th-century Ottoman fortress, inciting a strong response from the Turkish government.

As a result of the ultraconservative Wahhabi ideology, even calligraphy—a very popular embellishment in religious architecture throughout the Middle East, as it provides decor while avoiding the depiction of human form—has been used sparingly in Saudi Arabia. Despite its heavy reliance on the holy word of the Quran, Wahhabi teachings often view the inscription of the text as an object in itself, posing a risk for a worshipper to be distracted by the beauty of the writing, when one is expected to focus fully on the prayer. Interestingly, the ideological preference of abstraction and simplicity of form, promoted by Wahhabism, created a welcoming ground for incorporating Western modernist forms in architecture in recent times.

Visual and fine arts on the Arabian Peninsula historically have been secondary to the many forms of literary expression, especially poetry. However, economic development brought a series of rapid and distinct cultural changes, including an emergence of a vibrant modern art scene in Saudi Arabia and the Gulf countries. Concurrently, Islamic art continues to grow and transform itself. The development of modern arts in Saudi Arabia reflects the country's focus on both modernization and preservation of Islamic and traditional values. Saudi Arabia was the first Gulf state to offer art education for male students at the university level since 1965. The government maintains its influence over the art scene through the Saudi Arabian Society for Culture and Arts, which sponsors and supports artists, facilitates exhibitions, and promotes the arts in the society. There is a gradual increase in opportunities for Saudi artists to present their works publicly in galleries and art shows. However, in order to exhibit their work, artists must follow the strict censorship guidelines defined by the country's religious establishment. Several members of the royal family support the modern art scene. For example, the Mansouria Foundation in Jeddah, established by Princess Jawaher Bint Majed Bin Abdulaziz Al-Saud, facilitates exhibitions, publications, and the kingdom's first official collection of contemporary Saudi art. Among other prominent patrons of the arts is Prince Khalid bin Faisal, who is a renowned painter and poet in his own right.

Among Saudi cities, Jeddah stands out as the center of contemporary Saudi art. It attracts a growing number of new artists by presenting an array of opportunities for them. For instance, the city commissioned sculptors to create over 300 large sculptures along the corniche, representing various aspects of modern and traditional art. Jeddah is also home to several major art galleries. Among these is Darat Safeya Binzagr, opened in 2000, which serves simultaneously as a studio and a gallery of Safeya Binzagr—one of Saudi Arabia's most prolific and acclaimed painters.

Further Reading

Ettinghausen, Richard, et al. *The Art and Architecture of Islam, 650–1250*. Penguin Books, 1987.

Foley, Sean. *Changing Saudi Arabia: Art, Culture, and Society in the Kingdom*. Lynne Rienner Publishers, 2019.

Khalili, Nasser D. *Islamic Art and Culture: A Visual History*. Overlook Press, 2005.

Martin, Rose, et al. "Reflections on Contemporary Arts Education in Egypt, Lebanon and Saudi Arabia." *The Palgrave Handbook of Global Arts Education*. Edited by Georgina Barton and Margaret Baguley. Palgrave Macmillan, 2017, pp. 171–185.

Abraj al-Bait

One of the most known symbols of contemporary Saudi cityscape is the Abraj al-Bait structure, which literally means "Towers of the House," in reference to the Kaaba—the house of God. The towers are owned by the Saudi government and constitute a part of a massive hotel complex in Mecca, consisting of seven skyscraper hotels. The

An aerial view of Abraj al-Bait in Mecca. (Samet Guler/Dreamstime.com)

structure is located next to the most sacred site in Islam—the Great Mosque (Masjid al-Haram) of Mecca and the Kaaba. Abraj al-Bait were built within the ambitious King Abdulaziz Endowment Project that aims to radically remodel the holy city for its pilgrims. Abraj al-Bait are located across the square to the south from the King Abdul-Aziz Gate, which serves as the main entrance to the Great Mosque. The towers have two large prayer rooms—one for male visitors, another for females—that can accommodate more than 10,000 people.

With the construction costs totaling $15 billion, Abraj al-Bait is one of the world's most expensive buildings. The central hotel tower, the Mecca Royal Clock Tower, has the world's largest clock face. This same tower contains a five-star hotel—a luxury lodging operated by Fairmont Hotels and Resorts. It is the world's third-tallest building and the fifth-tallest freestanding structure. The towers feature 26 bright searchlights that reach the height of over 6 miles into the sky. The call to prayer is announced from Abraj and is heard at the distance of over 4 miles across the valley.

Towering over the city and the Great Mosque, Abraj al-Bait have become a visual marker of the new Mecca, which was transformed—at a breathtaking speed—from the traditional and relatively small desert town into a neon-lit techno city. Over just a few decades, the developers changed the dense urban growth of low-rise courtyards and narrow streets into a repeatable pattern of steel and glass. The new buildings do include some traditional elements, such as mosaics and inlay, as well as the *mashrabiyah* panels—beautiful latticework openings originally designed as ventilating covers, but in this case used as decoration.

The construction of Abraj generated a lot of local and international controversy as it was built directly on the site of the historic 18th-century Ottoman Ajyad Citadel. The stone fortress was built in 1781 as a protection from invaders and was one of the very few remaining Ottoman structures of its kind in the world. The fortress covered about 250,000 square feet and was situated on Bulbul Mountain overlooking the Great Mosque from the south. The citadel was completely demolished and the mount was erased to the ground to make room for the new project. The demolition sparked an international outcry in 2002 and a strong response from the Turkish government.

See also: Chapter 1: Mecca. Chapter 2: Muhammad, Prophet of Islam; Pre-Islamic Arabia. Chapter 4: Tourism. Chapter 5: Five Pillars or the Tenets of Islam; Hajj. Chapter 12: Great Mosque of Mecca; Modernization of Saudi Architecture; Traditional Architecture.

Further Reading

Sadi, Muhammad Asad, and Joan C. Henderson. "A Saudi Arabian Perspective: Local versus Foreign Workers in the Hospitality and Tourism Industry." *The Cornell Hotel & Restaurant Administration Quarterly*, vol. 46, no. 2, May 2005, pp. 247–257.

Sidawi, Bhzad. "The Tale of Innovation in Two Departments of Architecture in the Kingdom of Saudi Arabia." *International Journal of Architecture, Engineering and Construction*, vol. 3, no. 4, 2014, pp. 275–286.

Bedouin Jewelry

Traditionally, silver was the primary material for making jewelry on the Arabian Peninsula. The most frequently used jewelry pieces are bracelets, necklaces, rings, hair ornaments, and belts. For many centuries, jewelry constituted the main part of the woman's dowry, and she continued receiving it throughout her life on different occasions, such as birth of children. This practice continues today, and jewelry often serves as the woman's capital of which she has an exclusive and undisputed ownership. Under Muslim law, in the case of divorce, a woman keeps all of her jewelry. Thus, jewelry pieces are often seen as a wearable investment, especially among the Bedouin community. Additionally, it serves as a visual marker of the woman's social status. Jewelry is worn very frequently and on various formal and informal occasions. It is expected from a woman to wear large amounts of jewelry on special occasions, such as weddings and other celebrations. But many women also wear various jewelry pieces in their homes when performing daily tasks.

An important cultural function of jewelry is that it serves as protection against various types of misfortunes and the evil eye. One of the most common amulets throughout the Arabian Peninsula and the Gulf is the *hirz*—a cylindrical or rectangular silver container where small scrolls with Quranic verses are placed. Usually, a *hirz* is worn around the neck as a pendant and has great variations in size. Jewelry pieces are often heavily embellished with various semiprecious stones, such as turquoise, amber, agate, cornelian, coral, and pearls, as well as their imitations made of glass. Red and blue are particularly important colors as they are believed to have protective qualities, regardless of whether they are a semiprecious stone or a glass bead—the color of the object is more important than the material. Additionally, jewelry pieces are usually decorated with intricate patterns and granulations of different styles, depending on geographical regions, tribal affiliations, and other factors. Necklaces and pendants often feature silver bells, balls, beads, coins, and links of intricate chainmail mesh. Most Bedouin jewelry pieces are large and dramatic, especially necklaces and bracelets, some weighing several pounds.

Silversmithing is done by both men and women, depending on regional customs. In the south of the Arabian Peninsula, Yemeni silversmiths were celebrated for their highly creative work. This craft was practiced by the Yemeni Jewish community and has been in decline after the 1950s, when their majority relocated to Israel. Oman is also known for its silver jewelry of high quality, both with regard to workmanship and high silver content. Craft centers such as Nizwa and Bahla traditionally supplied the whole Gulf region with beautiful jewelry.

Sources of silver were primarily the Maria Theresa dollar, or thaler, and other colonial coinage. In the 20th century, Saudi riyal was also used for silversmithing. According to the Bedouin custom, jewelry is passed from mothers and grandmothers to women of younger generations. Therefore, much of the silver in use today has been used and reused for many years and, in some cases, contains ancient silver. Old Bedouin jewelry is highly valued and sought after by collectors and museums.

See also: Chapter 6: Bedouins and Nomadism.

Further Reading

Ross, Heather Colyer. *The Art of Bedouin Jewellery: A Saudi Arabian Profile.* 3rd ed. Arabesque, 1989.

Topham, John, et al. *Traditional Crafts of Saudi Arabia.* Rev. ed. Stacey International, 2005.

Calligraphic Art

A number of cultural and religious factors helped Arabic calligraphy to evolve into a primary form of visual arts throughout the Middle East and North Africa. From its inception, Islam emphasized the uniqueness of one God and strongly condemned idol worshipping in any form. Representing the divine in a visual or material form was and still is considered blasphemy and strictly prohibited—a religious practice known as aniconism. Over time, Sunni teachings expanded the prohibition to include any living thing, since each was seen as containing an element of the divine. It is important to note, however, that cultural attitudes toward representing living beings were markedly different among Muslim societies, which while largely accepting core Islamic values,

An example of Arabic calligraphic art. (Nabeel Zytoon/Dreamstime.com)

embraced various local traditions. In fact, several Muslim societies did not practice aniconism and developed distinct traditions in figurative art, especially during the Umayyads and the Fatimids, and later under the Ottomans. Among the most prominent examples of such art are the genre of Persian miniatures, which focused on depictions of people, often in large numbers.

Nevertheless, in the absolute majority of cases, Islamic art avoided figurative representations, but instead focused on the Arabic language itself—considered the divine word as the language of the Quran—as a means of creative expression. The flexibility of Arabic letters allowed a great deal of variation. The multitude of calligraphic styles allowed the artists to create masterpieces, many of which survived in the form of architectural details and ornaments.

The earliest form of Arabic writing, historically known as al-Jazm, was the foundation of what is considered to be the first Arabic script—Kufi. It is believed that this script was developed and received its name from the city of Kufa in Iraq (about 110 miles south of Baghdad), an important cultural center in the early days of Islam. Kufi was used to record the Quran: its earliest surviving copies (8th–10th centuries AD) feature the early simple version of this angular script. It was also frequently used on tombstones, coins, pottery, and for architectural purposes. In later centuries, other more elaborate forms of Kufi appeared, including floral, foliated, interlaced, bordered, and squared Kufi styles. The main aesthetic features of the early Kufi calligraphy were round letters and horizontal strokes of the extremes—either very elongated or very compact. The end of the 7th century, vowels were introduced into the text in the form of red dots, which were placed above or below characters. Around the 12th century, Kufi gradually stopped being used for writing, although it continues to be widely employed for decoration.

Naskh is another historically important script. It first appeared in the cities of Mecca and Medina around the 7th century AD, but it was refined and acquired its character much later—by the prolific calligrapher Ibn Muqlah, who transformed it into an elegant cursive script in the early 10th century. Due to its clarity and ease in writing, Naskh quickly became the main calligraphic style for copying of the Quran and composition of manuscripts. Naskh's harmonious proportions and clear connections made it the most suitable script for printing purposes. Currently, most printed publications, such as newspapers and periodicals, have Naskh typefaces. It also remains the most commonly used style for recording and publishing the Quran.

Thuluth is an elegant Arabic script that was especially popular in the Middle Ages and widely used for religious purposes. In Arabic, the word *thuluth* means "one-third." There are different theories about the origin of its name, but the most probable reason was given by Ibn Muqlah himself—the inventor of both Naskh and Thuluth scripts—who explained that the name is related to the calligraphic categorization of letters in this script: one-third of the letters in this script are straight and two-thirds are round. Thuluth is closely associated with Islamic culture and is frequently used for decorating mosques and other religious purposes. The letters in Thuluth are usually large but compact, and round shapes dominate.

Ruq'ah calligraphic script was invented and refined in the Ottoman government offices in Istanbul in the mid-19th century. Before its arrival, the Ottoman officials used four different script styles: Ta'liq, Siyakat, Diwani, and Jaly-Diwani. Each of these styles was assigned a particular practical function, such as legal or financial documents. To resolve the complexities of the four-style system, Ruq'ah was designed as a uniform script for handwriting, having combined the elements from Ta'liq and Diwani. Stripped of elongation, decorations, and lifting of the pen, Ruq'ah was meant to be fast and efficient. It became the simplest form of Arabic calligraphy. Among the central features of Ruq'ah were short, straight lines and simple curves, as well as even lines of text. Mümtaz Efendi was the inventor of this style, but a different calligrapher—Mehmed Izzet Efendi—was the one to develop the canonical form of Ruq'ah.

Each of the Arabic calligraphic scripts has a distinct history and a set of specific functions. Some of them became widely used throughout the Arabic-speaking world, while others remained local. Among those, the Maghribi script was developed and used primarily in North Africa and Spain. The elegant style of Nastaliq originated in Iran and Central Asia and continued to spread eastward, becoming a commonly used script in Mughal India and Ottoman Turkey.

Calligraphers are considered artists, whose work is celebrated in Islamic culture. Through the centuries, the calligraphic art, its techniques, and traditions were passed down from masters to their students, who often belonged to the same family—keeping and refining the art through generations. If one strived to be formally recognized as a master calligrapher, they were required to be fully dedicated to the craft and to train for many years. This was a long and rigorous process, which included a long period of meticulous copying in order to perfect the skill before attempting to produce one's own calligraphic art. Most calligraphers were highly educated individuals. Some belonged to privileged social classes, as it was a common practice for a ruler to be trained by the best calligraphers. Although traditionally calligraphy was practiced by men, some women from wealthy families were also educated in the craft. Nowadays, calligraphy is widely practiced by both men and women.

The numerous tools and materials used in calligraphy are very particular and must follow strict regulations and traditions, since they are considered to play a major role in the quality and value of the final product. The knowledge of how to prepare and use such tools as pens, inks, and paper constitutes an essential part of training to become a professional calligrapher. A calligraphic pen is called *qalam*. It is usually made from a reed that grows around water, due to its flexibility. Thick pens can also be made from bamboo, and thin ones from the stems of roses. In the long process of making this important calligraphic instrument, hollow reeds were harvested and dried up. Then the calligrapher needed to cut the tip in a specific way to match a particular script to be created with this pen. The shape, width, and angle of the cut needed to be very precise.

Inks were made of a variety of natural materials, including soot, ox gall, and plant essences. Specific formulas of ingredients to make calligraphic ink were always treated as valued secrets among calligraphers. Most renowned calligraphers had their own recipes for making ink. Usually, soot from a hemp oil lamp, mixed with Arabic gum, served as the base of the ink mixture. Additional ingredients included henna leaves, indigo, and gallnuts. They would let the final mixture sit for five days, then strain it, and finally thin it with water and add perfume. A hedgehog quill was used for stirring the mixture—a very important part of the process, so that the ink has the right consistency. Finally, the finished product was poured into inkwells that contained a small ball of raw silk (*lika*), which was meant to absorb some of the ink to prevent spillage and control the amount of ink on the pen.

Early Arabic manuscripts were produced on papyrus and parchment. Then, around the 8th century, paper was introduced to the Islamic world from China. The instruments and materials used to create calligraphy were considered artistic works in their own right and were often made of precious materials, elaborately decorated and collected by calligraphers and rulers alike.

See also: Chapter 2: The Abbasids; The Golden Age of Islam in Arabia; The Rise of Islam. Chapter 3: Sharia Law and Judicial System. Chapter 5: Quran.

Further Reading

Blair, Sheila. *Islamic Calligraphy*. Edinburgh University Press, 2006.

George, Alain. *The Rise of Islamic Calligraphy*. Saqi, 2010.

Gharipour, Mohammad, and Schick Irvin Cemil. *Calligraphy and Architecture in the Muslim World*. Edinburgh University Press, 2013.

Khatibi, Abdelkebir, and Mohamed Sijelmassi. *The Splendor of Islamic Calligraphy*. Thames and Hudson, 1996.

Osborn, J. R. *Letters of Light: Arabic Script in Calligraphy, Print, and Digital Design*. Harvard University Press, 2017.

Contemporary Art

Throughout the 18th and 19th centuries, most of the Arabian Peninsula lingered outside of the burgeoning artistic and cultural developments happening in other parts of the Middle East and the Mediterranean. Even with the discovery of oil in the 20th century and the subsequent rapid transformation of the country and its culture, Saudi Arabian society remained closed and traditional. However, when in the 1950s the government began establishing a new educational system largely modeled after Western systems, art teachers were brought from Egypt, Lebanon, and Palestine and introduced students to artistic methods in other parts of the Middle East and beyond. In the 1980s, the political and ideological climate in Saudi Arabia underwent some radical changes, caused the Iranian Revolution and the siege of the Holy Mosque in Mecca by Islamist extremists. During this period, Saudi Arabia became extremely conservative. Various religion-based constraints, such as the ban on gender mixing, restrictions on women's dress, mobility, and employment, and reinforcement of the ban on the depiction of the human form greatly restricted the development of the arts.

In addition to the hostile ideological environment, the few Saudi artists working in the country were facing difficulties in obtaining the materials they needed to create their work and were forced to buy the basics such as paint and canvas from abroad. It was also almost impossible to find art books, since many of them contain images of the human body. Given restrictions on women's mobility, female artists often were not able to attend the openings of exhibits featuring their own work. At the beginning of the 21st century, the contemporary art scene was virtually nonexistent in Saudi Arabia. The country was lacking the basic infrastructure to support the development of the arts, without any schools, journals, galleries, or other venues and opportunities.

However, by 2012, Saudi Arabia had developed a legitimate contemporary art scene. There was and continues to be an unprecedented growth in the number of artists—both men and women—who show a great diversity of artistic forms and methods. These include installations, conceptual art, digital and video art projects, performance art, pop and street art, comic books and graphic art, and many more. The artists are actively forming networks and collaborations all over the country.

Among the most important and influential initiatives for the development of Saudi art is Edge of Arabia—a nonprofit initiative conceptualized in 2003, when Saudi artists Ahmed Mater and Abdulnasser Gharem met British artist Stephen Stapleton at the al-Meftaha Arts Village, an artists' community in the Asir region. Described as "Saudi Arabia's first independent platform for contemporary art," Edge of Arabia has quickly become one of the most influential institutions on the Saudi art scene; since its base in

> **ART GALLERIES**
>
> Lam Gallery, opened in an upscale mall in Riyadh in 2005, became one of the important sites of contemporary Saudi art. Originally, it was established as a gallery for female artists from the Gulf and the Arabian Peninsula, but gradually widened its focus to include a broad range of paintings, photographs, and sculptures from across the Middle East. As is typical of women-run businesses in Saudi Arabia, Lamya al-Rashed, Lam's founder and director, needed her male guardian's written permission to open the gallery. She has also consistently faced problems with the religious police. For example, the *mutawwa* confiscated her art books because they contained photographs of ancient Greek statues of nude men and women.
>
> Another prominent gallery, Alaan Artspace, opened in Riyadh in 2012 and became the city's first curated contemporary art platform. The gallery focused on art created by women, and its first exhibit, "Soft Power," featured three female artists—Sarah Mohanna al-Abdali, Sarah Abu Abdallah, and Manal Al Dowayan. According to the founding director of Alaan Artspace, Neama Alsudairy, the gallery highlights the current trend in the world of art that a significant number of leading artists, dealers, and curators in the Middle East are women.

London opened in 2008, the initiative has sponsored seminars, art shows, and publications, with the goal of making Saudi and Arab artists known to international audiences. The initiative's first public exhibition in Saudi Arabia opened in January 2012 under the title "We Need to Talk." The exhibition was groundbreaking; it was the first contemporary art show to take place in the kingdom, and it opened to both local and international acclaim. "We Need to Talk" was installed in an unfinished portion of the al-Furisiya Marina and Mall in Jeddah. Prior to the opening, the exhibition was inspected by officials from the Ministry of Culture and Information, whose approval was required to open it to the public. A total of 40 works by 22 Saudi artists, half of whom women, were offered to the audiences. The exhibit was carefully curated to make the show accessible to local Saudi audiences, taking into consideration that many were completely unfamiliar with contemporary art. The title of the event emphasized the need for open dialogue regarding the accessibility of the arts in contemporary Saudi Arabia, while individual art pieces engaged controversial issues such as freedom of speech, human rights, religion, and women's roles in Saudi society. The success of Edge of Arabia and its artists is a powerful testimony to the unprecedented growth of all forms of art in Saudi Arabia.

See also: Chapter 3: Wahhabi Ideology. Chapter 7: Guardianship; Hijab and Dress Code; The *Mutawwa*: Saudi Religious Police. Chapter 16: Tradition vs. Globalization.

Further Reading

Danforth, Loring M. *Crossing the Kingdom: Portraits of Saudi Arabia*. University of California Press, 2016.

Foley, Sean. *Changing Saudi Arabia: Art, Culture, and Society in the Kingdom.* Lynne Rienner Publishers, 2019.

Hassanein, Saffaa. "I Am My Own Guardian: Reflections on Resistance Art." *JMEWS: Journal of Middle East Women's Studies,* vol. 14, no. 2, 2018, pp. 234–241.

Trevathan, Idries, and Manal Alghannam. "Bringing It Back Home: Redefining Islamic Art in Saudi Arabia." *Representing the Nation: Heritage, Museums, National Narratives, and Identity in the Arab Gulf States.* Edited by Pamela Erskine-Loftus, Mariam Ibrahim Al-Mulla, and Victoria Hightower. Routledge, 2016, pp. 13–26.

Great Mosque of Mecca

The Great Mosque of Mecca was built to enclose the Kaaba—the holiest shrine in Islam and the site at which Muslim prayers are directed. Its name in Arabic is al-Masjid al-Haram, literally "the Holy Mosque." The mosque serves as the center of Islamic pilgrimage rituals and receives millions of worshippers each year. It consists of a rectangular central courtyard surrounded by covered prayer areas. Pilgrims perform the circumambulation of the Kaaba around the courtyard, in the ritual called *tawaf*. In addition to the Kaaba, the Great Mosque's central area hosts two other sacred sites. One of them is Maqam Ibrahim, or Abraham's Station—a stone that Islamic tradition associates with the rebuilding of the Kaaba by Ibrahim (Abraham) and Ismail (Ishmael). It is believed that the stone contains Ibrahim's footprint. The other sacred site is

The Great Mosque of Mecca (Masjid al-Haram) and the sanctuary of Kaaba. (Ayşegül Muhcu/Dreamstime.com)

the well of Zamzam, which according to the Islamic tradition, miraculously sprang when infant Ismail and his mother Hajar were left in the desert and suffered from thirst. Pilgrims drink from Zamzam when they come to circumambulate around the Kaaba. An important part of the pilgrimage ritual involves two small hills—al-Safa and al-Marwah—located to the east and north of the courtyard. The pilgrims must run or walk between them seven times, which is called *sa'y*, an obligatory action within the pilgrimage rituals. According to the Islamic hadith, Hajar went back and forth between the two hills in search of water for Ismail, and the ritual is meant to commemorate this event.

The current structure of the Great Mosque is the product of centuries of development, with the oldest parts dating back to the 16th century. Before Islam, the Kaaba was an important pagan shrine and stood in an open space, where worshippers gathered to pray and perform rituals. The second caliph, Umar ibn al-Khattab, ordered the building of the first Muslim structure on the sacred site in 638—a wall around the Kaaba. In subsequent decades, partial ceilings, columns, and architectural decorations were added. A more extensive renovation was accomplished under the guardianship of the Abbasid caliph al-Mahdi in the second half of the 8th century AD. The overall structure of the mosque was rebuilt and significantly expanded. One important change was implemented at that time: the external walls of the structure were moved to position the Kaaba at the center of the courtyard, giving it the iconic look it is known for today. In the early 14th century, the Great Mosque was badly damaged by fire and floods and almost entirely rebuilt. In 1571, another series of significant architectural changes were done to the site, when the celebrated Ottoman architect Mimar Sinan ("Architect Sinan"), who was considered one of the most prominent architects in history, made a number of improvements to the building at the directives of Sultan Selim II, such as the replacement of the flat roof with small domes. The architectural elements implemented during the Ottoman era are the oldest remaining parts of the current Great Mosque.

Throughout the 20th century, the Great Mosque underwent several major renovations. The building of the mosque was electrified during the reign of Hussein ibn Ali, who was the Sharif of Mecca from 1908 until 1924. In the second half of the 20th century, the Great Mosque experienced the most drastic changes, as the number of pilgrims rapidly increased thanks to the commercial air travel, whereas oil revenues enabled the Saudi government to undertake ambitious construction projects. The year 1955 marked when the first of the series of significant enlargements was implemented, and the changes continued through 1973. The project expanded the total area of the structure from about 290,000 square feet to about 1,630,000 square feet, and thus significantly increased its maximum capacity to 500,000 people.

Another significant expansion of the mosque was initiated by King Fahd in 1984, in order to accommodate the constantly increasing numbers of pilgrims, which in the 1980s rose to over a million of visitors annually. Several historical buildings around the mosque were completely erased to expand the open space around the mosque. Various pedestrian tunnels, escalators, and passageways were added to the building to improve the flow of people during the Hajj.

The mosque's new size was about 3,840,000 square feet, with the increased capacity to fit 820,000 pilgrims. The most recent effort to further expand the Great Mosque was initiated by King Abdullah in 2011, with a budget of $10 billion and plans to increase the structure's capacity to accommodate 2.5 million worshippers. This project was halted in September 2015 when a construction crane fell during a storm, killing 111 people and injuring 394 others. The construction resumed in 2017.

On November 20, 1979, the Great Mosque was violently attacked by several hundred Islamic militants, who seized the building and took pilgrims hostage. They were led by Juhayman al-Utaybi and Muhammad bin Abdullah al-Qahtani, whereas the latter was proclaimed the Mahdi—an Islamic messiah. The insurgents called for the overthrow of the House of Saud. The fighting between the Saudi forces and the militants continued for over two weeks. The government had to receive a special *fatwa* from the *ulama*, allowing the use of deadly force within the Great Mosque. Having obtained the permission, the Saudi forces captured the mosque in a bloody battle in December 1979, with over 200 casualties among the pilgrims, troops, and insurgents, and several hundred of the injured. The siege resulted in a stricter enforcement of Sharia, implemented by King Khaled. The *ulama* and the religious police were given substantially more power over the next decade, which had a particularly strong impact on women and the further narrowing of their rights.

See also: Chapter 1: Mecca. Chapter 2: Muhammad, Prophet of Islam; Rise of Islam; Sharifs of Mecca. Chapter 5: Five Pillars or the Tenets of Islam; Hajj. Chapter 12: Abraj al-Bait; Modernization of Saudi Architecture; Traditional Architecture.

Further Reading

Isma'il, Muhammad Kaml. *The Architecture of the Holy Mosque, Makkah*. Hazar, 1998.

Serageldin, Ismail, and James Steele. *Architecture of the Contemporary Mosque*. Academy Editions, 1996.

Trofimov, Yaroslav. *The Siege of Mecca: The Forgotten Uprising in Islam's Holiest Shrine and the Birth of Al Qaeda*. Doubleday, 2007.

Modernization of Saudi Architecture

In the mid-20th century, revenues from the Saudi oil industry generated a wide-scale building boom all over the country, which continues into the 21st century. In the span of only several decades, the majority of old cities have been overtaken by new developments and sometimes rebuilt anew. This, in turn, resulted in rapid and often radical urbanization, especially of the Bedouin population, many of whom gave up their nomadic way of life to settle in towns and take wage jobs. The growing demand for housing was met by the Saudi government by introducing Western-style accommodation, such as villas and apartment blocks at low or no cost to citizens. Open spaces, which were a typical feature of settlements and towns on the Arabian Peninsula, quickly vanished under highways, skyscrapers, housing complexes, airports, stadiums, and other contemporary construction projects. Architects and city planners abandoned the traditional setup of the Arab city with its walled residential areas, narrow paths, courtyards, and palm gardens.

However, one dominant feature of Islamic architecture—gender segregation—survived and persisted even in luxurious villas and apartment complexes, which continue to feature two distinct spaces, one for guests and one for family members. Single-family homes with high walls and separate entrances became a symbol of affluent and middle classes. Nowadays, only poor families and foreign workers reside in government-built apartment blocks. In the 1970s, modernist European and American architectural plans began to dominate the Saudi construction industry. Most urban planning was designed by Western and Western-educated architects. The pace of change in Saudi Arabia over the last half century has been tremendous and is most notable in the modern look of the cities and the infrastructure. Extensive building programs and large-scale urbanization made most Saudi cities unrecognizable compared to 50–60 years ago. Among the most obvious changes to the architecture in the entire region was in the method of climate control, where traditional ventilation methods have been replaced with modern air conditioning systems.

The unfortunate consequence of the unprecedented building boom was the virtual disappearance of traditional architecture of the Arabian Peninsula—the process that began in the 1950s. The remaining structures serve as museums or heritage projects and are no longer inhabited on a regular basis. The modern cosmopolitan architecture changed the appearance of the entire region. Only very recently, one may note a growing awareness of the past, reflected in incorporation of regional and Islamic elements into contemporary architectural structures.

See also: Chapter 4: Diversification and Development Plans; Oil Industry and Aramco. Chapter 6: Urbanization. Chapter 12: Abraj al-Bait; Great Mosque of Mecca; Traditional Architecture. Chapter 16: Tradition vs. Globalization.

Further Reading

Abu-Ghazzeh, Tawfiq M. "Privacy as the Basis of Architectural Planning in the Islamic Cultures of Saudi Arabia/Tawfiq Abu-Gazzeh." *Faith and the Built Environment: Architecture and Behaviour in Islamic Cultures.* Edited by Suha Özkan. Comportements, 1996, pp. 93–111.

Naim, Mashary A. "Conservatism versus Modernism: Hesitant Urban Identity in Saudi Arabia." *Architecture and Urbanism in the Middle East. Viewpoints.* The Middle East Institute, Special Edition, 2008, pp. 29–33.

Trevathan, Idries, and Manal Alghannam. "Bringing It Back Home: Redefining Islamic Art in Saudi Arabia." *Representing the Nation: Heritage, Museums, National Narratives, and Identity in the Arab Gulf States.* Edited by Pamela Erskine-Loftus, Mariam Ibrahim Al-Mulla, and Victoria Hightower. Routledge, 2016, pp. 13–26.

Sadu Weaving

For centuries, Sadu weaving was central to traditional Bedouin lives, as it provided many essential objects while showing a great deal of artistry. Woven geometric and figurative patterns and symbols are indicative of the traditional tribal lifestyle, the desert environment, and the weavers' self-expression. Generations of Bedouin women weavers produced rugs, dividing curtains, cushions, saddlebags, and other domestic accessories—both for their family use and for sale. The woven objects were strong, flexible and light, and at the same time, decorative and functional. Especially impressive were large handwoven tents called *bait al-sha'ar* ("house of hair"), created by the women weavers out of goat hair. Many traditional decorative textiles were also made from camel hair and sheep wool. Nomadic Bedouin tribes depended strongly on camels for survival. Camels were used not only for transportation and food, but also for textile production. The inclusion of camel symbols and tribal animal brandings created complex visual codes in the highly prized Sadu textiles. Tribal affiliation was indicated with special markers called *wasm*.

The environment had a big impact on traditional weaving. Geometrical patterns were essential to the Sadu design, where the patterns and shapes reflected the natural environment of the desert. A number of tools were used for carding and spinning threads, and special wooden or metal ground looms—for weaving. Bedouin weavers use a ground loom with no movable parts that allows for it to be easily moved during frequent relocations. Natural dyes made from indigo, onions, pomegranates, iron, and copper ores were used, but synthetic dyes became widely popular following their introduction in the late 1940s and early 1950s. In addition to the traditional camel, goat, and sheep hair, a number of imported materials were used as well. These were mainly silk, metal, and cotton threads brought from India, China, and Egypt. When these threads were available, Bedouin weavers used them to make more delicate objects.

The Sadu cloth is usually red or black. Although it usually has a simple look, many hours of intricate workmanship go into each product. It can take from several days to months to complete a project. The weavers learn the techniques at an early age, and the craft is frequently passed through generations of women from the same family. Each experienced weaver develops their own style. In Bedouin communities, Sadu weaving is considered an artform, and it is often said that designs have meanings and can be read, like poetry.

See also: Chapter 6: Bedouins and Nomadism.

Further Reading

Hilden, Joy Totah. *Bedouin Weaving of Saudi Arabia and Its Neighbours*. Arabian Publishing, 2010.

Hussain, Fahad Ali. "Traditional Mat Weaving in Al-Hassa Province." *Al-Ma'thurat Al-Sha'Biyyah*, vols. 59–60, July 2000.

Topham, John, et al. *Traditional Crafts of Saudi Arabia*. Stacey International, 2005.

Traditional Architecture

Traditional architecture in Saudi Arabia has several distinct styles that developed in different geographical regions of the country, namely, the Najd, the Hijaz, the Arabian Gulf coastal region, and the Asir in the southwest. Although these styles show significant differences, what they all have in common is the simplicity of the form and practicality of implementation. Each of the styles took advantage of the available building materials in its corresponding region to create a comfortable living environment for the inhabitants. Thus, architectural forms depended on specific climate conditions, such as the hot and dry deserts of Central Arabia or the cool and wet regions of the southwest. Following the oil boom, the kingdom embraced very modern styles and contemporary materials for its building projects, and architecture has radically transformed in the course of only several decades. However, the need to preserve the remaining pieces of Saudi architectural heritage is receiving increased recognition, especially as the country is trying to balance the influence of modernity with its traditional character.

The most striking feature of traditional architecture in the central region of Saudi Arabia is its emphasis on simplicity, where often the only distinction between the houses of the rich and the poor are their sizes. Both highly conservative cultural values and the harsh environment of the Najd emphasized seclusion, defense, and simplicity as central features of human dwelling. The Najdi architectural style was informed by unique demands of life in a hot and dry climate. The main building material was sun-dried mud brick. The mud was collected during specific times in the year when the usually dry streambeds became wet after a short rainy season. It was mixed with water, straw, and other available materials and made into bricks. Then the bricks were sun dried and laid along horizontal layers to form walls. The walls were deliberately made thick for added structural integrity. Roofs were made out of tree trunks, most often those of the date palm and palm fronds, covered with mud. These houses usually had small windows—both for privacy and to keep out the elements. The resulting structure featured excellent insulation, keeping cool in the summer and warm in the winter. The only decorative element of these buildings was mud or clay plaster covering the walls.

The architecture in the Hijaz has a number of unique characteristics, as found in the region's main cities—Mecca, Medina, and Jeddah. Although the climatic conditions are quite different in these locations—hot and dry in Mecca and Medina, and hot and humid in the coastal Jeddah—they show a number of common features. The multistory building design was common, usually consisting of five or six floors. These structures are shaped as towers where functional rooms were positioned toward the external facades with windows, to allow cross ventilation on each floor. Sleeping rooms were located on upper floors, to take advantage of cool breezes. The buildings often had *mashrabiyah* screens—a unique architectural feature that provided natural ventilation while offering privacy. Due to its location and spiritual significance, the Hijaz has always been a cosmopolitan center of the peninsula. Strong ties with international trade lines and incoming pilgrims influenced the way Hijazi residents built their houses, incorporating building materials and techniques from elsewhere. For example, the concept of the *mashrabiyah* panels was developed due to the Egyptian architectural influences. In the Red Sea coastal areas of the Hijaz, massive coral columns were used as a structural skeleton, with added wooden floors and roofs.

The traditional architecture of the Eastern Province resembles the styles of the neighboring Gulf countries, which illustrate strong Ottoman and Persian influences. Building materials included coral blocks, stone, lime, mud brick, and wood from mangroves and palm trees. The most common design featured a house with rooms opening into a courtyard and arcaded verandas surrounding it. Typical of most regional designs, courtyard houses had separate areas for family and guests and were surrounded by thick walls. The usual features of the architectural style of the Gulf region include pointed keel arches and the *mashrabiyah* screens. The most visible difference between buildings in the Eastern Province and those in other parts of Saudi Arabia is the presence of gypsum decorations, inspired by the architecture of the neighboring Gulf countries and Iran. Another common feature of the local architecture is wind towers called *barajil*, derived from the Persian word *badger* (meaning wind-catcher or wind tower). They were often built into the roofs and had openings to catch the coastal breeze.

The Asir region is home to two distinct building styles. One was developed on the Tihamah coastal plain and featured cylindrical huts made from reed and palm fronds. The other emerged in the mountainous areas around Abha and Baha and introduced multistory tower houses. The buildings' outer walls had layers of flat stones, protecting the mud brick wall from eroding from rains, which are much more frequent here than in other parts of the country. Gypsum stucco embellishments were a common decor on the outer walls and rooflines. Doors were painted with bright colors and floral designs, while colorful geometric patterns were featured on the inner walls.

Unfortunately, many of the local architectural traditions have disappeared in Saudi Arabia, due to the adoption of Western building and planning regulations without considering the environmental and cultural specificities of the region. In the early 1950s, Western methods and zoning ordinances started to rapidly take over the construction plans throughout the country, ignoring hundreds of years of local architecture and its outstanding sustainability features. One of the earlier big projects that adopted Western building regulations was al-Malaz—a 500-acre satellite suburb of Riyadh, which was completed in the late 1950s. It introduced the hierarchic patterns of streets and square land lots, which at the time were new concepts in Saudi architecture. Around 1968, the Greek architect C. A. Doxiadis began planning Riyadh and introduced the style dubbed by anthropologists "containment urbanism," which had the underlying objective to urbanize the migrating rural class in a way that prevents the emergence of subversive political movements. Since then, the Saudi government continued to plan other Saudi cities relying almost exclusively on Western principles and showing little or no attention to the local building traditions.

See also: Chapter 6: Urbanization. Chapter 12: Abraj al-Bait; Great Mosque of Mecca; Modernization of Saudi Architecture. Chapter 16: Tradition vs. Globalization.

Further Reading

Abu-Ghazzeh, Tawfiq M. "Domestic Buildings and the Use of Space: Al-Alkhalaf Fortified Houses-Saudi Arabia." *Vernacular Architecture*, vol. 26, 1995, pp. 1–17.

Babsail, M. O., and J. Al-Qawasmi. "Vernacular Architecture in Saudi Arabia: Revival of Displaced Traditions." *Vernacular Archetecture: Towards a Sustainable Future*. Edited by C. Mileto, F. Vegas, L. Garcia Soriano, and V. Cristini. Taylor & Francis, 2015.

Hawker, Ronald William. *Traditional Architecture of the Arabian Gulf: Building on Desert Tides*. WIT, 2008.

King, G. R. D. *The Traditional Architecture of Saudi Arabia*. I. B. Tauris, 1998.

Traditional Garments

Traditional Saudi dress represents both the country's culture and its harsh environment. In pre-Islamic times, comfort dominated style and the region's climate called for loose, flowing garments. *Izar*—one of the earliest forms of dress on the peninsula—was made of a large piece of cloth, worn as a mantle or wrapped around the waist. One can still find a similar sarong-shaped male garment, called *wizra* or *futah*, in the southwestern regions of Saudi Arabia. Additionally, the Hajj rituals require that male pilgrims wear a similar dress that consists of two garments—one seamless garment wrapped around the waist and another over the shoulder.

By the 7th century AD, the traditional dress included five main categories of clothes, divided by their function, for both men and women. Remarkably, the general structure of the clothes remained unchanged through the course of centuries. The first category was the basic dress, consisted of long flowy and simple shirts with long sleeves. The second category was the outer dress, mainly featuring long seamless robes. The third was undergarments for lower and upper body. The fourth—different types of headwear were worn by both men and women. Finally, the fifth category, footwear, consisted of shoes, sandals, and slippers.

Throughout history, regional clothing continued to serve as the protection from the harsh climate, but its utility and simplicity also fit with the Islamic emphasis on modesty. Gradually, with the spread of Islam, the Arabian dress also spread from the peninsula throughout the region. Although traditional clothes have different names and styles in different Arab countries, one can notice their general resemblance. Saudi Arabia is one of the few remaining countries in the world and the region that maintained its traditional dress styles. Although specific clothing styles continued to evolve over time, the process of change had a much slower pace and, thus, does not show nearly as much foreign influence as the majority of other Arab countries. Traditional Saudi dress has regional variations in cut and style and a number of local names for different garments.

The physical isolation of Najd, its desert environment, and the revivalist movement of Ibn Abd al-Wahhab were the main factors in the development of the dress codes of this area. These dress codes remained essentially the same through the centuries. Men would usually wear a long and simple kaftan garment, called *thawb*, in solid colors. The outer garment worn over *thawb* was an ankle-length robe with long sleeves. The basic garment worn by women was also a long kaftan-style dress, which has several names based on stylistic variations, including *thawb, dura'ah,* and *kurtah*. Bedouin and young women would often wear a style called *fustan*, featuring long narrow sleeves, decorated with long embroidered cuffs and small silver bells. Women's overdress was also called *thawb* and was made of two sewn pieces of rectangular cloth with an embroidered neckline. Head coverings included long embroidered scarves: *bukhnugs* or *mukhnugs*. A black veil was used to fully cover the faces, only leaving the eyes uncovered.

Before the annexation of the Hijaz by Ibn Saud and his forces in 1926, local urban dress styles showed a marked influence of the Ottoman styles popular in the 19th century. In contrast to Najd, men's *thawbs* often featured bright colors and stripes. As an outer coat, they usually wore ankle-length robes with elaborate embroidery, called *jubbah* or *daqlah*. Main headgear was a high cap, *taqiyah*, with a long cloth wrapped around it, called *'usbah*. At the time, urban Hijazi women who lived in cities wore elaborate kaftan robes, which were covered with long shrouds, called *jamah*, in public. A typical head dress was the *mahramah*, with multiple holes around the face. Rural Hijazi women wore heavily embroidered tribal caftans.

The Asir area remained isolated until recent times, and the traditional dress did not undergo any substantial changes. In the eastern area of Asir, men also wore the regionally popular *thawb*, with either narrow or wide sleeves, and traditional head cloths called *ghutrah*. In the mountains and on the Red Sea coast, *wizar* garments (a male sarong) and turbans were a common attire. Men's robes were often made of sheepskin or heavy wool and embroidered at the shoulders and neck. Women living in the western part of Asir would usually wear the common black *abayah* as the basic outer garment, complemented with headscarves of various styles that differed by area and social class. The multitude of head coverings included basic headscarves, hoods, heavily decorated face masks called *burqah*, and simple black veils called *tarhah*. It was also relatively common for both urban women and rural women to keep their faces uncovered, whereas Bedouin women were fully covered.

In the eastern part of the country, men wore *thawbs* similar in style to those of Najd. It was also common along the Gulf coast to see a different version of this dress, which is called *dishdashah* and features wider sleeves. Women's clothes of this area often reflected regional influences from Persia, as well as South, Central, and East Asia, in both the materials (such as silk, largely unavailable in other parts of the country) and decorative details. For their outer garments, women wore *abayahs*, long embroidered headscarves, and black veils.

Over time, with the establishment of the Saudi rule throughout the Arabian Peninsula, the Najdi style of male garment has replaced most local styles, creating a national homogeneity of dress. Women's traditional attires have also become more similar, although some continue to reflect regional features, especially in the case of clothes worn to weddings and other festive occasions.

See also: Chapter 7: Hijab and Dress Code. Chapter 10: Dress Etiquette.

Further Reading

Quamar, Mohamed Muddassir. "Sociology of the Veil in Saudi Arabia: Dress Code, Individual Choices, and Questions on Women's Empowerment." *Domes: Digest of Middle East Studies*, vol. 25, no. 2, 2016, pp. 315–337.

Rabolt, Nancy J., and Judith C. Forney. "Contemporary Saudi Arabian Women's Dress." *Clothing and Textiles Research Journal*, vol. 7, no. 3, 1989, pp. 22–32.

Stillman, Yedida Kalfon, and Norman Stillman. *Arab Dress: A Short History: From the Dawn of Islam to Modern Times.* Rev. 2nd ed. Brill, 2003.

Yamani, Mai. "Changing the Habits of a Lifetime: The Adaptation of Hejazi Dress to the New Social Order." *Languages of Dress in the Middle East.* Edited by N. Lindisfarne-Tapper and B. Ingham. Curzon, 1997, pp. 55–66.

CHAPTER 13

MUSIC AND DANCE

OVERVIEW

The Arabian Peninsula is home to diverse musical genres and dance forms, despite the fact that conservative teachings, promoted by the followers of the Wahhabi movement, discouraged performance of any and all musical forms outside of the Quranic recitations. Several distinct indigenous traditions developed in different parts of the peninsula, most notably Najd and the Hijaz. Additionally, local music incorporated various influences from other regional traditions, including those coming from Iran, Iraq, Syria, Egypt, Sudan, the East African coast, Ethiopia, and India. The local diversity incorporates the music of the Bedouins, rural populations, distinct genres of the Gulf coast, and urban folk music. As a result of these various influences and local developments, the Arabian Peninsula has some of the most interesting music traditions in the Arabic-speaking world.

Arabian music has five main types, which showcase the cultural and social diversity of the Peninsula: Bedouin music; songs by farmers when working in the field; wedding music; maritime and pearling music; and the complex musical genre of *sawt*. In recent times, a contemporary genre of music, which incorporated these various genres and traditions, developed on the Arabian Peninsula and the Gulf: it is called *khaliji* (literally "belonging to the Gulf") and is popular throughout the whole Arab world. Throughout centuries, Bedouin music had a major impact on the development of all other regional traditions, including basic rhythmic patterns, poetry, and specific types of songs. In the latter category, the most common songs were those of celebration, war, solidarity, and songs accompanying various types of work, such as special chants of camel riders. An interesting feature of local music traditions is the gender specific genres. Women have their own distinct tradition of songs, which are sung within family circles and during rites of passage, such as weddings and births.

Sawt is one of the principal music genres and singing styles throughout the Arabian Peninsula and the Gulf. In Arabic, the literal meaning of *sawt* is "voice," highlighting the central position of the singer in this genre. Music related to maritime activities and pearling is particularly important in the eastern regions of Saudi Arabia, bordering the Persian Gulf. It incorporates a great variety of genres, based on specific occupations and activities. These include ship-building songs, songs for moving the ships from the dockyards to the sea, and a variety of songs accompanying the operation of a sailing ship, such as raising and lowering sails, using oars, raising the anchor, and so on. Each of these song genres has a name: for example, a song for raising a sail is called *al-rafi'ah*, and for lowering a sail is called *al-khatifah*. Pearl-diving songs are called *al-nahim*. Some of these seafaring genres are tied to specific areas, such as the *hasawi* music, which is named after the al-Hasa Oasis.

Both Bedouin and sedentary populations of the Arabian Peninsula have a rich history of performing arts, where dance is the main form of artistic expression. Arabian traditional dance combines unique movements with indigenous folk songs and poetry. The origins of the dance tradition go back to pre-Islamic times and incorporate elements from several regional ethnic traditions, both Arab and Persian. In the tribal culture, dance was both a form of entertainment and a ritual marking major events, such as celebrations, rites of passage, and wars. Most genres of the Arabian dance are highly interactive, allowing and encouraging the audience's participation. Dancing traditions can be generally divided into formal and informal, depending on the social setting. Formal dances are connected to various events accompanying rites of passage, such as weddings, births, circumcisions, and religious occasions. Informal dances are usually performed at home, in a family setting, or during work. Dances with different types of weapons, such as rifles, swords, and daggers, are very popular throughout the peninsula. In recent decades, dances are increasingly performed at official events, such as national celebrations and other political occasions, or at sporting events—despite apprehension expressed by conservative clerics, many of whom consider dancing a shameful practice.

Many dancing genres are tied to particular regions or specific social occasions. For example, there is a special form of dance performed during wedding celebrations by the mother of the bride or the groom, who dances with a tray on her head, covered with lit candles. The skill of this dance is to keep the candles lit throughout the performance. In Asir, there is a traditional line dance called *al-khatwah* (literally "the step"), which is performed by women. One area in Asir, Muhayil, features a women's warlike dance where they stamp, while wearing ankle bracelets and holding small swords. Although the belly-dancing tradition is not indigenous to the Arabian Peninsula, due to its popularity throughout the Middle East, it is often performed in private gatherings among women.

Further Reading

Hardy Campbell, K., and K. H. Campbell. "Folk Music and Dance in the Arabian Gulf and Saudi Arabia." *Images of Enchantment: Visual and Performing Arts of the Middle East.* Edited by Sherifa Zuhur. American University in Cairo Press, 1998, pp. 57–69.

Reynolds, Dwight Fletcher. *Arab Folklore: A Handbook.* Greenwood Press, 2007.

Urkevich, Lisa. *Music and Traditions of the Arabian Peninsula: Saudi Arabia, Kuwait, Bahrain, and Qatar.* Routledge, 2015.

Ardha Dance

The *ardha* sword dance is perhaps the single most important dance of the Arabian Peninsula and performed by men holding up their weapons and moving slowly to the beat

A group of men prepare to perform the *ardha* sword dance. (Hansmusa/Dreamstime.com)

of drums. Originally performed before going to war, it is now considered the national dance of Saudi Arabia and some other Gulf States, particularly the United Arab Emirates (UAE) and Bahrain. It is often performed by political leaders at all major public occasions. The origins of this dance are traced back to Najd, where it has long been an established local war-singing tradition, whose intent was to instill fear in the enemy and prepare for the battle. The word *ardha* is thought to derive from the verb *aradha*, which means "to show" and "to parade." This points to the main objective of the ritual—to publicly display the might of the tribe and its warriors and boost the morale, while intimidating the enemy.

The lyrics accompanying the performance are called *hidwah*. They are antiphonal and syllabic, and the content focuses on praising the tribe, its honor, its leader, and its warriors. In the past, *ardha* was performed by both men and women together, but the current tradition is limiting it to male performances with swords. The Najdi variation of *ardha* is danced to a six-beat rhythm, produced both by a double-skinned drum (*tabl*) and a single-skinned drum (*daff* or *tar*). The dance is performed by two lines of men, whose movements are accompanied by singing in chorus and waving swords. There is a tradition among Saudi rulers, including the kings, to dance *ardha* in various public occasions. Various versions of *ardha* are popular throughout the Gulf. For example, the version popular in Bahrain and the UAE is called *ayalah* and is often performed with a double chorus. The Omani variation of *ardha* is called *wahhabiyyah*.

See also: Chapter 1: Najd: Central Arabia. Chapter 3: Gulf Cooperation Council. Chapter 6: Bedouins and Nomadism.

Further Reading

Campbell, Kay Hardy. "Days of Song and Dance." *Aramco World*, vol. 50, no. 1, 1999, pp. 78–87.

Campbell, Kay Hardy. "Saudi Folk Music: Alive and Well." *Saudi Aramco World*, vol. 58, no. 2, 2007, pp. 2–13.

Hardy Campbell, K., and K. H. Campbell. "Folk Music and Dance in the Arabian Gulf and Saudi Arabia." *Images of Enchantment: Visual and Performing Arts of the Middle East*. Edited by Sherifa Zuhur. American University in Cairo Press, 1998, pp. 57–69.

Urkevich, Lisa. "Battle Song-Dance Forms of Arabia: Men's 'Ardha and Women's Badawi.'" *Hadith Al-Dar*, vol. 31, 2010, pp. 2–7.

Bedouin Music

Bedouin music has historically played an important role in the development of different musical genres throughout in the Arabian Peninsula and the Gulf. The central feature of Bedouin music is that it is primarily a vocal performance, with very few instruments. The main Bedouin instrument is the one-string fiddle or *rababah*, sometimes also called *rabab*. The *rababah* has a wide, flat, and square shape, with a short neck. It is made of wood covered in goat leather, whereas the string is usually made of horsehair and occasionally from gut. The string is played with a large horsehair bow. The instrument is placed on the player's knee and held upright. The *rababah* has a mournful sound and is used as musical accompaniment for sung poetry, performed exclusively by men. The poet is expected to show his skill of improvisation, or he could be asked to sing traditional ballads about the glorious past.

Drumming is another element of Bedouin music. Local traditions of Najd, Qasim, and the Eastern Province have large drum groups of up to 50 men, which remain an important aspect of the tribal culture and a ritual that showcases bravery. Drum groups accompany all of the main Bedouin dances, including *ardha*, *ayalah*, and *razif*. Certain styles of drumming have become more popular throughout the region, such as the style from Ta'if called *majrur*, in which 12 small tars are played together. Drumming styles from Najd and Qasim are used in most public performances of *ardha* to such an extent that the dance is often called *al-ardha al-najdiyah* (the Najdi *ardha*). The most spectacular drumming styles are those coming from Qasim and the Eastern Province, where the drums are decorated with large colorful tassels and the drummers sway them up and down and back and forth in unison during the performance.

See also: Chapter 1: Eastern Arabia: Al-Hasa; Najd: Central Arabia. Chapter 6: Bedouins and Nomadism; Major Tribes.

Further Reading

Campbell, Kay Hardy. "Days of Song and Dance." *Aramco World*, vol. 50, no. 1, 1999, pp. 78–87.

al-Manaser, Ali. "Traditional Music or Religious Ritual? Ancient Rock Art Illumined by Bedouin Custom." *To the Madbar and Back Again: Studies in the Languages, Archaeology, and Cultures of Arabia Dedicated to Michael C. A. Macdonald*. Edited by Laïla Nehmé and Ahmad Al-Jallad. Brill Academic Publishers, 2018, pp. 81–95.

Racy, Ali Jihad. "Heroes, Lovers, and Poet-Singers: The Bedouin Ethos in Music of the Arab Near-East." *The Journal of American Folklore*, vol. 109, no. 434, 1996, p. 404.

Contemporary Saudi and *Khaliji* Music

Regional commercial music is usually called *khaliji* music (literally "from the Gulf" or "of the Gulf") or "Saudi," referring to Saudi Arabia. It has become very successful throughout the Arab world. The beginnings of its modern form can be traced to the 1950s. Most early recordings of the genre were short songs noted for their cheerful melodies; they quickly became popular throughout Saudi Arabia and the Gulf. Many of these early songs remain popular even today. Kuwaiti and Bahraini singers faced fewer official restrictions than their Saudi counterparts and were the first in the region to record with local companies. Prior to that, traditional music, mainly the *sawt* genre, dominated local radio stations, along with the more widely distributed music from Egypt, Lebanon, Syria, and Iraq. The early *khaliji* singers were influenced by Egyptian musicals, songs from the radio station Sawt al-Arab ("Voice of the Arabs") broadcast from Cairo, and popular Indian musical films.

The first Gulf-style song to become a hit throughout the whole Arab world was "Maqadir," released in 1976 by the Saudi singer Talal Maddah. The song's tempo and rhythmic patterns sounded very different from popular Egyptian and Lebanese songs. The use of different types of drums beating out their own rhythms created a complicated, syncopated sound. These unusual features made the new genre appealing to the audiences, and its popularity quickly grew in Arab countries. In a televised interview in 1996, the Saudi singer Abd al-Majid Abdallah highlighted the unique aspects of the Saudi and Gulf music, in that it contains 20 different rhythmic patterns, whereas Egyptian and Lebanese music uses fewer than 10. Additionally, songs from Saudi Arabia and the Gulf almost always used poems of recognized high quality, which attracted Arab listeners. The growing popularity of this musical genre prompted various collaborations between local poets and singers. This group of musicians and poets even included princes from the ruling houses, such as the Saudi Khalid al-Faysal and the Emirati Muhammad bin Rashid al Maktum.

Among other popular *khaliji* singers were Muhammad Abduh and Nabil Sha'il, both of whom were not limited to the recording market but were frequently played on radio and television. The Saudi singer Muhammad Abduh comes from the Hijaz, and many of his songs have definite Hijazi features. However, he also recorded several albums featuring folksongs from different Saudi regions. He remains one of the best-known singers from Saudi Arabia, especially recognized for the high quality of his songs. He carefully chooses the poems that serve as a lyrical foundation for his songs. Another major star of the *khaliji* genre is Nabil Sha'il, whose album *Ana Mansak* became an instant hit in 1987.

The 1990s saw an even greater rise in popularity of the *khaliji* music, when several Saudi and other Gulf singers rose to major stardom. The Saudis Abd al-Majid Abdallah and Rashid al-Majid found success beyond the Arab world—in Europe, North America, and Asia. In North Africa, their albums even rival the popularity of the recognized stars of the local Rai genre Shab Khalid and Shab Mami. Several singers from other countries of the Arab world recorded entire albums in the *khaliji* style of music due to the genre's popularity. Among those are the Lebanese Diana Hadda and the Tunisian Lutfi Bushnaq. Kuwaiti stars of the genre include Muhammad al-Balushi and Asalah, whereas female singers Ahlam and Samar represent the genre in Bahrain and the United Arab Emirates, respectively.

Various studios and music labels have been created to support and promote the *khaliji* genre in Saudi Arabia and other Gulf countries, especially Kuwait and the United Arab Emirates. Kuwait was among the first countries to invest in the contemporary music industry, and its major company al-Nazir is one of the largest distributors of Gulf music. Saudi Arabia's Stallion and Rotana are also among major producers of Gulf and Saudi music, while also recording and promoting many other singers from across the Arabic-speaking world.

See also: Chapter 1: Hijaz and Tihamah. Chapter 3: Gulf Cooperation Council.

Further Reading

Abdel Aziz, Moataz. "Arab Music Videos and Their Implications for Arab Music and Media." *Music and Media in the Arab World*. Edited by Michael Frishkopf. American University in Cairo Press, 2010, pp. 77–89.

Campbell, Kay Hardy. "Recent Recordings of Traditional Music from the Arabian Gulf and Saudi Arabia." *Middle East Studies Association Bulletin*, vol. 30, no. 1, 1996, pp. 37–40.

Ulaby, Laith. "Mass Media and Music in the Arab Persian Gulf." *Music and Media in the Arab World*. Edited by Michael Frishkopf. American University in Cairo Press, 2010, pp. 111–127.

Janadiriyah Heritage and Cultural Festival

The annual Janadiriyah Festival is one of the country's biggest events to preserve the traditional Arabian culture, which takes place in late winter or early spring outside Riyadh. It happens over a two-week period and features an open-air arena with pavilions and showcases that celebrate traditions of every Saudi region. The festival offers various events and performances, and includes a military air show, world's fair, dance and music shows, poetry competitions, food stands, and other cultural features. It also includes various sporting events, celebrating traditional sports, such as camel racing and falconry. The camel race is a particularly popular attraction, which usually has over

2,000 participating camels and jockeys. Members of the royal family frequently attend the races and grant large monetary prizes for the winners.

Only a few decades ago, Janadiriyah was a small, quiet village in the Qasim Province near Riyadh, visited occasionally by Bedouin tribes during the dry summer season. The festival was initiated in 1985 and was sponsored by the Saudi Arabian National Guard Forces—a military unit primarily composed of tribal forces. The festival was the brainchild of King Abdallah, who at the time was the commander of the National Guard. Since then, it grew into a major event that draws thousands of visitors from all over the country. Most importantly, this event captures and preserves the changing traditional culture of the kingdom—the culture that is in danger of disappearance in the face of rapid urbanization. In addition to cultural preservation, other objectives of the Janadiriyah Festival focus on reinforcement of the country's unity, highlighting of its religious and social values, and demonstration of the achievements of the modern society.

Each Saudi province is represented with a separate pavilion, which usually features local architectural styles. There are various representatives eager to talk to the visitors about history and customs of the region. There are also many food stands, offering samplings of various Saudi cuisines and the traditional cardamom coffee. Janadiriyah became the cultural space where local and regional aspects blend into a national Saudi culture—a process that historically has been far from smooth, given the attempts of Najd to dominate and homogenize the country's cultures and traditions. Thus, the festival became a welcome outlet for various regions of the peninsula to showcase and preserve their heritage and claim their own space in the cultural composition of the country. The festival is very popular among the Saudis, including the youth, because of the wide variety of entertainment—in a country that lacks public entertainment venues outside of shopping malls and sporting events.

See also: Chapter 1: Najd: Central Arabia. Chapter 6: Bedouins and Nomadism. Chapter 16: Tradition vs. Globalization.

Further Reading

Campbell, Kay L. "Folk Music and Dance in the Arabian Gulf and Saudi Arabia." *Images of Enchantment: Visual and Performing Arts of the Middle East.* Edited by Sherifa Zuhur. American University of Cairo Press, 1998, pp. 57–69.

Clark, Arthur. "A Festival at Janadriyah." *Saudi Aramco World,* vol. 36, no. 5, 1985, pp. 2–7.

Long, David. *Culture and Customs of Saudi Arabia.* Greenwood Press, 2005.

Music of Hijaz and Asir

Among the regionally specific instruments used in the south of the Arabian Peninsula is *qanbus* (southern Arabian flute), often used in various musical performances in the area. But over the course of the 20th century, *qanbus* was gradually replaced by the 'ud. A typical feature of the Hijazi music is that a musical piece contains a segment of improvisation, which is called *mawwal* or *majass*. The improvisation is usually played in the middle of the piece that is mainly composed in one of the traditional rhythms.

Mizmar is a very popular Hijazi dance performed by men. The dance is an imitation of a fight, where male dancers perform with long wooden canes. It is similar to the dance with canes performed in the south of Egypt by the Sa'idis. The name of the dance comes from *mizmar*—a double-reed pipe that is also used in the music of Southern Egypt. The melodies performed within the *mizmar* style have the name of *zawamil*, which are usually accentuated by the beats from special drums called tar. Today, *mizmar* is a staple at the male wedding parties in the Hijaz.

The songs called *sahbah* are another important musical form of the region. They were performed by the Hijazi fishermen during their trip back home after spending the season at sea. There is a variety of *sahbah* music in the Medina region, but musically, it is different from the one sung by the fishermen and bears more resemblance to the *muwashshah*—the traditional songs of the Levant.

The term *yanbawiyyah* refers to a special musical rhythmic model in songs usually sung by sailors. The name comes from the Yanbu area on the Red Sea coast. Among its typical instruments is *simsimiyyah*—a six-string lyre, popular through the whole Red Sea region. In some areas, this instrument is known as *tanburah*. *Simsimiyyah* is also the name of the musical genre that uses the instrument and incorporates the *yanbawi* rhythm. An interesting feature of these songs is that they are accompanied by dancing movements that imitate various sea chores, such as raising the sail or pulling an imaginary sailing rope. Today, the *simsimiyyah* genre is widely performed in a variety of occasions, including wedding celebrations and family parties.

Khobayti music was originally performed in the Hijaz during *zar* rituals (the ancient practice of spirit exoticism). However, since *zar* is condemned by the conservative Islamic traditions of Saudi Arabia, *khobayti* is now considered party music, but many musicians hesitate to call it so—because of the negative association with *zar*—and refer to it as "mukhalifa" music, which literally means "different" or "unique."

Majrur is a musical art genre of the Ta'if and Asir regions, which is performed by men and women alike and combines singing with dancing. The genre is believed to be one of the oldest in the area—almost a millennium old. In Arabic, *majrur* literally means "to pull" or "to extend," in reference to the way it is sung—with longer note durations and holding the last syllable of each verse. The lyrics represent several styles—romantic poem, philosophical poem, or eulogy. All participants play a treble *tar*, except for the lead drummer, who plays a low-pitched *tabir* together with *tar*. The leader of the group is positioned between two lines of players during the performance. The dancers sing while performing movements. The performers typically take turns in leading the group with each change in the rhythm. The dancers performing the *majrur* of Ta'if wear long garments with circular skirts and make twirling moves.

See also: Chapter 1: Asir; Hijaz and Tihamah; Jeddah; Mecca; Medina. Chapter 13: Traditional Instruments.

Further Reading

Campbell, Kay Hardy. "Saudi Folk Music: Alive and Well." *Saudi Aramco World*, vol. 58, no. 2, 2007, pp. 2–13.

Urkevich, Lisa. *Music and Traditions of the Arabian Peninsula: Saudi Arabia, Kuwait, Bahrain, and Qatar*. Routledge, 2015.

Religious Music

Unlike most Western musical traditions, Islamic religious music and chanting are seen as a tradition completely different from secular music, which is called *musiqa*. This separate category includes not only the Quranic recitations, *tajwid*, but also religious songs that are rooted in various folk musical forms.

The Muslim call for prayer, *adhan*, is performed by a special trained individual, *mu'adhdhin* (literally, "the one who performs *adhan*"). *Adhan* is announced five times a day and its schedule is based on sun movements. Following the call, Muslims are expected to perform the corresponding prayer (*salat*) of the day. In the early days of Islam, when the majority of practices and rituals were developed and canonized, the call to prayer was announced by human voice, to differentiate it from Jewish, Christian, and other traditions. One of Muhammad's followers by the name of Bilal was chosen to be the first *mu'adhdhin* because of his beautiful, clear, and strong voice. Within the Muslim community, *mu'adhdhin* holds a highly respected position. During the

---

MAQAMAT: MUSICAL MODES

Maqamat (singular: *maqam*) are musical modes constructed around an ascending and descending scale, with prominent tonalities. Each *maqam* is believed to affect the mood of the listener in a special way. Saudi Arabian music, both in its art form (*fann*) and traditional popular form (*shaabi*), is melodically organized around *maqamat*. They are comparable to modes more than scales, since the tonalities may vary quite narrowly. Each *maqam* has a name and a typical melodic pattern that emphasizes particular dominant tones. An important feature of *maqamat* is that they have microtonality—which are tones narrower than the half pitch between the black and white notes of the Western piano. The poet-singer plays an essential role in delivering this kind of music.

Maqamat are further subdivided into smaller subsets, which are usually sets of five notes. Improvisation on *maqamat* and the use of call-for-response structures are common musical features. Harmony is uncommon, with the exception of some forms of choral singing, such as those featured in the music of pearl divers from the Gulf. An important aspect of music from the Arabian Peninsula is its strong use of rhythm and multiple rhythms, which are performed on a variety of drums, in addition to the traditional clapping technique, called *tasfiq*.

Ottoman times, *mu'adhdhins* even had their own guild. Different *mu'adhdhins* offer different melodic renditions of the *adhan*, based on different *maqams* (Middle Eastern musical modes). Some prefer a very simple and melodically unembellished style, which is based on only two notes and sometimes referred to as *adhan shar'i*.

Quranic recitation, which is called *qira'ah* (literally "reading"), is performed by a special reciter called *qari'* ("reader"). The art of recitation is called *tajwid* and is not technically considered a musical form. It is strictly differentiated from secular music, although there is historical evidence that during the times of the Islamic caliphate, elaborate performances of *tajwid* were common. There are two types of melodic recitation: *murattal*, which is done at a slower pace and used for study and practice, and *mujawwad*, which employs technical artistry and requires a great deal of skill.

Pilgrimage songs, referred to as *tahlil*, have many ancient traditions, and consist of those played during the pilgrims' departure, while on the Hajj, and upon their return. *Tahlil* songs reflect many national traditions, depending on where the pilgrims are coming from. Saudi Arabia has its own indigenous styles of *tahlil*, since many local residents regularly participate in the Hajj. Traditionally, musical bands would play for the departing pilgrims and use a special Hajj drum, called *tabl al-hajj*.

A special genre of religious singing, called *al-inshad al-dini*, is popular in Mecca. These songs have a number of themes, including preaching, glorifying God, praising the prophet and his family, and asking for forgiveness. There are also songs dedicated to Islamic holidays and occasions. The chanters performing *al-inshad al-dini* are called *munshadin*.

See also: Chapter 2: The Rise of Islam. Chapter 5: Quran.

Further Reading

Graham, William A., and Navid Kermani. "Recitation and Aesthetic Reception." *The Cambridge Companion to the Quran*. Edited by Jane Dammen McAuliffe. Cambridge University Press, 2006, pp. 115–141.

Linden, Neil van der. "Hajj Music from Egypt, Syria and Lebanon: Some Reflections on Songs for the Pilgrimage." *Hajj: Global Interactions through Pilgrimage*. Edited by Luitgard Mols and Marjko Buitelaar. Sidestone, 2015, pp. 229–236.

Shieh, Rana. "Music and Islamic Law." *Transcendent Philosophy: An International Journal for Comparative Philosophy and Mysticism*, vol. 17, 2016, pp. 47–72.

Shiloah, Amnon. *Music in the World of Islam: A Socio-Cultural Study*. Wayne State University Press, 1995.

Sawt Music

The *sawt*—which literally means "voice" in Arabic—is a sophisticated musical genre that developed in the urban areas of the Arabian Peninsula. It is also often called *fann* or "art music." The origins of *sawt* are a matter of debate, but it is generally believed that it began as court music in Baghdad during the Abbasid period. One of the main researchers of *sawt*, Abdallah al-Faraj, pointed out that the sister of the legendary caliph Harun al-Rashid (786–809), Aliyah bint al-Mahdi, was the first person to reference *sawt* music.

This genre employs several musical instruments, including *'ud*, *qanun* (a string instrument similar to a harp), and *kaman* (a string instrument of the violin family). Among these, *'ud* is the principal instrument, which can also be accompanied by *nay* (a flute) and *qanun*. As is the case with all genres of classical Arabic music, *sawt* uses Middle Eastern musical modes called *maqamat*. Most *sawt* performances are based on the typical *maqamat* of the Bayati, Rast, Sikka, and Hijaz types, but this genre also has accompanying rhythms that make it truly unique.

Historically, *sawt* performances would take place in private homes or houses that belonged to the local community. A typical performance featured the lead singer, who also played the *'ud*, and four other musicians who played a range of other instruments, including the *marawis* (small double-skinned drums), and did special rhythmic hand-clapping, called *tasfiq*. The instrument choices depended on regional varieties. The lyrics of the *sawt* music are most often taken from classical Arabic poetry, but sometimes include colloquial poetry as well, especially in more recent times. The genre has a special musical sequence, which begins with an instrumental introduction (*istihlal*), then followed by a short poem (*istima*), and finally the main segment is sung to one of the two main rhythms. The performance was concluded with another short poem (*tawashih*). The dance accompanying the *sawt* performance is called *zifan*. The dancers move together in preset steps, alternating between walking toward the musicians and away from them. In urban settings, *sawt* performances usually take place in a *majlis al-tarab*—a special large room designated for guests and separate from the living quarters.

See also: Chapter 13: Contemporary Saudi and *Khaliji* Music; Music of Hijaz and Asir; Traditional Instruments.

Further Reading

Urkevich, Lisa. "Sawt: The Art Song of Kuwait." *Ḥadīth Al-Dār/Hadeeth Ad-Dar*, vol. 24, 2007, pp. 22–25.

Urkevich, Lisa. *Music and Traditions of the Arabian Peninsula: Saudi Arabia, Kuwait, Bahrain, and Qatar*. Routledge, 2015.

Traditional Instruments

A wide range of instruments are used in different genres of Saudi music. Some of them are commonly used throughout the Middle East, while others are unique to the Arabian Peninsula. The traditional instruments represent three major categories: string, wind, and percussion. String instruments include the *'ud* (a type of lute), the *qanun*

A classic 'ud instrument. (Berkay/Dreamstime.com)

(zither), the *rababah* (one-string fiddle), the *kaman* (three-string fiddle), now often alternating with a modern violin; and the *tanburah* or *simsimiyah* (a type of lyre). The one-string *rababah* has a wooden frame, covered with a stretched skin of wolf, goat, camel, or gazelle. Wolf skin is believed to be the best, as it makes the instrument "howl like a wolf." The string and the bow are made of rattan and a special kind of horsehair. According to the local folklore, the *rababah* was created by the Tayy tribe in the area around Ha'il.

Wind instruments include the *mizmar* (single-reed instrument), the *surnai* (a double-reed instrument), the *nay* (end-blown reed flute), and *habban* (bagpipe). The term *mizmar* has a wide range of meaning in regional music. It can function as a general term for any woodwind instrument, or specifically apply to an end-blown flute used in the Asir, or refer to the stick dance popular in the Hijaz. *Habban*, which is also sometimes called *jirba*, is both the name of the bagpipe instrument and the term of the music genre it produces. In the Gulf region, bagpipe music is associated with Persian musical traditions and has been historically more popular among the Shia communities.

Percussion instruments include the *darabukah* (single-headed hourglass drum), *tar* (large, circular, single-headed drum), *riq* (tambourine), *mirwas* (a small, double-headed drum), and *mesondo* (a tall one-headed drum of East African origin). *Mirwas* is often used as a generic term for any double-headed barrel drum, which can have a range of sizes. Maritime musicians usually play it horizontally while standing. A large barrel drum can also be called *maradd*. The goblet drum, *tabl*, is also common, although it is not used to play complex rhythms as its Egyptian counterpart. *Tabl* has variations, such as *shaqwah, kasir, sif tabl*, and the largest of the group, *tabl 'ud*. Among other percussion instruments is *sajat*—a type of cymbals that have a range of sizes. These include dancing finger cymbals and small hand cymbals, which are particularly popular with the female musicians of the Hijaz and the seamen of Yanbu. *Jihal* is a ceramic jar that produces a hollow sound. *Batu*, or *bib*, is a metal container (often an empty petrol can), placed upside down and struck with two sticks. In addition to the various percussion instruments, rhythmic accompaniment is produced by means of hand-clapping, called *tasfiq*, which is often used in various music genres in Saudi Arabia and the Gulf. *Tasfiq* is a sophisticated technique, requiring great skill and substantial practice, as the participants are clapping at different speeds and rhythms simultaneously.

See also: Chapter 13: Bedouin Music; Contemporary Saudi and *Khaliji* Music; *Sawt* Music.

Further Reading

Baird, Jo Ann. "Arabic Musical Instruments." *Music Educators Journal*, vol. 76, no. 3, 1989, pp. 11–13.

Racy, Ali Jihad. "The Lyre of the Arab Gulf: Historical Roots, Geographical Links, and the Local Context." *Turn Up the Volume! A Celebration of African Music.* Edited by J. Cogdell DjeDje. UCLA Fowler Museum of Cultural History, 1999, pp. 134–139.

Robson, J. "Some Arab Musical Instruments." *Islamic Culture*, vol. 32, 1958, pp. 171–185.

Wedding Music and Dance

Traditional Saudi weddings consist of various ceremonies and rituals, spread over five to six days of preparatory celebrations and leading up to the final wedding day. Each of the preparatory ceremonies for the wedding is accompanied by special songs and dances, which have subgenres depending on whether they are played at the groom or the bride party, which have traditionally been separate. Bridal ceremonies have significantly more music and entertainment than the groom's. Often, all-female music groups were hired to perform at the women's gatherings, whereas all-male groups—for the men's parties, although the latter would frequently be a more somber gathering without any music. Nowadays, female music bands continue to perform on the wedding night for the bridal party, called *haflat al-zafaf*. A variety of songs are performed at these gatherings, including *sammari* and the Hijazi *majrur*, often accompanied by instruments such as the *'ud* and the *tar*. During the party, younger women would usually participate in dances, often performing traditional dances of their native region. One distinct dancing movement during the celebration includes hair tossing, called *na'ish*, when women loosen their long hair and swing it in circles. *Na'ish* is believed to be native to the Bedouin culture but has become popular throughout the Arab world.

Laylat al-henna—the henna night prior to the wedding ceremony—is an occasion of extensive dancing. Female members of the family and friends perform various dances to entertain the bride, who herself cannot move as she is patiently waiting for the henna dye to dry. Unlike other Middle Eastern wedding celebrations, Saudi men are expected to show reserve at these occasions and are much less likely to participate in public dances. However, rural weddings are much more inclusive and dancing often involves the whole local community.

The Hijaz has two local types of the wedding song: *majass* and *dana*. They are usually sung by men and continue to be performed at many Hijazi weddings. A professional male singer, *jassis*, would normally perform the *majass* song, which is meant to praise the groom and to cheer both families on the marriage. These songs often include a great deal of improvisation. The *dana* songs, which emerged in Mecca, are not improvised but are part of the traditional compilation of old songs, which are transmitted from generation to generation. These songs have intricate movements up and down the *maqamat* (musical modes) and can be performed by both men and women.

See also: Chapter 7: Marriage Law and Tradition; Traditional Wedding.

Further Reading

Tawfiq, Wijdan, and Sara Marcketti. "Meaning and Symbolism in Bridal Costumes in Western Saudi Arabia." *Clothing & Textiles Research Journal*, vol. 35, no. 3, July 2017, pp. 215–230.

Urkevich, Lisa. *Music and Traditions of the Arabian Peninsula: Saudi Arabia, Kuwait, Bahrain, and Qatar*. Routledge, 2015.

CHAPTER 14

FOOD

OVERVIEW

Saudi Arabia has a fascinating food culture that reflects the region's history, social groups, traditions, religious practices, and ways of life. Saudi cuisine offers a great deal of diversity, informed by three main factors: (1) regional variation of terrains and climates; (2) traditions and customs of different ethnic groups, including influences from neighboring food cultures; and (3) culinary customs and specific regulations dictated by Islam. In ancient times, the different lifestyles of the Arabian Peninsula's inhabitants determined the types of foods they produced and consumed. Nomadic Bedouins survived off the products of their camels, particularly milk and other types of dairy. The sedentary population had a limited variety of agricultural products, where dates were particularly popular for their preservation qualities. Dates were a valuable product among the Bedouins too. Today, Saudi dates continue to be highly valued on both domestic and global food markets. Throughout history, the Arabian Peninsula was at the center of important trade routes with Central Asia, the Levant, Africa, and the Indian subcontinent. These trade relationships resulted in culinary influences from these regions. Gradually, a variety of new dishes and spices entered the Bedouin cuisine, which was largely based on dates and dairy. Soon, a flavorful and diverse Saudi cuisine emerged, having combined local traditions and regional influences.

Historically, water resources have been scarce everywhere on the peninsula, with the exception of the western mountains and the great oases. Thus, both the variety and quantity of food were limited, particularly in central regions of the country. Despite the region's severe conditions, sedentary farmers in oasis villages managed to cultivate various grains, vegetables, and fruit. The most common grains were wheat and barley. Traditional vegetables and fruit included tomatoes, melons, squash, beans, root vegetables, and—of course—the always important dates. Bedouin pastoralists provided meat and cheese from sheep and goats, which were grazing in the desert in winter months. Nomadic and sedentary populations heavily relied on each other in providing the necessary products that the other group was lacking. The diet of those living in the coastal areas was based on various fish and seafood. Trade routes that for centuries crisscrossed the peninsula brought foreign items that became popular locally, such as rice, tea, and spices. Coffee came from its birthplaces in Yemen and Ethiopia and became a beloved drink among the Bedouins. Sweetening was based on local honey until granulated sugar was introduced from the West. Some areas of the peninsula had a more favorable climate and were able to grow a wider variety of agricultural products. For example, the rainier conditions of the Hijaz, Baha, and Asir allowed the local population to grow grapes, pomegranates, peaches, apricots, almonds, and bananas.

Various grain products were and still are the main source of food throughout the Arabian Peninsula. Wheat products include different kinds of unleavened bread, pies, and desserts. Barley, which is more resistant to drought than many other grains, was used to make *burghul* (a dish that resembles cereal) and *jarish* (ground wheat). Saudis eat bread with virtually every meal. The most common and popular type is the traditional round, flat, unleavened bread called *khubz*—this word generally means "bread" in Arabic. This type of bread is consumed by the population throughout the Middle East and North Africa. Among other popular traditional breads are the paper thin and crisp *raqayiq*; *samuli*, which is similar to French bread; and *hab*, made from wheat kernels. Some types of bread were imported from other regional cuisines, such as *luhuh*, a thick and moist bread from Somalia and Yemen, and *tamiz*, an Afghani bread. Rice is an important staple used in main courses for lunch and dinner. Saudi Arabian cuisine has more than 15 popular cooking methods of rice. In addition to several varieties of white rice, there are also yellow saffron-colored biryani rice called *sayyidiyyah*, and the popular reddish Bukhari rice, which is cooked with tomatoes, nuts, and raisins in a method that was adopted from Central Asian pilgrims (Bukhari means "Bukharian" in Arabic).

Milk has always been a core ingredient in all local cuisines throughout the peninsula. Butter, yogurts, *laban* (fermented milk), and several types of cheese are made of goat, sheep, and camel milk. Yogurt is a particularly important type of diary, and many Saudi families continue to make their own traditional yogurt. When mixed with olive oil and salt, this homemade yogurt has an ability to preserve its qualities for many months. This is an ancient method of preserving milk before refrigeration became available and is still popular today. Yogurt can be eaten either plain, or with various other ingredients, such as fruit, honey, or sugar. It can also be drunk as a beverage, served as a side dish, or be used as an ingredient in a wide range of salads, rice, and meat dishes and desserts.

Vegetables and legumes constitute an important aspect of the cuisine throughout the peninsula. Of these, the most common types are tomatoes, cucumbers, zucchini, onions, okra, garlic, peppers, carrots, eggplants, lettuce, parsley, lentils, and chickpeas. Vegetables constitute an important component in many traditional dishes and are also consumed raw. Pickling is one of the common food conservation methods throughout the Middle East, including Saudi Arabia, and many vegetables are used in a pickled form. Seasonal fresh fruits are served with every meal. Local fruits include dates, figs, oranges, melons, grapes, lemons, pomegranates, peaches, apricots, and apples. The few Saudi areas that have tropical climate harvest bananas, mangos, and papayas. The two most popular types of the Arabian indigenous fruit are dates and figs. Due to their excellent preservation qualities, they are available throughout the year in a dried form. Historically, dried figs and especially dates, both of which have high nutritional value, were a popular product in the exchange trade between Bedouins and the settled population. Until now the date is considered the most versatile product of Arabian cuisine and offers a great range of sizes and tastes.

The most common types of meat are mutton, goat, chicken, and camel. Meats are often spiced the with salt, pepper, garlic, thyme, and coriander or marinated in vinegar, oil, and rose water. The local cuisine relies on oils, spices, and fat—both for preparation and preservation of foods. The most popular oil is olive, followed by sesame and coconut oil. The main spices and seasonings are salt, pepper, garlic, and paprika. Garlic is particularly common, as many believe in its medicinal qualities. Among other seasonings that are frequently used are thyme, cumin, peppermint, coriander, cardamom, cinnamon, sumac, anise, fennel, cloves, and saffron. In regions along the Red Sea and the Persian Gulf coasts, a variety of seafood products are used, including different types of fish, such as tuna, mackerel, bass, and mahi mahi, as well as shrimp, crabs, and turtles. Different kinds of nuts and seeds are eaten raw or used as ingredients in dishes, including almonds, hazelnuts, pistachios, as well as melon, sunflower, and pumpkin seeds. Traditional desserts have high sugar content.

As a rule, Saudi Arabians have three meals a day. A distinct feature of the Saudi food tradition is that, unlike most other countries where daily schedules were usually defined by the mealtimes, here the main factor in arranging one's daily life is the five Muslim daily prayers. The times when meals are consumed are closely connected to the prayer times. Prayer times change daily, since they are based on the sun movements. A traditional day begins at dawn when people get up to perform the dawn prayer (*fajr*), but many go back to bed following the prayer and sleep for another one or two hours. The daily routine begins with breakfast (*futur*), which has a relatively simple menu. The usual breakfast foods among the inhabitants of rural areas include bread with honey and raw butter (*saman*), dates, fresh milk, cheeses made of sheep and goat milk, tea, and coffee. Urbanites usually eat olives, homemade jam, eggs, cream, and yogurt in their morning meals. Bedouin breakfast may also include dried camel and goat milk. In the past, lunch (*ghada*) was the main meal of the day, but in modern times dinner (*'asha*) has also become a substantial meal, especially in the cities. It was served in the early afternoon, and the exact timing was determined by the afternoon prayer (*asr*). By law, all stores and businesses in Saudi Arabia close for the prayer times. Men would normally return home for lunch and prayers, followed by an afternoon nap. Typical lunch meals in the rural areas are variations of meat and rice combos. Urban lunch has a wider variety, but usually also include dishes based on rice or cracked wheat (*bulghur*) combined with lamb, mutton, chicken, or fish. Yogurt, salad, tea, and desserts are also commonly eaten for lunch. Dinner (*'asha*) is usually consumed late in the evening—which is not unusual for hot-climate cultures—but in Saudi Arabia it can be served as late as midnight. Dinner menus are similar to lunch. In addition to prayer times, the daily schedule including meal consumption on the Arabian Peninsula was largely dictated by the climate conditions, where extreme heat during the daytime hours moved many activities late into the night.

Hospitality is a key aspect of food culture throughout the Arabian Peninsula. In the old days, it was even common for hosts to eat only after their guests have finished their meal, so that they can focus on serving the guests. Generosity to a guest is expected and widely practiced in poor and wealthy families alike.

Further Reading

Harrigan, Jane. *The Political Economy of Arab Food Sovereignty*. Palgrave Macmillan, 2014.

Nawwab, Ni'mah. "The Culinary Kingdom." *Aramco World*, vol. 50, no. 1, 1999, pp. 88–97.

Parker, Jessie Kirkness. *A Taste of Arabia*. Jerboa, 2010.

Zayani, Afnan Rashid. *A Taste of the Arabian Gulf*. A. R. Zayani, 1988.

Zubaida, Sami, et al. *A Taste of Thyme: Culinary Cultures of the Middle East*. Tauris Parke Paperbacks, 2000.

Arabic Coffee, Tea, and Other Traditional Beverages

The word "coffee" originated from the Arabic *qahwah*, as the earliest accounts of coffee drinking are traced back to Yemen. The legend says that the stimulating properties of coffee were discovered by a goat herder who noticed that his animals are unusually energized after eating coffee beans. Throughout history, coffee was banned for a significant period by conservative Muslim clerics due to its invigorating quality, as they considered it a form of intoxication. Its legality in the Muslim world was accepted only in the late 16th century. Yemen was traditionally the main producer of coffee beans and its port city, Mocha (or al-Makha), gave its name to one of the most popular coffee drinks. Members of the Sufi order (Sufism is a mystical denomination in Islam) helped spread coffee throughout the Arab world, since they would often drink it to be able to stay up all night for their rituals.

Two main types of coffee preparation are common throughout the Arabian Peninsula: Turkish and Arabic. The so-called Turkish coffee, *qahwah Turkiyah*, is strong, thick, and bitter, although in more recent times large amounts of sugar are often added to it. Generally speaking, Turkish coffee is the drink of coffeehouses and city people. It is prepared in a special brass pot called *kanakah*. The coffee is brought to boil several times, then poured into special small cups and served hot. Strong sweet Turkish coffee is often served to visitors during morning hours. In the last several centuries, this type of coffee has become very popular throughout the whole Middle East.

Arabic coffee, *qahwah arabiyah*, has a different preparation method. Although it is much lighter in color, it has the same strength as Turkish coffee. The preparation of traditional Arabic coffee starts by roasting coffee beans over an open flame. Then the beans are allowed to cool in a special wooden dish called *mabrad* or *mubarrad* (from the Arabic word *bard*, which means "cold"). Afterward, the cooled beans are put into a large wooden mortar, *mihbaj*, and are manually ground with a long wooden pestle into a fine powder. The person grinding the beans produces special beats and rhythms with the pestle to let the neighbors know that coffee is being made. The ground beans are then put in a brass pot designated specifically for coffee making, called *dallah*. At this phase, cardamom is added for flavor and aroma—an important aspect of Arabic coffee. The coffee is served in special small cups, or *finjan*. An old custom expects from a guest to drink three cups of Arabic coffee. There is also a special signal indicating that one had enough coffee and does not need more serving: the guest would wiggle the cup and say *da'iman* ("remain blessed"). This type of coffee, which is unique to the Arabian Peninsula, is also called "white" due to its color contrast with Turkish coffee. In addition to the traditional spicing with cardamom, it can include other spices such as cinnamon, ginger, or saffron. Arabic coffee never contains sugar and is often served with dates.

A traditional coffeepot, *dallah*, with cups and dates. (Alju21/Dreamstime.com)

Both tea and coffee are very popular among all populations and social classes in Saudi Arabia. People consume them throughout the day—usually after each meal and sometimes between the meals. While in the past both drinks would normally be served without sugar, in recent times they are often heavily sweetened. The main suppliers of tea to the region were traditionally India and Shri Lanka, but now imported Western brands, such as Lipton and Tetley, are also available. Tea is often consumed black (without milk) and may contain various herbal additions, among which mint is the most frequent. It is usually served in small glasses with handles. Drinking tea is a particularly common custom during visitations among women, although coffee is usually available as well. Both drinks are served with sweets. Tea-serving sweets have a large variety, but the most popular is perhaps the delicious *asabi' al-sitt* (literally "ladyfingers"). These are rolled-up pastries that are deep fried, filled with sugar, cinnamon, and almonds, and served with sugar syrup. Tea and coffee have an important ceremonial function in Saudi culture. Both are offered as a way of greeting guests on any occasion, including formal meetings between government officials and business professionals. Tea is usually served first, then followed by the Arabic ("white") coffee, served with dates.

Among other historically important drinks in the region is milk. For millennia, it was the main drink among the tribal community that practiced nomadic pastoralism. Its nutritional value was central for survival in the harsh natural environment. Milk is sourced from various livestock, including camel, sheep, and goat. Other dairy drinks are common as well. Yogurt is normally made into a drink called *laban* (also known as fermented milk throughout the Middle East). It has a number of preparation methods, which include salted, sweet, and smoked varieties.

Sobia is a cold drink which originated in the Hijaz and gradually spread throughout the country. It is particularly popular during Ramadan. Sobia is made from a light fermented mixture of barley, brown bread, sap from a date palm, sugar, cinnamon, cardamom, and other spices. Traditionally, it is prepared by soaking brown bread and barley in a large pot for a whole day with enough water to cover the mixture. Then it is boiled, supplemented with cinnamon and cardamom, and left to soak for one more day. Finally, the mixture is filtered to separate the liquid from the bread, and sugar is added. Depending on the type of flavor, sobia may be either white or colorful. It is also found to have health benefits. In recent years, a new drink, called "Saudi champagne," emerged and became popular with the youth. It does not actually contain any alcohol, since alcohol is illegal in Saudi Arabia and drinking it has serious legal punishments. "Saudi champagne" is a combination of sliced fruits, apple cider, and sparkling water, and was given this name because of its color and bubbly appearance.

See also: Chapter 6: Bedouins and Nomadism. Chapter 7: Social Life, Kinship, and Friendships. Chapter 10: *Majlis*; Social Life.

Further Reading

Elmadani, Abdalla. *Finjan Gahwa (a Cup of Coffee) and a Bit of Everything*. Alwafa Printing Press, 1997.

Parker, Jessie Kirkness. *A Taste of Arabia*. Jerboa, 2010.

Ukers, William H. *All about Coffee*. Tea and Coffee Trade Journal Company, 1935.

Islamic Dietary Laws

Islamic dietary laws have a major impact on local cuisine. They are closely related to ancient Jewish dietary rules, due to these groups' common ethnic background and the similarity of their basic cuisines. All food is categorized as pure (*tayib*) and impure (*najis*), or as lawful (*halal*) and unlawful/prohibited (*haram*). Pork is considered impure and alcohol as unlawful. Religious dietary rules are meant to reinforce the group's collective identity and emphasize its exclusiveness. Islamic dietary laws that divide the foods into allowed and forbidden categories are fairly straightforward. However, the instructions on proper slaughtering of animals, in order to produce lawful meat, are more complicated.

Muslims are allowed and encouraged to eat "good" types of food, as prescribed by the following Quranic verse: "O mankind, eat from whatever is on earth [that is] lawful and good and do not follow the footsteps of Satan" (Quran 2: 168). In other words, Muslims should consume food and drink that is identified as pure, clean, wholesome, tasty, and nourishing. In general, everything is automatically allowed (*halal*), except for several explicitly forbidden categories and concrete foods. But under certain circumstances, such as in starvation or similar hardship, even prohibited food and drink can be excused and not considered sinful, if no *halal* foods are available. In other words, a rational rule of necessity removes prohibition, if there is no viable alternative.

Required abstention from eating certain foods is considered to be not only an act of obedience to God's will, but also in the interest of health and hygiene. The types of foods and drinks that are strictly prohibited (*haram*) are explicitly defined by various Quranic verses:

- Dead meat, referring to the carcass of an already-dead animal as opposed to being slaughtered by a proper method.
- Pork meat.
- Meat from which wild animals have already eaten.
- Meat of an animal that was killed for sacrifice to idols.
- Meat of an animal that died from electrocution, strangulation, or blunt force.
- All intoxicating drinks. For particularly conservative Muslims, this category includes not only explicitly alcoholic drinks, but also sauces or supplementary liquids that include miniscule amounts of alcohol.
- Blood.

Islam places a great deal of importance on the manner in which the lives of animals are taken to provide food to humans. According to the Islamic tradition, all life is sacred, and one must kill only to meet one's lawful need for food. Thus, a series of specific rules are to be followed. The livestock must be slaughtered only by slitting the animal's throat in a swift and merciful manner. The rule prescribes that the animal should not suffer, either physically or psychologically, and should not even see the blade before slaughter. The knife's blade needs to be very sharp and clean, without any residual blood from the previous slaughter. The act of slaughtering is performed by a professional who usually recites the following verse: "In the name of God, God is the greatest." The animal's blood must be completely drained before meat can be consumed. The meat that comes from a proper slaughtering technique is called *halal* meat. These rules do not apply to fish or other seafood, which is collectively considered *halal* food. In contrast with Jewish dietary laws that consider only aquatic life with fins and scales as kosher, Islamic dietary law views all forms of seafood *halal*.

See also: Chapter 3: Sharia Law and Judicial System. Chapter 5: Quran.

Further Reading

Chand, Muhammad Umar. "The Prohibited and the Permitted Foods and Drinks According to Islam." *Islamic Thought and Scientific Creativity*, vol. 5, no. 4, 1994, pp. 24–58.

Cook, Michael. "Early Islamic Dietary Law." *Jerusalem Studies in Arabic and Islam*, vol. 7, 1986, pp. 217–277.

Waines, David, and Sami Zubaida. "Food: Muslim and Jewish Food and Foodways." *The Routledge Handbook of Muslim-Jewish Relations*. Edited by Josef Meri. Routledge, 2016, pp. 475–495.

Kabsah

Although the Arabian Peninsula shows a great regional variety of traditional cuisines, there is still one dish that can be considered Saudi Arabia's national dish. This very popular dish is *kabsah*—a rice casserole prepared with lamb, chicken, fish, or *ful* (fava beans). It originated in Najd but has quickly spread throughout the peninsula. The main ingredients of *kabsah* are saffron rice, tomatoes, onions, spices, and meat, where the latter can be of several kinds. Given the great regional variety of *kabsah*, technically, the term represents a family of dishes. Its name comes from the verb "to press," referencing the cooking technique where all of the ingredients are pressed in one pot. Although it is generally associated with Najd, where it is usually served with lamb, different versions of the dish can be found all over the country. There is a saying that there are as many ways of cooking *kabsah* as there are cooks. The choice of meat is based on regional availability and local cuisine traditions. Among the popular meats are lamb, mutton, goat, camel, chicken, fish, and shrimp. Due to harsh weather and terrain conditions, chicken was considered a delicacy until modern poultry farming facilities and air transportation made it widely available. Fish, shrimp, and other seafood ingredients are typical of *kabsah* made in the coastal areas.

The spices used in *kabsah* are largely responsible for its taste, and there is a large variety of those as well, including bay leaves, cardamom, saffron, black pepper, cloves,

---

***KABSAH* RECIPE**

The roots of the famous Saudi dish can be found in Yemen, from which it spread throughout the rest of the Arabian Peninsula. In addition to Saudi Arabia, *kabsah* is considered a traditional dish in Qatar, Kuwait, the United Arab Emirates, and Jordan. *Kabsah* has many varieties; each one is unique as it incorporates the local culinary traditions. The usual components of this dish are rice, meat, vegetables, and various blends of spices. The traditional meat component of *kabsah* can be lamb, mutton, or chicken, but in some areas the cooks also use beef, camel, goat, fish, or shrimp. The mix of spices is the part of the dish that has the widest variations. Some families have their own recipes for *kabsah* spices, which are passed from generation to generation. In addition to the core ingredients, the dish can contain nuts, such as almonds and pine nuts, onions, and sultanas (raisins made of white grapes). *Kabsah* can be served with *daqqus*—a homemade tomato sauce.

cinnamon, lime, and nutmeg. Nowadays, premixed *kabsah* spices are sold under several brand names. Given the labor-intensive and time-consuming nature of this dish, these mixes reduce preparation time, but many cooks believe that they alter the original taste of *kabsah* and prefer to cook it using traditional methods. *Kabsah* meat can be cooked in a number of ways. One of the popular methods is called *mandi*: this is an ancient cooking technique coming from Yemen, where meat is barbecued in a deep hole in the ground, which has to be covered during the cooking. Another common method is *mathbi*, in which the meat is heavily seasoned and then grilled on flat stones, which are sitting on top of burning embers. Another technique, which emerged recently and is called *madghut*, cooks the meat in a pressure cooker.

See also: Chapter 14: Traditional Foods and Regional Variations.

Further Reading

Nawwab, Ni'mah. "The Culinary Kingdom." *Aramco World*, vol. 50, no. 1, 1999, pp. 88–97.

Riolo, Amy. *Arabian Delights: Recipes & Princely Entertaining Ideas from the Arabian Peninsula*. Capital Books, 2008.

Traditional Foods and Regional Variations

In Saudi Arabia, dishes originating from the Hijaz had the biggest impact on the national cuisine. Islamic dietary laws made a profound impact on local culinary traditions, as they banned some foods and promoted others. The increasing numbers of pilgrims from various countries flocked to Mecca and Medina every year. Some of them stayed behind and assimilated into the Hijazi society, adding to its diversity and cosmopolitanism. While these newcomers were ultimately assimilated, their culture and customs became a part of the indigenous population. Expectedly, various cooking traditions brought by the pilgrims greatly enriched Hijazi cuisine. A number of foreign dishes have been assimilated so completely that many people do not know about their foreign roots and consider them a part of the indigenous cuisine. These include *harisah,* which is made of meat with crushed wheat and served with sugar. *Aysh abu laham* is another one of these dishes: it is made with meats, leeks, and *tahinah* sauce and often called the Saudi pizza. Other assimilated dishes include *ma'sub*—bananas mashed with sweetened homemade whole-wheat Arab bread; *lahuh*—crepes with meat and yogurt; *jubniyyah*—a goat cheese dessert; and *mutabbaq*—a popular pastry with minced meat or cheese, bananas, or cream. One of the typical representatives of the Hijazi cuisine that illustrates the cosmopolitan nature of the region is called *sayadiyyah*—a combination of rice and fish, which spread from the coastal Jeddah and became popular in Mecca. In ancient times, Meccans did not eat fish due to the area's inland location, but as travel between the two cities became easier, fish dishes gained popularity.

As the coastal region of the Red Sea, famous for its diverse and plentiful sea life, Jeddah's relationship with seafood has deep historical roots. Given the region's hospitality

Fish *kabsah*, a variation of the traditional Saudi dish, is popular in coastal areas. (Станислав Саблин/Dreamstime.com)

traditions, the locals often present a stunning array of seafood dishes to honor a special guest. The series of dishes begin with a fish soup and fish salad. Then one or more fish courses follow, such as fish patties, baked fish, fish cooked in coconut milk in Indonesian style, and other varieties based on regional traditions and family preferences. The seafood array ends with *sayadiyyah*, or *biryani* prepared with fish or shrimp. In the meantime, Meccans historically relied on vegetable and meat dishes. The main vegetables were okra, potatoes, white beans, and peas, which were prepared with meat and various spices and sauces. Meccan cuisine is famous for its meat recipes. They include a variety of cooking methods, such as lamb shank and chicken cooked in gravy, or ground meat patties (*kuftah*) which are typically served with round bread, lemon wedges, and rice. *Dubbah arabi* is one of the region's typical dishes, made of squash, yellow lentils, and lamb, cooked in a tomato-based sauce and heavily flavored with dill—the latter being rare in Saudi cooking. Another popular Meccan dish, which is usually cooked for special occasions, is *mabshur*. It is made of very lean and finely ground lamb, which is pressed by hand onto skewers, grilled, and served on a bed of rice. There is also a special salad served exclusively with *mabshur*: it is based on thick yogurt and enriched with a mixture of clarified lamb fat and butter (*samn baladi*). In modern times, *mabshur* is usually prepared by professional cooks who bring their grills, skewers, and ingredients.

Special occasions, which are plentiful in the Hijaz and include religious holidays, fast-breaking meals during Ramadan, weddings, births, and funerals, call for a variety of special traditional meals. A number of them are rice-based. Among those are *saliq*—a popular dish for weddings, made of rice and lamb or rice and chicken. *Saliq* originates from Taif and is usually prepared by professional cooks, like *mabshur*. *Ruzz bi hummus* (literally "rice with chickpeas") is often served to family members and visitors at funerals. This dish is usually served with a green salad and a special hot sauce called *duqqus*. The latter is a typical Hijazi ingredient, which has become popular throughout the rest of country. *Duqqus* is made from hot chili peppers, fresh coriander, garlic, tomatoes, and lemon juice.

Traditionally, a Hijazi meal ends with fresh fruit and desserts. The local tradition is rich in desserts, where some of the most popular are *labaniyyah*, fudge made with milk; *jubniyyah*, made with Taif goat cheese; and *ridha al-walidyan*, milk pudding whose name literally means "parental approval." A cultural reminder of the Ottoman presence in the area, Turkish culinary influences are visible in sweets. Several desserts were also adapted from Syrian, Egyptian, and Indian cuisines. Among those are the traditional Egyptian Umm Ali (literally, "Ali's mother") and *aysh al-saraya*, coming from the Levant. The dessert part of the meals is usually followed by coffee and mint or green tea.

The ancestral cuisine of Najd, known for its isolation and severe climate, was relatively simple and straightforward, mainly based on wheat, rice, milk, dates, and a limited variety of vegetables grown in the oases. However, due to trade relations with Syria, India, and other countries, as well the increased mobility brought by the oil boom, the Najdi cuisine quickly diversified and now offers a rich assortment of dishes. A typical Najdi dish incorporates whole-wheat or rye bread, vegetables, and meat. *Tharid* is one of the oldest regional dishes, known from pre-Islamic times. It is made of layers of thin wheat dough rounds, saturated with broth and topped with meat and vegetables. *Marquq* is another traditional dish, very similar to *tharid*. Among other common meals is *mataziz,* which is made from lamb and vegetable dumplings and served with white rice. Unlike their ancestors who had limited food choices due to harsh conditions, contemporary Najdis incorporate a large variety of vegetables into their dishes.

A common feature of Najdi recipes is that they are very time consuming. One of these is *haris*—a combination of wheat and meat. Although it is popular in all countries of the Gulf, the Najdi cuisine has elevated it into a culinary art. The preparation method requires an overnight soaking of wheat, which is then pounded by the cook until is turns mushy. Then it is boiled with red meat or chicken, after the latter is deboned and cleaned of fat. The cooking process continues until the ingredients are indistinguishable. Rice can be added to the mixture to give it a smooth consistency. *Haris* is typically garnished with another flavorful mixture, *hashwah,* which is made of browned onions, dried limes, black pepper, and cardamom. Finally, the dish is topped with regular or clarified butter (*samn*). In the old days, the women of the family would take turns in the long and manually intense job of pounding the wheat, but now Saudi women often use modern food processors.

The dish called *jarish* is based on cracked wheat and features two variations. One is creamy and made with yogurt, and another includes tomatoes. The latter is called *jarish nathri* or *mufallaq*. Najd is famous for its desert truffles, *faq',* which are typically collected during the spring, especially after the rain. Preparation of truffles is a laborious job, as they have to be carefully cleaned of sand and rid of skin. They continue to be included in many traditional dishes, including *tharid* and *ruzz mutabbaq*, a layered rice dish.

A typical aspect of Najdi meals is the tradition of a skillful combination of multiple dishes into one dish. One of them is *al-badiyah*, usually prepared for celebration of Eid al-Adha. On the first day of the holiday, whole Najdi neighborhoods participate in this multilayered dish. It is cooked in lamb broth, garnished with onions, and covered with a layer of dough sheets cooked with vegetables and tomato sauce, and then garnished with more onions. The next layer is saffron rice sprinkled with rose water and topped with meat. Then the dish is garnished with yet another layer made of sliced tomatoes, boiled eggs, dried limes, and peppers.

Although Najdis became accustomed to various international desserts in the course of the 20th century, many still prefer the local desserts, most of which incorporate the legendary homegrown date. *Qishdah* stands out among these dishes: it is made of whole dates cooked with butter, flour, and yogurt, and served warm. In winter months it is often served for breakfast. Najdis eat dates in a variety of forms, including puddings, round pastries, and more.

In the Eastern Province of Saudi Arabia, spicy foods are popular—an obvious impact of historical trade and cultural ties with the neighbors famed for their spices, namely, Iran, India, Pakistan, and Afghanistan. Although spices are used throughout the Arabian Peninsula, the Gulf region of the country offers a particularly expansive and sophisticated variety. Among the most common spices and herbs in this region are saffron, *shaybah* (lichen), cumin, cloves, coriander, artemisia, and dried black limes, originating from Oman. Usually, households have different traditional blends of spices for meat, fish, and vegetable dishes. The Eastern Province is also known for its diversity of fresh seafood. The most common kinds of fish are grouper, mackerel, red snapper, parrotfish, and other reef-dwellers. Traditional coastal dishes include *hubul*, which is a fried mackerel roe served with rice or salad. *Muhashsha* is also very popular—an elaborate dish of rice and a fried type of fish of a meaty variety, such as *kan'ad* or mackerel.

An array of sophisticated rice dishes is another specialty of the Eastern Province. They are made for all kinds of occasions and feature a great range of cooking methods. Rice can be flavored with rose water and saffron, garnished with raisins, onions, and dried limes, and mixed with various spices. Locals prefer the long-grained and fragrant basmati rice, which is the most popular type of rice throughout the kingdom. *Mashkhul* is a popular rice dish throughout the Gulf; it is made with mutton, chicken, fish, or shrimp. *Fi qa'atuh*, which literally means "at the bottom of the pot," is a typical example of the local cuisine—a layered dish made with spiced shrimp, chicken, or meat, cooked with green peppers and potatoes. Among foreign borrowings that were fully assimilated is *ruz Bukhari* ("the Bukhari rice")—one of various originally foreign rice dishes known in the province. An interesting fact is that Saudis in the Eastern Province usually call rice *aysh* (meaning "life" in Arabic), which highlights the importance of this food for the region. In many other Arabic-speaking regions, inside and outside of the Arabian Peninsula, *aysh* refers to bread. As a rule, people end their meals with a serving of dates or watermelons that come from Qatif.

In addition to the many indigenous dishes, Saudis adopted a large number of dishes from other Arab countries, which acquired a number of local variations. The famous Egyptian *mulukhiyyah* is among the favorite imports, made of the mallow plant, which is cooked with chicken or meat in a soup-like mixture, served with bread or rice. Stuffed vegetables of different varieties, called *mahshi*, are also very popular. They include grape and cabbage leaves, tomatoes, zucchini, green peppers, and other vegetables, stuffed with rice and meat and cooked in a spiced tomato-based sauce. Other dishes popular throughout the Arabic-speaking world include *falafel* (deep-fried chickpea patties) and *shawarmah* (sliced lamb or chicken sandwiches).

Saudi cuisine includes dishes that are prepared only for special occasions, such as religious holidays. For example, there are a number of foods that people eat for the breaking of the fast during Ramadan, which include *ful mudammas* (fava beans cooked in a sauce of clarified butter, cumin, and lemon juice), *minazzalah* (pieces of lamb, chopped tomatoes, and *tahinah*), and *qatayif* (small turnovers fried on one side and stuffed with nuts, fruits, and sweet spices, and dipped in sugar syrup). People ate only twice during Ramadan, both taken at nighttime: *iftar* is the breaking of the fast meal that takes place immediately after sunset, and *suhur* is eaten just before sunrise.

See also: Chapter 1: Eastern Arabia: Al-Hasa; Hijaz and Tihamah; Jeddah; Mecca; Medina; Najd: Central Arabia; The Persian Gulf; The Red Sea. Chapter 4: Agriculture. Chapter 5: Hajj. Chapter 6: Bedouins and Nomadism; Settled Population: *Hadar*.

Further Reading

al-Hamad, Sarah. *Cardamom and Lime: Flavours of the Arabian Gulf.* IMM Lifestyle Books, 2016.

Musayqar, ʿAbd al-Rahman. *Traditional Foods in the Arabian Gulf Countries.* FAO/RNEA, 1993.

Nawwab, Niʾmah. "The Culinary Kingdom." *Aramco World*, vol. 50, no. 1, 1999, pp. 88–97.

Yamani, Mai. "A Taste of Mecca." *A Companion to Muslim Cultures.* Edited by Amyn B. Sajoo. I. B. Tauris, 2012, pp. 185–199.

CHAPTER 15

LEISURE AND SPORTS

OVERVIEW

Saudi Arabia is known for its homogenous social culture, which is largely dictated by religious and societal norms and expectations. These include gender segregation, resulting in markedly different social roles of men and women, and the moral appropriateness of particular activities, defined by religious institutions. Most leisure activities are family oriented and separated by gender. Men usually spend several hours after work socializing with their peers at coffee shops and specially designated leisure areas (*istirahah*). Socializing activities include exchanging news, playing cards and board games, and seeking advice from more senior and authoritative members of the group—while drinking tea and coffee and, sometimes, smoking traditional water pipes (*shishah*). This leisure time is an important element of Saudi communal life and a crucial tool for building and maintaining social and career networks. Visitation of friends, acquaintances, colleagues, and especially family members is an unspoken social requirement for both men and women. Gender segregation, which is not only a social norm but a formal law in Saudi Arabia, results in separate social lives led by men and women, especially those belonging to older generations. Social visitation, even of close friends and family, is usually gender segregated as well, and takes place in different quarters of the house.

The culture of mutual visitation is particularly important for women, given the very few socializing opportunities they have in Saudi society. Married women typically pay visits to their friends and family members after finishing their chores at home or after work. Like men's, these activities center on exchanging the news while drinking tea and coffee with dessert. Public spaces—as limited as they are in Saudi Arabia (e.g., cinemas have been banned until 2018)—are significantly less accessible for women, in comparison to men. Although women often attend playgrounds with the children, they have traditionally been much less involved in physical leisure activities. However, in recent years a new and exciting grassroot initiative emerged where women self-organize to run in the streets. Additionally, most Saudi cities now offer segregated sport facilities for women, such as gyms and fitness clubs.

Saudi youth culture and social life are noticeably different from that of older generations. The youth are facing many difficulties and restrictions in enjoying leisure activities of their choice. Young men and women are expected to obey local customs and traditions, as well as to show respect to the elders who define the socially accepted norms of behavior. Those deviating from these norms are at risk of being ostracized within their community and even within their own family. Nevertheless, even the most strictly controlled social standards cannot stop the change. The new ways of communication presented by the Internet and social media had a major impact on the culture of young Saudis. Additionally, the mall culture has been growing exponentially in the last decade. Strolling around shopping malls and window shopping have become a popular pastime among both young men and women.

Traditionally, the majority of leisure activities in Saudi Arabia are family oriented. In recent years, weekend trips to the desert or the beach became popular in many families. Television remains the primary source of entertainment—as it is in many other Arabic-speaking countries. Ramadan programming is especially popular and brings the entire family together to watch various television series after the *iftar* (the breaking of the fast). Reading of Arabic fiction—both Saudi and from other Arabic-speaking countries—has been on the rise, especially since several prominent Saudi authors have emerged on the literary scene and have received regional and international acclaim.

Leisure activities popular among men include various popular and traditional sports, such as soccer, horse and camel racing, falconry, and hunting, although the latter has been significantly restricted in recent years to protect the wildlife. Races are very popular and always attract large crowds of almost exclusively male spectators. The Riyadh camel race and the Dubai World Cup horse race are the most prestigious regional events that offer sizable prizes. One major difference with races in the West is that betting is illegal in Sharia, thus all forms of racing are purely a spectatorship. Football, or soccer, remains the most popular sport and has been increasingly promoted by the Saudi government. The number of stadiums and sporting facilities is constantly increasing, and the government makes considerable investments into the development of the sport. Per the Saudi Vision 2030 plan, which places a great deal of focus on the development of sports and promotion of an active lifestyle among Saudi citizens, soccer will play an even greater role. This globally popular sport is seen as a way of promoting a cosmopolitan image of contemporary Saudi Arabia, in addition to serving as a tool of national unity. For decades, women were banned from attending sporting events in public, but in 2017, the government issued a statement reversing the ban. In January 2018, women were allowed to attend a football match for the first time, which took place at the King Abdullah Sports City stadium, although they had to enter the facility through designated areas.

The Saudi Vision 2030 reform plan estimates that currently only 13 percent of the Saudi population exercises at least once a week. Several factors contribute to the low levels of engagement in fitness by Saudis. These include difficult environmental conditions, rapid urbanization and the accompanying lifestyle transformation, and new eating habits, particularly with the growth of fast food chains. Most importantly, this low percentage of fitness participation reflects almost complete isolation of the women population from physical activities. Even with the recent positive changes regarding women's participation in sports, they remain largely void of opportunities to do fitness and physical training. Although Saudi Arabia had participated regularly in the Olympics, until very recently not a single female athlete represented the country internationally. However, slowly the changes are taking place. A number of measures are being implemented within the Vision 2030 reform to address these challenges. For instance, in 2017, the government announced that it will implement mandatory physical education for girls in secondary schools starting in the fall of 2018.

Further Reading

Seddon, Philip J., and Abdul-Rahman Khoja. "Youth Attitudes to Wildlife, Protected Areas and Outdoor Recreation in the Kingdom of Saudi Arabia." *Journal of Ecotourism*, vol. 2, no. 1, 2003, pp. 67–75.

Shaheed, Aisha Lee. "Saudi Arabian Women and Sport: Bodies, Rights and Public Spaces." *Women's Sport as Politics in Muslim Contexts*. Edited by Homa Hoodfar. Women Living Under Muslim Laws, 2015, pp. 248–261.

Shavit, Uriya, and Ofir Winter. "Sports in Contemporary Islamic Law." *Islamic Law & Society*, vol. 18, no. 2, May 2011, pp. 250–280.

Camel Racing

Camel racing is one of the oldest sports on the Arabian Peninsula—a native habitat of the dromedary. For millennia, camels have been essential for the survival of the local population, both nomadic and sedentary. They served as the main means of transportation, as they are able to cross long stretches of desert, and also provide milk, meat, and hides. The history of camel racing in this region goes back to at least the 7th century AD. Although horse racing was always a more popular sport on the peninsula—since it is also home to the world-renowned Arabian horse—the camel racing was also an important event at festivals and other gatherings.

Historically, these competitions were informal, until camel racing received a new following in the 1970s and became a formally recognized sport, akin to horse racing. At that time, a number of organizations and associations were established to govern and promote camel-racing events. Rules and regulations have been defined as well, although they show certain variations in different countries. The sport quickly became popular—not only in Saudi Arabia, but in many other countries throughout the Middle East, Africa, and beyond, including countries as diverse as Egypt, Sudan, Kenya, India, and Australia. Several supporting industries grew in parallel to the development of the sport, such as training, breeding, and research industries. Since the 1970s, camel racing has been formally recognized as an international sport and has become a big draw for tourists and enthusiasts. The sport centers on camels running at high speeds over a predetermined course, with a rider astride. The racing is generally limited to the dromedary, or camels with one hump, as opposed to the Bactrian camel which has two humps. Historically well-known for their speed, the very name "dromedary" comes from the Greek verb which means "to run" (*dramein*).

In Saudi Arabia, weekly races are held at the Riyadh stadium during the cool months of winter. In the year 1974, the Annual King's Camel Race was established, which is now considered one of the sport's most important contests and attracts riders and fans from the region and the rest of the world. Camels are bred and raised specifically for the

A camel-racing competition. (Klights/Dreamstime.com)

sport and track running, implementing various methods of breeding, training, and nutrition. A well-bred racing camel is highly valued. Camel-racing events are often accompanied by cultural festivals that reflect local customs and keep them relevant for younger generations.

See also: Chapter 2: Pre-Islamic Arabia. Chapter 6: Bedouins and Nomadism; Major Tribes.

Further Reading

Khalaf, Sulayman. "Camel Racing in the Gulf: Notes on the Evolution of a Traditional Cultural Sport." *Anthropos (Anthropos-Institut)*, vol. 94, no. 1–3, 1999, pp. 85–106.

Khan, Majeed. "About the Discovery of Al Jawf 'Camel Figures' in Saudi Arabia." *Rock Art Research*, vol. 36, no. 1, May 2019, pp. 115–116.

Pesce, A., and E. Garbato Pesce. *Marvel of the Desert: The Camel in Saudi Arabia*. IMMEL, 1984.

Falconry

Hunting with falcons is an ancient occupation on the Arabian Peninsula and an important part of regional heritage. Archaeological surveys indicate that the relationship between Arabs and their falcons is over 12 centuries old. According to Saudi Arabia's

General Authority for Tourism and National Heritage, archaeological findings related to falcons go back to the ancient civilizations around 9000 BC. Falconry, which is also often referred to as hawking, has its own unique culture. It is one of the very few cultural and recreational activities that has remained almost unchanged from the earliest days of its history, having preserved its unique features, gestures, language, and its cultural values. The fans of this ancient sport compare falconry with art, literature, and music.

Falconry remains popular among many Saudis. They see it as an important aspect of their Bedouin identity and the region's cultural heritage, which should be preserved and cherished. Being simultaneously a sport and a cultural activity, falconry is practiced with passion and has lifelong admirers who often pass the skill to the next generations of the family. Saudi falconry changed very little throughout history due to the surrounding environment that for many centuries remained untouched by agriculture and urban development. In the past, falcons were not used as a sport or a pastime but mainly as a means of survival in the desert, supplementing a sparse diet.

Of all Middle Eastern countries where falconry is practiced, Saudi Arabia is perhaps the only one to have retained the ancient tradition of using wild hawks to hunt wild targets. The capturing and training of falcons is a complex process that requires a lot of skills and patience. Traditional Saudi falconry begins with an important ritual of capturing of falcons during the migration season. Some consider this practice as significant as the hunt itself. June and July are the two months when falconers prepare for the trapping season. Wild young falcons around two years of age are the best raptors for falconry, as they have already developed their hunting skills naturally. In the world of falconry, a bird caught in Saudi Arabia has a high value because it is assumed that the raptor has strong survival skills and hunting abilities, as it was able to survive in a harsh habitat of the Arabian Peninsula. After the capture, the bird is placed in a tent for two to seven days. Gradually, falconers begin training the raptors—first in close proximity, and later in the desert. In the beginning, the falconer works on making the bird get used to its human. Arab falconry uses exclusively female birds, who are usually released back into the wild at the end of the hunting season. Having gone through extensive training, by October or November, the falcons are ready to catch prey and return to their falconers from great distances. Amazingly, by the end of the training period, most of these falcons are able to recognize their names—a testimony to the great skills of the falconers who succeed in training a completely wild raptor in a short period of time.

Falconry continues to be popular in various regions of Saudi Arabia. Various festivals and celebrations include live falcon presentations. There are also specialized courses in falconry breeding and training. However, the country has unfavorable environmental conditions for breeding falcons, with high temperatures and humidity limiting hatching. Saudi Arabia and other Gulf Cooperation Council states join efforts to reduce overhunting and implement various measures to protect endangered species.

Since the 1970s, falconry has been increasingly promoted by the Saudi government both inside the country and on a global level. The most prominent government decision to promote falconry was the royal order to establish the Saudi Falcons Club, whose goal is to preserve the sport's traditions. In 2019, the club organized the King

Abd al-Aziz Falcons Festival, which entered the Guinness Book of Records as the world's largest tournament in falcon racing. In a 10-day event, 1,723 falcons participated, with over $4.5 million allocated for cash prizes for Saudi and international falconers.

See also: Chapter 6: Bedouins and Nomadism.

Further Reading

Koch, Natalie R. "Gulf Nationalism and the Geopolitics of Constructing Falconry as a 'Heritage Sport.'" *Studies in Ethnicity and Nationalism*, vol. 15, no. 3, 2015, pp. 522–539.

Remple, David, and Christian Gross. *Falconry and Birds of Prey in the Gulf.* Motivate Publishing, 1993.

Subramanian, Meera. "A Heritage Takes Wing." *Saudi Aramco World*, vol. 63, no. 2, 2012, pp. 20–31.

Golf

Golf came to Saudi Arabia in the 1930s, but in these early years it was mainly played in the expatriate communities, who began to arrive to the country with the discovery of oil. In recent years, as the country is undergoing major cultural and social changes, Saudi Arabia seems to have embraced the global obsession with golf—much like other Gulf countries have done in previous years. Golf is one of the key components in Vision 2030 reform, which aims to substantially reduce Saudi Arabia's dependence on oil and develop public service sectors, placing particular focus on sports and tourism. The first professional golf tournament took place in Saudi Arabia in 2019 when it hosted the European Tour. The government saw this as an opportunity to promote the country's image as a destination for global tourism and leisure, as well as creating a domestic infrastructure to promote a more active lifestyle among its citizens. The four-day event had over $3.5 million in prize money, and the World Number 1 Dustin Johnson won the tournament. However, several big-name players, including Tiger Woods, declined invitation to participate after the global political scandal that followed the murder of Saudi journalist Jamal Khashoggi.

If in the early 20th century Saudi golf was played mostly on sand-based greens commonly known as "browns," many of the golf development projects that are currently under way show almost unprecedented magnitude, at least in the context of the Middle Eastern countries. For example, the ambitious Royal Greens project has a massive course stretching over 6,900 yards along the Red Sea coast, approximately 100 miles north of Jeddah. It is situated at the center of the al-Muruj residential district, which is the largest privately funded city development in the world and the first dedicated golf community in Saudi Arabia. A lush desert oasis with scenic views, Royal Greens is currently the only grass course on Saudi Arabia's west coast, but there are plans under way to significantly expand golf culture throughout the nation: as many as 13 more golf courses are set to open in the near future.

See also: Chapter 4: Vision 2030.

Further Reading

Baabood, Abdullah. "Sport and Identity in the Gulf." *Popular Culture and Political Identity in the Arab Gulf States*. Edited by Alanoud Alsharekh and Robert Springborg. Saqi, in association with London Middle East Institute SOAS, 2008, pp. 97–120.

Ben Sulayem, Mohammed, et al. *Sport Management in the Middle East: A Case Study Analysis*. Routledge, 2013.

Horse Racing

Horses have been central to life on the Arabian Peninsula for many centuries. Saudi Arabia in particular is known for its strong desert-bred Arabian horses, who are among the most celebrated horse breeds in the world. The Arabian horse is closely linked with the history of Najd and the local tribes, where this breed was first developed around 3,500 years ago.

Purebred Arabian horses with a long lineage are rare and are characterized by the special traits valued by the traditional Bedouin community—loyalty, endurance, speed, intelligence, beauty, and courage in battle—qualities that are applicable equally to riders and their horses.

Many Saudis are fans of equestrian sport and regularly patriciate in competitions, both inside the kingdom and internationally. Elite horses belonging to the Saudi elite frequently compete and win the biggest and most prestigious international equestrian competitions in the world. Among these, the win of Kentucky Derby in 2002 by the horse named War Emblem particularly stands out, as it is perhaps the most important horse race in the United States. The owner of War Emblem, Prince Ahmed bin Salman bin Abd al-Aziz, was the first Arab owner to win at Kentucky Derby since it was launched in 1875.

Horse racing has always been popular in Saudi Arabia, where public cinemas have been banned until recently, and opportunities for public spectatorship are very limited. As a result of the country's interest in equestrianism, the King Abd al-Aziz Arabian Horses Center was established in Dirab in 1961. The center registers Arabian horses in the kingdom and represents the country in international equestrian organizations. It is also a member of the World Arabian Horse Organization (WAHO), which organizes regular equestrian beauty contests.

Many Saudis also get involved in horse breeding, including members of the royal family. Historically, the Saudi royal family, as well as the tribal leaders, have been preoccupied with collecting and breeding the best Arabian horses. King Abdullah was a particularly well-known sponsor and promoter of equestrian sports. In addition to serving as the patron of the King Abd al-Aziz Arabian Horses Center, he served as president of the Arriyadh Equestrian Club and founder of the Saudi Arabian Equestrian Federation. The King Abd al-Aziz Arabian Horses Center and al-Janadiriyyah farm are among the most distinguished horse-breeding establishments in the world.

The Arabian Horses Festival is an important event that takes place in Riyadh in the course of 10 days in winter. Among various events of the festival is a long-distance endurance race of 46.6 miles. Resulting from enthusiastic petitioning and sponsorship from riders and racers, this type of race has been accepted into the Olympics. The race is traditionally held in the Thumamah National Park, located north of Riyadh. It is divided into three sections of 25 km each, and is sometimes called the race of a million steps. The sporting events of the Arabian Horses Festival also include show jumping and a beauty contest for the horses. An important aspect of horse racing in Saudi Arabia is that betting is illegal for religious reasons and is banned at all events. However, some enthusiasts argue that this gives a special character to Saudi horse racing and other equestrian sports as they are driven by the spectators' pure passion for the horses.

Show jumping is not an indigenous sport and was introduced to Saudi Arabia in the 1980s. Arabian horses are not well suited for this sport, but the country began importing other thoroughbreds specifically for jumping. Particularly important for the development of jumping in Saudi Arabia have been the contributions of brothers Khalid and Fayad al-Eid, who were members of the Olympic slow-jumping team, and the two trained consistently in England, Germany, and the United States. While placed 30th in the 1996 Olympics, Khalid al-Eid continued to train, completed again in 2000, and won the bronze medal.

See also: Chapter 1: Najd: Central Arabia. Chapter 6: Bedouins and Nomadism.

Further Reading

Ammon, K. W. *Historical Reports on Arab Horse Breeding and the Arabian Horse: Collected Reports from Early Travellers to Arabia.* Olms, 1993.

Collie, K. *Spirit of the Wind: The Horse in Saudi Arabia.* Immel, 1982.

Schiettecatte, Jérémie, and Abbès Zouache. "The Horse in Arabia and the Arabian Horse: Origins, Myths and Realities." *Arabian Humanities*, vol. 8, 2017.

Upton, Peter. *The Arabian Horse: History, Mystery and Magic.* Thames & Hudson, 2005.

Maqha: Traditional Coffeehouse

Coffeehouses (*maqha* in singular, *maqahi* in plural) historically played an important cultural role on the Arabian Peninsula. The coffeehouse culture comes from Egypt where they first appeared in Cairo in the early 16th century. From there they spread to Syria and further eastward to Istanbul, quickly gaining popularity throughout the whole region. Despite the centuries-long popularity of coffeehouses throughout the Middle East, conservative Muslim clerics have been questioning whether coffee is permitted in Islam, due to its intoxicating properties. Moreover, these new social spaces were a point of concern for the religious establishment, as they challenged the status of mosques as centers of communal socializing and discussion. However, with time, coffee and coffeehouses were accepted by the majority of Islamic jurists, and both the drink and the gathering place continue to thrive throughout the Muslim world.

In their early history, coffeehouses often offered entertainment to the guests, which usually took the form of folklore and poetry recitations, often accompanied with music. The storyteller would play a one- or two-string fiddle, whereas a group of musicians would play drums. Smoking was often as important a ritual as coffee drinking. Coffeehouses often offered large selections of flavored tobaccos that were usually inhaled through a traditional water pipe popular throughout the Middle East, which is called *narjilah* or *shishah* in Arabic. Historically, coffeehouses were built in busy parts of town near places of business, and quickly became important spaces to conduct negotiations, make deals, and reach agreements—where the informal environment encouraged friendly and mutually respectful conversation. Even nowadays coffeehouses continue to play this role in Saudi Arabia and elsewhere in the Middle East. Overall, they remain key social spaces and are frequented by regular customers on a daily basis. Coffeehouses are primarily urban institutions, but due to their social popularity, even the smallest village usually has at least one. They remain a male space—not only in Saudi Arabia, but in most other Arabic-speaking countries.

In recent years, a new tradition emerged throughout the neighboring Gulf countries, where a new type of coffeehouse has become an increasingly popular part of Ramadan celebrations. These places serve traditional coffees, teas, and water pipes, and also other regional drinks, such as *sahlab*, made of hot milk with arrowroot, nuts, and coconut; and the popular Egyptian drink *karkadeh*, made of boiled hibiscus flowers and

---

SHISHAH: TRADITIONAL WATER PIPE

The traditional Middle Eastern water pipe has many names and varieties, based on different geographical regions and cultural traditions. Its origins are traced to 15th-century India, from where it spread to Persia and then throughout the Middle East. The earliest term of this vaporizing instrument is *huqqa* or *hookah*—a Hindustani word. In Persian it is known as *qalyan*. *Hookah* became particularly popular during the Ottoman times, when even the sultans regularly smoked it. *Argileh* is the most common term in the Levant area, including Syria, Lebanon, Jordan, and Palestine, as well as Kuwait, Uzbekistan, and Azerbaijan. Another version of the same word, *nargileh*, is used in Turkey, Greece, and Eastern Europe. The term *shishah* was initially the name of the glass base of the pipe, derived from the Persian word *shishe*, which means "glass." Currently, *shishah* is one of the most popular names of the Middle Eastern water pipe, used most commonly throughout the Arabian Peninsula, Egypt, and the Sudan.

believed to have blood-pressure-stabilizing properties. These modern coffeehouses are not exclusive to men but are also frequented by women and family groups, who come here to socialize in the evening after *iftar* (the breaking of Ramadan fast). Live entertainment is often offered in these places and includes both traditional Arabic music and poetry recitations, and large-screen televisions similar to those installed in Western sports bars.

See also: Chapter 7: Social Life, Kinship, and Friendships. Chapter 10: *Majlis*; Social Life.

Further Reading

Bowman, Jim. "Time to Smell the Sweet Smoke: Fantasy Themes and Rhetorical Vision in Nargile Café Cultures." *Journal of Popular Culture*, vol. 42, no. 3, June 2009, pp. 442–457.

Elmadani, Abdalla. *Finjan Gahwa (a Cup of Coffee) and a Bit of Everything*. Alwafa Printing Press, 1997.

Hattox, Ralph S. *Coffee & Coffeehouses: The Origins of a Social Beverage in the Medieval Near East*. University of Washington, Department of Near Eastern Languages and Civilization, 1986.

Kirli, Cengiz. "Coffeehouses: Public Opinion in the Nineteenth-Century Ottoman Empire." *Public Islam and the Common Good*. Edited by Armando Salvatore and Dale F. Eickelman. Brill, 2004, pp. 75–97.

Ukers, William H. *All about Coffee*. Tea and Coffee Trade Journal Company, 1935.

Popular Consumerism

The traditional shopping area in Saudi Arabia and in most of the Middle East was made up of small shops, often situated along a street. Shopping malls evolved from the traditional form of bazaars, where people would frequent to buy goods from local artisans, craftsmen, as well as farm products from local farmers. But with the oil boom of the late 20th century, especially in the late 1970s to the 1980s, Saudi Arabia experienced a rapid growth of mall culture, and many of them have been built—and continue to grow—throughout the country. Gradually, investors also started incorporating various leisure facilities into the mall structures. This was particularly necessary due to the lack of nature parks and other recreational areas, attributed both to the difficult climate conditions and strict ultraconservative regulations that control the types and numbers of public spaces. With the rapid growth of Saudi Arabia's shopping malls, they have become an important social space, especially for younger people, not unlike the mall culture popular in the United States in the 1980s. Without nightclubs, music shows, or movie theaters, malls perform the function of entertainment, in addition to shopping. These are especially favored by the women, considering that this is one of the few public spaces where they can enjoy their free time, and they often come in groups of friends or relatives. Saudi malls are generously sized and often host numerous restaurants and fun parks, in addition to the usual shopping areas.

Every shopping mall has a specially designated area for women, where men are not allowed to enter. For example, one of Riyadh's biggest upscale shopping centers, al-Mamlakah, has a whole floor reserved solely for women. These areas are where women meet not only to shop, but for social purposes and even for conducting business. In a way, they have become similar to coffeehouse gatherings of men. High fashion has many followers in Saudi Arabia, where wealthy women often wear the latest Western trends under the mandatory black *abayah* and inside their homes. In addition to the always popular European labels, Saudi Arabia has its own up-and-coming designers, such as Wijdan al-Sharyoufi, Siraj Sanad, and Summer Olayan.

The Al Faisaliah mall in Riyadh. (Giuseppemasci/ Dreamstime.com)

For the most part, Saudi malls are very similar to any such shopping center abroad, offering the same globally popular brands. The unique shopping experiences can be found in a traditional *suq*. These outdoor markets, which remain very popular throughout the Middle East, offer various handmade and folk products, including the famous intricately decorated Saudi daggers, jewelry, incenses, traditional baskets, pottery, woven products, etc. The *suqs* attract tourists as much as they do the locals. Among the best known *suqs* is Riyadh's Suq al-Thumairi, the antique market located next to the Masmak Fortress. Several *suqs* specialize in certain kinds of products, like Jeddah's gold *suq* and the Al-Basha market for food and spices. As in all *suq* culture of the Middle East, haggling is expected and considered an important aspect of the buying-selling ritual.

All Saudi shops must close during the five daily prayers. As a result of this policy, some stores remain closed all afternoon, but reopen in the evening and continue to welcome customers well after midnight. They also have late closures during Ramadan and many remain closed during the hours of fasting, which is throughout the day until sunset. For a long time, salespeople in Saudi shops were exclusively men. However, in recent years, the Saudi Ministry of Labor began to implement an ambitious plan to gradually change its retail sector by employing exclusively women. In 2012, women were allowed to work in cosmetics and perfume shops. The focus on women's employment is an important aspect of the government's Saudization efforts, which aim to radically increase the number of Saudis working in various sectors of the economy.

See also: Chapter 7: Gender Segregation. Chapter 10: Social Life.

Further Reading

Aldossry, Theeb, and Matthias Zick Varul. "A Time to Pray, a Time to Play? Everyday Life in the Kingdom of Saudi Arabia between the Temporalities of Religion, Tradition and Consumerism." *Time & Society*, vol. 25, no. 3, 2016, pp. 471–492.

Le Renard, Amélie. "Engendering Consumerism in the Saudi Capital: A Study of Young Women's Practices in Shopping Malls." *Saudi Arabia in Transition: Insights on Social, Political, Economic and Religious Change.* Edited by Bernard Haykel, Thomas Hegghammer, and Stéphane Lacroix. Cambridge University Press, 2015, pp. 314–331.

Soccer

Certain types of sport are considered a national obsession, and in the case of Saudi Arabia it is particularly true of soccer, which appears to function as a source of unifying national and regional identity. Soccer is also extremely popular in the neighboring Gulf countries and in most other Arabic-speaking countries throughout the Middle East and North Africa. In the late 1920s, soccer fans in Jeddah founded al-Ittihad Club (literally "the unity club"), making it the oldest soccer club in Saudi Arabia and one of the oldest in the region. The Saudi Arabian Football Federation was established in 1956 under the leadership of Prince Sultan bin Fahd ibn Abd al-Aziz. The team wears green and white colors, and they are known as the Green Falcons.

In the 1990s, the federation became a professional league, which currently includes 12 teams from the main regions of the country. In 1994, it successfully entered FIFA qualification. The Saudi Football League is known for its focus on national players and has a restricted number of foreign players. The Saudi Arabian national soccer team has been regularly participating in the World Cup but has yet to achieve significant success at the global level. They have been more successful in the Asian Cup, where the Saudi team won several titles. Football players have celebrity status at home, especially with the young generations. Sami al-Jabir is one of the most popular Saudi players, having played for al-Hilal Club and scored at four Saudi Arabian World Cup appearances. In 2006, at the Soccer World Championship for the Disabled, the Saudi team beat the Netherlands to win the title.

Al-Hilal Club is the most well known and popular among Saudi soccer teams. It is based in Riyadh and plays at the massive King Fahd Stadium that has a 67,000-seat capacity. Al-Nasr and al-Shabab clubs are also based in Riyadh. Among other popular domestic teams are the original al-Ittihad Jeddah and al-Ahli. There are soccer clubs in other Saudi cities, including Mecca, Dammam, Abha, and Tabuk.

Saudi Vision 2030, with its new emphasis on entertainment and sports, includes a substantial increase of investment in football, as an important area to attract and energize youth. The globally popular sport is seen as another venue to display Saudi Arabia's reforms, meant to increase social openness and improve its international image. The kingdom's new ambition in soccer is led by Turki al-Sheikh—the new head of the Saudi General Sports Authority and a close adviser to Crown Prince Muhammad bin Salman. Since his appointment, the country quickly ventured into various sports initiatives, some of them crushing the country's cultural taboos, such as the invitation to host World Wrestling Entertainment events for the next 10 years.

See also: Chapter 4: Vision 2030.

Further Reading

Abuzayed, Bana. "Sport and Emerging Capital Markets: Market Reaction to the 2022 World Cup Announcement." *International Journal of Islamic and Middle Eastern Finance and Management*, vol. 6, no. 2, 2013, pp. 122–141.

Shavit, Uriya, and Ofir Winter. "Sports in Contemporary Islamic Law." *Islamic Law & Society*, vol. 18, no. 2, May 2011, pp. 250–280.

Women in Sports

Saudi Arabia's strict regulations have long banned women from participating and even attending public sport events. Only in January 2018, women were allowed to attend a soccer match in a public setting for the first time. But Saudi women still cannot participate in state-sponsored sports leagues or national tournaments. Of about 150 official sports clubs, none is open to women.

If the state-mandated curriculum in boys' schools makes gym classes compulsory, no physical education for girls is currently offered in Saudi Arabia—although the government has recently announced plans to gradually incorporate sports and physical education into the curricula of public schools for girls. The only possibility for exercise outside of home has become available only in recent years through memberships in private fitness clubs, which have been growing rapidly throughout the country.

In 2008–2010, the staunch critic of Saudi Arabia and its policies Ali al-Ahmed, a Saudi dissident who founded the Institute of Gulf Affairs in Washington, DC, began a campaign encouraging the International Olympic Committee to take a stance and ban Saudi Arabia from participating in the games, unless it allowed women to compete. His reasoning was that the policy of banning women's participation violated the

Saudi Arabia's Olympic team during the opening ceremonies of the 2016 Rio Olympics. (Zhukovsky/Dreamstime.com)

committee's policies in that it was similar to South Africa's exclusion of black athletes under apartheid. Others have joined the call that resonated with the committee and resulted in issuing the ultimatum to Saudi Arabia, requiring that female athletes be represented on the team as a condition to the country's participation in the 2012 Olympics. Unwilling to accept disqualification, Saudi officials rushed to recruit a number of women to represent the country. On July 12, 2012, the Saudi Olympic Committee chose two women to compete in London. The two female athletes were Wojdan Shaherkani competing in judo, and 800-meter runner Sarah Attar. In the following summer Olympics that took place in 2016 in Rio de Janeiro, Saudi Arabia sent four women to represent the country on the national team: runners Sarah Attar and Cariman Abu Al-Jadail, fencer Lubna Al-Omair, and judoka Wujud Fahmi. Given the complete lack of internal infrastructure to promote women's participation in sports and physical training, the government was forced to recruit those athletes who were either foreign-born or who were trained abroad. Among the four athletes, the two runners, Sarah Attar and Cariman Abu Al-Jadail, and Judoka Wujud Fahmi trained in the United States, while fencer Lubna Al-Omair—in Egypt. Thus, paradoxically, all four female athletes had to leave the very country they were representing to be able to reach the appropriate athletic level and skills, in order to compete in the Olympics.

In the equestrian and horse-racing circles, Arwa Mutabagani has been a prominent contributor to the development of this sport in Saudi Arabia. She was the founder of the Trio Ranch Country Club that opened in 1990 and became one of the first and best riding schools in the country. Herself a talented show jumper, Mutabagani established Trio Ranch with the goal of offering appropriate riding education to Saudi children and young adults—including her own daughter, Dalma Malhas. Since girls are not allowed to officially compete, they would often organize mock horse shows among girls. Given the great limitations of Saudi physical education, Mutabagani knew that her daughter had to move abroad if she wanted to fulfill her potential as a rider, and the two moved to Italy when Malhas turned 12. Arwa Mutabagani's active participation in nurturing Saudi equestrian sport was officially recognized by the government in 2008, when she was appointed to the Saudi Olympic Committee by the king, becoming the first female member of the Saudi Olympic delegation in the country's history. Additionally, she is a board member for the Saudi Arabian Equestrian Foundation.

A fascinating grassroot movement for women's participation in sports and physical training—openly or by tricking the system—is currently on the rise throughout the country. Many women of different generations began regular exercises at home, including yoga, Pilates, kickboxing, and other fitness classes at their houses, as well as exercising with equipment, such as treadmills and elliptical machines. Because of the tricky licensing rules, the women often have to find creative solutions to open gyms, often fronting them with a seamstress shop or opening a fitness studio in places that do not require licensing, such as hospitals and hotels. Others join running groups and fitness classes that take place inside gated communities, which are home to foreign workers. The most exciting trend within this movement are self-organized running clubs where women, covered in hijabs, jog in groups—openly, in the streets, claiming their right for an activity long considered inappropriate for their gender. This movement is growing throughout various regions in Saudi Arabia—from the western seaport Jeddah, to Riyadh, to eastern Khobar.

The development of an active sporting culture being one of the central objectives in Vision 2030, the role of women in improving the lifestyle and health of Saudi citizens has been increasingly highlighted by the government. Recently, Princess Reema bint Bandar al-Saud was appointed to head a specialized women's section of the General Sports Authority. In the past, the princess oversaw the initiation of girls' fitness in schools and the licensing of women's health clubs. Additionally, starting in January 2018, women are allowed to attend public sporting events, although in special segregated sections that are being added to main major stadiums throughout the country, including large soccer arenas in Dammam, Jeddah, and Riyadh.

In 2008, a historical first-ever Saudi women's football match was played in Dammam between two university teams. The first women's football club, King's United, was founded in 2006 and currently has 35 players who range from 13 to 35 years of age.

See also: Chapter 3: Wahhabi Ideology. Chapter 4: Vision 2030. Chapter 7: Gender Segregation; Guardianship; Women's Mobility and Driving Ban. Chapter 8: Education of Women.

Further Reading

Abedalhafiz, Abedalbasit. "The Perspective of Headmistresses of Al-Madinah Al-Munawarah Schools for Girls toward Physical Education Course for Comprehensive Health." *International Journal of Academic Research (IJAR)*, vol. 4, no. 4, part B, 2012, pp. 5–19.

Shaheed, Aisha Lee. "Saudi Arabian Women and Sport: Bodies, Rights and Public Spaces." *Women's Sport as Politics in Muslim Contexts.* Edited by Homa Hoodfar. Women Living Under Muslim Laws, 2015, pp. 248–261.

CHAPTER 16

MEDIA AND POPULAR CULTURE

OVERVIEW

Since the very inception of the Saudi state, its government has been actively involved in defining the country's media culture, and it continues to control news outlets and publications across all platforms. The Ministry of Culture and Information directly oversees radio, television, and other forms of media, both with regard to operation and content. The first formal government body to oversee media was the Ministry of Information, formed in 1963. Prior to that, a number of government entities succeeded one another in different branches of the media. In 2003 the Ministry of Information went through a reform and was renamed into Ministry of Culture and Information. Its staff in different departments regulated and licensed all print, broadcast, and online media services. In June 2018, the ministry was split into two—Ministry of Culture and Ministry of Media—to address the rapid expansion of media forms and outlets.

The first Arabic-language newspapers appeared in the Hijaz around World War I and were published by educated merchant families. Saudi Arabia's first newspaper, *Umm Al Qura*, was founded in 1925. It continues to be in circulation and currently serves as the country's official news source. As for the birth of Saudi television, a royal decree of 1949 established Saudi Broadcasting. In modern times, mass media in the Arabic-speaking world, including Saudi Arabia, has become incredibly diverse. Currently, various forms of Internet and mobile sources are widely available, in addition to the more traditional forms of spreading information, such as newspapers, television, and radio.

Despite the fact that the majority of newspapers and other periodicals are privately owned, they are as limited in expressing unofficial and unsanctioned information as are government-run news sources, as it is common among the editorial staff to practice self-censorship. In addition to that, members of the Saudi royal family have bought significant shares in Saudi and other Arabic-speaking media in the region and thus exert control over a wide range of publications. Any criticism of the government and the royal family is likely to bring dire consequences to both individual journalists and their media outlets. Any questioning of Islamic tenants or the Islamic faith is impossible as apostasy is legally punishable. However, although various regulations imposed on Saudi media are famously strict, the age of mass communications, especially with the rise of social media, has made it increasingly difficult for those in power to exercise control over the entire media sector.

Paradoxically, Saudi Arabian money is financing some of the most open and critical daily newspapers of the region, *al-Hayat* and *al-Sharq al-Awsat*, both published in

London. They are considered among the top multinational newspapers in the area and often cover controversial social and political issues in the Gulf. Due to wide-ranging investments by Saudi businessmen across the Middle East, the country's media industry has influence outside of the borders of the kingdom. For example, large shares of several major regional networks, including the Middle East Broadcasting Center (MBC), based in Dubai, and Orbit Showtime, based in Bahrain, are owned by Saudi media moguls. In 1993, Saleh Abdullah Kamel established Arab Radio and Television Network, which became an important hub for entertainment, music, and sport news in the region. Another known Saudi media mogul, Prince Al-Waleed bin Talal is the founder and owner of the Rotana Group media entertainment conglomerate. Moreover, in 2011 he bought a $300 million share in Twitter, thus plunging into the global media market. In sum, despite being home to one of the most rigorously controlled and censored media environments in the world, Saudi Arabia's investors play an important role in the regional media industry.

The Saudi Broadcasting Corporation (SBC) remains under full government control. It currently operates a number of television channels and radio stations. Television channels include the Arabic-language channel Al Saudiya focusing on news and entertainment; the Arabic rolling news channel Al Ekhbariya; Saudi 2, broadcasting news and entertainment programming in English; and the most recently launched channel, branded "SBC," geared toward younger audiences. Among other media outlets owned by the state are the Saudi Radio station and the Saudi Press Agency. The Ministry of Culture and Information held a monopoly on broadcasting in the kingdom until the advent of Saudi-owned, pan-Arab satellite broadcasters such as Rotana and Middle East Broadcasting Center (MBC) in 1987 and 1991, respectively. Pan-Arab TV operator OSN is owned by Panther Media Group, which is based in the Dubai International Finance Centre, but the equity in the business is shared between KIPCO, Kuwait's national project company, and the Mawarid Group, the Saudi conglomerate, with a stake of just under 40 percent.

Electronic and broadcast media appeared much later in Saudi Arabia than many other Arab countries, mostly because of the high costs and lack of an adequate number of specialists. But with the introduction of satellite technology and computers, mass media in the whole region has grown and changed profoundly. Through satellite dishes, cellular technologies, the Internet, and social media, a new level of communication and information exchange has been reached, a level that is difficult to control by central authorities. Global and local news are now quickly available, and censorship is increasingly difficult to maintain, even though the authorities openly acknowledge that widespread filtering takes place, targeting sites that contain political, religious, or sexually explicit content. It has been reported that in 2016, there have been over 20.8 million Internet users in Saudi Arabia, and this number is certainly much higher today.

Further Reading

Ayish, Muhammad I., and Ali Qassim. "Direct Satellite Broadcasting in the Arab Gulf Region: Trends and Policies." *International Communication Gazette,* vol. 56, no. 1, 1996, pp. 19–36.

Fandy, Mamoun. *(Un)civil War of Words: Media and Politics in the Arab World*. Greenwood Press, 2007.

Hafez, Kai, and David Paletz. *Mass Media, Politics, and Society in the Middle East*. Hampton Press, 2001.

Kazan, Fayad E. *Mass Media, Modernity, and Development: Arab States of the Gulf.* Praeger, 1993.

Khalil, Joe. "New Televisions in the Gulf: Period of Transitions." *Global Media Journal*, vol. 5, no. 8, 2006.

Rugh, William. *Arab Mass Media: Newspapers, Radio and Television in Arab Politics*. Greenwood, 2004.

Cinema

All aspects of the film industry of Saudi Arabia are subject to strict censorship and various regulations. These regulations apply equally to local and foreign productions. Moreover, until 2018, movie theaters were banned throughout the country for over 30 years. However, the situation with Saudi cinema has not always been so repressive. In fact, in the 1970s, going to the movies was a norm for many Saudi families, and numerous theaters were in operation in Saudi Arabia. Most of the movie theaters were located in the more culturally open Hijaz. Cinema was not considered un-Islamic, although conservative clerics did resist the industry's growth—but it was no different from their protests against television or, in earlier years, the appearance of the automobile. Up until the 1980s, Arabic-language films (especially Egyptian), as well as some Indian and Turkish productions were regularly screened.

However, things changed rapidly following the tragic events of 1979, when Islamic militants seized the Grand Mosque in Mecca. King Khaled's consequent decision to give more power to religious conservatives, who had long objected to any and all cultural influences from the West, brought about radical changes to all spheres of Saudi society. Complete closure of all public theaters was one of the subsequent measures, which also included numerous additional restrictions to Saudi women's already limited rights. During the many years of the cinema ban, the only open venue available for screening films was an IMAX cinema in Khobar at the Sultan Bin Abdulaziz Science and Technology Center. When it opened in 2005, it was designated solely to showing educational films. In the rest of the country, there were no cinemas between 1983 and 2018. The only way for the Saudis to watch films was on recorded media, such as videotapes and DVDs, and, more recently, satellite television.

A number of important changes to the Saudi entertainment culture came with King Salman's ascent to the throne in 2015, the designation of his son Muhammad bin Salman as the crown prince, and the announcement of wide-scale modernization of all spheres of Saudi society. On December 11, 2017, the Saudi government announced that public movie theaters would be allowed to open throughout the country, and in early 2018 the Ministry of Culture and Information began issuing licenses to movie theaters. The first public film screening after the end of the cinema ban took place in April 2018 at the King Abdullah Financial District in Riyadh. The film was *Black Panther* (Marvel and Walt Disney Studios, 2018). In line with the Saudi Vision 2030 modernization plan, it is expected that by 2030, Saudi Arabia will have as many as 300 public cinemas with over 2,000 movie screens. However, it is important to note that although the cinema ban has been lifted, all screened films remain subject to existing strict media laws and censorship.

Saudi Arabia's film industry is very small, although it continued to produce a number of films prior to the lifting of the ban. The first Saudi big-budget feature film *Keif al-Hal?* (*How Are You?*) was produced by Prince Al-Walid bin Talal's Rotana Group and released in 2006. Although it was promoted as Saudi Arabia's first film, it was filmed on location in Dubai. The 2012 *Wadjda* became the first feature film shot entirely in Saudi Arabia and was also produced by Rotana. *Wadjda* (the name of the main character) was written and directed by Haifaa al-Mansour—the country's first female filmmaker—and told the story of a 10-year-old girl and her dream of owning and riding a bicycle. Al-Mansour's film premiered at the Venice Film Festival and received critical acclaim worldwide. It was selected as Saudi Arabia's entry for the Best Foreign Language Film at the 86th Academy Awards—this was the first time Saudi Arabia submitted a film for the Oscar Award. Another prominent Saudi feature film was released in 2015—it was Mahmoud Sabbagh's *Barakah Yuqabil Barakah* (*Barakah Meets Barakah*), filmed in Jeddah and told a romantic story between representatives of different social classes. It became the first Saudi feature film to participate in the Berlin International Film Festival.

See also: Chapter 3: Ulama; Wahhabi Ideology. Chapter 4: Vision 2030. Chapter 16: Government Censorship.

Further Readings

Gibbons, Bob. "Cinema Renaissance: Saudi Arabia Welcomes the Movies, and Has a Vision for the Future." *Film Journal International*, vol. 121, no. 7, July 2018, pp. 68–71.

Gorvett, Jon. "Saudi Filmmakers Find Their Voice." *Middle East*, no. 390, June 2008, pp. 56–58.

Sakr, Naomi. "Placing Political Economy in Relation to Cultural Studies: Reflections on the Case of Cinema in Saudi Arabia." *Arab Cultural Studies: Mapping the Field*. Edited by Tarik Sabry. I. B. Tauris, 2012, pp. 214–233.

Freedom of Speech

In February 2017, Human Rights Watch issued a report regarding multiple and consistent violations of freedom of speech in Saudi Arabia. According to the report, since 2010, dozens of prominent Saudi dissidents have been jailed or banned from international travel, as a result of participation in protests or other forms of government criticism. Saudi Arabia has one of the strictest forms of censorship in the world. Criticism of the government, the royal family, or religious leaders is legally punishable and can carry a death penalty. Apostasy is illegal and punishable by death, and any criticism of Islam or even a deviation from the formally accepted doctrines can result in accusation of apostasy. Despite the strict regulations and extreme measures in suppressing dissent, Saudi activists continue their work both inside the country and from abroad.

Nadhir al-Majed, a prominent writer and human rights activist, was arrested in 2011 for his participation in pro-Shia protests and for maintaining contact with foreign media and human rights organizations. On January 18, 2017, he was sentenced to seven years in prison and a seven-year travel ban. In the same month, another prominent human rights activist Abd al-Aziz al-Shubaily, whose charges included incitement against the government and judiciary, was given a sentence of eight years in prison, in addition to an eight-year ban on travel and on using social media following his release from prison. Yet another activist, Essam Koshak, was detained without charge, also in January 2011, and in 2018 sentenced to a prison term and a travel ban. The subsequent years saw a consistent expansion of the crackdown on dissidents and activists, and since 2014, nearly all well-known Saudi dissidents and protesters have been sentenced to long jail terms and issued travel bans. The Saudi Civil and Political Rights Association (ACPRA), which was formed by Saudi activists and served as a hub for human rights activism and peaceful protests, was dissolved by the government in 2013. Earlier, all of its 11 founding members have been arrested and imprisoned.

The government campaign to silence dissident voices includes charges in apostasy and anti-Islamic behavior, which are serious legal violations in Saudi Arabia. In 2013, the Palestinian poet and contemporary artist Ashraf Fayadh was detained by the religious police, allegedly for promoting atheism in his collection of poems *Instructions Within*, published in 2008. In 2015 he was charged with apostasy and given a death sentence, which was later overturned by the Saudi government and changed to an eight-year prison term. Fayadh's numerous supporters believe that his prosecution was a consequence of his circulating a video online that showed a public lashing by the religious police in Abha. The content of his poetry was simply used as an excuse.

A similar charge was given to the prominent Saudi activist and writer Raif Badawi, who is known as the creator of the website Free Saudi Liberals. He was arrested in 2012 on charges of apostasy and "insulting Islam through electronic channels." In 2013, he was convicted on several charges and sentenced to seven years in prison and 600 lashes. Badawi's arrest and sentencing caused international outcry with various human rights organizations attempting to intervene on his behalf. In 2015, he was awarded the Sakharov Prize, which is the EU's highest tribute to human rights. Badawi's sister Samar Badawi is also a known activist for human rights and women's rights. She was arrested on several occasions on the charges of disobeying her male guardian—her father. Her last arrest took place in 2018, and she is being held in the Dhahban Central Prison. In the summer of 2018, Canada's Minister of Foreign Affairs Chrystia Freeland voiced concerns on behalf of her government over the arrest of Samar Badawi and demanded the release of both siblings. Saudi Arabia's reaction to this intervention was to expel the Canadian ambassador and to freeze all trade with Canada. As of 2019, the relationship between the two countries remains strained.

The case that generated particularly intense international scrutiny was the murder of journalist Jamal Khashoggi in 2018. Khashoggi was a veteran reporter and served as foreign correspondent for various Arab newspapers throughout his career. Between 1999 and 2003, he worked as a deputy editor-in-chief of *Arab News*. He also worked as the editor-in-chief for *Al Watan*. For decades, Khashoggi was a loyalist to the Saudi government, since his family had deep ties with the royal family that went back generations (Khashoggi's grandfather was doctor to King Abd al-Aziz, the founder of the Saudi state). However, in the last years of his life, he fell out of favor and became critical of various members of the royal family. Ultimately, he went into a self-imposed exile in the United States, where he published a monthly column in the *Washington Post*. The main focus of Khashoggi's column was on criticizing policies initiated by Crown Prince Mohammed bin Salman, known as MBS. Following the journalist's murder, many accused the prince in playing a role in it. On October 2, 2018, Khashoggi went missing in Istanbul. After weeks of conflicting reports, in November 2018, Saudi authorities announced that he was killed inside the Saudi consulate in Istanbul by means of lethal injection, following a physical altercation. Following his death, his killers dismembered the body. In the wake of Khashoggi's murder, over 20 Saudi nationals were detained by the Saudi government. Additionally, two senior officials have been fired—Deputy Intelligence Chief Ahmad al-Assiri and Saud al-Qahtani—a senior aide to Crown Prince Muhammad bin Salman. As of early 2019, 11 people have been charged over the journalist's death.

See also: Chapter 3: Human Rights and Censorship; Political Dissent and Opposition. Chapter 16: Government Censorship.

Further Reading

Laachir, Karima, and Saeed Talajooy. *Resistance in Contemporary Middle Eastern Cultures: Literature, Cinema and Music*. Taylor & Francis, 2012.

Swazo, Norman K., and Hamza Kashgari. "The Case of Hamza Kashgari: Examining Apostasy, Heresy, and Blasphemy under Shari'a." *Review of Faith & International Affairs*, vol. 12, no. 4, 2014, pp. 16–26.

Government Censorship

The tightly regulated censorship is exercised over all forms of media in Saudi Arabia, including print publications, such as newspapers, magazines, journals, and books; radio, films, and TV programming; and—in recent times—the Internet content. Not only does the Saudi government closely monitor media, but there is also an official law that regulates and mandates censorship. Indeed, a number of important changes have been implemented in recent years to reduce these restrictions, increase the allowed content, and improve Saudi media's reputation globally. But despite these positive changes, Reporters Without Borders continue to rank Saudi Arabia at the bottom of the list for freedom of press: in 2018, it was ranked 169th out of 180 countries.

Saudi Arabia's strict regulation of media stands out even in comparison with other conservative Gulf countries. At least formally, constitutions of other GCC states include protection of freedom of expression, whereas the Saudi Basic Law of Governance, in contrast, formally limits and regulates free speech. Specifically, Article 39 of the Basic Law mandates all mass and publishing media to "use decent language and adhere to state laws" and to "contribute towards educating the nation and supporting its unity," while simultaneously prohibiting it from anything that may lead to "sedition and division, or undermines the security of the state or its public relations, or is injurious to the honor and rights of man." The government body responsible for overseeing Saudi media is the Ministry of Information. Its administrative structure includes a special unit, the Department of Management of Publications, whose job is to regularly examine all forms of publications and to instruct media sources on how particular topics and issues should be presented to the public. This rigorous system of government control promotes the culture of self-censorship among journalists.

Following the events of the Iranian Revolution and the seizure of the Grand Mosque by Islamic militants in 1979, the Saudi government dealt with these external and internal threats to its authority by caving to the conservative agenda. It began implementing a series of reforms that further limited the freedoms of Saudi citizens. Among these measures was an increasingly strict form of censorship. However, most of the regulating processes were taking place informally, until an official regulatory measure of media was implemented by the government in 1992—to combat the new wave of people's discontent with the government. This was the time when a special media policy statement was released and formalized, and journalists were mandated to cover all issues related to Islam and the government with utmost respect. Since then, the government's control over mass media continued to expand. The Law of Printing and Publication was issued in 2003. It increased the methods of regulation and expanded onto virtually all forms of media, such as photographic images, films, television broadcasts, and audio recordings, in addition to the more traditional forms, such as books and printed press. The law formalized various restrictions and required from the published material not to jeopardize public security, or appear in conflict with the Sharia law, or to "stir up discord among citizens"—all of which are very broad areas, allowing to ban virtually anything that the government deems inappropriate. Although the law focused on print media, it extends to digital publications as well. Additionally, it requires government licensing for any activities and publications related to mass information.

In reaction to the rapid growth of the Internet and social media use in the country, the Anti-Cyber Crime Law was issued in 2007 and defined punishing measures specific to cybercrimes. This law further expanded the already broad categories of banned content and now includes anything that can negatively impact public order or offend religious and moral values of Saudi citizens. Under these broad definitions, the banned content can take virtually any form—from online endorsements of drug use, pornography, and terrorism to promotion of atheism. The range of punishments for cyber violations include imprisonment and fines.

A royal decree of 2011 augmented the licensing requirement to include digital publications, such as blogs and online newspapers. Additionally, the new law increased penalties for violations outlined by the 2003 law, to include large monetary fines, removal of the content from the web, barring responsible persons or groups from future publishing, and even closure of the media source that published the offensive content. Moreover, charges related to media censorship violations can and often are applied in conjunction with terrorism charges, given Saudi Arabia's extended legal definition of terrorism, which includes any content that is damaging to the state's stability and security or its reputation.

The strict and all-encompassing system of censorship extends far beyond Saudi Arabia's borders. Many non-Saudi journalists writing in Arabic tend to be cautious about criticizing Saudi Arabia, in fear of jeopardizing their future careers, especially considering that many prestigious journalistic positions are made available by the networks owned by Saudi media moguls. Additionally, a great number of advertising deals in regional media sources comes from Saudi Arabian companies—often between 40 and 70 percent. As a result, most networks, TV channels, and publications exercise caution when covering Saudi Arabia, careful not to risk their advertising income.

See also: Chapter 3: Human Rights and Censorship; Political Dissent and Opposition.

Further Reading

Fandy, Mamoun. "CyberResistance: Saudi Opposition between Globalization and Localization." *Comparative Studies in Society and History*, vol. 41, no. 1, Jan. 1999, pp. 124–147.

Kraidy, Marwan M. "Saudi-Islamist Rhetorics about Visual Culture." *Visual Culture in the Modern Middle East: Rhetoric of the Image.* Edited by Christiane Gruber and Sune Haugbolle. Indiana University Press, 2013, pp. 275–292.

Martin, Justin, et al. "Desire for Cultural Preservation as a Predictor of Support for Entertainment Media Censorship in Saudi Arabia, Qatar, and the United Arab Emirates." *International Journal of Communication*, vol. 10, Jan. 2016, pp. 3400–3422.

Internet and Social Media

The introduction and rapid growth of new technologies, including the Internet and mobile phones, transformed and broadened the means of personal and mass communication in Saudi Arabia. These technologies have been playing a particularly important role in the kingdom, where they offered free access to information and entertainment, and became a new form of communication allowing to subvert the strictly regulated relationships between sexes.

Although limited and censored, access to the Internet is now a basic technological asset in the country. Internet access has been available at Saudi universities and other research institutions since 1994, and individuals were allowed to purchase hardware and modems through foreign providers. Driven by the high demand, Saudi Arabia began to register first public providers in 1999. But before the entire population was allowed to go online, the government established a set of specific guidelines, with the goal of prohibiting all sites with content that is considered explicit and illegal per Saudi law. New Internet rules and regulations were issued by the government, mandating all online publications—whether media source-based (newspapers and magazines) or individual (blogs)—to obtain a special license from the Ministry of Media. Online activity of Saudi activists is tracked and scrutinized on a regular basis. Online activities are monitored both on blogs and on social media. In a very public case in 2012, a known blogger and the leader of the Saudi Liberal movement Raif Bawadi was sentenced to a long prison term and 1,000 lashes, in addition to a 10-year ban on foreign travel and media publishing—as a punishment for his online publications that promoted liberal ideas. The formal charge was apostasy; in Saudi Arabia this is a very serious crime that can carry a death sentence.

Local Internet providers are connected to a single government-controlled proxy farm housed in Riyadh at the King Abd al-Aziz City for Science and Technology (KAACST). It controls and blocks web content that is deemed inappropriate. For example, access to Yahoo and other sites offering private clubs was banned by the authorities. The authorities in Saudi Arabia and other Gulf Cooperation Council (GCC) states tend to censor everything that seems offensive to the country's religious and government establishment. Banned sites and topics include pornography, homosexuality, alcohol and drugs, political opposition groups, Israeli issues, women's rights, etc. The Internet Services Unit maintains two lists of banned sites. The first list contains what is conceived as "immoral" content, as well as content promoting Shia ideology. The second list targets a much wider range of online sites and publications: it is based on the findings of the special security committee that belongs to the Ministry of Media and usually targets content critical of Saudi government. Like many other countries, Saudi Arabia utilizes some globally common content-filtering technologies, such as SmartFilter, which employs automatic screening and filtering of websites based on particular topics and keywords. The government also tracks unusual spikes in Internet traffic when it relates to censored or sensitive content. A noteworthy feature of this system of strict control is that it contains a mechanism for individual reporting of "immoral" websites by regular citizens, who are encouraged to use a special form on the government website. However, despite the existence of a sophisticated and constantly updated control system of blocking the banned sites, tech-savvy Saudis keep finding new ways to bypass these regulations.

In July 2006, both Wikipedia and Google Translate were blocked by the government, as they were used to bypass the filters on the blocked sites through translation. Wikipedia is not blocked currently, especially considering that encrypted HTTPS connections made censorship more difficult for individual wiki pages. YouTube is also operational in Saudi Arabia, but in 2014 the government announced that it would oversee and regulate locally produced content for YouTube. In response to the digital revolution that accelerated the events of Arab Spring, the Saudi government began blocking applications that offered virtual means of communication, such as Skype, Snapchat, and WhatsApp, as they were widely used by activists. The newly formed government censorship body, the General Authority for Audiovisual Media, was tasked with censoring any material deemed "terrorist" in nature. Taking into consideration Saudi Arabia's very broad legal definition of terrorism, this can apply to any content that "disturbs public order, jeopardizes security, obstructs the ruling system, or harms the reputation of the state." In sum, any criticism of the government or the royal family can be labeled a terrorist activity. However, in 2017, some of the restrictions related to digital content were lessened and the ban on virtual communication apps was lifted, in light of the Vision 2030 plan to modernize and diversify the economy, and given the importance of virtual communication for international business networks.

Despite various consistent efforts by the government to control digital media, social media platforms are very popular in Saudi Arabia, especially Twitter and Facebook. Nearly 30 percent of Twitter users in the Arabic-speaking region are located in Saudi Arabia. The app has become an important platform for expressing dissent, especially after playing a key role during the Arab Spring as a tool of social networking. There are numerous cases when citizens have been arrested and sometimes prosecuted for criticizing the government on social media. Some recent reports claim that the Saudi government has been employing bots and human trolls to counteract its criticism on Twitter. Nevertheless, the number of social media users continues to rise consistently. Saudi Arabia is considered among the largest markets for social networking apps in the Middle East. Besides Twitter, Facebook and WhatsApp are also very popular. Virtually all Saudi Internet users—about 97 percent of them—use Facebook, and 81 percent use WhatsApp.

See also: Chapter 3: Human Rights and Censorship; Political Dissent and Opposition. Chapter 16: Government Censorship; Tradition vs. Globalization.

Further Reading

Almestad, Ida Nicolaisen, and Stig Stenslie. "Online Mobilization for Civil and Political Rights in Saudi Arabia." *Asian Politics & Policy,* vol. 6, no. 3, 2014, pp. 500–504.

Fandy, Mamoun. "CyberResistance: Saudi Opposition between Globalization and Localization." *Comparative Studies in Society and History,* vol. 41, no. 1, Jan. 1999, pp. 124–147.

Golesorkhi, Lara-Zuzan. "Cases of Contention: Activism, Social Media and Law in Saudi Arabia." *Arab Media & Society,* vol. 20, 2015.

Samin, Nadav. "Dynamics of Internet Use: Saudi Youth, Religious Minorities and Tribal Communities." *Middle East Journal of Culture & Communication,* vol. 1, no. 2, July 2008, pp. 197–215.

Printed Press

Saudi Arabia has over a dozen dailies, and the following are considered the major national newspapers: *al-Sharq al-Awsat, al-Riyadh, al-Hayat, al-Watan, al-Ukaz, al-Yawm, al-Jazirah, Arab News,* and *Saudi Gazette.* Newspapers in Saudi Arabia are created by royal decree. Pan-Arab newspapers are available as well, although they are subject to censorship.

Before the introduction of print media on the Arabian Peninsula, oral communication was the main tool for disseminating information. Public debate occurred in the weekly meetings with local leaders—the *majlis*, and this tradition continues today. The first newspapers were published around World War I in the Hijaz, around the time when the region gained its independence from the Ottomans. Mostly family owned, they were more interested in conveying political and cultural news and opinions than in making profit.

The prominent *Umm al-Qura* newspaper was initially a weekly literary journal, until it turned into the official announcer of royal decrees and other legal and political events. Two other newspapers from that time reached a larger audience in the Hijaz, *Sawt al-Hijaz* and *al-Madinah al-Munawwarah*, both of which reappeared after an interruption during World War II. In the early years since the establishment of the Saudi state, daily newspapers were published in Jeddah, until the discovery and profitable production of oil changed the demographics and the economic and political setup of the kingdom. With the introduction of the education reform and opening of school throughout the kingdom, the literacy rates of the Saudi population rapidly increased. Advanced publishing and distribution technologies also led to a major growth in demand and supply of newspapers. In the Eastern Province and the capital Riyadh, new dailies emerged, turning the print media into a nationwide operation. The 1960s opened an era in which newspapers were actually read, trusted, and used as a primary source of information. The quickly growing economy used newspapers for advertisement and promotion.

Saudi newspapers have always been privately owned. As a rule, influential business families published their newspapers, until in 1963 a new press law called for multiple ownerships and professional management. Since the turn of the century, two major publishing companies, al-Yamamah and Saudi Research and Marketing Group (SRMG), came to own the majority of the domestic newspapers—in addition to several Middle Eastern newspapers, such as *al-Sharq al-Awsat* and *al-Hayat.* Although these periodicals are privately owned, everything that is published in Saudi Arabia is subject to official control and censorship. In addition to a complex system of censorship, the government also has the power to appoint and dismiss publishers and editors. Moreover, a number of newspapers and publishing houses have been bought by members of the royal family and have thus fallen under the establishment's control.

The underdevelopment of the Saudi press is more complex than simply the case of strict government censorship. An important reason for its lack of development is a distinct tradition of private, interpersonal, and therefore primarily verbal communication to distribute news and opinions. After all, Saudi Arabia remains a culturally conservative society, where most lines of communication stay within one's family and close circle of friends. Another reason stems from the Press Law of 1963, which required a broader base of private ownership. If the post–World War II period was a time when the journalistic profession was thriving, the 1963 law put businessmen in charge of many publishing houses, and profit-based changes followed, with little interest to invest in raising professional standards. As a result, the quality of newspapers quickly declined. Salaries remained low, and many reporters were expats from Egypt and Palestine who were more interested in covering pan-Arab issues than purely domestic Saudi matters.

In 1991, with an increasing threat of an attack by Saddam Hussein's military forces, the Saudi government was not informing the population about the ongoing crisis. As a result, most Saudis were receiving the news from foreign sources of information. On the one hand, the vacuum of information has become a turning point in the Saudi media world and prompted newspapers to take on a more active stance. On the other hand, this crisis led to an increasing outreach to other media sources, such as electronic and broadcasted media.

With the rapid rise of digital media, newspapers' circulation is now limited to particular social groups—mainly highly educated intellectuals, politicians, and other journalists. In the meantime, the majority of the population receive the news either through satellite television or the Internet. Traditional verbal communication still takes place, especially through the medium of *majlis* and women's gatherings, although it is increasingly replaced by the Internet and mobile messaging and social media platforms, particularly in the case of younger generations.

See also: Chapter 4: Public vs. Private Sectors. Chapter 6: Urbanization. Chapter 16: Government Censorship.

Further Readings

Boyd, Douglas A. "Saudi Arabia's International Media Strategy: Influence through Multinational Ownership." *Mass Media, Politics, and Society in the Middle East.* Edited by Kai Hafez. Hampton Press, 2001, pp. 43–60.

Hammond, Andrew. "Maintaining Saudi Arabia's Cordon Sanitaire in the Arab Media." *Kingdom without Borders: Saudi Political, Religious and Media Frontiers.* Edited by Madawi Al-Rasheed. Hurst, 2008, pp. 335–352.

Kamalipour, Yahya R., and Hamid Mowlana. *Mass Media in the Middle East: A Comprehensive Handbook.* Greenwood Press, 1994.

Long, David E. *Culture and Customs of Saudi Arabia.* Greenwood Press, 2005.

Television

Saudi Arabia was among the first Arabic-speaking countries to introduce television (the second Arab country after Iraq). From the moment it came to Middle Eastern markets, television quickly became an essential part of Saudi culture. It offered a popular and highly accessible form of entertainment in a system that makes public socializing very difficult. Saudi broadcasting began in 1965, when King Faysal contracted the American National Broadcasting Corporation (NBC) to build a national television network, and by 1969, it became available to the public. Early programming focused on religious and educational topics, such as the basic news, readings, and lessons from the Quran, and children's cartoons. During the early phase, two national television channels were in operation. One was an Arabic-language channel that offered conservative programming, whereas the other channel broadcasted in English for the expatriate community. Color television came to Saudi Arabia in 1976. It continued to offer conventional television programming, such as coverage of the pilgrimage and religious holidays in Mecca and Medina. Other programs included poetry recitals, television series aired during the month of Ramadan, and reruns of classical Egyptian movies. Any political content, other than official announcements from the government, remained very limited.

Notwithstanding the highly conservative and strictly regulated content on Saudi television, the religious establishment strongly opposed it. In earlier years, conservative clerics similarly opposed the telegraph, the radio, the telephone, and even the automobile—as inventions of the Western world that should be avoided at all cost. The introduction of television by King Faysal, who is considered one of the most progressive Saudi kings, provoked violent protests from the radical opponents—some of whom were members of the royal family, including Prince Khalid Bin Musa'id, who was one of the leaders and organizers of the protests. During one particularly violent attack on a television station in 1966, he was shot dead by the police. Ten years later, his brother Faysal Bin Musa'id avenged the death of his brother by killing King Faysal himself—the one who introduced television to Saudi Arabia.

The television market in Saudi Arabia and the rest of the Arab world changed rapidly in the early 1990s with the emergence of private satellite television. The Arab Satellite Communications Organization—which is known as Arabsat and is headquartered in Riyadh—became the first satellite operator in the Arab world. The first satellite was launched in 1985, but the operational costs were very high up until the 1990s, when technological development made satellite television commercially viable. Egypt was the first country to adopt satellite television in the region, although in early years its programming did not significantly differ from traditional broadcasting.

With the outbreak of the First Gulf War in 1991, its news coverage—or lack thereof—served as a catalyst for establishing and promoting private satellite television in the region. The stark contrast between CNN's technologically superior 24-hours coverage and the local channels lagging behind and, at times, avoiding the news altogether, made the public eager for diverse television content. In the same year, the Middle East Broadcasting Center (MBC) was founded by two Saudi entrepreneurs, Salah Kamel and Walid Ibrahim. It was the first private satellite channel in the Arab world, with the headquarters in London that was relocated to Dubai in 2001. Despite the growing competition, MBC remains one of the most popular and technologically advanced Arabic-language channels. Among other television networks, in which Saudis have financial stakes, are Orbit Showtime Network (OSN) and Salah Kamel's Arab Radio and Television Network (ART), known for its exclusive broadcasts of sporting events.

The news station Al Jazeera, launched in 1996 and headquartered in Doha, Qatar, became a true game changer in the development of Arabic-language satellite television. It expanded the global media landscape by offering views from the Middle Eastern perspective, which often challenge perspectives presented by Western media sources. Al Jazeera English was launched in 2006.

Television series are a highly popular form of entertainment throughout the Middle East. In Arabic, they are called *musalsalat* (originating from the word *silsilah* which means "series" or "chain") and generally refer to dramatic or comedic series made for television. *Musalsalat* were first developed in Egypt in the early days of radio, and initially had the form of fictionalized stories based on historical and contemporary issues. *Musalsalat* are made for year-round viewing, but the high season traditionally falls on the month of Ramadan. The series released during Ramadan often have large budgets, cast major stars, and are heavily promoted. Families all over the Arabic-speaking world gather in front of the television following the *iftar*—the meal that breaks the fast at sunset. The watching of *musalsalat* has become an important social event and a part

---

STAR ACADEMY: **REALITY TELEVISION AS A CULTURE WAR**

In 2003, LBC Channel adapted *Star Academy* from an Endemol format, and the show became an unprecedented pop cultural phenomenon throughout the Arabic-speaking world. The 2004 season featured 16 amateur performers (8 men and 8 women), selected as finalists from a pan-Arab pool of 3,000 applicants. The finalists agreed to spend four months in the "Academy" and take classes in performing arts. During this time, the participants—hailing from Egypt, Lebanon, Syria, Saudi Arabia, Kuwait, Morocco, and Tunisia—were monitored by 60 cameras. On Mondays, a jury of media personalities announced two "nominees" to be expelled at the end of the week, which launched a weeklong pan-Arab voting via Internet and cell phones. *Star Academy* aired nightly, showcasing the day's events and culminating in a weekly two-hour Friday episode with live performances by the contestants and the announcement of voting results.

The popularity of *Star Academy* in Saudi Arabia was truly remarkable. It broke all ratings in broadcasting and emptied streets during aired episodes in busy cities like Riyadh and Jeddah. The show generated heated national debates and religious sermons and, reportedly, distracted Saudi students during the final exams in May 2004. In response to the viewers' questions on whether watching the show would be considered *haram* (forbidden) or *halal* (permitted), Saudi clerics issued a series of *fatwas*, prohibiting watching, discussing, voting in, or participating in the show. Nevertheless, many Saudi journalists and media personalities praised *Star Academy* as an alternative to the extremist dogma and used the program to discuss the culture and aspirations of Saudi youth. A major voice against the clerics even emerged from the royal family. A prominent businessman and media mogul Prince Al-Waleed Bin Talal became a vocal supporter of *Star Academy*.

of a daily ritual during Ramadan. In contrast with the regular programming that is regulated by authorities, the Ramadan series are given significantly more freedom in addressing various controversial topics, such as terrorism, religious intolerance, addiction, infidelity, family dynamics and women's issues, and many more. *Musalsalat* are extremely popular, widely discussed in social gatherings and on social media, and are covered by the press. On average, about a hundred new and returning series are made for the month of Ramadan. New episodes are usually released on a daily basis.

See also: Chapter 4: Public vs. Private Sectors. Chapter 6: Urbanization. Chapter 16: Government Censorship.

Further Reading

Khalil, Joe. "New Televisions in the Gulf: Period of Transitions." *Global Media Journal*, vol. 5, no. 8, 2006.

Kraidy, Marwan M. "Reality Television, Gender, and Authenticity in Saudi Arabia." *Journal of Communication*, vol. 59, no. 2, 2009, pp. 345–366.

al-Qasimi, Noor. "Shampoo: Editing, Advertising, and Codes of Modesty on Saudi Arabian Television." *Camera Obscura: A Journal of Feminism, Culture, and Media Studies*, vol. 26, no. 77 [2], 2011, pp. 91–121.

Rugh, William. *Arab Mass Media: Newspapers, Radio and Television in Arab Politics*. Greenwood, 2004.

Samin, Nadav. "Our Ancestors, Our Heroes: Saudi Tribal Campaigns to Suppress Historical Docudramas." *British Journal of Middle Eastern Studies*, vol. 41, no. 3, 2014, pp. 266–286.

Tradition vs. Globalization

Media culture is set to play a crucial role in Saudi Arabia's ambitious set of reforms, branded Saudi Vision 2030 and aimed at modernization and diversification of the country's economy.

The government has earmarked substantial spending—almost $900 million by 2020—for the development of culture and media, with the hope of attracting substantial private investments. Significant efforts are given to encouraging foreign entertainment industries to participate and invest in the modernization of Saudi popular culture and mass media. A number of high-stakes agreements have been made since the announcement of Vision 2030 plans—from AMC and IMAX plans to open a large number of new movie theaters, to Richard Branson's participation in the country's tourism projects, to Cirque de Soleil performances. However, several of these plans were put on hold by the foreign participants following the murder of Jamal Khashoggi.

The need for dynamic development of media culture emphasizes the conflict between the new and the traditional in Saudi culture, which stems from the deep cultural divergences between different generations in Saudi Arabia. The government that strives to modernize media culture and make it more competitive on the global market, at the same tries to maintain the rigid system of control and censorship and to comply with the demands of the country's religious establishment. Still, a substantial number of reforms is taking place despite protests from the conservatives—in order to energize younger generations and address their needs. In December 2017, the government announced the reopening of commercial cinemas, following a ban that lasted 35 years. It is expected that a renaissance of cinema culture (300 licensed cinemas are anticipated to open by 2030) will not only have cultural impact, but will also have a positive economic effect by creating over 30,000 permanent jobs and over 130,000 temporary ones. In April 2017, the Public Investment Fund announced its plans to invest in a new entertainment city, which will be built near Riyadh and will cover the area of about 334 square kilometers. It will include a Six Flags theme park, a safari experience, and various sports facilities—designed to encourage Saudi families to spend more of their income at home, rather than traveling abroad. The development is set to open in 2022.

Among the various media-related changes is the creation of a new public TV channel run by the Saudi Broadcasting Corporation and branded "SBC." It launched in 2018, aiming to lure younger audiences and further promote the kingdom's modern image. The channel's content is geared toward youth between 15 and 35 years old, and will broadcast exclusive content, including films, talk shows, and cooking programs. An important aspect of the new channel is that it plans to employ a large number of women—both on screen and off.

See also: Chapter 4: Vision 2030.

Further Reading

Fandy, Mamoun. "CyberResistance: Saudi Opposition between Globalization and Localization." *Comparative Studies in Society and History*, vol. 41, no. 1, Jan. 1999, pp. 124–147.

Mellor, Noha. "Bedouinisation or Liberalisation of Culture? The Paradox in the Saudi Monopoly of the Arab Media." *Kingdom without Borders: Saudi Political, Religious and Media Frontiers*. Edited by Madawi Al-Rasheed. Hurst, 2008, pp. 353–374.

Mellor, Noha. "'More Than a Parrot'—The Case of Saudi Women Journalists." *Journal of Arab & Muslim Media Research*, vol. 3, no. 3, 2010, pp. 207–222.

APPENDIX A

A DAY IN THE LIFE

Note: The following accounts have been fictionalized, but are based on the lives of real people.

A DAY IN THE LIFE OF A YOUNG PROFESSIONAL WOMAN

Mariam is a young unmarried woman in her late twenties, who works in a bank and lives with her middle-class family in a Riyadh suburb. Her family consists of her parents and two younger siblings. Her father, who received his PhD in economics from the University of Michigan, is a head of a department in a large private company. Her mother is a housewife, but she also studied in the United States in her youth—she has a master's degree in political science from Penn State. Both Mariam's parents are fluent in English and made sure that all their children studied English from a young age. Mariam also has an older married brother. He works for Aramco and lives in the Eastern Province with his wife and infant daughter.

Mariam has always been an excellent student—both in secondary school and during her studies at the Princess Nourah Bint Abdul Rahman University, where she received her bachelor's degree in international finance from the College of Business Administration. She initially wanted to be a dentist, but her parents thought that she should use her talents in math and convinced her to study finance instead. Mariam's father is her male guardian and has to formally approve all of her life decisions, from studies to travel to opening a bank account. Although she has arguments with him every now and then, she knows that he is much more open minded than some of her girlfriends' fathers and older brothers. Still, she wishes she could just do what she aspired to do, without needing to convince her family first.

Mariam gets up every morning for a *fajr* prayer (dawn prayer). Her younger siblings do not pray in the morning, but she really enjoys this time by herself and feels spiritually uplifted as she says the prayers. Sometimes she goes back to sleep for another hour or so, but on most mornings, she likes to do an hour of yoga—a habit she picked up from her girlfriends when she lived in California. Mariam spent two years at the University of California in Santa Barbara studying for an MA in economics, together with her older brother, who was getting his PhD in chemical engineering from the same university. Both of them had substantial study-abroad stipends from the Saudi government that allowed them to focus on their studies. Even though they did not need to work, both Mariam and her brother had internships, to get as much experience as possible before returning to Saudi Arabia.

Around 6:30 am she has breakfast with her mom—the two really enjoy having some "girl time" in the morning, exchange the news, and plan their next shopping spree together. They usually eat *ful* (fava beans), flat bread with zaatar (Middle Eastern herb), fruit jams, labna (yogurt), and drink some strong Bedouin coffee, which Mariam's mom loves to make as a sign of her Bedouin heritage. The mother, Hamida, especially enjoys listening to Mariam's stories about her work at the large bank. Hamida never had a job, despite her excellent grades and her MA degree from the United States. Although her father let her study both in Saudi Arabia and even in the United States, where she lived with her uncle's family, she could not find a job when she returned home. Then she got married, had four children, and her dream to work was never realized. However, as her children are getting older, Hamida hopes to start looking for a job in a year or two—encouraged by the government's new push for Saudization of the workplace, which promises to focus on creating more jobs for Saudi women.

Around 7:15 am Mariam puts on her *abayah* and head cover and heads off to work; her workday is set to begin at 8:00 am. Despite the terrible traffic, she loves this part of her day because, as of last month, she drives her own car to work. Before 2018, women were not allowed to drive in Saudi Arabia. This was the main reason some of her girlfriends ended up not working, because they had no one to drive them and could not afford a daily driver. However, Mariam insisted on keeping her job and traveling to work every day, even though she was paying about half of her salary for a hired driver, whom she and her female colleague living nearby hired to drive them to work and back. Right after the government lifted the driving ban in June 2018, Mariam changed her U.S. driver's license, which she got when living in California, to a Saudi license. She bought her first car using her savings and a financial contribution from her father and older brother. Most of Mariam's girlfriends either got their licenses already or are studying for it.

After arriving to work, Mariam goes to her department in the bank. Women and men have separate offices, in accordance with the Saudi law that prevents *ikhtilat* (gender mixing). At noon, the employees leave for a long lunch/fiesta break, and Mariam usually spends it at her aunt's house who lives nearby. The work resumes at 3:30 pm and lasts until 6:00 pm. Mariam really enjoys her job. She works at the international banking department, where she gets to use her English and her knowledge and experience with both Islamic and Western banking systems. Due to her hard work, she has already received her first promotion.

Upon returning back home a little before 7:00 pm, Mariam helps her mother with the house chores and cooking dinner for the family. After dinner, she spends time chatting on social media with her friends, listening to music, and watching some new TV shows on Netflix. She spends at least a couple of hours on social media, checking the news from people she follows and international news in both Arabic and English. Recently, Mariam and some of her friends decided to join the newly opened gym for women, where they would exercise and socialize after work and on the weekend, which in Saudi Arabia falls on Friday and Saturday. On most Fridays, Mariam and her family visit her grandparents' house, where she gets to see her cousins, several of whom are her close friends and chat buddies on social media. Mariam is close with her grandmother and always enjoys the Fridays when she gets to see her.

See also: Chapter 4: Financial Institutions and Saudi Riyal; Saudization. Chapter 6: Urbanization. Chapter 7: Gender Segregation; Guardianship; Parents and Children; Women's Mobility and Driving Ban. Chapter 8: Education of Women; Princess Nourah Bint Abdulrahman University. Chapter 14: Arabic Coffee, Tea, and Other Traditional Beverages.

Further Reading

AlMunajjed, Mona. *Women in Saudi Arabia Today.* St. Martin's Press, 1997.

Alshahrani, Bandar. "A Critical Legal Analysis of the Impact of Male Guardianship System on Women's Rights in Saudi Arabia." *Journal of Islamic State Practices in International Law,* vol. 12, no. 2, 2016, pp. 31–70.

Yamani, Mai. *Changed Identities: The Challenge of the New Generation in Saudi Arabia.* Royal Institute of International Affairs, 2000.

A DAY IN THE LIFE OF A BEDOUIN

Every morning, Abu Samir slowly sips the light-colored cardamom-spiced Bedouin coffee in his tent, which is always open to guests and visitors. At 72, Abu Samir has seen some incredible changes—in the environment, in his own family, and in families of the other members of his tribe. In his childhood and youth, he used to feel that they owned the desert, as his tribe would travel around the Eastern Province. But as the oil industry rapidly expanded, many grazing areas were disrupted and destroyed, and their tribe had to relocate to the northern part of the Arabian Peninsula. But cities, industrial areas, and highways continue to mushroom throughout the desert. Abu Samir and his friends like to reminisce about the old days and complain about the new generation, who do not seem to love the desert the way their forefathers did. However, Abu Samir's oldest son, Samir, continues the Bedouin lifestyle—as difficult as it may be these days—and this makes his father proud. Abu Samir literally means "the father of Samir." This is a common way in the Bedouin community and generally throughout the Middle East of calling parents by their oldest son's name. Abu Samir's wife is referred to as "Umm Samir," respectively, which means "the mother of Samir."

Abu Samir wakes up with the sun to pray *fajr* (dawn prayer). Then he goes to check on his sheep and his camels. The desert is overgrazed, and it is getting more difficult every year to find suitable pasture, but Abu Samir refuses to settle down and move to the city where all of his younger sons now live. His wife, Umm Samir, is also awake by now, and they are about to have their first coffee of the day and light breakfast together. Then Abu Samir, Samir, and Samir's two sons spend most of the day with the livestock. They pray the rest of the daily prayers together. Abu Samir always knows the right time for each of the remaining four prayers as he closely follows the positions of the sun— *dhuhr* (midday), *'asr* (mid-afternoon), and then upon returning back to the tents, *maghrib* (dusk) and *'asha* (evening). In the evening, after eating their dinner together, the men sit around the fire, while the women are finishing their house chores. Here in the desert, the stars are bright, and one can almost forget those busy cities and oil plants that are taking over the steppes—until a distant airplane crosses the skies. Sometimes they read poetry to each other. Abu Samir feels so happy and proud when his grandsons recite old Bedouin poems by heart. He hopes that even when they move into the city—he knows it will happen one day—they will keep their Bedouin identity in their hearts and will pass it on to their children.

Abu Samir and his family's lives are tough. Despite the advances of civilization, the desert environment is as harsh as ever, with scorching days and cold winds at night. Pastures are few and far between, and it is increasingly difficult to find good grazing areas. But Abu Samir refuses to settle down. He knows though that their days in the desert are counted, as almost all of the other tribes and families became sedentary a long time ago. But he often says that civilizations came and went, but the desert, the Bedouin, and his camel survived and persisted through it all.

See also: Chapter 5: Five Pillars or the Tenets of Islam. Chapter 6: Bedouins and Nomadism; Major Tribes; Urbanization. Chapter 7: Parents and Children. Chapter 11: Poetry. Chapter 14: Arabic Coffee, Tea, and Other Traditional Beverages.

Further Reading

Ginat, J., and Anatoly M. Khazanov. *Changing Nomads in a Changing World*. Sussex Academic Press, 1998.

Maisel, Sebastian. "The New Rise of Tribalism in Saudi Arabia." *Nomadic Peoples*, vol. 18, no. 2, 2014, pp. 100–122.

Naimi, Ali. *Out of the Desert: My Journey from Nomadic Bedouin to the Heart of Global Oil*. Portfolio Penguin, 2016.

A DAY IN THE LIFE OF A RURAL WIDOW

Umm Said wakes up with the sun every single day. She is 52 years old and lives about a hundred miles north of Najran in a small governorate called Thar. Everyone calls her Umm Said, "the mother of Said," because parents are commonly called by the name of their oldest son—especially as they (parents) become older. She got married when she was very young, as is customary in her rural community. She has 15 children—eight sons and seven daughters, many of whom remained in this community after getting married.

Umm Said's husband had a stroke three years ago, which severely disabled him. He was almost completely bedridden for a year and could barely talk. With all major hospitals and rehabilitation centers many miles away, Umm Said and her older children took out a loan to travel to Riyadh and treat him there. But he was unable to recover and passed away a year after the stroke. The death of the earner of the family brought a lot of hardship to Umm Said, who needed to support her children who were still living with her. She was especially worried about her younger daughters who were still unmarried.

At first, Umm Said decided to make some handicraft products and sell them in her community. She had to teach one of her sons to drive a car, so that he could take her to the nearest city to buy supplies. Despite the driving ban, most women in Umm Said's and other rural and Bedouin communities drive cars and trucks regularly—otherwise the families wouldn't be able to survive. Sometime ago, the religious police, *Mutawwa*, requested from the local police at a nearby village to take measures against women driving cars, but the tribal sheikhs and the local police simply ignored these orders. Umm Said was never worried about that—no *Mutawwa* ever come here, the local men would never let them through. But driving alone to the city was problematic—until the driving ban was officially lifted throughout the country last year. Unfortunately, the handicraft business was not very successful—she was earning some money but not enough to get by. But then Umm Said, known for her excellent cooking skills, came up with another idea: to make bread together with her daughters and sell it. She borrowed some startup money from her brother and opened a bakery shop in her community.

Umm Said eats a quick breakfast—some bread, eggs, and milk—and starts prepping the dough at home before bringing it to the bakery, where they will do the baking. It is a physically hard job to knead large quantities of dough every single day, mixing it with eggs, oil, and milk. But Umm Said and her daughters are happy to do it, because the bakery started to bring good money. Not only her community is happy to buy her bread, but people from the neighboring communities often come to her shop too. Sometimes, they get special orders to prepare large amounts of bread and other baked products for weddings and other celebrations. As their orders continue to increase, two of Umm Said's daughters-in-law will soon join them at the shop.

Umm Said loves being independent and taking care of their small house and her family, not needing to ask for money from her brothers. She often says: "I didn't and still don't need anyone. My children and I can take care of ourselves." Moreover, Umm Said was even able to support one of her sons when he had an accident, broke both his legs, and was unable to work for months. Using her earnings, she hired a worker to assist with his agricultural work, and she also continued to take care of his wife and their two children until he got better.

Like most businesses and shops, Umm Said's bakery closes at noon and then reopens again at 4:00 pm when people come to buy bread for dinner. Her daughters clean the bakery while she goes home to cook dinner for them. She is tired but also excited to cook for them, especially since they can now afford to eat meat. After dinner, her girls are asleep in mere minutes, but Umm Said keeps thinking about her daughters' future. Both youngsters know how to read and write, but they are too busy with the bakery and house chores to continue their studies. Umm Said hopes that they can marry well, now that they are earning extra money. She keeps thinking of her daughters and whispering protective prayers until she falls asleep.

See also: Chapter 6: Bedouins and Nomadism; Settled Population: *Hadar*; Urbanization. Chapter 7: The *Mutawwa*: Saudi Religious Police; Parents and Children; Women's Mobility and Driving Ban.

Further Reading

AlMunajjed, Mona. *Women in Saudi Arabia Today*. St. Martin's Press, 1997.

Rahmaan, Bushra A. "Village Cluster Centers of Saudi Arabia: Integrating and Transforming Rural Habitat." *Ekistics*, vol. 59/354–355/1992, 1996, pp. 166–169.

A DAY IN THE LIFE OF A YOUNG URBAN MAN

Abdallah is the youngest son in his large conservative family of 10, which includes his parents, six older siblings, and a younger sister. He is in his early twenties and lives with his family in Riyadh. Last year, Abdallah graduated from King Saud University with a degree in computer science. He initially wanted to study Islam and the Arabic language, but getting a job with this kind of degree is next to impossible these days. He wanted to make his parents proud by studying diligently, and as a result, he graduated with high marks and quickly found a job with a government organization. He was lucky to get a position so quickly; several of his friends remain unemployed after graduation. Given his field of study, there were several opportunities to continue his education and complete professional training in the United States or the United Kingdom—and he would have qualified for a full government study-abroad stipend. But he never went because he thought it would be very difficult to maintain his traditional lifestyle in a foreign non-Muslim country.

Abdallah wakes up with the *adhan* for the *fajr* prayer (dawn prayer). Sometimes he prays at home, but he likes to do the first prayer of the day in a nearby mosque. When he returns home, he sleeps for another hour or two, then has breakfast with his parents and sister, and gets ready to work. Abdallah always wears the traditional white *thawb* and finds Western clothes uncomfortable and going against Saudi traditions. As most working residents of Riyadh, he drives to work. When stopping at the light, he looks around and sees several women at the wheel. Abdallah shakes his head, sighs, and begins thinking about the main issue that has been bothering him lately—he feels as if he is having a culture shock in his own country. He is not against lifting the driving ban per se, as he knows how much easier it made life for his two older sisters, who work at the hospital. But he sees it as just another glaring sign of the many cultural changes that have been happening in his society with a dizzying speed. Abdallah notices three women wearing colorful headscarves and heels and a group of young men in jeans and T-shirts, and he quickly looks away and sighs again. This would be unthinkable in a Saudi Arabia of only a few years ago, where all public places looked like a sea of black and white—all women were wearing black *abayahs* and men were in white *thawbs*. Abdallah misses these days.

His workday begins at 8 am. Only men work on his floor, according to the official policy of avoiding *ikhtilat* (gender mixing). "At least we still have that," he says to himself, and proceeds to his office that he shares with another young man of the same age. His colleague, Muhammad, is very friendly and hardworking, but he also leads a very different lifestyle. They frequently eat lunch together and also pray together when they hear *adhan*. Abdallah has recently learned that Muhammad dates a young woman whom he met on social media, and they even are able to meet in coffeeshops sometimes.

His family has no idea, and while not saying it to his friend directly, Abdallah thinks that this is definitely *haram* (an unlawful, unethical thing or action from the Islamic point of view). Not that he was shocked, as this kind of "dating" is becoming more and more common among people of their age. Abdallah likes Muhammad but cannot really relate to him. For himself, Abdallah cannot even imagine doing something like this. He would like to get married soon though, relying on his mother's and older sisters' efforts to find a suitable bride for him. Because he has a job, a car, and will soon have his own apartment, he hopes to get engaged before the end of the year.

Since Abdallah works in a government office, his workday ends around 2:30–3:00 pm. After work, he likes to socialize with several of his friends, two of whom are his cousins, and they normally spend the time in one of their houses, drinking tea, exchanging the news, and asking each other for all kinds of advice. Abdallah really enjoys these *majlis* gatherings (traditional gathering of men, a form of social networking), as he gets to spend some time with a like-minded group of friends. As a rule, they pray *maghrib* (sunset prayer) together in a mosque, and then Abdallah returns home to have dinner together with his family.

Abdallah prays the last prayer of the day, *asha'* (evening prayer), and then browses through social media on his phone—he and his friends have a Facebook group, where they read and discuss religious texts together. He does not watch television, with rare exceptions during Ramadan, when it is impossible to avoid all these *musalsalat* (television series) that everyone is watching and talking about. Abdallah actually likes TV but thinks there is too much *haram*, as many of the shows are becoming increasingly risqué, both in the content and the visuals. Before going to bed, Muhammad likes to read the Quran, which always puts his mind at ease. Tomorrow is Friday, and he really looks forward to going to the mosque and hearing the sermon from his favorite imam. He drifts away while reciting Surat al-Nas (the 114th and last chapter of the Quran), which should ward off the evil temptations.

See also: Chapter 4: Migrant Workers and Unemployment. Chapter 5: Five Pillars or the Tenets of Islam; Quran. Chapter 6: Urbanization. Chapter 7: Gender Segregation; Parents and Children; Women's Mobility and Driving Ban. Chapter 8: Key Universities. Chapter 10: Dress Etiquette; *Majlis*; Workweek and Holidays.

Further Reading

Fadaak, Talha H., and Kenneth Roberts. *Youth in Saudi Arabia*. Palgrave Macmillan, 2019.

Yamani, Mai. *Changed Identities: The Challenge of the New Generation in Saudi Arabia*. Royal Institute of International Affairs, 2000.

APPENDIX B

GLOSSARY OF KEY TERMS

Abayah: A long and loose black traditional cloak that women are expected to wear in public. It covers the entire body and serves as an outer garment, with other clothes worn underneath.

Adhan: Muslim call for prayer. Performed five times a day by a *muadhdhin* (a title of a person who performs a call for prayer).

Aramco: Aramco, or Saudi Arabian Oil Company, is the state-owned petroleum and natural gas company, with the headquarters in Dhahran. It is one of the biggest oil companies in the world.

Ardha: A traditional Bedouin dance with swords. It is a ceremonial row dance, usually performed by men. In recent decades, it came to function as a performative aspect of one's Bedouin identity. Many Saudi rules regularly participate in public performances of *ardha*.

Bedouins: Nomadic Arab tribal people, who historically occupied the desert regions of the Arabian Peninsula, the Levant, Iraq, Egypt, and North Africa. Their primary occupation was nomadic pastoralism. The word "Bedouin" comes from the Arabic word *badawi* (singular) and *badu* (plural).

Caliph: The ruler of the Islamic Empire, who was simultaneously a political, military, and religious leader. The word comes from the Arabic *khalifah*, which means "successor"—implying that they were successors of Muhammad. The first four caliphs are often called the Righteous Caliphs, as they were from among the earliest followers of Muhammad and his close companions (*sahabah*). Caliphs were ruling the Muslim Empire in Baghdad until 1258, when the city was captured and destroyed by the Mongol armies, and then in Egypt until the Ottomans came in 1517. Following that, the title "Caliph" was held by the Ottoman rulers simultaneously with the title "Sultan," until the former was abolished in 1924 by Ataturk.

Fatwa: A nonbinding legal opinion issued by a qualified Islamic jurist, called a *mufti*. *Fatawa* (the word's plural form) can be issued as a response to a question posed by an individual, a group, or a government body. *Fatwa* is meant to determine the lawfulness or a particular situation or topic, from the Islamic point of view.

Hadar: Sedentary population historically inhabiting towns and oases on the Arabian Peninsula, in contrast to the nomadic Bedouins.

Hadith: A collection comprised of sayings and actions of the Prophet Muhammad. Hadith occupies a central place in Islam, and as a religious text, it is second in importance to Quran. Together with the Sunnah, which is a record of Muhammad's daily practice and customs, Hadith is a major source of guidance for Muslims and constitutes the backbone of the Islamic law (Sharia). The meaning of the word *hadith* in Arabic is "speech" or "record."

Hajj: An annual pilgrimage to Mecca. It is one of the Five Pillars of Islam. All Muslims who are physically and financially able to partake in pilgrimage, are required to do so once in a lifetime. It is also called the Great Pilgrimage, in contrast to *Umrah*, a lesser pilgrimage. The person who has completed the *Hajj* receives the honorary title of *hajj* or *hajji* (for a man) and *hajjah* (for a woman).

Hijab: Women's headscarf. A mandatory covering for Saudi women when they appear in public.

Hijrah: The emigration of Muhammad and his followers from Mecca to Medina, which took place in 622 AD. This event serves as the beginning of the Islamic lunar calendar. The word *hijrah* means "migration" or "emigration" in Arabic.

Ikhtilat: Literally, "mixing." This word is used as a term for intermingling of the sexes. In Saudi Arabia, it is forbidden by law for unrelated men and women to socialize or even just to be in a physical proximity from each other. All public places are required to provide accommodations for gender segregation.

Ikhwan: Literally, "brotherhood." The term refers to the army of Wahhabi warriors who fought under the leadership of Ibn Saud in the early 20th century to unify the Arabian Peninsula under his rule. These warriors previously belonged to Bedouin tribes but, inspired by the religious ideology of Wahhabism, they left their nomadic lifestyle and settled in special settlements called *hujar*. One may also frequently encounter this term used to identify a religious group in Egypt, Ikhwan, or al-Ikhwan al-Muslimeen (the Muslim Brotherhood). This is an entirely different Islamist organization, founded in Ismailiyah, Egypt, in 1928.

Imam: This term is used in a number of Islamic contexts. First, it could mean a leader of the Islamic state or a Muslim community (*ummah*). This title implies both spiritual and political leadership. Secondly, specifically in reference to the history of Saudi Arabia, the title Imam was claimed by the rulers from the House of Saud, from the late

18th century onward. Ibn Saud preferred the title "King," and thus "imam" was no longer used to refer to the country's rulers. Third, imam can be an honorific title given to renowned Islamic scholars. Fourth, for Shia, imam references Ali and all of his descendants who are honored as the leaders of the Islamic world. Finally, this term can simply mean a prayer leader.

Jihad: Literally, "striving" or "struggle." In Islam, this concept has two connotations. The greater jihad refers to the personal spiritual quest of each Muslim to fulfill the ideals and requirements of the Muslim faith. The lesser jihad refers to fighting for the faith. Throughout most of the Islamic history, jihad was used primarily in the first, spiritual meaning of the word. In modern times, however, several reformist Islamic ideologies emphasized the second meaning of the term, the lesser jihad, which implied military action. It is in this second meaning that jihad is currently used in political discourse.

Majlis: Literally, "seating." A traditional gathering or a council, which can have two purposes. It could be a setting where leaders have open meetings with the people who come to seek mediation or help. *Majlis* can also mean a gathering or a party with one's (male) guests. The word is also used to name the part of the house where the *majlis* gathering takes place—which is always an area separate from the rest of the house.

Male Guardianship: A legal system in Saudi Arabia that requires each female, regardless of age, to have a male guardian. The woman's father, husband, brother, or another male relative can be her guardian, and in some cases, this role can even be taken by her son. The guardian is given the authority to make all critical decisions on behalf of the woman, such as to acquire passport and other important documents, to travel abroad, to marry, to take a job, to open a business, and even to choose a field of study. In sum, a Saudi female effectively remains a legal minor throughout her whole life. Only in 2017 did King Salman issue a decree allowing women to access government services without a male guardian's consent. For many years, Saudi women have been protesting against this discriminatory system and demanding its termination.

Mutawwa: Saudi Arabia's religious police. Its official name is the Committee for the Promotion of Virtue and Prevention of Vice. Colloquially, it is also often called *hayah* or the "committee." The *Mutawwa* means "pious" and "volunteer," with the plural form *mutawwiyun*, referencing the fact that membership in this organization is voluntary. The religious police are tasked with monitoring and reinforcing public behaviors according to the strict Wahhabi requirements for moral and modest conduct and gender segregation. Until very recently, they had the power to make arrests. In April 2016, the Saudi government stripped the *Mutawwa* of most of its powers.

OAPEC: The Organization of Arab Petroleum Exporting Countries. This is a multinational organization created with the objective of defining and regulating energy policies among oil-producing Arab states. In its concept, OAPEC is similar to OPEC, with the main distinction that the former is limited to Arab countries producing significant amounts of oil, whereas the latter is open to any significant oil-producing country. OAPEC's headquarters are in Kuwait.

Qasidah: An ancient form of Arabic poetry. The *qasidah*, plural *qasa'id*, emerged among the Bedouin tribes of the Arabian Peninsula in pre-Islamic times. Even in its earliest history, Arabic *qasa'id* had a highly sophisticated system of meter and rhyme. Although many other poetic genres and forms developed in Arabic oral and written literary traditions, *qasidah* persevered throughout its long history into the present.

Qiblah: The orientation of the Muslim prayer toward Mecca. Muslims perform the daily prayers facing that direction.

Quran: The holy book of Islam, the record of the divine revelation received by Muhammad, according to the Islamic tradition. It consists of 114 chapters, or Surahs, of varying lengths. All surahs are categorized as Meccan or Medinan, based on the place of revelation. The revelation is believed to have begun in 610 AD with the first five verses of Surah 96.

Ramadan: The holy month of the Islamic lunar calendar. Muslims are required to fast throughout the whole month of Ramadan (if they are physically able to), where no food or liquid can be consumed during the daylight hours. The fast is broken daily at sunset. The breaking of the fast meal is called *Iftar*.

Saudization: Officially known as Saudi nationalization scheme, made of various labor policies and measures. Its objective is to increase the employment of Saudi nationals in the private sector of the country's economy.

Sawt: Literally means "voice"; a musical genre popular throughout the Arabian Peninsula, featuring a solo male singer and the *'ud*—a traditional string instrument.

Sharia: The system of canonical Islamic law, which is based on the Quran and the traditions of the prophet, namely the Hadith and the Sunnah.

Sharif: Traditional title of the ruler of Mecca. Sharifs were the descendants of Muhammad's tribe, the Quraysh. This position was eliminated by Ibn Saud when he conquered the Hijaz. The title "Sharif" was also used in a more general sense, to refer to a prominent religious or tribal leader. The word *sharif* means "noble," "highborn," and "honorable."

Sheikh: The term of utmost respect, it can be used for an elder of a Bedouin tribe or an Islamic scholar.

Shia Islam: One of the two main denominations in Islam (the other one is Sunni). Shia Muslims believe that the descendants of Ali—Muhammad's cousin and son-in-law, who was the fourth Righteous Caliph—are the rightful leaders of the Muslim community. In contrast to Sunni Islam that emphasizes Muslim customs, Shia place particular importance on the relatives of the prophet (*ahl al-bayt*—"the people of the House").

Sunnah: Sunnah means "habitual practice." It is a compilation of literature that defines social and legal practices and customs of the Muslim community. Together with the Quran and the Hadith, it constitutes a foundation of the Islamic law, Sharia.

Sunni Islam: One of the two main denominations in Islam (the other one is Shia). The name "Sunni" is an adjective of Sunnah, which is a compilation of the prophet's customs and habits. For Sunni Muslims, the fundamental principle of the Muslim faith is to follow the practices and traditions of Muhammad and the first community of Muslims.

Ulama: Islamic scholars who are formally recognized as the guardians, interpreters, and teachers of Islamic law. The word *ulama* means "the learned" and originates from the Arabic word *'ilm* (knowledge). *Ulama* is a broad term and includes various narrower categories of Islamic scholars, such as theologians, teachers, canon lawyers (*muftis*), and judges (*qadis*). *Ulama* can also be used in a narrower sense to indicate a formal government council in various Muslim countries, including Saudi Arabia.

Vision 2030: The latest economic development plan of Saudi Arabia, which aims to reduce the country's dependence on oil, diversify its economy, improve its social infrastructure, and modernize the Saudi society as a whole.

Wahhabism: This revivalist Islamic movement and theological doctrine were conceptualized in the 18th century by Muhammad ibn Abd al-Wahhab (1703–1792). Wahhabism promotes one of the strictest interpretations of Islam. It received the name "Wahhabism" in modern times, whereas the followers of Wahhabism never call themselves "Wahhabi" and consider it a demeaning term. Instead, they refer to themselves as "Salafi" or simply "Muslims." They generally do not accept any other interpretations of Islam as legitimate.

Zakat: Charity; donation of a portion of one's money to the poor. One of the Five Pillars of Islam. In most Muslim countries, it is a voluntary tax, but some countries, including Saudi Arabia, utilize mandatory zakat taxation.

APPENDIX C

FACTS AND FIGURES

Table 1: GEOGRAPHY

Location	Occupying most of the Arabian Peninsula in southwestern Asia, Saudi Arabia is bordered by Iraq, Jordan, and Kuwait to the north, Yemen to the south, Oman to the southeast, and the United Arab Emirates and Qatar to the east. It has a long western coastline on the Red Sea facing Egypt, Sudan, and Ethiopia, and a shorter coastline on the Persian Gulf facing Iran.
Time Zone	8 hours ahead of U.S. Eastern Standard
Land Borders	2,744 miles
Coastline	1,640 miles
Capital	Riyadh
Area	864,869 square miles
Climate	Although most of the country is arid desert, the coastal regions have high humidity with temperatures between 100°F and 120°F in the summer. Temperatures in the interior reach up to 129°F, and some areas go without rainfall for several years. With the exception of mountainous regions, winters are mild.
Land Use	1.6% arable land; 0.4% temporary crops; 0.1% permanent crops; 79.1% permanent meadows and pastures; 0.5% forest land; 18.3% other (2015)
Arable Land	1.6% (2015)
Arable Land Per Capita	0.11 hectares per person (2015)

Table 2: POPULATION

Population	28,572,000 (estimate) (2017)
World Population Rank	46th (2017)
Population Density	13.3 people per square kilometer (2017)
Population Distribution	83.8% urban (2018)
Age Distribution	
0–14	26.10%
15–24	18.57%
25–54	46.86%
55–64	5.03%
65+	3.44% (2017)
Median Age	27.5 years (estimate) (2017)
Population Growth Rate	1.4% per year (estimate) (2018)
Net Migration Rate	–0.5 (estimate) (2018)
Languages	Arabic
Religious Groups	Muslim (100%)

Table 3: HEALTH

Average Life Expectancy	75.7 years (2018)
Average Life Expectancy, Male	73.6 years (2018)
Average Life Expectancy, Female	77.9 years (2018)
Crude Birth Rate	18.2 per 1,000 people (2018)
Crude Death Rate	3.4 per 1,000 people (2018)
Maternal Mortality	16 per 100,000 live births (2013)
Infant Mortality	13 per 1,000 live births (2013)
Doctors	2.6 per 1,000 people (2016)

Table 4: ENVIRONMENT

CO_2 Emissions	19.5 metric tons per capita (2014)
Alternative and Nuclear Energy	0.0% of total energy use (2014)
Threatened Species	434 (2017)
Protected Areas	234,840 square miles (2014)
Total Renewable H_2O Resources per Year	76 (estimate) (2014)

Table 5: ENERGY AND NATURAL RESOURCES

Electric Power Generation	318,000,000,000 kilowatt hours per year (estimate) (2016)
Electric Power Consumption	292,800,000,000 kilowatt hours per year (estimate) (2016)
Nuclear Power Plants	0 (2018)
Crude Oil Production	10,134,000 barrels per day (2017)
Crude Oil Consumption	3,302,000 barrels per day (2017)
Natural Gas Production	103,000,000,000 cubic meters per year (estimate) (2013)
Natural Gas Consumption	103,000,000,000 cubic meters per year (estimate) (2013)
Natural Resources	Petroleum, natural gas, iron ore, gold, copper

Table 6: NATIONAL FINANCES

Currency	Saudi riyal
Total Government Revenues	$185,600,000,000 (estimate) (2017)
Total Government Expenditures	$246,900,000,000 (estimate) (2017)
Budget Deficit	−8.8 (estimate) (2017)
GDP Contribution by Sector	Agriculture: 2.6%; Industry: 44.2%; Services: 53.2% (2017)
External Debt	$212,900,000,000 (estimate) (2017)
Economic Aid Extended	$4,773,290,000 (2011)
Economic Aid Received	$0 (2017)

Table 7: INDUSTRY AND LABOR

Gross Domestic Product (GDP)—Official Exchange Rate	$790,905,000,000 (estimate) (2015)
GDP per Capita	$25,320 (estimate) (2015)
GDP—Purchasing Power Parity (PPP)	$1,773,551,000,000 (estimate) (2017)
GDP (PPP) per Capita	$54,777 (estimate) (2017)
Industry Products	Petroleum products, refined petroleum, petrochemicals, fertilizers, cement, crude steel, plastic products
Agriculture Products	Wheat, dates, tomatoes, barley, watermelons, vegetables, sheep, goats, poultry
Unemployment	5.5% (2016)
Labor Profile	Agriculture: 6.7%; Industry: 21.4%; Services: 71.9% (estimate) (2005)

Table 8: TRADE

Imported Goods	Transportation equipment, machinery, base metals, textiles, chemical products, vegetable products, pearls and precious stones, live animals, scientific instruments, foodstuffs
Total Value of Imports	$136,800,000,000 (estimate) (2017)
Exported Goods	Crude and refined petroleum products, chemicals, resins, plastics, rubber
Total Value of Exports	$231,300,000,000 (estimate) (2017)
Import Partners	China: 15.4%; U.S.: 13.6%; UAE: 6.5%; Germany: 5.8%; Japan: 4.1%; India: 4.1%; South Korea: 4% (2017)
Export Partners	Japan: 12.2%; China: 11.7%; South Korea: 9%; India: 8.9%; U.S.: 8.3%; UAE: 6.7%; Singapore: 4.2% (2017)
Current Account Balance	$4,322,000,000 (estimate) (2017)
Weights and Measures	The metric system is in use.

Table 9: EDUCATION

School System	Primary education in Saudi Arabia begins at the age of 6 and lasts for six years. Students then attend three years of early secondary education, followed by three years of either academic or technical upper secondary education.
Mandatory Education	6 years, from ages 6 to 12
Average Years Spent in School for Current Students	17 (estimate) (2013)
Average Years Spent in School for Current Students, Male	17 (estimate) (2013)
Average Years Spent in School for Current Students, Female	17 (estimate) (2013)
Primary School–Age Children Enrolled in Primary School	3,678,391 (2016)
Primary School–Age Males Enrolled in Primary School	1,894,048 (2016)
Primary School–Age Females Enrolled in Primary School	1,822,115 (2016)
Secondary School–Age Children Enrolled in Secondary School	3,419,441 (estimate) (2016)
Secondary School–Age Males Enrolled in Secondary School	1,951,648 (estimate) (2016)
Secondary School–Age Females Enrolled in Secondary School	1,467,793 (estimate) (2016)
Students per Teacher, Primary School	11.7 (estimate) (2016)
Students per Teacher, Secondary School	11.0 (2016)

Enrollment in Tertiary Education	1,622,441 (2016)
Enrollment in Tertiary Education, Male	829,609 (2016)
Enrollment in Tertiary Education, Female	792,832 (2016)
Literacy	95% (2016)

Table 10: MILITARY

Defense Spending (% of GDP)	10% (2017)
Total Active Armed Forces	251,500 (2015)
Annual Military Expenditures	$63,673,000,000 (2016)
Military Service	Service in the Saudi armed forces is voluntary (2016).

Table 11: TRANSPORTATION

Airports	214 (2013)
Paved Roads	21.0% (2016)
Registered Vehicles	6,599,216 (2015)
Railroads	5,410 miles (2017)
Ports	Major: 11 (including Jeddah, Jizan, Ad Dammam, Ras Tanura, Al Jubayl, Yanbu al Bahr, Duba)

Table 12: COMMUNICATIONS

Facebook Users	18,000,000 (estimate) (2017)
Internet Users	20,768,456 (2016)
Internet Users (% of Population)	74.0% (2016)
Land-Based Telephones in Use	3,637,442 (2016)
Mobile Telephone Subscribers	47,932,521 (2016)

Table 13: RULERS OF SAUDI ARABIA

Ruler	Years of Reign
King Abd al-Aziz Al-Saud (1880–1953), founder of the Saudi state	1932–1953
King Saud ibn Abd al-Aziz Al-Saud (1902–1969)	1953–1964
King Faisal ibn Abd al-Aziz Al-Saud (1906–1975)	1964–1975
King Khalid ibn Abd al-Aziz Al-Saud (1913–1982)	1975–1982
King Fahd ibn Abd al-Aziz Al-Saud (1923–2005)	1982–2005
King Abdullah ibn Abd al-Aziz Al-Saud (1923–2015)	2005–2015
King Salman ibn Abd al-Aziz Al-Saud (b. 1935)	2015 currently

APPENDIX D

HOLIDAYS

Date/Day	Holiday
10th day of Dhu al-Hijjah month of the Islamic lunar calendar	Eid al-Adha (Feast of the Sacrifice), falls on the 10th day of the Hajj pilgrimage and commemorates Abraham's sacrifice. The lunar calendar has a shorter year, and therefore the holiday does not have a fixed date on the Western calendar, but it moves every year.
End of Ramadan month of the Islamic lunar calendar	Eid al-Fitr (Festival of the Breaking of the Fast) concludes the month of Ramadan of the Islamic lunar calendar.
September 23	Saudi National Day. This is the only holiday celebrated using the Western calendar. It marks the formal establishment of the Kingdom of Saudi Arabia in 1932.

Note: In Saudi Arabia, the only formally sanctioned holidays are the two major Islamic holidays, Eid al-Adha and Eid al-Fitr. All non-Islamic holidays are banned, with the exception of Saudi National Day. Even other minor Muslim holidays that are often celebrated in other countries of the region, such as Mawlid al-Nabi (birthday of Prophet Muhammad), are prohibited in accordance with the ultraconservative Wahhabi doctrine.

Selected Bibliography

Aarts, Paul, and Gerd Nonneman. *Saudi Arabia in the Balance: Political Economy, Society, Foreign Affairs*. New York University Press, 2005.

Abd al-Jabbar, Falih, and Hosham Dawod. *Tribes and Power: Nationalism and Ethnicity in the Middle East*. Saqi Books, 2001.

Abdulfattah, Kamal. *Mountain Farmer and Fellah in Asir—Southwest Saudi Arabia: The Conditions of Agriculture in a Traditional Society*. Erlangen, 1981.

Abu-Zinada, A. H. *Protecting the Gulf's Marine Ecosystems from Pollution*. Birkhauser, 2008.

Al Obaida, Abdulaziz, Muhammad Babilli, and Elizabeth Greenberg. *Rub Al Khali: Empty Quarter*. Desert, 2009.

Al Zawad, Faisal. *Climate Change in Saudi Arabia on a Regional Scale: Impacts on Evaporation, Surface Runoff and Soil Moisture*. VDM Verlag Dr. Müller, 2009.

Alangari, Haifa. *The Struggle for Power in Arabia: Ibn Saud, Hussein and Great Britain, 1914–1924*. Ithaca Press, 1998.

Alghafis, Ali. *Universities in Saudi Arabia: Their Role in Science, Technology & Development*. University Press of America, 1992.

Ali, Kecia, and Oliver Leaman. *Islam: The Key Concepts*. Routledge, 2008.

AlMunajjed, Mona. *Women in Saudi Arabia Today*. St. Martin's Press, 1997.

Alshamsi, Mansoor. *Islam and Political Reform in Saudi Arabia: The Quest for Political Change and Reform*. Routledge, 2011.

Alsharhan, A. S. *Hydrogeology of an Arid Region: The Arabian Gulf and Adjoining Areas*. Elsevier, 2001.

Altorki, Soraya. *Women in Saudi Arabia: Ideology and Behavior among the Elite*. Columbia University Press, 1986.

Anderson, Irvine. *Aramco, the United States, and Saudi Arabia: A Study of the Dynamics of Foreign Oil Policy, 1933–1950*. Princeton University Press, 1981.

Antar, Ziad, and Hans Ulrich Obrist. *After Images: Stories from the Mountains of Asir*. KAPH, 2016.

Arabi, Oussama. *Studies in Modern Islamic Law and Jurisprudence*. Kluwer Law International, 2001.

Arebi, Saddeka. *Women and Words in Saudi Arabia: The Politics of Literary Discourse*. Columbia University Press, 1994.

Armstrong, Karen. *Muhammad: A Biography of the Prophet.* Harper San Francisco, 1992.

Armstrong, Karen. *Islam: A Short History.* Modern Library, 2000.

Ayoob, Mohammed, and Hasan Kosebalaban. *Religion and Politics in Saudi Arabia: Wahhabism and the State.* Lynne Rienner, 2009.

al-Azab, M., W. El-Shorbagy, and S. Al-Ghais. *Oil Pollution and Its Environmental Impact in the Arabian Gulf Region.* Elsevier, 2005.

Babar, Zahra, ed. *Arab Migrant Communities in the GCC.* Oxford University Press, 2017.

Bagader, Abubaker, et al. *Assassination of Light: Modern Saudi Short Stories.* Three Continents, 1990.

Bagader, Abubaker, et al. *Voices of Change: Short Stories by Saudi Arabian Women Writers.* Lynne Rienner Publishers, 1998.

Bal, C. *Production Politics and Migrant Labour Regimes: Guest Workers in Asia and the Gulf.* Palgrave Macmillan, 2016.

Beeston, A. F. L. *The Arabic Language Today.* Georgetown University Press, 2006.

Bemert, Gunnar, and Rupert Ormond. *Red Sea Coral Reefs.* Kegan Paul International, 1981.

Bengio, Ofra, and Meir Litvak. *The Sunna and Shi'a in History: Division and Ecumenism in the Muslim Middle East.* Palgrave Macmillan, 2011.

Bennison, Amira K. *The Great Caliphs: The Golden Age of the Abbasid Empire.* Yale University Press, 2009.

Bianchi, Robert. *Guests of God: Pilgrimage and Politics in the Islamic World.* Oxford University Press, 2004.

Bin Hethlain, Naif. *Saudi Arabia and the U.S. since 1962: Allies in Conflict.* Saqi Books, 2010.

Birashk, Ahmad. *A Comparative Calendar of the Iranian, Muslim Lunar, and Christian Eras for Three Thousand Years: 1260 B.H.–2000 A.H./639 B.C.–2621 A.D.* Mazda Publishers, 1993.

Black, Antony. *The History of Islamic Political Thought: From the Prophet to the Present.* Edinburgh University Press, 2011.

Blankinship, Khalid Yahya. *The End of the Jihâd State: The Reign of Hishām Ibn 'abd Al-Malik and the Collapse of the Umayyads.* State University of New York Press, 1994.

Bobrick, Benson. *The Caliph's Splendor: Islam and the West in the Golden Age of Baghdad.* Simon & Schuster, 2012.

Bonney, Richard. *Jihād: From Qur'ān to Bin Laden.* Palgrave Macmillan, 2004.

Bowen, Wayne. *The History of Saudi Arabia.* Greenwood, 2015.

Bower, Tom. *The Squeeze: Oil, Money and Greed in the Twenty-First Century.* Harper, 2009.

Bronson, Rachel. *Thicker Than Oil: America's Uneasy Partnership with Saudi Arabia.* Oxford University Press, 2006.

Brown, Anthony. *Oil, God, and Gold: The Story of Aramco and the Saudi Kings.* Houghton Mifflin, 1999.

Brown, Brian. *Three Testaments: Torah, Gospel, and Quran.* Rowman & Littlefield, 2012.

Buchan, James. *Jeddah: Old and New.* Stacey International, 1996.

Caudill, Mark. *Twilight in the Kingdom: Understanding the Saudis.* Praeger Security International, 2006.

Citino, Nathan. *From Arab Nationalism to OPEC: Eisenhower, King Saʻud, and the Making of U.S.-Saudi Relations.* Indiana University Press, 2002.

Cole, Donald Powell. *Bedouins of the Empty Quarter.* Aldine Transaction, 2010.

Coleman, Robert. *Geologic Evolution of the Red Sea.* Oxford University Press, 1993.

Collie, K. *Spirit of the Wind: The Horse in Saudi Arabia.* Immel, 1982.

Commins, David Dean. *The Wahhabi Mission and Saudi Arabia.* I. B. Tauris, 2006.

Commins, David Dean, and Malise Ruthven. *Islam in Saudi Arabia.* Cornell University Press, 2015.

Cook, David. *Understanding Jihad.* University of California Press, 2015.

Cook, Michael. *Muhammad.* Oxford University Press, 1983.

Cooper, Andrew. *The Oil Kings: How the U.S., Iran, and Saudi Arabia Changed the Balance of Power in the Middle East.* Simon & Schuster, 2011.

Corbin, Henry. *History of Islamic Philosophy.* Kegan Paul International, 1993.

Cordesman, Anthony. *Saudi Arabia: Guarding the Desert Kingdom.* Westview Press, 1997.

Cordesman, Anthony. *Saudi Arabia Enters the Twenty-First Century.* Praeger, 2003.

Cordesman, Anthony, and Nawaf Obaid. *National Security in Saudi Arabia: Threats, Responses, and Challenges.* Praeger Security International, 2005.

Cotran, Eugene. *The Rule of Law in the Middle East and the Islamic World: Human Rights and the Judicial Process.* I. B. Tauris, 2000.

Crone, Patricia. *From Arabian Tribes to Islamic Empire: Army, State and Society in the Near East c. 600–850.* Ashgate, 2008.

Crone, Patricia, and Martin Hinds. *God's Caliph: Religious Authority in the First Centuries of Islam.* Cambridge University Press, 1986.

Cuddihy, Kathy. *Saudi Customs and Etiquette.* Stacey International, 2002.

Daftary, Farhad. *A History of Shi'i Islam.* I. B. Tauris, 2013.

Danforth, Loring. *Crossing the Kingdom: Portraits of Saudi Arabia.* University of California Press, 2016.

Daun, Holger, and Reza Arjmand, eds. *Handbook of Islamic Education.* Springer, 2018.

Davis, Rohan, ed. *Western Imaginings: The Intellectual Contest to Define Wahhabism.* American University in Cairo Press, 2018.

Dehau, Etienne, and Pierre Bonte. *Bedouin and Nomads: Peoples of the Arabian Desert.* Thames & Hudson, 2007.

DeLong-Bas, Natana. *Wahhabi Islam: From Revival and Reform to Global Jihad.* Oxford University Press, 2004.

Déroche, François. *Qur'ans of the Umayyads: A First Overview.* Brill, 2014.

Dupret, Baudouin. *Ethnographies of Islam: Ritual Performances and Everyday Practices.* Edinburgh University Press, 2012.

Durrani, Nadia. *The Tihamah Coastal Plain of South-West Arabia in Its Regional Context, 6000 B.C.–600 A.D.* Archaeopress, 2005.

Edgell, H. Stewart. *Arabian Deserts: Nature, Origin and Evolution.* Springer, 2006.

El-Baz, Farouk, and R. M Makharita. *The Gulf War and the Environment.* Routledge, 2017.

El-Hibri, Tayeb. *Parable and Politics in Early Islamic History: The Rashidun Caliphs.* Columbia University Press, 2010.

El Mallakh, Ragaei, and Dorothea H. El Mallakh. *Saudi Arabia, Energy, Developmental Planning, and Industrialization.* Lexington Books, 1982.

al-Enazy, Askar. *The Long Road from Taif to Jeddah: Resolution of a Saudi-Yemeni Boundary Dispute.* Emirates Center for Strategic Studies and Research, 2005.

Esposito, John. *The Oxford History of Islam.* Oxford University Press, 1999.

Ettinghausen, Richard, Oleg Grabar, and Sheila Blair. *The Art and Architecture of Islam, 650–1250.* Penguin Books, 1987.

Exell, Karen, and Trinidad Rico. *Cultural Heritage in the Arabian Peninsula: Debates, Discourses and Practices.* Ashgate, 2014.

Facey, William. *Riyadh, the Old City: From Its Origins until the 1950s.* IMMEL, 1992.

Facey, William, and Philip Hawkins. *Dir'iyyah and the First Saudi State.* Stacey International, 1997.

Fadaak, Talha, and Kenneth Roberts. *Youth in Saudi Arabia.* Palgrave Macmillan, 2019.

Fandy, Mamoun. *Saudi Arabia and the Politics of Dissent.* St. Martin's Press, 1999.

Fandy, Mamoun. *(Un)civil War of Words: Media and Politics in the Arab World.* Greenwood Press, 2007.

Faroqhi, Suraiya. *Pilgrims and Sultans: The Hajj under the Ottomans, 1517–1683.* I. B. Tauris, 1994.

Farsi, Hani M. S. *Jeddah, City of Art: The Sculptures and Monuments.* Stacey International, 1991.

Farsy, Fouad. *Modernity and Tradition: The Saudi Equation.* Kegan Paul International, 1990.

Fisher, Greg, ed. *Arabs and Empires before Islam.* Oxford University Press, 2015.

Foley, Sean. *Changing Saudi Arabia: Art, Culture, and Society in the Kingdom.* Lynne Rienner Publishers, 2019.

Frishkopf, Michael, and Federico Spinetti, eds. *Music, Sound, and Architecture in Islam.* University of Texas Press, 2018.

al-Gailani, Noorah, and Chris Smith. *The Islamic Year: Surahs, Stories and Celebrations.* Hawthorn Press, 2002.

Galaty, John, and Philip Carl Salzman. *Change and Development in Nomadic and Pastoral Societies.* Brill, 1981.

George, Alain. *The Rise of Islamic Calligraphy.* Saqi Books, 2010.

George, Alain, and Andrew Marsham, eds. *Power, Patronage, and Memory in Early Islam: Perspectives on Umayyad Elites.* Oxford University Press, 2018.

al-Ghadeer, Moneera. *Desert Voices: Bedouin Women's Poetry in Saudi Arabia.* Tauris Academic Studies, 2009.

Gharipour, Mohammad, and Schick Irvin Cemil. *Calligraphy and Architecture in the Muslim World.* Edinburgh University Press, 2013.

Ginat, J., and Anatoly M. Khazanov. *Changing Nomads in a Changing World.* Sussex Academic Press, 1998.

Ginena, Karim, and Azhar Hamid. *Foundations of Shari'ah Governance of Islamic Banks*. John Wiley & Sons, 2015.

Gordon, Matthew. *The Rise of Islam*. Greenwood Press, 2005.

Gray, Matthew. *Global Security Watch—Saudi Arabia*. Praeger, 2014.

Gruendler, Beatrice. *The Development of the Arabic Scripts: From the Nabatean Era to the First Islamic Century According to Dated Texts*. Scholars Press, 1993.

Habib, John. *Ibn Sa'ud's Warriors of Islam: The Ikhwan of Najd and Their Role in the Creation of the Sa'udi Kingdom, 1910–1930*. Brill, 1978.

Hafez, Kai, and David Paletz. *Mass Media, Politics, and Society in the Middle East*. Hampton Press, 2001.

Halevi, Leor. *Muhammad's Grave: Death Rites and the Making of Islamic Society*. Columbia University Press, 2007.

Hamdan, Amani, ed. *Teaching and Learning in Saudi Arabia: Perspectives from Higher Education*. Sense, 2015.

Hammond, Andrew. *The Islamic Utopia: The Illusion of Reform in Saudi Arabia*. Pluto Press, 2012.

Hammond, Philip. *The Nabataeans: Their History, Culture and Archaeology*. P. Åström (S. vägen 61), 1973.

Hammoudi, Abdellah, and Pascale Ghazaleh. *A Season in Mecca: Narrative of a Pilgrimage*. Hill & Wang, 2006.

Hanieh, Adam. *Money, Markets, and Monarchies: The Gulf Cooperation Council and the Political Economy of the Contemporary Middle East*. Cambridge University Press, 2018.

Hart, Parker. *Saudi Arabia and the United States: Birth of a Security Partnership*. Indiana University Press, 1998.

Hatina, Meir. *Guardians of Faith in Modern Times: 'Ulama' in the Middle East*. Brill, 2009.

Hawker, Ronald. *Traditional Architecture of the Arabian Gulf: Building on Desert Tides*. WIT, 2008.

Hawley, T. M. *Against the Fires of Hell: The Environmental Disaster of the Gulf War*. Harcourt Brace Jovanovich, 1992.

Hawting, G. R. *The First Dynasty of Islam: The Umayyad Caliphate AD 661–750*. Routledge, 2000.

al-Hazimi, Mansour, Salma Khadra Jayyusi, and Ezzat Khattab, eds. *Beyond the Dunes: An Anthology of Modern Saudi Literature*. I. B. Tauris, 2006.

Hazleton, Lesley. *After the Prophet: The Epic Story of the Shia-Sunni Split in Islam*. 1st ed. Doubleday, 2009.

Healey, John. *The Religion of the Nabataeans: A Conspectus*. Brill, 2001.

Heer, Nicholas, and Farhat Jacob. *Islamic Law and Jurisprudence*. University of Washington Press, 1990.

Hefner, Robert. *Shari'a Politics: Islamic Law and Society in the Modern World*. Indiana University Press, 2011.

Hefner, Robert, and Muhammad Qasim Zaman. *Schooling Islam: The Culture and Politics of Modern Muslim Education*. Princeton University Press, 2007.

Hegghammer, Thomas. *Jihad in Saudi Arabia: Violence and Pan-Islamism since 1979.* Cambridge University Press, 2010.

Hertog, Steffen. *Princes, Brokers, and Bureaucrats: Oil and the State in Saudi Arabia.* Cornell University Press, 2010.

Hilden, Joy. *Bedouin Weaving of Saudi Arabia and Its Neighbours.* Arabian Publishing, 2010.

Hoigilt, Jacob, and Gunvor Mejdell, eds. *The Politics of Written Language in the Arab World: Writing Change.* Brill, 2017.

Holes, Clive. *Dialect, Culture, and Society in Eastern Arabia: Ethnographic Texts.* Brill, 2005.

House, Karen. *On Saudi Arabia: Its People, Past, Religion, Fault Lines—and Future.* Alfred A. Knopf, 2012.

Hoyland, Robert. *Arabia and the Arabs: From the Bronze Age to the Coming of Islam.* Routledge, 2001.

Hunt-Ahmed, Karen. *Contemporary Islamic Finance: Innovations, Applications, and Best Practices.* John Wiley & Sons, 2013.

Ibrahim, Fouad. *The Shi'is of Saudi Arabia.* Saqi Books, 2006.

Inamdar, Subhash. *Muhammad and the Rise of Islam: The Creation of Group Identity.* Psychosocial Press, 2001.

Ingham, Bruce. *Bedouin of Northern Arabia: Traditions of the Al-Dhafir.* KPI, 1986.

Ingham, Bruce. *Najdi Arabic: Central Arabian.* J. Benjamins Publishing, 1994.

Ingham, Bruce. *Arabian Diversions: Studies on the Dialects of Arabia.* Ithaca Press, 1997.

Ismail, Muhammad, and Damluji Salma Samar. *The Architecture of the Prophet's Holy Mosque, Al Madinah.* Hazar, 1998.

Izraeli, S. *Politics and Society in Saudi Arabia: The Crucial Years of Development, 1960–1982.* C. Hurst, 2012.

Jabbur, Jibrail Sulayman, et al. *The Bedouins and the Desert: Aspects of Nomadic Life in the Arab East.* State University of New York Press, 1995.

Jain, Prakash, and Ginu Zacharia Oommen, eds. *South Asian Migration to Gulf Countries: History, Policies, Development.* Routledge, Taylor & Francis Group, 2016.

Jamal, Ahmad, et al., eds. *Islamic Tourism: Management of Travel Destinations.* CABI, 2018.

Jones, Toby Craig. *Desert Kingdom: How Oil and Water Forged Modern Saudi Arabia.* Harvard University Press, 2010.

Jordan, Ann. *The Making of a Modern Kingdom: Globalization and Change in Saudi Arabia.* Waveland Press, 2011.

Joseph, Suad, ed. *Gender and Citizenship in the Middle East.* Syracuse University Press, 2000.

Joseph, Suad, and Susan Slyomovics, eds. *Women and Power in the Middle East.* University of Pennsylvania Press, 2001.

al-Juhany, Uwidah Metaireek, and Darat al-Malik Abd al-Aziz. *Najd before the Salafi Reform Movement: Social, Political, and Religious Conditions during the Three Centuries Preceding the Rise of the Saudi State.* Ithaca Press, 2002.

Kahn, Tamam. *Untold: A History of the Wives of Prophet Muhammad.* Monkfish Book Publishing, 2010.

Kazan, Fayad. *Mass Media, Modernity, and Development: Arab States of the Gulf.* Praeger, 1993.

Keay, John. *The Spice Route: A History.* University of California Press, 2006.

Kechichian, Joseph. *Succession in Saudi Arabia.* Palgrave, 2001.

Kechichian, Joseph. *From Alliance to Union: Challenges Facing Gulf Cooperation Council States.* Sussex Academic Press, 2016.

Kelly, Kathleen, and R. T. Schnadelbach. *Landscaping the Saudi Arabian Desert.* Delancey Press, 1976.

Kennedy, Hugh. *When Baghdad Ruled the Muslim World: The Rise and Fall of Islam's Greatest Dynasty.* Da Capo Press, 2005.

al-Khalili, Jim. *Pathfinders: The Golden Age of Arabic Science.* Allen Lane, 2010.

Khalili, Nasser D. *Islamic Art and Culture: A Visual History.* Overlook Press, 2005.

King, G. R. D. *The Traditional Architecture of Saudi Arabia.* I. B. Tauris, 1998.

Kirkby, Bruce. *Sand Dance: By Camel across Arabia's Great Southern Desert.* McClelland & Stewart, 2000.

Korstanje, Maximiliano, ed. *Risk and Safety Challenges for Religious Tourism and Events.* CABI, 2018.

Kostiner, Joseph, et al. *The Making of Saudi Arabia, 1916–1936: From Chieftaincy to Monarchical State.* Oxford University Press, 1993.

Kurpershoek, P. M. *Oral Poetry and Narratives from Central Arabia.* Brill, 1994.

Kurpershoek, P. M. *Arabia of the Bedouins.* Saqi Books, 2001.

Lacey, Robert. *Inside the Kingdom: Kings, Clerics, Modernists, Terrorists, and the Struggle for Saudi Arabia.* Viking, 2009.

Langermann, Y. Tzvi. *Avicenna and His Legacy: A Golden Age of Science and Philosophy.* Brepols, 2009.

Lassner, Jacob. *Jews, Christians, and the Abode of Islam: Modern Scholarship, Medieval Realities.* University of Chicago Press, 2012.

Le Renard Amélie. *A Society of Young Women: Opportunities of Place, Power, and Reform in Saudi Arabia.* Stanford University Press, 2014.

Lecker, Michael. *Jews and Arabs in Pre- and Early Islamic Arabia.* Ashgate, 1999.

Lecker, Michael. *People, Tribes, and Society in Arabia around the Time of Muhammad.* Ashgate, 2005.

Lippman, Thomas. *Inside the Mirage: America's Fragile Partnership with Saudi Arabia.* Westview Press, 2004.

London Middle East Institute, and Gulf Cooperation Council. *The Gulf Family: Kinship Policies and Modernity.* Saqi in Association with London Middle East Institute, SOAS, 2007.

Long, David E. *Culture and Customs of Saudi Arabia.* Greenwood Press, 2005.

Long, David E., and Sebastian Maisel. *The Kingdom of Saudi Arabia.* University Press of Florida, 2010.

Maddy-Weitzman, Bruce. *A Century of Arab Politics: From the Arab Revolt to the Arab Spring.* Rowman & Littlefield, 2016.

Maisel, Sebastian, and John A. Shoup III. *Saudi Arabia and the Gulf Arab States Today: An Encyclopedia of Life in the Arab States*. ABC-CLIO, 2009.

Makki, M. S. *Medina, Saudi Arabia: A Geographic Analysis of the City and Region*. Bucks, Avebury, 1982.

Mandaville, James. *Flora of Eastern Saudi Arabia*. Taylor & Francis, 2013.

Mansour, Nasser, and Saeed Al-Shamrani, eds. *Science Education in the Arab Gulf States: Visions, Sociocultural Contexts and Challenges*. Sense, 2015.

Matthiesen, Toby. *Sectarian Gulf: Bahrain, Saudi Arabia, and the Arab Spring That Wasn't*. Stanford Briefs, an Imprint of Stanford University Press, 2013.

Matthiesen, Toby. *The Other Saudis: Shiism, Dissent and Sectarianism*. Cambridge University Press, 2015.

al-Mazrouei, Noura Saber. *The UAE and Saudi Arabia: Border Disputes and International Relations in the Gulf*. I. B. Tauris, 2016.

Mazuz, Haggai. *The Religious and Spiritual Life of the Jews of Medina*. Brill, 2014.

McLoughlin, Leslie J. *Ibn Saud: Founder of a Kingdom*. St. Martin's Press, 1993.

McMillan, M. E. *The Meaning of Mecca: The Politics of Pilgrimage in Early Islam*. Saqi Books, 2011.

McMurray, David A., and Amanda Ufheil-Somers, eds. *The Arab Revolts: Dispatches on Militant Democracy in the Middle East*. Indiana University Press, 2013.

McNally, Robert. *Crude Volatility: The History and the Future of Boom-Bust Oil Prices*. Columbia University Press, 2017.

Ménoret, Pascal. *The Saudi Enigma: A History*. Zed Books, 2005.

Ménoret, Pascal. *Joyriding in Riyadh: Oil, Urbanism, and Road Revolt*. Cambridge University Press, 2014.

Mernissi, Fatima. *The Veil and the Male Elite: A Feminist Interpretation of Women's Rights in Islam*. Addison-Wesley Publishing, 1991.

Metz, Helen Chapin. *Saudi Arabia: A Country Study*. Federal Research Division, Library of Congress, 1993.

Monferrer Sala, Juan Pedro. *Redefining History on Pre-Islamic Accounts: The Arabic Recension of the Martyrs of Najrân*. Gorgias Press, 2010.

Morton, Michael. *Buraimi: The Struggle for Power, Influence and Oil in Arabia*. I. B. Tauris, 2013.

Mouline, Nabil. *The Clerics of Islam: Religious Authority and Political Power in Saudi Arabia*. Translated by Ethan S. Rundell. Yale University Press, 2014.

Muaikil, Khalil Ibrahim. *Study of the Archaeology of the Jawf Region, Saudi Arabia*. King Fahd National Library, 1994.

Munif, Abd al-Rahman, and Peter Theroux. *Cities of Salt: A Novel*. Random House, 1987.

Munt, Harry. *The Holy City of Medina: Sacred Space in Early Islamic Arabia*. Cambridge University Press, 2014.

Murata, Sachiko, and William Chittick. *The Vision of Islam*. Paragon House, 1994.

Musayqar, Abd al-Rahman. *Traditional Foods in the Arabian Gulf Countries*. FAO/RNEA, 1993.

Muslu, Cihan Yüksel. *The Ottomans and the Mamluks: Imperial Diplomacy and Warfare in the Islamic World*. I. B. Tauris, 2014.

Nahouza, Namira. *Wahhabism and the Rise of the New Salafists: Theology, Power and Sunni Islam*. I. B. Tauris, 2018.

Nasr, Seyyed Hossein, and Kazuyoshi Nomachi. *Mecca the Blessed, Medina the Radiant: The Holiest Cities of Islam*. Turtle Publishing, 2017.

Nasr, Seyyed Vali Reza. *The Shia Revival: How Conflicts within Islam Will Shape the Future*. W. W. Norton, 2007.

Nicholson, Eleanor. *In the Footsteps of the Camel: A Portrait of the Bedouins of Eastern Saudi Arabia in Mid-Century*. Transworld Arabian Library, 1983.

Nicolle, David. *Historical Atlas of the Islamic World*. Mercury Books, 2004.

Nigosian, S. A. *Islam: Its History, Teaching, and Practices*. Indiana University Press, 2004.

Ochsenwald, William. *The Hijaz Railroad*. University Press of Virginia, 1980.

Owens, Jonathan. *A Linguistic History of Arabic*. Oxford University Press, 2006.

Pampanini, Andrea. *Cities from the Arabian Desert: The Building of Jubail and Yanbu in Saudi Arabia*. Praeger, 1997.

Parker, Chad. *Making the Desert Modern: Americans, Arabs, and Oil on the Saudi Frontier, 1933–1973*. University of Massachusetts Press, 2015.

Parker, Jessie. *A Taste of Arabia*. Jerboa, 2010.

Pesce, A., and E. Garbato Pesce. *Marvel of the Desert: The Camel in Saudi Arabia*. IMMEL, 1984.

Peters, F. E. *The Hajj: The Muslim Pilgrimage to Mecca and the Holy Places*. Princeton University Press, 1994.

Peters, F. E. *The Arabs and Arabia on the Eve of Islam*. Ashgate, 1999.

Petraglia, M. D., and Jeffrey Rose. *The Evolution of Human Populations in Arabia: Paleoenvironments, Prehistory and Genetics*. Springer, 2009.

Power, Timothy. *The Red Sea from Byzantium to the Caliphate: A.D. 500–1000*. American University in Cairo Press, 2012.

Prochazka, Theodore. *Saudi Arabian Dialects*. Kegan Paul International, 1988.

Quraishi, Asifa, and Frank E. Vogel. *The Islamic Marriage Contract: Case Studies in Islamic Family Law*. Islamic Legal Studies Program, Harvard Law School, 2008.

Raj, Razaq, and Kevin Griffin, eds. *Religious Tourism and Pilgrimage Management: An International Perspective*. CABI, 2015.

Ramady, M. A. *The Saudi Arabian Economy: Policies, Achievements and Challenges*. Springer, 2010.

Rapoport, Yossef. *Marriage, Money and Divorce in Medieval Islamic Society*. Cambridge University Press, 2005.

al-Rasheed, Madawi, ed. *Politics in an Arabian Oasis: Rashidis of Saudi Arabia*. I. B. Tauris, 1992.

al-Rasheed, Madawi, ed. *Contesting the Saudi State: Islamic Voices from a New Generation*. Cambridge University Press, 2007.

al-Rasheed, Madawi, ed. *A Most Masculine State: Gender, Politics and Religion in Saudi Arabia*. Cambridge University Press, 2013.

al-Rasheed, Madawi, ed. *Salman's Legacy: The Dilemmas of a New Era in Saudi Arabia*. Oxford University Press, 2018.

Reynolds, Dwight. *Arab Folklore: A Handbook*. Greenwood Press, 2007.

Rice, Michael. *The Archaeology of the Arabian Gulf, c. 5000–323 B.C.* Routledge, 1994.

Rich, Ben. *Securitising Identity: The Case of the Saudi State*. MUP Academic, 2017.

Riedel, Bruce. *Kings and Presidents: Saudi Arabia and the United States since FDR*. Brookings Institution Press, 2018.

Rihan, Mohammad. *The Politics and Culture of an Umayyad Tribe: Conflict and Factionalism in the Early Islamic Period*. I. B. Tauris, 2014.

Rodgers, Russ. *The Generalship of Muhammad: Battles and Campaigns of the Prophet of Allah*. University Press of Florida, 2012.

Rogerson, Barnaby. *The Heirs of Muhammad: Islam's First Century and the Origins of the Sunni-Shia Split*. Overlook Press, 2007.

Ross, Heather. *The Art of Bedouin Jewellery: A Saudi Arabian Profile*. Arabesque, 1989.

Rugh, William. *Arab Mass Media: Newspapers, Radio and Television in Arab Politics*. Greenwood, 2004.

Ryad, Umar, ed. *The Hajj and Europe in the Age of Empire*. Brill, 2017.

Safran, Nadav. *Saudi Arabia: The Ceaseless Quest for Security*. Belknap Press of Harvard University Press, 1985.

Samin, Nadav. *Of Sand or Soil: Genealogy and Tribal Belonging in Saudi Arabia*. Princeton University Press, 2015.

Sardar, Ziauddin. *Mecca: The Sacred City*. Bloomsbury, 2014.

Scott, Noel, and Jafar Jafari. *Tourism in the Muslim World*. Emerald, 2010.

Serageldin, Ismail, and James Steele. *Architecture of the Contemporary Mosque*. Academy Editions, 1996.

Shiloah, Amnon. *Music in the World of Islam: A Socio-Cultural Study*. Wayne State University Press, 1995.

Shoult, Anthony. *Doing Business with Saudi Arabia*. Kogan Page, 2002.

Simmons, Matthew R. *Twilight in the Desert: The Coming Saudi Oil Shock and the World Economy*. John Wiley & Sons, 2005.

Simons, G. L. *Saudi Arabia: The Shape of a Client Feudalism*. St. Martin's Press, 1998.

Sonbol, Amira El Azhary. *Women, the Family, and Divorce Laws in Islamic History*. Syracuse University Press, 1996.

Soucek, Svatopluk. *The Persian Gulf: Its Past and Present*. Mazda, 2008.

Spuler, Bertold. *The Age of the Caliphs*. Markus Wiener, 1995.

Steinmetz, George. *Empty Quarter: A Photographic Journey to the Heart of the Arabian Desert*. Abrams, 2009.

Stephenson, Marcus, and Ala Al-Hamarneh, eds. *International Tourism Development and the Gulf Cooperation Council States: Challenges and Opportunities*. Routledge, 2017.

Stillman, Yedida, and Norman Stillman. *Arab Dress: A Short History: From the Dawn of Islam to Modern Times*. Rev. Brill, 2003.

Strathern, Andrew, and Pamela Stewart. *Contesting Rituals: Islam and Practices of Identity-Making*. Carolina Academic Press, 2005.

Sudayri, Abd al-Rahman. *The Desert Frontier of Arabia: Al-Jawf through the Ages*. Stacey International, 1995.

Suhail, Mohammad. *Introduction to General Geography and Water Resources of Saudi Arabia*. LAP Lambert Academic Publishing, 2016.

Suleiman, Yasir. *The Arabic Language and National Identity: A Study in Ideology*. Georgetown University Press, 2003.

Taylor, Jane. *Petra and the Lost Kingdom of the Nabataeans*. I. B. Tauris, 2001.

Teitelbaum, Joshua. *The Rise and Fall of the Hashimite Kingdom of Arabia*. New York University Press, 2001.

Thompson, Andrew. *Origins of Arabia*. Fitzroy Dearbourn, 2000.

Tønnessen, Liv. *Women's Activism in Saudi Arabia: Male Guardianship and Sexual Violence*. Chr. Michelsen Institute, 2016.

Topham, John, et al. *Traditional Crafts of Saudi Arabia*. Stacey International, 2005.

Trofimov, Yaroslav. *The Siege of Mecca: The 1979 Uprising at Islam's Holiest Shrine*. Anchor Books, 2008.

Turner, John. *Inquisition in Early Islam: The Competition for Political and Religious Authority in the Abbasid Empire*. I. B. Tauris, 2013.

Upton, Peter. *The Arabian Horse: History, Mystery and Magic*. Thames & Hudson, 2005.

Urkevich, Lisa. *Music and Traditions of the Arabian Peninsula: Saudi Arabia, Kuwait, Bahrain, and Qatar*. Routledge, 2015.

Vasil'ev, A. M. *The History of Saudi Arabia*. Saqi Books, 1998.

Vincent, Peter. *Saudi Arabia: An Environmental Overview*. Taylor & Francis, 2008.

Wagner, Walter. *Opening the Qur'an: Introducing Islam's Holy Book*. University of Notre Dame Press, 2008.

Wald, Ellen. *Saudi, Inc.: The Arabian Kingdom's Pursuit of Profit and Power*. Pegasus Books, 2018.

Walker, Philip. *Behind the Lawrence Legend: The Forgotten Few Who Shaped the Arab Revolt*. Oxford University Press, 2018.

Watt, W. Montgomery. *Muhammad: Prophet and Statesman*. Oxford University Press, 1974.

Weeks, Lloyd R., ed. *Death and Burial in Arabia and Beyond: Multidisciplinary Perspectives*. Archaeopress, 2010.

Weston, Mark. *Prophets and Princes: Saudi Arabia from Muhammad to the Present*. John Wiley & Sons, 2008.

Wick, Alexis. *The Red Sea: In Search of Lost Space*. University of California Press, 2016.

Wilson, Peter, and Douglas Graham. *Saudi Arabia: The Coming Storm*. M. E. Sharpe, 1994.

Wolfe, Michael. *One Thousand Roads to Mecca: Ten Centuries of Travelers Writing about the Muslim Pilgrimage*. Grove Press, 1997.

Wynbrandt, James. *A Brief History of Saudi Arabia*. Facts on File, 2010.

Yamani, Hani. *To Be a Saudi*. Janus Publishing, 1997.

Yamani, Maha. *Polygamy and Law in Contemporary Saudi Arabia*. Ithaca Press, 2008.

Yamani, Mai. *Changed Identities: The Challenge of the New Generation in Saudi Arabia*. Royal Institute of International Affairs, 2000.

Yamani, Mai. *Cradle of Islam: The Hijaz and the Quest for an Arabian Identity*. I. B. Tauris, 2004.

al-Yousef, Yousef Khalifa. *The Gulf Cooperation Council States: Hereditary Succession, Oil and Foreign Powers*. Saqi Books, 2017.

Zahran, M. A., and Francis S. Gilbert. *Climate—Vegetation: Afro-Asian Mediterranean and Red Sea Coastal Lands*. Springer, 2010.

Zarabozo, Jamaal al-Din. *The Life, Teachings and Influence of Muhammad Ibn Abdul-Wahhaab*. International Islamic Publishing House, 2010.

al-Ziad Aseeri, Ahmed Mater. *Sculptures of Jeddah: Twentieth-Century Sculpture in the Arabian Peninsula*. Booth-Clibborn Editions, 2015.

Zuhur, Sherifa. *Saudi Arabia*. ABC-CLIO, 2011.

Index

Note: Page numbers in *italic* indicate photographs; page numbers followed by *t* indicate tables.

Abbasids, 36–37, 63, 142, 144–145, 242, 253, 273; Golden age of culture and, 43, 207–208, 227; history, 20, 29, 32, 49–50, 66–67

Abd al-Aziz ibn Saud, xiii, 33–34, 38, 44, 85, 93, 95, 116, 158, 332–334; House of Saud and, 89, 11, 155–156; Ikhwan and, 44, 46, 82, 138 (*see also* Ikhwan); relations with the United States and, 44–45, 91–92; role in establishment of Kingdom of Saudi Arabia, 13, 29, 50, 64–65, 70, 130, 151, 161; role in oil industry, 39, 45, 110

Abdelrahman Munif, 228, 229–230, 234

Abdullah ibn Abd al-Aziz Al Saud (King Abdullah), 35, 65, 71, 141, 156, 187, 254, 341*t*; political and economic reforms, 47–48, 73, 87, 89; role in education, 48, 109, 118–119, 190, 195, 198–199; women's rights, 83, 87, 104, 167, 185

Abraj al-Bait, 16–17, 242, 243–245

Abu Bakr (1st Caliph), 31, 52, 59–60, 61

Abu Talib, 30, 51–52, 61

Adnan (tribal branch), 148, 150, 158

Agriculture: modern industry, 2–4, 7, 100–102, 116, 200; role in history, 18–19, 46–47, 160, 277–278. *See also* Hadar

Aishah (prophet Muhammad's wife), 31, 59–60

Ajman (tribe), 148–149, 157, 212

Ali ibn Abi Talib (4th Caliph), 31, 59, 61, 161, 333, 335; Shia ideology and, 60, 66, 131, 142–143

Arab League. *See* League of Arab States

Arab Revolt, 33, 37–38, 51, 126

Arab Spring, 35, 71–73, 92, 141, 316

Arabian Gulf. *See* Persian Gulf

Arabic language, 193, 200, 234, 235, 238, 307–309; dialects, 209–210, 211–213; history of, 66, 203–204; role in Islam, 196, 206–207, 215, 228, 247

Aramco, 10–11, 33–34, 36, 108, 114–115, 331; education and social programs, 118, 191, 193–194; oil industry and, 8, 22, 39–40, 110–111 (*see also* Oil industry); political role of, 6, 39; Shia community and, 7, 111; women's issues and, 171, 178

Architecture, 55, 199, 247; modernization, 26, 163, 254–255; traditional, 206–207, 241–242, 253–254, 257–259

Ardha, 264–266, 331

Asir, 71, 82, 164, 250, 257–258, 260, 264, 269–270; geography, 1–3, 7, 10, 13, 29, 278; historical significance, 40, 46, 50, 155–156; relations with Yemen and, 5, 24; tourism, 122–123

Ataturk, 144, 331

Ayyubids, 145, 161

Baghdad, 4, 32, 34, 53, 112, 229, 247; role in Abbasid empire, 20, 36–37, 43, 49, 63, 67, 207–208, 273, 331

Bahrain, 30, 100, 158, 203, 210, 213, 230, 236; culture, 222, 267; geography and resources, 21–22, 57, 110; political relations with, 35, 71–72, 78, 112–113; religious communities, 139, 143

Banu Tamim (tribe), 157–158

Basic Law of Saudi Arabia, 35, 71, 75–76, 89–90, 313

Battle of the Trench, 31, 62, 158
Battle of Uhud, 18, 31, 61–62
Bedouins, xiv–xv, 10, 220, 229, 241–242, 269, 331, 332, 334; Arabic language and, 204–205, 211–212; crafts of, 245–246, 256; customs and culture of, 217–220, 260, 263–264, 266, 277–278, 279, 295–296, 297–298; history of, 11–12, 16, 19, 37–38, 50; Ikhwan movement, 44, 46, 64; Islam and, 52; poetry of, 227–228, 232–233; pre-Islamic society and, 16, 52, 57–58, 149–152, 159; society of and tribal relations among, 148, 157–158, 160, 162, 186, 254
Bukharis, 153, 278, 288
Buraydah, 19, 123, 158, 236
Byzantine, 31, 58, 59, 145

Cairo, 32, 38, 49–50, 63, 139, 208, 230–231, 267, 298
Calligraphy, 206–209, 241–242, 246–250
Camel, 100–101, 135, 151, 256, 263, 277–279, 282, 284; domestication of, 30, 57, 150; racing of, 268–269, 292–294, 325–326
Censorship, 79–81, 228, 243, 307–312, 313–317; in literature, 231, 234, 238; religious authorities and, 234, 322
Cinema, xiv, 35, 297, 309–310, 322
Coffee, 2, 4, 181, 204, 269, 277, 279–281, 287, 324; coffeeshop culture, 291, 298–301, 328; religious customs and, 96
Committee for the Promotion of Virtue and the Prevention of Vice. *See Mutawwa*

Dates (fruit), 19, 26, 56, 100–101, 277–279, 288–289, 339*t*; cultural importance of, 132, 281, 287
Deserts: environment issues, 9–11; geography, 1–3, 6–7, 11–12, 20, 121; impact on society, 19, 26, 57, 211, 232, 256–257
Dhahran, 7–8, 23, 34, 110, 115, 164, 193–194, 197, 331. *See also* Aramco
Diriyah Emirate, 32, 40–42, 53, 122, 155
Dress codes, 96, 135, 165, 173–174, 218–220, 250, 259–260, 332
Driving ban, xv, 35, 87, 109, 167, 171, 181, 186, 222; activism against, 80, 83, 86, 166, 187–188

Eastern Arabia, 2, 7, 10, 26, 29, 36, 42, 64, 213
Education, xiii, 69, 72, 81, 122, 147, 170, 176, 189–190, 340–341*t*; government investment in, 47–48, 102–103, 117–119, 127, 317; post-secondary, 48, 109, 154, 192–194, 196–199; role of religious authorities in, 71, 73, 90, 195–196; secondary, 200; in sports, 293, 303, 305; of women, 87, 94–95, 167, 171, 184, 186, 191–192, 235
Egypt, 198, 203–204, 210, 229–231, 293, 304, 331, 332, 337*t*; cultural influences, 225, 234, 256, 258, 309, 319–320; geography, 1, 25, 149; historical role, 14, 31–32, 105, 144–145, 227; influences on Saudi cuisine, 287, 289, 298–299; influences on Saudi music, 263, 267, 270, 274; migrant workers from, 108, 147, 152, 190, 192, 213, 250, 318; Ottoman Empire and, 41–42, 49, 155; political relations with, 4, 34, 56, 79, 112–113, 156
Eid al-Adha, 133, 135–136, 224, 288, 343*t*
Eid al-Fitr, 136, 224–225, 343*t*
Elections, 35, 71–72, 82–83, 87, 141, 167, 185

Fahd ibn Abd al-Aziz Al Saud (King Fahd), 34–35, 47, 65, 156, 231, 253, 341*t*; political reforms, 71, 75, 89
Faisal ibn Abd al-Aziz Al Saud (King Faisal), 34, *91*, 95, 190–192, 197, 222, 341*t*
Falconry, 20, 151, 268, 292, 294–296
Fatimids, 14, 29, 32, 63, 161, 225, 247
Fatwa, xiii, 73, 93–94, 96, 237, 254, 320, 331–332 (*see also* Ulama); women's rights and, 71, 165, 167, 174, 186
fiqh (Islamic jurisprudence), 43, 75, 195
fitna (dissent), 173, 186
fitna (Muslim Civil War), 31–32, 60, 66
Freedom of speech. *See* Censorship

Gamal Abdel Nasser, 34, 229
GCC (Gulf Cooperation Council), 34, 138, 313, 315; economic relations with, 79, 107, 120–121, 127; political relations with, 4–5, 78–79, 91, 175
Gender segregation (anti-*ikhtilat* policy), 83, 165, 174, 192, 221, 223, 291, 332; architecture and, 163, 255; impact on workplace, 117, 171–172; *mutawwa* and, 178

Ghazi al-Gosaibi, 230–231
Golf, 122, 296–297
Great Britain (United Kingdom): Arab Revolt and, 33, 37–38; political relations with, 64, 47, 84, 86, 113, 156, 198, 231
Great Mosque in Mecca (Grand Mosque), 16, 47, 133, 244–245, 252–254; 1979 Siege of, 34, 65, 86, 94, 167, 235, 250, 309, 313
Guardianship (of women), xv, 80, 88, 109, 165–166, 170, 172–173, 253, 333
Gulf War, 5, 8–9, 34, 66, 94, 103, 113, 186, 319

Hadar, 148–151, 160, 162, 332
Hadith, 52, 61, 140, 253, 332; Islamic jurisprudence and, 71, 75, 144, 334–335; role in culture and education, 134, 180, 191, 196, 219, 232
Hail, 19, 71, 82, 187
Hajj (Muslim pilgrimage): customs of, 259, 272; history of, 34, 43, 63, 65, 173, 224 (*see also* Islam; Kaaba; Mecca); impact on Saudi economy, 15, 48, 100, 115, 135, 253; religious doctrine, 13–14, 16, 52, 130, 132–134, 332, 343*t*
Harb (tribe), 148–149, 157–158
Al-Hasa. *See* Eastern Arabia
Hasan ibn Ali, 63, 66, 131, 142, 161
Hashemites, 33, 38, 46, 63, 155, 161
Hijab. *See* Dress codes
Hijaz: cuisine of, 282, 285–287; culture of, 207, 217, 233, 257–258, 260, 307, 309; establishment of Saudi state and, 33, 37–38, 64, 106–107, 138, 155, 334; geography, 1–3, 10, 13–14, 17, 19, 24, 147, 278; Islamic history, 32, 40–41, 43–44, 46, 49–50, 63, 93, 158–159, 161; language of, 210–211; literature of, 227–228, 233; music of, 263, 267, 270, 273, 274–276; pre-Islamic history, 54, 224; society of, 85, 130, 152, 167, 184, 189, 191, 215
Hijrah: Ikhwan community, 33, 46; migration of Muhammad, 30–31, 52, 61, 139, 332. *See also* Muhammad, prophet of
House of Saud, 40–41, 44–45, 69, 87, 155–156, 254, 332–333
Hufuf, 7, 123, 193, 230

Hussein ibn Ali (last Sharif of Mecca), 33, 37–38, 253
Hussein ibn Ali (son of Caliph Ali), 31–32, 136, 142, 161

Ibn Saud. *See* Abd al-Aziz ibn Saud
Ikhtilat. *See* Gender Segregation
Ikhwan, 33, 44, 46–47, 64, 82, 138, 332
Iran, 73–74, 114, 209, 213, 248, 258, 288 (*see also* Iran–Iraq War); Iranian Revolution, 65, 112, 250, 313; oil industry, 39, 110; political relations with, 6, 21–22; religion, 34, 94, 141, 143–144, 177
Iran–Iraq War, 78, 92
Iraq, 203, 210, 213, 227, 229–230, 263, 267, 318, 337*t* (*see also* Gulf War); geography, 21; history, 59–60, 66, 136, 161, 207, 247; Iran–Iraq War, 78, 92; oil industry, 29, 110, 112–113; political relations with, 4–5, 34, 37–38, 65; religion, 139, 143–144; tribal connections with, 20, 149, 157–158
Islam: customs and rituals, 133–135, 217, 224–225, 259, 271–272; dietary laws, 178, 277, 282–283, 285, 299; early history, 20, 51–52, 56, 58–62, 132, 204, 232; education and, 189, 193, 195–196; foundations and doctrine, 55, 129, 130–133, 140, 206–207, 242, 246–247 (*see also* Islamic Law); Islamic Empire, 31–32, 36–37, 43, 49, 65–67, 161, 207–208; landmarks of, 13, 16, 18, 29, 121, 244, 252–253; Saudi economy and, 106, 120; Saudi state and, 64–65, 69–71, 73, 76, 80–81, 156, 227–228, 307, 311–313; Shia sect (*see* Shia Islam); Sunni sect (*see* Sunni Islam); tribal culture and, 148, 151, 215–216; Wahhabism and, 40–41, 46, 53–54, 80, 96, 130, 138, 178–179 (*see also* Wahhabism); women's issues, 166, 168–169, 174, 176–177, 180, 184, 191
Islamic calendar, 18, 136, 224–225
Islamic Law (Sharia): customs and, 176–177, 292; foundations and doctrine of, 93, 168–169, 196, 332, 334–335 (*see also fiqh*); Saudi state and, 47, 64, 73–76, 90, 107, 120, 171–172, 178, 313
Ismaili Islam, 32, 80, 141, 143–144, 147

Israel, 120, 149, 203, 246, 315; Arab-Israeli War, 20, 34, 91, 113
Istanbul, 35, 41, 80, 248, 298, 312

Jamal Khashoggi, 35, 80, 85–86, 296, 312, 321
Janadiriyah, 268–269, 298
Jeddah: culture, 211, 243, 251, 257, 285, 301–303, 305, 310, 320; economy, 83, 105, 116, 122–123, 125–127, 296; education in, 193–195, 197; geography, 16; history, 5, 13–14, 50, 59, 158, 317; urbanization of, 15, 18, 23, 163; women's issues, 167, 184, 187, 191
Jihad, 41, 96, 137–138, 333
Jordan, 4, 10, 190, 203, 210, 229, 299, 337t; history, 20, 38, 54, 57, 126, 149, 161
Jubail, 8–9, 100, 102, 114–115, 127, 195

Kaaba: before Islam, 31, 52, 62, 151, 232, 241; Islamic significance, 16, 131, 133–134, 217, 243–244, 252–253. *See also* Hajj; Mecca
Karbala, 32, 41, 66, 131, 136
KAUST (King Abdullah University of Science and Technology), 48, 109, 118–119, 178, 195, *197*, 198
Khadijah (prophet Muhammad's wife), 17, 30, 51–52, 61
Khaliji music, 263, 267–268
Khamis Mushayit, 123, 164
Khobar, 8, 23, 35, 123, 127, 164, 194, 305, 309
King Saud University, 34, 193, 196–197, 236, 328
Kufa, 31, 59–60, 144, 205, 207, 247
Kuwait: culture, 158, 222, 236, 267–268, 284, 299, 320; geography, 21, 337t; history, 30, 40, 44, 105, 155; language, 203, 210, 213; oil industry, 8–9, 39, 110, 334; political relations with, 4, 33–34, 78, 92, 103, 112–113, 186; religion, 143. *See also* Gulf War; Iraq

Lawrence of Arabia, 14, 37–38
League of Arab States (Arab League), 21, 34
Loujain al-Hathloul, 80, 83, 187–188

Mabahith (secret police), 81–82
Majlis: as cultural concept, 181, 215–216, 221–222, 317–318, 333; as political body, 69–70, 76, 87, 89–90, 94, 185. *See also* Shura Council
Mall culture, 223, 238, 251, 292, 300–301
Mamluks, 32, 49–51, 161, 208
Mecca: architecture and urbanization, 116, 163, 241–243, *244*, 252–253, 257; before Islam, 57, 59, 148, 151, 224, 227, 232, 241, 159; culture and cuisine, 207, 248, 272, 276, 285–286, 303; economic development of, 107, 115, 119, 121–123, 125, 127, 193; geography, 2, 13, 16, 71, 82–83, 211; in literature, 234–235; religious significance, 46, 50–52, 130–135, 195, 209, 332, 334; role in Islamic history, 30–32, 36, 43, 60–63, 67, 139, 155, 161; society of, 147–148, 153; 20th century history, 33–34, 37–38, 41, 47, 64–65, 167, 178, 250, 309. *See also* Hajj; Qiblah
Medina: culture, 207, 211, 248, 319; economic development, 107, 115–116, 121–123, 125–127, 163; education, 73, 193, 195; during early days of Islam, 18, 30, 51–52, 56; geography, 2, 4, 13–14, 17, 71, 82–83, 270, 285; during Islamic Empire, 43, 50, 58–63, 66, 142, 144–145, 155; religious significance, 129–130, 132, 135–136, 147, 242, 332, 334; society, 153, 158–159
Mongols, 32, 36, 49, 196, 208
Mosque: architecture and structure, 131–132, 242, 248, 299; customs, 208, 217, 223, 225; early history of, 59, 196; historical mosques, 17–18, 20, 66, 123. *See also* Great Mosque in Mecca
Muawiyya, 31, 60, 65–66
Muhammad Abd al-Wahhab, xiv, 53–54, 69, 95, 130, 259, 335; pact with Al Saud, 32, 40, 50, 155; religious teachings, 41, 46, 75, 96. *See also* Wahhabism
Muhammad Ali, 32, 41
Muhammad bin Salman, 39, 70, 80, 156, 303, 312; political activity and reforms, 77, 87–88, 103, 127–128, 167–168, 309
Muhammad ibn Saud, 32, 40–41, 53
Muhammad, prophet of Islam, 16–18, 30–31, 51–52, 56, 161, 209, 343t; companions of, 58–61, 65–66, 136, 331; military campaigns, 61–62, 158–159; religious teachings, 96, 131–135, 139–140, 196, 224–225, 332, 355

al-Murrah (tribe), 148–149, 157, 212
Musalsalat television series. *See* Television
Mutawwa (religious police), 81, 111, 178, 187, 228, 251, 333; 2016 reform, 71, 95, 179
Mutayr (tribe), 149, 157–158

Nabateans, 30, 54–55, 122, 206–207, 241
Najd: Abd al-Wahhab and, 53, 96, 155; Al Saud family and, 29, 32–33, 39–42, 63–64; cuisine, 284, 287–288; culture, 177, 210–213, 217, 224, 257, 259–260; geography, 2, 13, 18–19, 26; music traditions, 263, 265–266, 269; society, 24, 43–44, 157–158, 167, 176, 184, 191, 215, 297
Najran: administration, 71, 82, 155–156; communities, 56, 138, 147, 212; geography, 3–5, 55, 123
Northern Arabia, 2, 20, 30, 55, 157–158

OAPEC, 34, 112–113, 333–334
Oil embargo of 1973, 34, 91, 94, 113
Oil industry, 23–24, 33, 108, 110–111, 115, 229, 339t; education and, 194, 228; international relations and, 79, 90–92, 112–113; other industries and, 104, 114, 119, 121, 124–125; urbanization, 163–164, 254–255
Oil reserves, 6, 8, 22; discovery of, 11, 39–40, 45; environment and, 9
Oman, 78, 100, 203, 210, 213, 224, 246, 288, 337t; geography, 5, 9, 21; history, 30, 40, 57; religion, 93, 143
Omar ibn al-Khattab (2nd Caliph), 31, 59, 61
OPEC, 34, 112–113, 156, 333
Ottomans, 7, 64, 107, 161, 204, 207, 215, 272, 317; Al Saud struggle against, 40–42, 44, 138, 155; Arab Revolt and, 14, 33, 37–38, 51; history, 17, 32, 49–50, 158, 331; influences in architecture and culture, 225, 242, 245, 247–248, 253, 258, 260, 299

Persian Gulf: culture, 213, 263, 279; economic development, 127, 163; geography and resources, 4–8, 21–22, 110, 122–123, 337t; political importance, 9, 78–79
Petrochemical industry, 8, 39, 102, 113–115, 127, 163, 339t
Pre-Islamic Arabia: culture, 136, 206, 224, 259, 264, 287; history, 56, 161, 163; poetry, 227, 232, 334; religion, 20, 52, 217; society, 57, 142, 151, 153, 158
Princess Nourah Bint Abdulrahman University, 171, 199, 323

Al-Qaeda. 35, 48, 237. *See also* Terrorism
Qahtan (tribal branch), 141, 148–150, 157–158
Qarmathians, 32, 63
Qassim (province), 19, 71, 82–83
Qatar: geography, 21, 337t; language and culture, 203, 210, 213, 284, 320; political and administrative system, 73–74, 78; political relations, 4–5, 35, 79, 112–113; religion, xiv, 143
Qiblah, 18, 62, 131, 334
Qiblah, preservation, 50, 67, 153, 242
Quran: Arabic language and, 203–204, 206–209, 247–248; as religious text, 16, 51, 129, 131, 139–140, 334; dietary laws and, 282–283; education and, 191, 193, 196, 319; in history, 30–31, 55–56, 58–59, 142, 159; influences on culture and customs, 133, 217, 224–225, 232, 245, 271–272; role in Islamic jurisprudence, 75–76, 93, 144; Saudi state and, 64, 71, 73, 94, 106, 171–172; Wahhabism and, 155, 242, 263
Quraysh (tribe), 30, 36, 51–52, 61–63, 148, 203, 334

Raja Alem, 234–235, 238
Ramadan (Islamic month): cuisine and, 101, 282, 286, 289; cultural impact of, 292, 300–301, 319–321; religious importance, 130, 132, 136, 224–225, 334, 343t
Rashids (House of Al Rashid), 33, 42, 44, 46, 50, 64, 155, 157–158
Red Sea: cuisine of, 279, 285; culture, 167, 211, 242, 258, 260, 270; economic development, 11, 122–123, 127, 198, 296; geography, 1–2, 5–6, 13–17, 19, 24–25, 337t; in history, 43, 158
Riyadh: as capital of Saudi Arabia, 34–35, 71–72, 77–78, 82–83, 92, 187; culture, 212, 251, 268–269, 292–293, 301–303, 305, 322; economic development, 115, 118, 125–126, 315; education, 171, 190–191, 193–194, 196–197, 199; geography, 2, 19, 123; House of Al Saud and, 29, 32–33, 41–42, 44, 64,

Riyadh (*cont.*)
155; in literature, 236–238; media, 310, 317, 319–320; society, 157–158, 167; urbanization, 14, 18, 23, 163, 258
Riyal (Saudi currency), 105–107, 120–121, 246, 339*t*

Sabaean Kingdom, 30, 56, 241
SABIC (Saudi Arabian Basic Industries Corporation), 99–100, 114–115
Saddam Hussein, 34, 318
Sadu weaving, 256
Salman ibn Abd al-Aziz Al Saud (King Salman), 35, 65, 89, 124, 166, 341*t*; political and economic reforms, 39–40, 70, 77, 87–88, 156, 309; ulama and, 71, 76, 86, 95; women's issues, 173, 188, 333
Saud ibn Abd al-Aziz (King Saud), 34, 156, 191–192, 341*t*
Saudia Airlines, 115, 118, 125–126
Saudization, 39, 100, 103, 108–109, 111, 117–118, 147, 200, 334; women's issues and, 302, 324
Sawt music, 263, 267, 272–273, 334
Sayyid (title), 161
September 11, 2001, events, 35, 86–87, 92, 184, 238. *See also* Terrorism
Shammar (tribe), 46, 64, 148–149, 155, 157–158, 212
Sharia. *See* Islamic Law
Sharifs of Mecca, 32–33, 37–38, 49–51, 63–64, 161, 253, 334
Sheikh Nimr, 72
Shia Islam (Shiites), 31–32, 36, 41, 63, 145, 274, 315, 333; doctrine and customs, 59–60, 66, 131, 136–137, 142–143, 177, 334–335; history of Shia community in Saudi Arabia, 7, 24, 69, 80–81, 111, 130, 147, 242; Shia activism and dissent in Saudi Arabia, 34, 65, 71–73, 74, 82–83, 85, 141, 311
Shura council (Muslim form of governance), 58, 142
Shura Council (Saudi political body), 35, 48, 69–70, 76, 87, 89–90, 167, 185, 216
SOCAL (Standard Oil of California), 33, 39
Soccer, 292, 302–303, 305
Social media, 238, 292, 307–308, 311, 316, 321; activism and, 166, 187; censorship and, 313, 315; social life and, 176, 222–223, 318

Spain, 29, 43, 248; Iberian Peninsula, 66, 204
Sufism, 96, 280
Sulubbah, 150, 157, 162
Sunni Islam: doctrine, 52–53, 58, 60, 66, 130–131, 137, 246, 335; jurisprudence and, 71, 75–76, 93, 144–145; Sunni communities in Saudi Arabia, 24, 147, 153, 158
Syria: Arab Revolt in, 37–38; Bedouins in, 149, 158–159; cultural influences from, 227, 263, 267, 287, 298–299; Islamic Empire in, 31, 49, 59–60, 66, 142, 144–145, 161, 225; language in, 203–204, 210; political relations with, 113, 191–192; pre-Islamic history in, 51, 54–55, 57, 139

Tabuk, 13, 71–73, 82, 303
Taif, 2, 5, 13, 33, 72, 125, 287
Television, 307–309; censorship and, 312–314; culture and, 209, 222, 267, 292, 300, 318–319, 320–322; women's issues and, 167, 170
Terrorism, 5, 35, 65, 92, 198, 321; government response against, 48, 74, 80, 82; vs. political dissent, 86, 88, 130, 314, 316
Tihamah, 3, 13–14, 16, 158, 213, 224, 258
Treaty of Taif, 2, 5, 33
Turkey, 9, 37, 248, 299
Turki al-Hamad, 228, 234, 236–237
Turki ibn Abdallah ibn Muhammad, 32, 42, 44, 155

UAE: culture, 210, 213, 265; geography, 21–22; political relations with, 5–6, 79, 112–113; society and religion, 73–74, 78, 158
Ulama: judicial infrastructure and, 70, 76, 90, 93–95, 254, 335; women's rights and, 71, 165, 174–175, 183–184, 186
Umayyads, 14, 18, 29, 31, 36–37, 65–67, 242, 247; beginnings of dynasty, 59, 61, 144
Unayzah, 19, 158
United Kingdom. *See* Great Britain
United States: cultural influences, 297–298, 300, 304; education and, 189, 198, 230, 236; military cooperation with, 84–85, 124; non-oil industries cooperation, 101, 106, 114; oil industry cooperation, 39, 110–111; political relations with, 33–35, 37–38, 77,

90–92, 113, 185, 312; Saudi kings and, 47, 65, 86, 156

Urbanization: architecture and, 244, 254–255; environment, 10–11, 295; social issues and, 23, 128, 147, 163–164, 176, 292; tribal culture and, 152, 158, 160, 162; urban culture, 269, 272–273, 279, 299

Uthman (3rd Caliph), 31, 59, 60–61, 65, 140, 142. *See also* Ummayads

Vision 2030, 35, 39–40, 103, 118, 127–128, 316, 321, 335; culture and, 310; economy and, 99, 104, 107, 115, 122, 126; education and, 198; sports and, 292–293, 296, 303, 305; women's issues and, 111, 117, 168

Wahhabism: history of, 29, 32, 41–44, 56, 69; ideology of, xiv, 53–54, 80, 95–96, 130, 138, 165–166, 335; Ikhwan and, 46–47, 64, 332; impact on culture, 242, 263, 343*t*. *See also* Muhammad Abd al-Wahhab

Walid bin Talal, 77, 184, 308, 310, 320

Water conservation, 3–4, 7, 9–11, 25, 100, 101–102

Wedding traditions: cultural aspects, 245, 260, 264, 270, 275–276, 286–287; social and legal aspects, 169, 176–177, 182–183

World Trade Organization, 35, 123

Yanbu: cultural aspects, 195, 211, 270, 274; industries, 13, 100, 102, 114, 127, 341*t*

Yathrib. *See* Medina

Yemen: cultural aspects, 203, 210, 213, 246, 277–278, 280, 284–285; geography, 1–3, 24–25; migrant workers from, 108, 147, 152; political relations with, 78, 156; pre-Islamic history, 13, 57, 138–139; Saudi-Yemeni War 1934 and 2015, 5–6, 33, 35–36, 56, 85, 124 (*see also* Treaty of Taif); social and religious aspects, 73, 120, 143

Youth: activism, 72; education of, 24, 48, 303; social issues, 23, 108, 147–148; vs. traditional values, xiv–xv, 179–181, 269, 291–292, 320

About the Author

Valerie Anishchenkova is an associate professor of Arabic studies and core faculty in film studies at the University of Maryland, College Park. Her research focuses on Arab culture; post–Cold War identity discourses in the Middle East, the United States, and Russia; and the relationship between identity and new forms of media. She is the author of *Autobiographical Identities in Contemporary Arab Culture* (University of Edinburgh Press, 2014).

www.ingramcontent.com/pod-product-compliance
Lightning Source LLC
Chambersburg PA
CBHW060506300426
44112CB00017B/2563